ROMANTICISM AND POPULAR CULTURE IN BRITAIN AND IRELAND

From the ballad seller to the Highland bard, from 'pot-house politics' to the language of low and rustic life, the writers and artists of the British Romantic period drew eclectic inspiration from the realm of plebeian experience, even as they helped to constitute the field of popular culture as a new object of polite consumption.

Representing the work of leading scholars from both Britain and North America, *Romanticism and Popular Culture in Britain and Ireland* offers a series of fascinating insights into changing representations of 'the people', while demonstrating at the same time a unifying commitment to rethinking some of the fundamental categories that have shaped our view of the Romantic period. Addressing a series of key themes, including the ballad revival, popular politics, urbanization, and literary canon-formation, the volume also contains a substantial introductory essay, which provides a wide-ranging theoretical and historical overview of the subject.

PHILIP CONNELL is a university lecturer at the University of Cambridge, and a Fellow of Selwyn College, His first book, *Romanticism, Economics and the Question of 'Culture'*, was published in 2001. He has also published a number of essays on the literature and culture of the eighteenth and nineteenth centuries, and has held an Early Career Fellowship at the Centre for Research in the Arts, Social Sciences, and Humanities (CRASSH) in Cambridge.

NIGEL LEASK is Regius Professor of English Language and Literature at the University of Glasgow. He has published widely in the area of Romantic literature and culture, including *Curiosity and the Aesthetics of Travel Writing, 1770–1840: 'From an Antique Land'* (2002) and *Land, Nation and Culture, 1740–1840: Thinking the Republic of Taste* (co-edited with David Simpson and Peter de Bolla, 2005).

ROMANTICISM AND POPULAR CULTURE IN BRITAIN AND IRELAND

EDITED BY

PHILIP CONNELL AND NIGEL LEASK

CAMBRIDGE
UNIVERSITY PRESS

CAMBRIDGE UNIVERSITY PRESS
Cambridge, New York, Melbourne, Madrid, Cape Town, Singapore, São Paulo, Delhi

Cambridge University Press
The Edinburgh Building, Cambridge CB2 8RU, UK

Published in the United States of America by Cambridge University Press, New York

www.cambridge.org
Information on this title: www.cambridge.org/9780521880121

First published 2009

Printed in the United Kingdom at the University Press, Cambridge

A catalogue record for this publication is available from the British Library

Library of Congress Cataloguing in Publication data
Connell, Philip.
Romanticism and popular culture in Britain and Ireland / Philip Connell and Nigel Leask
p.   cm.
Includes bibliographical references and index.
ISBN 978-0-521-88012-1
1. English literature – 18th century – History and criticism.   2. English literature – 19th century –
History and criticism.   3. Popular culture in literature.   4. Popular culture and literature –
Great Britain – History – 18th century.   5. Popular culture and literature – Great
Britain – History – 19th century.   6. Popular culture and literature – Ireland – History – 18th
century.   7. Popular culture and literature – Ireland – History – 19th century.
8. Romanticism – Great Britain.   9. Romanticism – Ireland.   I. Leask, Nigel, 1958–
II. Title
PR447.C596 2009
820.9′145–dc22   2008052568

ISBN 978-0-521-88012-1 hardback

For Marilyn Butler

Contents

vii

Illustrations

Notes on contributors

JOHN BARRELL was until recently Co-Director of the Centre for Eighteenth Century Studies at the University of York. He is the author of a number of books on the history and culture of the eighteenth and nineteenth centuries, most recently *Imagining the King's Death: Figurative Treason, Fantasies of Regicide, 1793–96* (2000) and *The Spirit of Despotism* (2006).

PHILIP CONNELL is a lecturer in the Faculty of English at the University of Cambridge, and a Fellow of Selwyn College. He is the author of *Romanticism, Economics and the Question of 'Culture'* (2001), and a number of essays on literature, culture, and politics in the eighteenth and nineteenth centuries. His current research concerns the relations between poetry, religion, and politics in the late seventeenth and early eighteenth centuries.

GREGORY DART is a senior lecturer in English Literature at University College London. He is the author of *Rousseau, Robespierre and English Romanticism* (Cambridge University Press, 1999), has edited Hazlitt's *Metropolitan Essays* (2005), and is soon to be producing an edition of the same author's *Liber Amoris and Related Writings*. He has also published academic articles on Dickens, Ford Madox Brown, and Thomas De Quincey. He is currently researching a monograph on Cockney Art and Literature 1820–40.

LEITH DAVIS is Professor of English at Simon Fraser University in Canada. She is the author of *Acts of Union: Scotland and the Literary Negotiation of the British Nation, 1707–1830* (1998) and *Music, Postcolonialism and Gender: The Construction of Irish National Identity, 1724–1874* (2005) as well as co-editor of *Scotland and the Borders of Romanticism* (Cambridge University Press, 2004). Her current project explores print culture and the articulation of transnational identity in the British Isles from 1689 to 1800.

INA FERRIS is Professor of English at the University of Ottawa, Canada. Her publications include a critical edition of Charlotte Smith's *The Old Manor House* (2006), *The Romantic National Tale and the Question of Ireland* (Cambridge University Press, 2002), and *The Achievement of Literary Authority: Gender, History, and the Waverley Novels* (1991). She is currently working on a project on antiquarianism and the culture of the book in the Romantic period.

KEVIN GILMARTIN is Professor at the Centre for Eighteenth Century Studies and the Department of English at the University of York. In addition to articles on the politics of literature and print culture in the Romantic period, he is the author of *Writing against Revolution: Literary Conservatism in Britain, 1790–1832* (Cambridge University Press, 2007) and *Print Politics: The Press and Radical Opposition in Early Nineteenth-Century England* (Cambridge University Press, 1996), and co-editor of *Romantic Metropolis: The Urban Scene of British Culture, 1780–1840* (Cambridge University Press, 2005).

MINA GORJI is a lecturer in Eighteenth-Century and Romantic Literature at the University of Cambridge. Her publications include articles on poetic awkwardness and literary allusion, an edited collection of essays, *Rude Britannia* (2007), and a critical monograph, *John Clare and the Place of Poetry* (2008). She is currently working on a study of Romantic Vulgarity.

IAN HAYWOOD is Professor of English at Roehampton University, London. His current research is focused on the relationship between popular visual culture and literature in the eighteenth and nineteenth centuries. His most recent books are *Bloody Romanticism: Spectacular Violence and the Politics of Representation 1776–1832* (2006) and *The Revolution in Popular Literature: Politics, Print and the People 1790–1860* (Cambridge University Press, 2004).

NIGEL LEASK is Regius Professor of English Language and Literature at the University of Glasgow. His most recent publications are *Curiosity and the Aesthetics of Travel Writing, 1770–1840: 'From an Antique Land'* (2002) and a co-edited collection of essays entitled *Land, Nation and Culture, 1740–1840: Thinking the Republic of Taste* (2005). He is currently working on a book entitled *Scottish Pastoral: Robert Burns, Improvement, Romanticism*.

KIRSTEEN MCCUE is a lecturer in the Department of Scottish Literature at the University of Glasgow where she is also Associate Director of the Centre for Robert Burns Studies. She has published widely on Scottish song, has co-edited Haydn's folk-song settings for George Thomson for the new *Haydn Werke*, and is currently editing *Songs by the Ettrick Shepherd* and *Hogg's Contributions to Musical Collections & Miscellaneous Songs* for the Stirling/South Carolina research edition of the *Collected Works of James Hogg*.

GILLIAN RUSSELL is Reader in English, School of Humanities, Australian National University, Canberra. She is the author of *The Theatres of War: Performance, Politics, and Society, 1793–1815* (1995) and *Women, Sociability and Theatre in Georgian London* (Cambridge University Press, 2007). Her current research is on the theatre, sociability, and the Romantic writer.

Acknowledgements

The idea for this volume evolved in conversations between the editors over a number of years, but its final shape has been determined to a significant extent by our contributors. We'd like to thank them for their dedication to the book, their patience, and their promptness in responding to editorial enquiries. We also received valuable support and advice on various aspects of the project from Valentina Bold, Gerry Carruthers, Matthew Craske, Suzanne Gilbert, Stuart Gillespie, Heather Glen, Sheila O'Connell, Murray Pittock, Corinna Russell, Samuel Smiles, Julia Swindells, and two anonymous readers for Cambridge University Press. Our introductory reflections on Romanticism and popular culture were first presented to the graduate seminar of the Centre for Eighteenth-Century Studies at the University of York, with encouraging results. We'd like to thank the Universities of Cambridge and Glasgow, and Selwyn College, Cambridge, for their institutional support, and especially Dr John Coyle, Head of Glasgow's English Department, for being generous with his time and *savoir faire* during the production of the final typescript. We owe a particular debt of thanks to our editorial assistant, Dr Emma Lister, who put in a huge number of hours in preparing the text for submission. Although an expert on hypertext and the novels of Alasdair Gray, she quickly adapted her professional and technical skills to deal with editorial problems specific to an earlier period, and showed good-humoured patience when it all took rather longer than planned. We are also very grateful to Linda Bree and other colleagues at Cambridge University Press for their encouragement and indulgence as the project took shape, and for seeing the volume into print. The book's dedication to Marilyn Butler reflects both editors' long-standing personal and intellectual debts and, more specifically, her pioneering contributions to the study of popular antiquarianism in the Romantic period.

PART I

Introduction

CHAPTER I

What is the people?

Philip Connell and Nigel Leask

– And who are you that ask the question? One of the people. And yet you would be something! Then you would not have the People nothing. For what is the People? Millions of men, like you, with hearts beating in their bosoms, with thoughts stirring in their minds, with the blood circulating in their veins, with wants and appetites, and passions and anxious cares, and busy purposes and affections for others and a respect for themselves, and a desire for happiness, and a right to freedom, and a will to be free.[1]

The opening sentences of William Hazlitt's celebrated essay suggest both the historical urgency of his eponymous question, and the irreducible plurality of its object. Published in a radical periodical in 1817, during an unprecedented era of plebeian political organization, 'What is the People?' speaks directly to a radicalized *demos*, yet remains acutely conscious of its textual abstraction from the diversity and particularity of popular experience. The essay's interrogatory frame enacts this tension, in the unstable *prosopopoeia* through which addressee and object ('you', 'the people') coalesce and diverge in unsettling succession. Hazlitt's vividly corporeal imagery proceeds, with a certain rhetorical inevitability, to describe the people's collective embodiment as 'the heart of the nation'; but the peculiar forcefulness of the essay's beginning relies as much on its address to a singular reader. The identity of that reader, moreover, remains very much at issue, as the personification of a universalized political nation – *vox populi* – which remains unambiguously masculine in its gender ('millions of *men* like you').

At one level Hazlitt's address evokes Rousseau's republican apotheosis of popular festival in the 1758 *Lettre à d'Alembert*, in opposition to the spectacular detachment of theatre: 'put the spectators into the show; make them actors themselves; contrive it that everyone sees and adores themselves in others, and everyone will be bound together as never before'.[2] Suspicious of the reactionary or revolutionary appeal to 'public opinion' as a dangerous abstraction, Hazlitt's rhetorical strategy assumes a rigorous inclusiveness, in contrast to a characteristic tendency of many Romantic writers to view 'the people' as 'other', implying 'a certain distance, a position from which the popular can be evaluated, analysed, and perhaps dismissed'.[3] Yet Hazlitt's career as a political and literary journalist was marked by a persistent equivocation between the 'popular' and 'polite' readerships created by widening literacy and an increasingly stratified marketplace of print. His question, even in its articulation, thus posits a more complex field of inquiry, concerning not just the changing nature of 'popular culture' in Britain and Ireland, but the relationship between that culture and the realm of polite arts and letters that would later come to be identified with the concept of Romanticism.

Although the question raised by Hazlitt's essay is still pertinent today, the chapters in this book are concerned with the practice and emergent discourse of popular culture within the Romantic period, and its entanglement with those concepts which would, in subsequent decades, come to define the meaning of Romanticism. (We are not concerned, therefore, with the representation of Romanticism in the popular literature, cinema, or music of the twentieth and twenty-first centuries: that would be the subject of another book.) As a point of entry, we might consider one of the most significant literary appropriations of the 'popular' within the Romantic period, and one with which Hazlitt was certainly well acquainted. In the 1800 Preface to the *Lyrical Ballads*, Wordsworth famously proposed 'a selection of the real language of men in a state of vivid sensation' as a model for his poetry, locating that language in the condition of 'low and rustic life'.[4] If Hazlitt's prose returns upon its relation to the demotic reader in a relation of rigorous inclusivity, Wordsworthian poetics, it is often assumed, is based on detached sympathy rather than identification, and addressed to a reader who, it is supposed, is *not* 'one of the people'. His appeal to the language and culture of a peasantry which was, by his own confession, in a condition of rapid attenuation signals the return of pastoral to late eighteenth-century poetic theory, as a means of criticizing 'the bourgeois sociolect that gives rise to poetic diction', although Wordsworth studiously avoids the word 'peasant' and always qualifies the word 'pastoral'.[5]

Wordsworth here appeals to rural vernacular speech, albeit a 'selection' thereof, as the model for an experimental poetry seeking to redress the ills of modern commercial society, a collective pathology characterized by 'a degrading thirst after outrageous stimulation'. Such a condition is the result, Wordsworth argues, of war, urbanization, 'the rapid communication of intelligence', and a national literature deformed by 'frantic novels, sickly and stupid German Tragedies, and deluges of idle and extravagant stories in verse'.[6] But despite a widely acknowledged sense that his 'poetic experiment' was inspired by the social experience and cultural forms of 'the people', it is hard to specify the exact nature of the debt. Riding the crest of a contemporary fashion for labouring-class poetry, as well as reflecting the powerful and under-acknowledged influence of Robert Burns and Scottish song, Wordsworth's Preface deterritorializes his Scottish and English regional sources in an impossible quest for a rustic lower-class vernacular that simultaneously transcends regional dialect.[7] In itself this need not reflect any disregard for vernacular poetry as such; the poet elsewhere attacks Adam Smith, a theorist of sympathy who 'could not endure the ballad of Clym of the Clough, because the [au]thor had not written like a gentleman'.[8] Yet as Jon Klancher has argued, *Lyrical Ballads* could 'claim no naïve mimesis . . . deprived of the real by the corruption of his own language, the self-conscious poet must now hypothesize another language – the language of the peasant poor – that preserves all the crucial referentials the poet can no longer summon himself'.[9] Such a 'popular' language is by its very nature an elusive object, at once removed (as contemporary reviewers frequently emphasized) from the actual vernacular speech of rural Britain, while at the same time 'all but inaccessible to the middle class mind'.[10]

In the same year in which Hazlitt sought to politicize the question of the 'People', Wordsworth's erstwhile collaborator Samuel Taylor Coleridge set out to extricate Romantic cultural theory from the 'levelling muse' of the revolutionary decade – and Wordsworth's early poetry, more parti-cularly – in the second volume of his *Biographia Literaria*. Ignoring Wordsworth's deterritorializing imperative, Coleridge attempted to root out any ambiguity which might still adhere to the *Lyrical Ballads*' 'jaco-binical' notion of a 'real language of men'. 'A rustic's language,' he wrote, 'purified from all provincialism and grossness, and so far re-constructed as to be made consistent with the rules of grammar . . . will not differ from the language of any other man of common-sense . . . except so far as the notions, which the rustic has to convey, are fewer and more indis-criminate.'[11] Coleridge substitutes a *lingua communis* (the cultural capital of which is signalled by its Latinity) for Wordsworth's 'real language of men', redirecting attention from the language and ordonnance of 'the market, wake, high-road or plough-field' to the professional, academic values of 'grammar, logic and psychology', whose models are Dante, Scaliger, and the Italian poets of the *Seicento*.[12] The mind's power of reflection, and its articulation in a language of philosophical inwardness, are the fruits of education and no instinctual property of the *demos*: 'though in a civilized society, by imitation and passive remembrance of what they hear from their religious instructors and other superiors, the most uneducated share in the harvest which they neither sowed nor reaped'.[13]

Coleridge's objection had to some extent been anticipated by Wordsworth himself, whose 1815 'Essay Supplementary to the Preface' offered a qualified withdrawal from his earlier demotic location of cultural value. Although Wordsworth praised Percy's *Reliques* and the humble vernacular ballad which had 'absolutely redeemed' the poetry of both Germany and Britain from false taste, he expressed reservations about the term 'popular', condemning 'the senseless iteration of the word, *popular*, applied to new works in poetry, as if there were no test of excellence in this first of the fine arts but that all men should run after its productions, as if urged by an appetite, or constrained by a spell!'[14] Wordsworth now understands the word not in the primary sense of '*belonging* to the people', but rather as 'finding favour with or approved by the people', thus associating it with the point of readerly consumption, rather than of production.[15] As Philip Connell points out in his chapter in this volume, Wordsworth's poetry was not obviously 'popular' in this secondary sense; but the alternative locus of poetic value was now precisely *depopulated*, translated into the terms of a bloodless abstraction.

Gone is any conception now of a popular source or inspiration for poetic creativity (as in the 1800 Preface), since 'grand thoughts . . . naturally and most fitly conceived in solitude . . . can . . . not be brought forth in the midst of plaudits, without some violation of their sanctity'.[16] But because Wordsworth, like Hazlitt's interlocutor, 'would not have the people nothing' in exchange for poetic solipsism, the Essay's celebrated conclusion struggles to distinguish a genuine *vox populi* from 'that small though loud portion of the community, ever governed by factitious influence, which, under the name of the PUBLIC, passes itself, upon the unthinking, for the PEOPLE'. Nevertheless, his reverence for 'the People, philosophically characterised' derives primarily from Wordsworth's concern to embody a select poetic audience, rather than from any sense of a common culture with which the poet might creatively sympathize, as in the 1800 Preface.[17]

It was the post-1815 position of Wordsworth and Coleridge, rather than Hazlitt's more heuristic questioning of the popular, which proved formative for the nineteenth-century rise of English literary studies, even as the demotic and vernacular elements within Romantic culture continued to be widely acknowledged. One legacy of these developments is an unfortunate ambiguity in the meaning of the term 'popular' which, in discussions of Romantic literature, tends to denote *either* the values of an idealized and evanescent peasantry (as in Wordsworth's earlier theorizations), *or else* what Pierre Bourdieu denominates 'heteronomous' cultural production, the commercially driven 'culture industry' spurned by post-Romantic aesthetic taste.[18] This ambiguity, added to the fact that the emergence of the English literary canon is historically dependent upon an objectifying distinction between high and low, 'the people' and 'the public' (a distinction which Romantic theory itself did much to entrench), may explain why recent studies of the relationship between Romanticism and popular culture have been few and far between.

In an attempt to redress this situation, the present volume revisits the terrain of 'the popular', albeit without the ability, or indeed inclination, to produce a singular and definitive answer to Hazlitt's question. One way of answering that question might lead us to contemporary political discourse. But what do Romantic attitudes to popular culture have to say about the relationship between country and city? And how might the relationship between elite and popular culture differ across the diverse territories of the 'Atlantic archipelago' (as, for instance, in the 'intensely bilingual and diglossic society' of eighteenth-century Ireland, the subject of Leith Davis's chapter in this volume)?[19] The chapters gathered here collectively acknowledge the irremediably protean, particularized character of 'the popular', while mapping some of the strategies through which writers and artists of the Romantic period sought to accommodate, incorporate, or exclude the realm of popular experience and tradition. From the urban ballad seller to the Highland or Irish bard, from 'pot-house' politics to the language of 'low and rustic life', the writers and artists of the Romantic period responded in eclectic and often contradictory ways to the realm of the demotic and the plebeian, even as they helped to constitute the field of popular culture as a new object of 'polite' consumption. In doing so, they also confronted an interpretative dilemma that continues to trouble modern scholarly treatments of this subject. For what does it mean to see 'people' as '*the* people' or, indeed, as the constitutive elements of 'popular culture'? 'They cannot represent themselves; they must be represented', in the words of Karl Marx's famous apothegm from *The Eighteenth Brumaire of Louis Napoleon*, cited by Edward Said as an epigraph to his 1978 study *Orientalism*.[20] And like a species of internal orientalism, translated from geographical into social space, 'the people' appear to demand acknowledgement, recuperation, representation; yet the product of such efforts – particularly at a historical distance – all too easily reflects the operations of distorting prejudice or idealizing projection, telling us more about the mediators than their object.

POPULAR CULTURE: A BRIEF SURVEY OF SCHOLARSHIP

If these questions have been more widely debated by historians than literary scholars, it is largely due to the stimulus of Peter Burke's influential study, *Popular Culture in Early Modern Europe*. Burke opens by defining culture as 'a system of shared meanings, attitudes and values, and the symbolic forms (performances, artefacts) in which they are expressed', and (more tentatively) defines 'popular culture' as 'the culture of the non-elite, the "subordinate classes" as Gramsci calls them'.[21] His first chapter describes the 'discovery of the people' by J. G. Herder and the Grimm brothers in the Romantic period, closely linked with the cultural and linguistic agenda of German proto-nationalism. Three elements of the German 'discovery' are underlined in particular: 'primitivism', 'purism', and 'communalism'. The first entails the belief that the 'songs and stories and festivals and beliefs' (p. 21) collected *circa* 1800 were thousands of years old, even if in fact they may have been invented not more than two generations before. The second heading, 'purism', anticipates Hazlitt's question, 'What is the People?', but answers it very differently. For Herder (to some extent like Wordsworth) 'the people' are the peasantry, living close to nature, untainted by new or foreign manners, emphatically not the town dwellers, least of all 'the mob of the streets, who never sing or compose but shriek and mutilate' (p. 22). The third heading, 'communalism', glosses Herder's famous theory of communal creation, *das Volk dichtet*, 'the folk creates', an idea which in imposing abstract unity on the people has the effect not only of denying creative agency to individuals, but of artificially isolating the peasantry (the concept is inapplicable to town dwellers) from external cultural influences or artefacts, not to mention print culture.[22]

Burke here perhaps overstates the relative importance of German theory, for, as we shall see, Scottish and English antiquarians had raised some of these issues half a century earlier, and many of the ideas of Herder and the Grimms – especially the notion of communal creativity – went virtually unnoticed in Britain and Ireland during the Romantic period. More useful is his location of 'the discovery of the people' 'in the main in what might be called the cultural periphery of Europe as a whole and of different countries within it' (pp. 13–14). Since the original publication of Burke's book, the rise of 'four nations' historiography has profoundly reshaped our sense of British historical and cultural identities, raising important questions about the emergence in this period of the vernacular canon, and a sense of the arts more generally, as a 'national' concern. Burke's notion of the peripheral (or especially 'northern'/Scottish or 'western'/Welsh and Irish) location of the inquiry still holds good, as is evident in the chapters in the present collection by Leask, McCue, Davis, and Ferris.

Also significant is Burke's contribution to theorizing the highly problematic relations between 'elite' and 'popular' culture. Possibly because of the 'objectifying' tendencies of commentators discussed above, analysis has often projected a form of conceptual dualism onto the social body itself. Burke was to some extent aware of this danger, revising Robert Redfield's bi-polar account of the relations between the 'great tradition' (a 'scholarly learned culture transmitted formally at grammar schools and universities') and a 'little tradition' of popular culture disseminated in marketplaces, taverns, and other places of popular assembly, by arguing that at least until the eighteenth century, 'there were two cultural traditions . . . but they did not correspond symmetrically to the two main social groups, the elite and the common people. The elite participated in the little tradition, but the common people did not participate in the great tradition' (p. 28).[23] Burke's asymmetrical model may itself be unduly restrictive for our period, however, given that in the course of the eighteenth century the 'great tradition' was itself increasingly democratized. It is certainly true that in 1763 James Boswell (following in the footsteps of Pepys and Selden and anticipating Scott) derived 'a pleasing romantic feeling' from the eighty-three chapbooks – which he labelled 'Curious Productions' – purchased from Dicey's Ballad Warehouse at Bow Church Yard.[24] But it is also the case that two decades later Robert Burns struggled to acquire the rudiments of French and Latin in his father's Ayrshire farm whilst familiarizing himself with Shakespeare, Milton, and Dryden; James Hogg read Burnet's *Sacred Theory of the Earth* as an eighteen-year-old shepherd boy in the Ettrick Valley; and the young John Clare saved up to purchase Thomson's *Seasons* at Peterborough Fair. Although the rise of the novel might be seen as itself an extension of the 'great tradition', in his *Memoirs* the radical publisher James Lackington embraced the eclipse of the 'little tradition' with glee rather than nostalgia: 'The poorer sort of farmers, and even the poor country people in general, who before that period spent their winter evenings in relating stories of witches, hobgoblins,

&c. now shorten the winter nights by hearing their sons and daughters read tales, romances, &c. and on entering their houses, you may see Tom Jones, Roderic Random, and other entertaining books, stuck up on their bacon-racks, &c.'[25] All this represented one aspect of what the eighteenth century denominated 'improvement', whether of land, economy, or plebeian manners.[26]

Burke concludes his study with the claim that around 1800, 'the clergy, the nobility, the merchants, the professional men – and their wives – . . . abandoned popular culture to the lower classes, from whom they were now separated, as never before, by profound differences in world view' (p. 270). Burke's chronology for upper-class withdrawal (of particular significance to Romanticists) is of course itself roughly coterminous with the date of what he calls the 'discovery of the people', and beyond acknowledging the fact that the owl of Minerva always takes wing at dusk, the temporal coincidence remains unexamined, particularly considering that the learned discourse of popular culture wasn't always either regulative or directly discriminatory. But the fact that the tone of polite 'discovery' is frequently elegiac or nostalgic (in contrast to Lackington's more 'progressive' views) suggests that it often served as a paradigm to set against the socially atomizing tendencies and cultural *anomie* of modernity, a dominant theme of Romantic cultural critique. Whatever the crises effecting the 'great tradition', the 'embourgoisement' of the 'little tradition' is undeniable, particularly in Scotland where a commitment to popular enlightenment co-existed in highly creative tension with traditional 'folklore' (as it would come to be known).

Despite its initial dependence on Redfield's two traditions, Burke's asymmetrical model is considerably less 'bi-polar' than that underlying E. P. Thompson's *Customs in Common*, which tends to ignore 'the middling sort', perhaps comprising as much as a third of the English population in the eighteenth century, in favour of a society cleanly divided between 'patricians' and 'plebs'.[27] More recent revisionist historians such as Tim Harris have proposed that an oppositional model of culture endemic to bi-polar theories should be replaced by an interactive theory which allows for the agency of 'the middling sort', straddling elite and plebeian classes, a two-way mediation of culture which prevents popular culture being seen as a mere 'residue' of elite culture, while at the same time jettisoning an essentialist account which is often forced to define 'the popular' purely in terms of what it is *not*.[28] Jürgen Habermas's influential but much-contested notion of the eighteenth-century 'bourgeois public sphere' is relevant here in considering the mechanism of cultural interaction: 'what is spoken or written, within this rational space, pays due deference to the niceties of class and rank; but the speech act itself, the *énonciation* as opposed to the *énoncé*, figures itself in its very form an equality, autonomy and reciprocity at odds with its class-bound content'.[29] The democratization of the 'great tradition' discussed above, symptomatic of the popular enlightenment which swept parts of eighteenth-century Britain and Ireland, might be seen as the result of an extension of Habermas's 'bourgeois public sphere', although the latter has frequently been seen as deeply hostile to popular culture as traditionally construed. The working-class reformers who sought (in Paul Keen's words) 'to storm the invisible walls of the republic of letters rather than the Houses of Parliament' in the 1790s could find intellectual inspiration in a variety of forms: from 'a proto-Victorian, self-help ideology' to the 'improving' discourse of pastoral sensibility discussed here in John Barrell's chapter.[30] But this by no means always entailed the rejection of communitarian concerns, including a commitment to more traditional forms of popular culture.

A word is due here about another body of theory that has proved influential in much recent work on popular culture, namely Bakhtin's notion of the carnivalesque as articulated in *Rabelais and His World* (first English translation 1968). Bakhtin has been far more important for literary critics than cultural historians, and it is strange that although Burke's book contains a whole chapter on popular carnival, and appropriates Bakhtin's concept of the carnivalesque, the Russian critic's name only occurs obliquely, in the book's endnotes. Bakhtin's appeal to literary critics is largely the result of his related work on language and stylistics, especially his theories of dialogism and privileging of 'heteroglossic' ('novelistic') over monologic ('poetic') discourse, important resources for late twentieth-century critics who sought to open the literary work to 'the social text'. Elements of Bakhtin's theory are undoubtedly productive for understanding the symbolic importance of the 'world turned upside down' (the carnival, the circus, the tavern, and other 'grotesque' sites and rituals) in the European cultural imaginary, instances of which are discussed below in Ian Haywood's account of Regency graphic satire and Gregory Dart's description of a 'mock election' in the King's Bench prison.

However, Bakhtin's theory is troubled by an uncritical equation between 'the people' and a collectivized 'grotesque body' celebrated in carnival rituals of feasting, drinking, belching, and fornicating. 'The material bodily principle is contained not in the biological individual, not in the bourgeois ego, but in the people, a people who are continually growing and renewed.'[31] To equate 'the people' with 'the grotesque body', and the ruling class with reason and moral judgement, represents an extreme version of the bi-polar model criticized above. It also risks essentializing our understanding of popular culture, which is too easily equated with a 'symbolic inversion' of social hierarchy, 'the world turned upside down'. Commenting on Bakhtin's influence in recent Shakespeare studies, Stuart Gillespie and Neil Rhodes fault the 'folkloristic' notion of popular culture as 'an entirely positive, liberating, body-focused phenomenon, which finds its apotheosis in the communal virtues of laughter'. Moreover, Shakespeare's use of the term 'popular' in *Coriolanus* (a play which contains four out of his total six usages) refers to 'the characters called citizens, who are eligible to vote, rather than . . . an inarticulate mob'.[32]

Historically, Bakhtin's focus on Rabelais and the sixteenth-century French festival calendar – the 'Battle between Carnival and Lent' – has limited applicability to eighteenth-century Protestant Britain.[33] More productive here is Peter Stallybrass and Allon White's nuanced consideration of carnival as one aspect of 'a generalized economy of transgression' in specific cultural sites and epochs and, in relation to our period, as the 'introjected other' of the eighteenth-century public sphere. In a version of Burke's 'withdrawal' theory, Stallybrass and White detail 'the self-exclusion of certain middling and professional classes from the popular ritual culture, irrespective of whether that culture was waxing or waning'.[34] The 'soft culture' of eighteenth-century masquerades, pleasure gardens, opera, and theatrical pantomimes 'ironized and sentimentalized . . . the carnival rituals of the open air', while the coffee house, exemplary locus of the emergent public sphere, 'demanded a withdrawal from popular culture and its translation into negative and even phobic representations' in the interests of rational intercourse.[35] While, to a certain degree, this analysis still depends on a folkloristic notion of 'the popular', Stallybrass and White's analysis of changing representations of Bartholomew Fair from Ben Jonson through Pope to Wordsworth is more productive, although arguably their turn to the language of psychoanalysis exposes the historical limitations of Bakhtin's model: 'like the scene of seduction, Bartholomew's Fair contained a phobic enchantment which, at least in Wordsworth, might be called traumatic. *Wo es war soll ich werden* could be the apt description of a poet-subject repulsed by social practices destined to become the very content of the bourgeois unconscious.'[36] Whatever its attendant problems, the theory of psychical introjection certainly has the virtue of offering one solution to the unresolved problem in Burke's account, the historical coincidence between the 'great withdrawal' of the upper classes and their simultaneous 'discovery of the people'.

A related alternative, endorsed by Burke himself in the introduction to the revised edition of his book, takes its departure from Roger Chartier's influential essay 'Culture as Appropriation' (1984). Basing his theory on the study of seventeenth- and eighteenth-century French popular literature, the *Bibliothèque bleue*, Chartier demolishes the binary social model with its neat distinction between elite and popular, literate and illiterate, by positing a reading public for these chapbooks that was 'neither cultured nor popular, a public made up in the city of merchants and wealthy artisans and, in the countryside, of low-ranking officials and the richer farmers and labourers'.[37] Going further, he attacks a 'sociology of distribution' which discovers a straightforward homology between the genres and contents of popular print and social groups. 'It is clear that the relation of appropriation to texts or behaviour in a given society may be a more distinctive factor than how texts and behaviour are distributed. The "popular" cannot be found readymade in a set of texts that merely require to be identified and listed; above all, the popular qualifies a kind of relation, a way of using cultural products such as legitimate ideas and attitudes.'[38] For Chartier, inspired by Michel de Certeau's 'art of doing', as theorized in *The Practice of Everyday Life*, popular culture is 'a kind of specific relationship with cultural objects', the creativity of which is in inverse proportion to the control exerted by the institutions of the school, the church, and the law.[39] The attraction of this ethnographic notion of popular culture as an inventive *bricolage* is its refusal of functionalist theories, whether their focus lies on the repressive function of state institutions, or the more diffuse sphere of Foucauldian bio-politics. This is not to say, as Emma Griffin has recently reminded us, that we can afford to overlook the ever-fluid relation between social structure, political power, and cultural form: the constantly exerted power of subordination exercised by the State or dominant class.[40] A suitably dynamic version of the 'appropriation theory' might, nevertheless, free popular culture from being seen as merely residual and, in the words of Tim Harris, 'the passive victim of the historical process, undermined and impoverished by various attempts at reform or suppression, or eroded by the effects of social, economic and intellectual changes'.[41]

Challenging an overly simplistic developmental view of 'the coffee house replacing the fair', some of the chapters in the present volume address varieties of popular culture which are distinct products of modern commercial society and the characteristic forms of urban leisure as they emerged in the long eighteenth century, a far cry from the life-world of the old peasantry. Because the political stakes are high here, as well as resisting any simple equation between popular culture and political radicalism, it is equally important to eschew a celebratory populism such as that which informs Goldby and Purdue's thesis in *The Civilization of the Crowd* (which views nineteenth-century popular culture as a product of the emancipatory influences of consumer capitalism, urbanization, and the availability of cheaper commodities, which together freed 'the people' from the hierarchical domination and cultural narrowness of the old rural society).[42] We rather follow John Mullan and Christopher Reid's agnostic response to these starkly opposed choices in conjecturing that 'the effects of commercialization could be destructive or liberating, that popular identities could typically be shaped by an ethos of consumption or by an ethos of custom depending on where (country or city?) one looks'.[43] Moreover, as Raphael Samuel reminds us, the commodification of popular tradition has never been wholly distinct from more democratic forms of 'unofficial knowledge'.[44]

THE 'DISCOVERY OF THE PEOPLE' AND POPULAR ANTIQUARIANISM

Peter Burke's acknowledgement that 'however much we may want to see these performances through the eyes of . . . craftsmen and peasants . . . we are forced to see them through the eyes of literate outsiders' is a fundamental problem that is, as we shall see, evident in a host of different contexts within the Romantic period (p. 65). The notion of popular culture as an 'elusive quarry' (in Burke's phrase) is also raised with peculiar self-consciousness by eighteenth-century inquirers, albeit for rather different reasons. Witness the preface to the Newcastle antiquary John Brand's *Observations on Popular Antiquities* (1777), itself a redaction of an earlier treatise on *Antiquitates Vulgares* by Henry Bourne (1725):

A Passage is to be forced through a Wilderness intricate and entangled: few Vestiges of former Labours can be found to direct us; we must oftentimes trace a tedious retrospective Course, perhaps to return at last weary and unsatisfied, from the making of Researches, fruitless as those of some antient enthusiastic Traveller, who ranging the barren *African* Sands, had in vain attempted to investigate the hidden Sources of the *Nile*.[45]

Although Brand's conceit is somewhat qualified by the fact that James Bruce had recently returned from Africa claiming to be the first explorer to have discovered the source of the Nile, he does insist that 'the prime Origin of the superstitious Notions and Ceremonies of the People is absolutely unattainable', so his aspiration must be limited to tracing them back as far as possible in the historical record.[46] The elusiveness of the quarry for Brand (one shared to some extent by Thomas Percy and eighteenth-century collectors of 'minstrel ballads', as Nigel Leask argues in his chapter in this volume) lies in the fact that ancient origins have been so mutilated and fragmented by tradition that it seems well nigh impossible to reconstitute them, a fact which licenses the mediator's 'mending and polishing'.

The question of scholarly motivation is important here too. Brand's precursor Henry Bourne had been impelled by a regulative desire to improve the legitimate rites and ceremonies of the people, and to abolish those which he considered 'sinful or wicked' (not to mention 'Papistical').[47] Brand himself writes as a revivalist, concerned that the best interests of the Nation are poorly served by the use currently made by the 'common people' of their leisure time: 'The revival of many [innocent Sports and Games], would I think, be highly pertinent at this particular Season, when the general Spread of Luxury and Dissipation threatens more than at any preceding Period to extinguish the Character of our boasted national Bravery.'[48] Like Percy, Brand emphasized the northern locus of his inquiry on the grounds that customs survive there which have long since disappeared in the metropolitan South. Entirely ignorant of Burke's German 'discoverers', he pleaded the essential humanity of his project by alluding to Gray's 'Elegy in a Country Churchyard', claiming that 'the People, of whom Society is chiefly composed, and for whose good, Superiority of Rank is only a Grant made originally by mutual Concession, is a respectable Subject to everyone who is a Friend of Man'.[49]

Marilyn Butler has discussed Brand's importance both as author and as Secretary of the Society of Antiquities from 1784, discovering in his 'resentment of metropolitan ascendancy' a characteristic of 'British fringe subcultures from mid-century to the 1780s'.[50] In this respect, and in the universalizing or primitivist tendency to trace modern popular rites and ceremonies back before the Reformation, to Anglo-Saxon, Celtic, or Roman antiquity, Brand resembles other 'fringe' antiquarians such as Sylvester O'Halloran in Ireland, Edward Williams (Iolo Morganwg) and William Owen Pughe in Wales, or the circle around David Erskine, Earl of Buchan, in Scotland. Brand's politics, a melange of Tory populism, provincial patriotism, and – after 1790 – Jacobinism, look relatively anodyne compared to those of the more famous Newcastle antiquary who followed him, Joseph Ritson. If Brand's celebration of 'the popular' proved a gentle irritant to contemporary Tory and Anglican apologists like Samuel Johnson and Thomas Warton, the irascible Ritson's frontal attack on Johnson's Shakespeare edition, Warton's *History of English Poetry* (1782) and Percy's *Reliques of Ancient English Poetry* contested the courtly pedigree for popular antiquities drawn by these scholars, in terms that candidly reflected an aggressively radical and anti-aristocratic political sensibility.[51] Ritson's most widely read book was *Robin Hood: A Collection of all the Ancient Poems, Songs and Ballads, now Extant, relative to that celebrated English Outlaw* (1795) which lauded 'a man who, in a barbarous age, and under a complicated tyranny, displayed a spirit of freedom and independence, which has endeared him to the common people, whose cause he maintained.'[52]

Butler usefully underlines the significance of popular antiquarianism for the literary productions of British and Irish Romanticism, generically concentrated on the popular ballad, the long verse romance, and the prose romance, as the latter shifted in the hands of a consummate practitioner like Walter Scott from the national tale to the historical novel.[53] Often the influence was direct, as in the case of Francis Grose, author of the *Antiquities of England and Wales* (6 vols., 1773–87), *Scotland* (2 vols., 1789–91), *Classical Dictionary of the Vulgar Tongue* (1796), and *Provincial Glossary* (1787). Although, as Mark Phillips has indicated, 'we cannot point to a British work of high literary standard or wide circulation styling itself as a history of manners', along the lines of Voltaire's *Histoire des Mouers*, the researches of Grose aren't too far off.[54] Like many popular antiquarians, and despite his immense corpulence, Grose was an enthusiastic fieldworker, a fact recorded by Robert Burns (whom he met *en route*) in his 1789 poem 'On the Late Captain Grose's Peregrinations, Thro Scotland Collecting the Antiquities of that Kingdom':

> Hear, Land o' Cakes and brither Scots,
> Frae Maidenkirk to Johnny Groat's! –
> If there's a hole in a' your coats,
>   I rede you tent it:
> A chield's amang you takin notes,
>   And, faith, he'll prent it.[55]

When Grose asked his fellow-Mason Burns to supply him with information concerning the antiquities of his native Alloway the result was a prose description about the haunting of Kirkalloway, subsequently transformed into Burns's poetic masterpiece *Tam O'Shanter*, published as a double-column footnote in the second volume of Grose's *Antiquities of Scotland* in 1791. Although Burns, like the plebeian poets Hogg and Clare, himself possessed an amphibious social cachet as a 'participant observer' of popular culture, his description of Grose as 'a chield amang you takin notes' elegantly captures the reaction 'on the ground' to learned antiquarian enquirers.

BROADSIDES, BALLAD SINGERS, AND POPULAR PRINT

We have preferred in this book to employ the term 'popular' rather than its cognate 'folk', even though both words often connote a specific opposition to 'mass' culture in the name of a rural working-class community and its oral traditions. But in contrast to 'popular' the term 'folk' had no currency in English during the Romantic period. In 1846, William John Thoms wrote to the *Athenaeum* suggesting that 'what we in England designate as Popular Antiquities, or Popular Literature' would be more 'aptly described by a good Saxon compound, Folk-lore – the lore of the People'.[56] The suggestion fell on fertile soil: by 1878 there was an English 'Folk-lore Society' (under the direction of Thoms himself) and 'folk-song' soon passed into common parlance. But Thoms's vernacularizing impulse disguises the fact that the provenance of such usage lay in German rather than British Romanticism: Morag Shiach notes that when Mary Howitt had employed the expression 'folk's-song' in 1847 she quite explicitly referred to Herder's notion of the *Volkslieder* and A. W. Schlegel's *Volkspoesie*. By 1871, the date of the first recorded use of the term 'folk-song' (in the *Cornhill Magazine*), it denoted the orally based production of an idealized, pre-industrial peasantry, at odds with modern industrial society.[57] William Barrett's *English Folk-Songs* (1891) was the first British collection to feature the term 'folk-song' in its title, although Francis James Child studiously avoided the term in the title of his landmark collection, *English and Scottish Popular Ballads* (1882–98), testifying to a residual Anglo-Saxon (as opposed to German) suspicion concerning collective 'folk' authorship and oral tradition.[58]

Such issues might recall us to Michel de Certeau's cautionary remarks on the futile search for 'the voice of the People'. There is, Certeau argues, 'no such "pure" voice, because it is always determined by a system (whether societal, familial, or other) and codified by a way of receiving it . . . orality insinuates itself, like one of the threads of which it is composed, into the network – an endless tapestry – of a scriptural economy'.[59] The very distinction between oral and print culture inspiring such a quest is itself a product of Romanticism and its aftermath. In his introduction to *Fragments of Ancient Poetry Collected in the Highlands of Scotland* (1760), James Macpherson claimed that the purity of oral transmission in a 'primitive'

Celtic society guaranteed the 'traditional' nature of its cultural productions: 'By the succession of these Bards, such poems were handed down from race to race; some in manuscript, but more by oral tradition. And tradition, in a country so free of intermixture with foreigners, and among a people so strongly attached to the memory of their ancestors, has preserved many of them in a great measure incorrupted to this day.'[60] Nick Groom has argued that 'even the name "Oscian" ... means "mouthy" (from the Latin *os*, a mouth)' and that the success of Macpherson's prose poetry depended upon the mastery of oral effects: the moment this failed, with the publication of part of the Gaelic manuscript of *Temora* in 1763, the fragments were denounced as a forgery.[61] As Leask's chapter argues, this did so much damage to the creditworthiness of oral sources that ballad editors from Percy to Scott – that is to say, up to and including the Romantic decades – preferred print and manuscript collection. Leith Davis, by contrast, proposes that Charlotte Brooke and her Irish contemporaries resisted the metropolitan preference for print, presenting 'ancient' Irish poetry as a continuous oral tradition passed down to the present day by harpers and composers like Turlough O'Carolan and Patrick Linden. Kirsteen McCue's chapter argues, further, that the transmission of songs and ballads in the Romantic period cannot be separated from the airs and melodies to which they were set, despite the fact that many collections published lyrics only. Melodic structure was as important in securing the popularity and currency of a song as its words, and in the case of national songs it was often the distinguishing feature. For instance, 'ancient Scottish airs' followed the modern diatonic scale with the fourth and seventh removed, a fact which tended to determine which melodies were collected by antiquaries, and which were excluded. In the long run, victory was assured for the Celtic fringe, as oral sources became increasingly important with the rise of the 'folk-song' movement in the nineteenth and twentieth centuries, affording a prestige to oral tradition which continues today.

It follows then that the distinction between oral and print culture which emerged during the Romantic period was, and is, a false trail. Although the problem of mediation in one way or another confronts every single chapter in this book, recent research suggests that the interweaving of orality in de Certeau's 'scriptural economy' (or its reverse, the interweaving of print in an oral economy) was just as much a feature of popular culture in the long eighteenth century as in modern academic discussions thereof. Influenced by Chartier's 'appropriation' theory discussed above, Jonathan Barry criticizes a common tendency of 'bi-polar' theories simply to equate popular culture with orality; 'rather than seeing literacy as a convenient dividing line between two cultures, we need rather to be aware of how far differential access to writing, and the forms of expression that writing encouraged, has structured our sources for popular culture'.[62] Barry demonstrates that in early modern Britain 'sign literacy' (the minimal ability to write one's name) was far less widely distributed than reading ability, and that 'the experience of print for many ordinary people may have been a public and communal one, in which clear boundaries between oral and literate culture would have been blurred', an experience epitomized in the popular ballad.[63] Nor should we forget the illustrated nature of many chapbooks and broadsides, completing their status as 'multi-media' artefacts often serving as transitional vehicles of literacy. Indeed, Patricia Anderson has argued that 'the imagery dispensed through the medium of print' between 1790 and 1832 'provided English workers with their most sustained source of aesthetic experience, visual information, and pictorial amusement', even if in the interests of economy the same woodcuts were frequently recycled to illustrate many different texts.[64]

Principal varieties of cheap books included chivalric romances, criminal biographies, histories, travels, and religious texts, although generic boundaries were often fluid. As Niall Ó Ciosáin writes, 'one form of transformation which applied frequently to all [these] texts was that they became oral recitations, performances, or simply rumours', especially via the widespread practice of reading aloud.[65] This was of course particularly true of the ballad, although given a common tendency to regard the ballad as an oral form, Albert Friedman's definition of the eighteenth-century understanding of the term still has the power to surprise: 'a ballad, so far as either men of letters or plain citizens were concerned, was a doggerel poem written to a familiar tune, printed on a folio sheet or long slip, and sold at bookstalls or hawked about the streets by ballad-singers'.[66] Robert S. Thomson has convincingly demonstrated that 'the availability of the broadside ballads supported, reinforced, and enlarged the folksong repertoire to a degree not hitherto suspected'.[67] Production and distribution of printed ballads and chapbooks in the eighteenth century was dominated by William and Cluer Dicey's printing house in Bow (later Aldermary) Churchyard, London.[68] Along with William Marshall, his successor John Pitts of Seven Dials, and the latter's rival James Catnach, from 1813 onwards famous for his 'cocks' and 'catchpennies' (fictitious ballad narratives printed when real news was scarce), the London ballad warehouses long dominated the nation's popular print industry. Leslie Shepard describes how the eighteenth-century popularity of chapbooks and garlands (song collections) was overtaken by ballad broadsides in the early nineteenth century, just before the introduction of cheap books and newspapers.[69]

With literacy levels estimated at 35–40 per cent in late eighteenth-century England and Ireland (higher in Scotland with its parochial schools) penny chapbooks and broadsides were often the only affordable reading matter for the populace.[70] Ó Ciosáin shows that much of the limited publication in the Celtic languages (Irish, Welsh, and Scottish Gaelic) in this period was devotional in nature, although some secular chapbooks and political tracts also circulated. A startling 3,000 works were printed in Welsh before 1820 (largely connected with the Methodist evangelical movement) compared to fewer than 200 in Irish, 'a statistic all the more striking when it is borne in mind that the population of Wales in 1800 was perhaps a tenth of the population of Ireland'.[71] But English of course dominated popular print, and London printers like the Diceys penetrated every corner of the United Kingdom by mid-century, although they encountered increasing competition from the provinces and from Scotland (where chapbooks were often printed in Scots as well as English) and Ireland, where, respectively, the 1709 copyright act was either flouted or not binding. The exclusion of Catholic printers from the flourishing Dublin trades guilds resulted in their monopolizing the chapbook 'country market' in rural areas of Ireland. This resulted in a 'culturally anglicizing and politically catholicizing' trend in Irish popular print, albeit one that was later challenged by the rise of provincial Gaelic language printing in the period 1800–50.[72]

Chapbook literature also crossed the barrier of social class, a fact well demonstrated by the example of James Boswell mentioned above. Boswell confessed to having read Dicey chapbooks like *Jack and the Giants* and *The Seven Wise Men of Gotham* as a child in Auchinleck in Ayrshire, suggesting either the extensive geographical reach of Dicey's broadsides and chapbooks over the Scottish border, or else, given the proliferation of provincial printing presses, the currency of pirated copies.[73] Boswell's enthusiasm for such material supports Barry's suggestion that 'for the upper classes . . . if there was a world of private reading [as opposed to the public texts of the university, church, and law court], it may have been in large part that of "popular literature". Certainly ballads, romances and the like were treasured by elite children as an enthralling alternative world of print to the authoritative texts they endured at school.'[74] Boswell's chapbooks emanated the utopian glow of childhood prior to his class-conditioning into the 'great tradition'. His countryman Walter Scott had assembled a collection of 114 chapbooks by 1810, 'formed by me when a boy from the baskets of the travelling pedlars', although his collection preserved in the library at Abbotsford yields several thousand more, attesting to a lifetime of collecting, upon which he drew subsequently in his poetry and fiction.[75]

The confusion wrought upon a two-tier model of cultural consumption by this instance is complemented by another anecdote mentioned by Dianne Dugaw, half a century later, and at the other end of the social scale. John Clare's delighted response to Percy's *Reliques of Ancient English Poetry*, which he first read in 1820, highlights the hidden links between printed and oral balladry: '[Edwin Drury] has sent me 3 vols call'd "Percy's Relics" there is some sweet poetry in them & I think it the most pleasing book I ever happend [*sic*] on the tales are familiar from childhood all the stories of my grandmother & her gossiping neighbours I find versified in these vols.'[76] Evidently ballads from the Dicey stock, incorporated without acknowledgement by Percy in the *Reliques* (including 'Chevy Chase', 'Jane Shore', 'Johnny Armstrong', 'The Dragon of Wantley', and others), were still current in rural Northamptonshire in the 1790s during Clare's boyhood, and it is significant that Clare's home was close to one of the distribution routes of Dicey's ballad sellers.[77]

The female sources named here by Clare (his grandmother and 'gossiping neighbours') also need to be underlined, for as Ann Wierda Rowland has argued, 'women who worked as nurses and mothers were the most common ballad singers in eighteenth-century Scotland and the most significant sources of traditional ballads for antiquarian collectors', an observation which seems to have been equally true of Clare's Northamptonshire.[78] Although plebeian women were less likely to be literate than men, the fact that many ballads envisage a female audience, or address subjects like the difficulties of courtship, betrayal by male lovers, or infanticide, suggests a female, domestic site for the singing or recitation of ballads. This shouldn't exclude consideration of more 'public' scenes of performance by women at markets and fairs (as well as street hawkers) to complement the male performance spaces of the tavern or workplace.[79] Deborah Symonds proposes that Scott and other male collectors 'never managed to erase the importance of women, either as [ballad] singers or heroines, despite their firm belief that ballads had originated in a male bardic tradition'.[80]

William St Clair has proposed that the chapbooks of this era should not be regarded as textual relics of 'pre-industrial Britain'. On the contrary, 'more chapbook titles, both old and new, were published, in larger numbers, and in many more towns, than at any previous time. Far from being an industry on the verge of decline, the chapbook industry of the Romantic period formed part of the explosion of reading which began in the late eighteenth century.'[81] Yet largely as a consequence of changes in the copyright regime explored in some detail by St Clair, an 'old' chapbook and ballad canon stretching back to Elizabethan and Jacobean times was in the process of being transformed by a new repertoire of cheap copies of titles such as *Gulliver's Travels* and *Robinson Crusoe*, along with popular pastoral songs of recent composition by the likes of Robert Burns, Tom Moore, and Charles Dibdin.[82] In contrast to Lackington's bullish view of this change quoted above, in attempting to form his own ballad collection, now recognized as the pioneer collection of English folk-songs, John Clare regretted that

nearly all those old & beautiful reccolections [*sic*] had vanished as so many old fashions & those who knew the fragments seemed ashamed to acknowledge it . . . those who were proud of their knowledge in such things – knew nothing but the sensless [*sic*] balderdash that is brawled over & sung at County Feasts Statutes & Fairs where the most sensless [*sic*] jargon passes for the greatest excellence & rudest indecency for the finest wit.[83]

Emphasis on the importance of printed broadsides in the period thus needs to be balanced by a sense of their relationship with oral transmission: it is certainly not the case that 'the folk' passively received their ballads ready-made from printed broadsheets distributed by monopolizing commercial networks. To argue that oral performance is merely a pale reflex of commercial print marketed by the big warehouses risks robbing popular culture of its appropriative power and creative agency.[84] In order to understand this process of cross-pollination between the oral and the printed ballad, it is necessary to grasp the mode of distributing broadsides and chapbooks in the seventeenth and eighteenth centuries. Printed ballads were distributed by 'flying stationers' who toured town and country, singing samples of their wares, and vending their broadside sheet to listeners for a penny or a halfpenny. The coverage of England by travelling chapmen was so highly organized that, as early as 1628, itineraries were being printed specifically to aid them in planning the most effective routes taking in provincial fairs and markets.[85] Broadsides and ballad sheets were commonly pasted up on the walls of cottages, taverns, and city streets, providing ample occasion for passers-by to memorize their narratives, or in taverns for solo or collective singing.[86] Some polite collectors were willing to admit wall ballads as sources; for example, in

1806 Robert Jamieson's notes to 'Young Bechan and Susie Pye' gives his principal source as the

recitation of Mrs Brown of Falkland . . . collated with two other copies procured from Scotland, one in MS, another very good one printed from the stalls; a third in the possession of the late Rev James Boucher of Epsom, taken from a recitation in the North of England, and a fourth, about as long as the others, which the Editor picked off an old wall in Piccadilly.[87]

A popular chapbook like *The History of John Cheap the Chapman* illuminates the rough-and-ready working conditions of its probable author, Stirling-born chapman and 'patterer' Dougal Graham (who also composed a 4d 'History of the Jacobite Rebellion' in verse, and scores of other chapbooks). Trade was just as hard for David Love of Nottingham, William 'Hawkie' Cameron of Glasgow, Charles Leslie ('Mussle-mou'd Charlie'), or James Rankin of Aberdeen, a blind beggar who was employed by the ballad collector Peter Buchan, and supplied material to Walter Scott, Robert Jamieson, and William Motherwell.[88] The fact that the chapmen mentioned here were of Scottish birth suggests not only that 'pattering' was an attractive option in relatively impoverished Scotland – and we might recall the Scottish provenance of Wordsworth's impeccably respectable Pedlar in *The Excursion* – but also that these disseminators of popular balladry were more likely to be memorialized in print in a culture obsessed with the question of working-class literacy.[89]

Pattering and oral performance (by singing and/or recitation) were thus fundamental to the ballad singer's sales pitch; so the fact that a ballad or song was printed didn't mean that it was 'frozen' and resistant to adaptation or variation. As Flemming G. Andersen has argued, 'many broadsides travelled from print into oral transmission in the rural districts and perhaps back to the printed page in the town, and many ballad versions were gleaned directly from oral circulation and then registered as broadsides in the Stationers' Company [Register]. Most ballads have been in and out of tradition.'[90] Questioning the exclusive claims of twentieth-century folklorists who adhere to the 'oral-formulaic' theory of ballad performance, Flemming Andersen analyses a broadside version of 'Lord Thomas and Fair Ellinor' in the Pepys collection, to show that 'the manner of narrative presentation, revealed by a structural analysis, is strikingly similar for the texts/songs we usually term oral traditional ballads'.[91]

Although, as Kirsteen McCue argues here, song melodies by and large remained constant, the creative mediation of printed ballads by common singers (as well as elite editors like Percy and Scott) is clear from historical anecdotage as well. John Clare wrote that he 'composed imitations of popular songs floating amongst the vulgar at the markets and fairs': Robert Burns had done the same in collecting songs for Johnson's *Musical Museum* and George Thomson's *Select Scottish Airs*, and although he often set new words to old tunes, he would frequently vary traditional settings.[92] This sometimes served to ironically inflect the new lyrics, as in his setting of the radical anthem 'Is there for Honest Poverty' to the old Jacobite song 'Tho' Geordie rules in Jamie's stead'. When James Hogg was asked by Walter Scott's servant during one of Scott's 'Liddesdale Raids' 'Are ye the chiel that maks the auld ballads and sings them?', the answer was coy: 'I said I fancied I was he that he meant, though I had never made ony very auld ballads.'[93] The London printer John Pitts increased his song stock by collecting songs and ballads from the Irish immigrants on his doorstep in the slum area of Seven Dials and 'enlisting printers in the countryside to tap the repertoires of provincial customers'.[94] The movement between printed and oral material, and between consumption and production, was in the nature of a constant feedback loop. At a different social level, McCue demonstrates the extent to which musical entrepreneurs like Thomson commissioned sophisticated settings for 'national airs' in order to introduce them to a polite audience previously ignorant of the richness of their national repertoires, another aspect of Burke's 'discovery of the people' in the Romantic period.

POPULAR POLITICS AND THE REFORMATION OF MANNERS

'Vulgar and indecent penny books were always common,' remarked the evangelical Hannah More in 1796, 'but speculative infidelity, brought down to the pockets and capacities of the poor, forms a new aera in our history.'[95] More's comments reflect growing alarm at the rapid spread of radicalism and irreligion through the lower orders, a process closely associated with the threat of plebeian literacy in the years following the French Revolution. Events across the channel, and burgeoning radical organization among the 'lower orders' within Britain and Ireland, gave new urgency to the representation of the people, in more senses than one. They also sharpened existing anxieties concerning the policing of plebeian society, exerting considerable pressure on contemporary representations of popular manners and traditions, and thus helped to shape an enduring ideologically motivated distinction between organic, traditionary, rural society and the dangerous, print-based world of popular enlightenment and militant literacy.

Recognizably 'popular' forms of political organization and expression were nothing new, of course, and nor were they necessarily identified with the cause of reform. The quintessential embodiment of English popular political consciousness, John Bull, was by turns independent and deferential, pugnacious yet stoical: an endlessly appropriable figure for the common people.[96] This ideological ambivalence (visually rendered as a kind of passive bemusement in many prints) reflects the predominantly constitutionalist idiom of eighteenth-century political discourse, which accorded a significant yet fundamentally contested role to the popular component of England's 'ancient' forms of government. As a result, from around the mid-eighteenth century, as Kathleen Wilson and others have shown, the 'sense of the people' assumed an unusually consequential place within the language and culture of English politics. Indeed, 'since it was the (largely mythical) role of the people in the constitution that in most contemporaries' minds distinguished English liberty from Continental absolutism, populist beliefs and discourses were a crucial plank in the construction of national ideologies and consciousness'.[97] The conflation of patriotic and plebeian political identities allowed popular politics to find unofficial expression within the 'quotidian domains of custom and culture', from clubs and alehouses to fairs, mock-elections, political ballads, jest books, and burlesque.[98] But 'popular' patriotism could also be fraught with political tension. In the case of Scotland, for example, the rebellious Jacobite 'Bonnie Hieland Laddie' was only reimagined as a loyal Briton in the course of the Napoleonic wars, after the heavy casualties suffered by Scottish regiments in the struggle against France.[99] And in Ireland, despite the best efforts of writers such as Maria Edgeworth and Lady Morgan, the recuperation of a 'loyal' Irish peasantry in the aftermath of the 1798 rebellion proved well-nigh impossible, despite the large numbers of Catholic Irishmen serving in the British army and navy.[100]

Adherents of E. P. Thompson's approach are apt to make a problematic equation between 'popular' and 'working class' although, as Patricia Anderson argues, popular culture was 'only in part expressive of worker radicalism and cannot on that ground be interpreted as an emergent class culture built wholly and exclusively on oppositional consciousness'.[101] It is worth recalling that Thompson in any case emphasized that the 'resistance' to the dominant culture mounted by eighteenth-century plebeians was often profoundly conservative and 'traditionary' in nature. There was undoubtedly a powerful strain of conservatism – religious and constitutional – in much popular political consciousness.[102] Yet in the decades following 1789, 'the people' would increasingly conjure either the spectre of revolution or the promise of constitutional reform.

It was, above all, the publication of Thomas Paine's *Rights of Man* in a cheap sixpence edition in 1792 that focused official attitudes to popular political literacy. The phenomenal success of Paine's work certainly provoked a concerted response, including More's notorious *Village Politics*, a mass-circulated attack on 'republicans and levellers' adapted to the idiom of the rural parish.[103] The series of *Cheap Repository Tracts* which followed constituted one of the largest publishing campaigns of the Romantic period, thanks in large part to the supportive efforts of voluntary societies, religious patrons, and wealthy benefactors, in Britain and Ireland.[104] Yet the counter-revolutionary politics of the *Tracts* cannot be separated from their broader moral and religious critique of late eighteenth-century popular culture. By colonizing the broadside and chapbook formats and styles, as well as the distribution networks of popular literature, the evangelicals sought 'to infiltrate and subvert, rather than legislate and overtly control, the day to day lives and culture of the poor'.[105] From this perspective, the evangelical conservatism of the *Cheap Repository* can be seen as part of a longer history of efforts to police the vulgar, stretching back to the 'reformation of manners' movement of the earlier eighteenth century.[106] It also demonstrates the degree to which the culture, traditions, religion, and 'manners' of the people were inseparable from increasingly urgent questions concerning popular political representation. The widespread campaigns against popular sports, pastimes, and holidays, which gathered pace in the later eighteenth century, were explicitly intended to instil social deference and labour discipline, restraining the 'riots and tumults' typically associated with plebeian recreation, but which could also assume the more threatening aspect of political protest (Figure 1.1).[107]

There is certainly little doubt that the world of popular print and balladry was regarded as a dangerous *demi-monde*, increasingly subject to the regulative concerns of Church and State – and often with good reason. While some popular prints enforced traditional morality and quiescent patriotism, others subordinated moral edification to impolite amusement, earning their description by Henry Thornton as 'corrupt and vicious little books and ballads'.[108] Anderson notes that of 735 broadside titles listed in Catnach's 1832 catalogue, only 17 are 'even remotely indicative of radical content', and of these, 'less than half imply any clear element of protest'.[109] But the broader moral tendency of popular literature could often appear distinctly

Fig. 1.1 The counter-revolutionary uses of popular print: [Hannah More], 'The Riot; or, Half a Loaf is Better than no Bread' (London, [1795]), Madden Ballad Collection, 15–69. Reproduced by permission of the Syndics of Cambridge University Library.

The *RIOT*;

Or, HALF a LOAF is better than no BREAD.

In a DIALOGUE between *Jack Anvil* and *Tom Hod*.

To the Tune of "A Cobler there was," &c.

TOM.

COME neighbours, no longer be patient and
   quiet,
Come let us go kick up a bit of a riot;
I am hungry, my lads, but I've little to eat,
So we'll pull down the mills, and seize all the meat:
I'll give you good fport, boys, as ever you faw,
So a fig for the Juftice, a fig for the law.
        Derry down.

Then his pitchfork Tom feiz'd—Hold a moment
   fays Jack,
I'll fhew thee thy blunder, brave boy, in a crack,
And if I don't prove we had better be ftill,
I'll affift thee ftraitway to pull down every mill;
I'll fhew thee how paffion thy reafon does cheat,
Or I'll join thee in plunder for bread and for meat.
        Derry down.

What a whimfey to think thus our bellies to fill,
For we ftop all the grinding by breaking the mill!
What a whimfey to think we fhall get more to eat
By abufing the butchers who get us the meat!
What a whimfey to think we fhall mend our fpare
   diet
By breeding difturbance, by murder and riot!
        Derry down.

Becaufe I am dry 'twould be foolifh, I think
To pull out my tap and to fpill all my drink;
Becaufe I am hungry and want to be fed,
That is fure no wife reafon for wafting my bread;
And juft fuch wife reafons for mending their diet
Are us'd by thofe blockheads who rufh into riot.
        Derry down.

I would not take comfort from others diftreffes,
But ftill I would mark how God our land bleffes;
For tho' in Old England the times are but fad,
Abroad I am told they are ten times as bad;
In the land of the Pope there is fcarce any grain,
And 'tis ftill worfe, they fay, both in Holland and
   Spain.
        Derry down.

Let us look to the harveft our wants to beguile,
See the lands with rich crops how they every
   where fmile!
Mean time to affift us, by each Weftern breeze,
Some corn is brought daily acrofs the falt feas,
Of tea we'll drink little, of gin none at all,
And we'll patiently wait and the prices will fall.
        Derry down.

But if we're not quiet, then let us not wonder
If things grow much worfe by our riot and plunder;
And let us remember whenever we meet,
The more Ale we drink, boys, the lefs we fhall eat.
On thofe days fpent in riot as bread you brought home,
Had you fpent them in labour you muft have had fome.
        Derry down.

A dinner of herbs, fays the wife man, with quiet,
Is better than beef amid difcord and riot.
If the thing can't be help'd I'm a foe to all ftrife,
And I pray for a peace every night of my life;
But in matters of ftate not an inch will I budge,
Becaufe I conceive I'm no very good judge.
        Derry down.

But tho' poor I can work, my brave boy, with
   the beft,
Let the King and the Parliament manage the reft;
I lament both the War and the Taxes together,
Tho' I verily think they don't alter the weather.
The King, as I take it, with very good reafon,
May prevent a bad law, but can't help a bad feafon.
        Derry down.

The Parliament-men, altho' great is their power,
Yet they cannot contrive us a bit of a fhower;
And I never yet heard, tho' our Rulers are wife,
That they know very well how to manage the fkies;
For the beft of them all, as they found to their coft,
Were not able to hinder laft winter's hard froft.
        Derry down.

Befides I muft fhare in the wants of the times,
Becaufe I have had my full fhare in it's crimes;
And I'm apt to believe the diftrefs which is fent,
Is to punifh and cure us of all difcontent.
—But harveft is coming—Potatoes are come!
Our profpect clears up; Ye complainers be dumb!
        Derry down.

And tho' I've no money, and tho' I've no lands,
I've a head on my fhoulders, and a pair of good
   hands;
So I'll work the whole day, and on Sundays I'll feek
At church how to bear all the wants of the week.
The Gentlefolks too will afford us fupplies;
They'll fubfcribe—and they'll give up their puddings
   and pies.
        Derry down.

Then before I'm induc'd to take part in a Riot,
I'll afk this fhort queftion—What fhall I get by it?
So I'll e'en wait a little till cheaper the bread,
For a mittimus hangs o'er each Rioter's head;
And when of two evils I'm afk'd which is beft,
I'd rather be hungry than hang'd, I proteft.
        Derry down.

Quoth Tom, thou art right; If I rife, I'm a Turk,
So he threw down his pitchfork, and went to his work.

        Z.

[*Entered at Stationers Hall.*]

Sold by J. MARSHALL,
(PRINTER to the CHEAP REPOSITORY for Moral and Religious Tracts) No. 17, Queen-Street, Cheapfide, and
No. 4, Aldermary Church-Yard; and R. WHITE, Piccadilly, LONDON.
By S. HAZARD,
(PRINTER to the CHEAP REPOSITORY,) at BATH; and by all Bookfellers, Newfmen, and Hawkers in Town
and Country.
☞ Great Allowance will be made to Shopkeepers and Hawkers.
Price an Halfpenny, or 2s. 3d. per 100.—1s. 3d. for 50.—9d. for 25.

subversive. As Pedersen puts it, broadside and chapbook literature of the later eighteenth century is remarkably

unified in tone: the vast proportion is profoundly irreverent and often amoral. It is equally sceptical of natural laws, social order, and religious duty. Often chapbooks present either a fantasy landscape or a world turned upside down: a world of giants and witches, of poor but valorous heroes, of scheming wives and successful crooks. Above all, they are hostile to respectability: to industry, chastity, piety, and other bourgeois values.[110]

Many radicals shared the prejudices of the tract societies regarding popular print. Writing to the future United Irishman Patrick Byrne, the radical Dublin printer Matthew Carey complained of 'the vile tales and burton books, whereof thousands are annually disseminated throughout Ireland, and which corrupt the taste (and may I not add, the morals) of the youth of both sexes'.[111] Nonetheless, radicals and conservatives alike appropriated the formats and distribution networks of cheap literature to promote their cause. As Kevin Gilmartin's chapter points out, Coleridge noted with concern, in 1812, that the speeches of leading political reformers were being 'printed in ballad form, & sold at a halfpenny each'.[112] And radical periodicals such as Thomas Spence's *Pig's Meat* or Daniel Isaac Eaton's *Politics for the People* broke with the rational protocols of 'respectable' radicalism in order to politicize the 'world turned upside down' of the chapbook tradition, as well as drawing upon the popular energy of tavern debating, 'filled with political argument, wild toasts and songs, and barbed humour'.[113] Yet the communal solidarity which found ritualized expression in such venues existed in a complex tension with the political, social, and indeed cultural aspirations of many plebeian reformers, a tension underlined in John Barrell's chapter in this volume.

Conservative fears of mass literacy were informed by a sociology of knowledge which remained considerably less nuanced in its representation of popular manners and opinion. As Penny Fielding has reminded us, 'in order for literacy to remain in the province of middle-class order and stability, popular literacy was generally thought of as *ill*iteracy'.[114] The prospectus for the *Cheap Repository* thus employed the language of poison and pathological corruption to characterize plebeian reading habits, even as it suggests the ubiquity of popular print at the turn of the nineteenth century:

The immediate object of this Institution is the circulation of religious and useful knowledge, as an antidote to the poison continually flowing through the channel of those licentious publications which are vended about our cities, towns, and villages, chiefly by the means of hawkers, of whom above 20,000 are supposed to be employed, more or less, in this pernicious traffic.

When it is considered what vast multitudes there are whose reading is, in a great measure, confined to these corrupt performances, which consist principally of immoral songs and penny papers, and what invention and pains are used to tempt people to the perusal of them, by hanging them on walls, exhibiting them at windows, as well as offering them to passengers in the streets, and at the doors of houses, it must be obvious, that it is become a point of no small consequence to correct so great an evil, which is not likely to be done effectually without condescending to supply tracts equally cheap, and adapted in like manner to the capacity of the common people.[115]

The titles of some of these ballads and tales, which had sold over two million copies by 1796, speak for themselves: 'The Riot; or, Half a Loaf is Better than no Bread', 'The Loyal Sailor; or no Mutineering', and so on. Although the wide circulation of such tracts might well have played some part in changing (or indeed reinforcing) popular attitudes, we should not assume that readers passively accepted their moralizing message. John Clare, for one, complained of

having a Tract thrust into my hand the other day by a neighbour containing the dreadful end of an atheist who shot his own daughter for going to a methodist chapple [*sic*] – this is one of the white lies that are suffered to be hawked about the country to meet the superstitions of the unwary – & though it may make the weak shake their heads & believe it – others will despise their cant & pity the weakness of those who propogate [*sic*] such absurditys [*sic*].[116]

As Deacon indicates, many readers of this kind of tract would perhaps have cared little for its attempts to frighten them from atheism or Methodism, being more likely to have taken it as just another 'awful murder' ballad.[117]

Yet the growth of plebeian reading audiences did not, of course, have a merely negative or destructive effect on traditional sources of popular recreation. Changing literacy rates, and the expanding market for print, created new forms of plebeian political consciousness, along with what has sometimes been called a 'counter-public sphere'. As the radical periodical the *Black Dwarf* put it, in 1819,

The political information so recently spread among the great bulk of the people, has produced an effect at which both Whigs and Tories are astonished. They start at finding politicians in every village, and orators in every town, that shame the boasted talents of wealth and education.[118]

Coleridge concurred: 'The Powers that awaken and foster the Spirit of Curiosity and Investigation, are to be found in every Village; Books are in every Cottage.'[119] Such manifestations of 'popular enlightenment' offered a considerable challenge to the conventional rhetorical deference to 'public opinion', or *vox populi*, on the part of the political classes. The radical response to the 'Peterloo massacre' of 1819, in which the Manchester yeomanry charged upon a peaceful mass reform meeting, crystallized a new-found sense of literate and constitutionally legitimate public opinion amongst the lower orders.[120] As Ian Haywood's chapter suggests, Peterloo offered a fundamental challenge to the Liverpool government's political intransigence, in the face of a dignified, 'respectable' – and in large part female – reformist body politic. Percy Shelley's imaginative response to the events in Manchester, in the *Mask of Anarchy*, draws much of its strength from the confidence and vitality of the popular reform movement in this period. Yet Shelley also remains implicitly attuned to the problems of agency involved in any such attempt to 'awaken & direct the imagination of the reformers' on the part of the enlightened poet.[121]

Coleridge himself, after his turn to political conservatism, sought not simply to submit popular opinion to the formative influence of a 'clerisy', but to redefine the idea of 'culture' itself in a politically consequential manner. In his most influential work of political prose, *On the Constitution of Church and State* (1829), Coleridge undertook what might be described as a philosophical reformation of 'manners', opposing mere civilization to *cultivation*, 'the harmonious development of those qualities and faculties that characterize our *humanity*'.[122] Such arguments would profoundly influence nineteenth-century debates on national education and the civic function of humanistic learning; more immediately, however, they also served to efface the complex dialectical relationship between commercial modernity and popular political consciousness, both of which could now be opposed, as the products of mere 'civilization', to an organic imagined community under the watchful tutelage of Church and State.

The terms of that opposition are already anticipated, with somewhat different ends, in the writings of William Cobbett. Disparaging the progressivist rhetoric of liberal whigs and 'respectable' radicals, Cobbett sought to articulate a form of popular political consciousness attuned instead to the traditional manners and customs of the country.[123] His attitudes to popular literacy, as a result, remained highly ambivalent; yet Cobbett turned his *Political Register* into one of the most important popular periodicals of the early nineteenth century. His truculent brand of 'rural radicalism' offered an influential alternative to those more eirenic and deferential representations of a contented British peasantry which, through the work of painters and poets such as Gainsborough, Goldsmith, and Bloomfield, helped to consolidate a conservative and predominantly rural vision of the nation's popular traditions until well into the nineteenth century.[124]

Indeed, while 'the people' were repeatedly appropriated by the dominant forms of 'high' Romantic culture, the traffic was by no means one-way. The strict legislative regulation of the press – much of it a direct result of anti-Jacobin reaction – did not deter a host of pirated editions of canonical Romantic writers marketed directly at plebeian audiences. The links between illicit publishers and political radicalism were both strong and enduring. From the 'radical underworld' of late eighteenth-century London to the Chartist publishers of the 1840s, the printed media of the reform movement played a crucial role in stimulating a truly popular audience for Romantic writers, while challenging the ideological grounds of literary canon formation.[125] The printing in 1817 of Southey's early Jacobin drama *Wat Tyler* is perhaps the most notorious example of such radical piracy in this period. The young Southey had sought to turn Tyler into a republican folk hero, and a spokesman for the grievances of the 'mighty multitude'; post-war popular radicalism turned the work back on its apostate author, to devastating effect.[126]

Meanwhile, reformist publishers such as William Benbow produced multiple illicit versions of the works of Shelley and Byron, 'retailed amidst obscenity, sedition, and blasphemy in inexpensive editions for working-class and artisan readers'.[127] Byron's *Don Juan*, in particular, achieved an extraordinary and lasting popularity through cheap pirated editions. For publishers such as William Hone, the poem's transgressive combination of 'sublime thought and low humour' made it eminently marketable to a popular audience, while simultaneously exposing the moralizing cant of Byron's 'respectable' readers.[128] As Mina Gorji discusses in her chapter, Hone went on to publish the *Every-Day Book* and *Table Book* – popular antiquarianism aptly described by its author as 'a kind of literary kaleidoscope, combining popular forms with singular appearances'.[129] Marilyn Butler has argued that 'it was this down-market publisher who gave the urban crowd the concept of a popular cultural history'.[130] But the impetus for such endeavours can be traced back to Hone's earlier activities as a radical publisher, and his persistent desire to challenge the hypocrisy and legislative repression which governed both popular political expression and the cultural division between 'high' and 'low' literature.

THE EXPERIENCE OF URBANIZATION

The 'discovery' of popular culture, we are accustomed to think, was profoundly connected with the rise of the town, and the accompanying desuetude of rural tradition. By 1801, nearly a third of the English population were urbanites of one sort or another. But while the displacement of the population into towns and cities generated new ways of experiencing and representing 'the people', the process of social and economic change was geographically uneven and chronologically extended, particularly when considered within the larger territorial context of Scotland and Ireland. Thus, while the process of urbanization proceeded slowly in Gaelic Ireland and Highland Scotland, the Scottish Lowlands experienced a far more rapid and unsettling demographic shift from country to city in the course of the later eighteenth century.[131] Patterns of migration, moreover, were more complex than is often assumed. Eighteenth-century Britain was indeed a highly mobile society, yet migration was often temporary, short-distance, and inhibited by the centripetal pull of parochial government.[132] If these factors preclude any simple opposition between 'country' and 'city', they also suggest the limitations of an exclusively ruralist approach to the popular culture of this period.[133]

We have seen in the foregoing discussion that eighteenth- and early nineteenth-century antiquarianism was often strongly oriented towards the traditional customs and manners of the country (anticipating the later bias of 'folklore' studies in this respect). Yet throughout this period, antiquarian discourse was just as likely to concern itself with the *urban* past. The eighteenth-century townscape was thus historicized as a legible repository of civic tradition and changing manners, a process treated here in Ina Ferris's chapter on Robert Chambers's *Traditions of Edinburgh*. As Ferris points out, civic antiquarians frequently pandered to the progressivist assumptions of their respectable readers within the 'middle orders', and the corresponding hostility of such readers to the traditional plebeian component of customary ritual and ceremony. In Rosemary Sweet's words, 'traditional forms of activity were marginalized to the status of popular customs or disappeared altogether and the civic rituals became more and more exclusive. What once commanded the participation of the town as a whole became stigmatized as "popular" and were rendered the objects of antiquarian curiosity.'[134] Such conclusions are clearly compatible with Peter Borsay's influential account of the English 'urban renaissance'. On this analysis, the architecture and topography of the eighteenth-century town increasingly served an exclusionary function, dividing the polite, enlightened world of circulating libraries, balls, assemblies, concerts, and clubs from the plebeian social milieu of artisans, labourers, and servants.[135] Although Borsay himself has qualified this binary model of urban social division, his account of cultural polarization provides a suggestive way of understanding both civic and regional identity in this period: 'The spatial perception embodied in traditional culture focused *inwards* on local customs and practices, whereas those of its polite counterpart looked *outwards* towards London and the continent.'[136]

Once polite provincial travellers actually arrived in Georgian London, however, their sense of social distinction was liable to be sorely tested. By the time of the 1801 census, the capital contained as many as 900,000 souls, around 10 per cent of the English population.[137] The sheer concentration of human life within London's boundaries offered an inescapable challenge to the spatial discrimination of high and low, popular and polite. This was, of course, a habitual complaint, vividly expressed in 1771 by Smollett's Matthew Bramble, on his first arrival in the metropolis: 'In short, there is no distinction or subordination left – The different departments of life are jumbled together – The hod-carrier, the low mechanic, the tapster, the publican, the shop-keeper, the pettifogger, the citizen, and courtier, *all tread upon the kibes of one another.*' This social anarchy is exemplified, for Bramble, in the city's cultural resorts and, above all, the pleasure gardens of Ranelagh and Vauxhall: 'The diversions of the times are not ill suited to the genius of this incongruous monster, called *the public*. Give it noise, confusion, glare, and glitter; it has no idea of elegance and propriety.' The entertainments of Vauxhall become a metonym for the chaotic and meretricious social miscibility of the town: 'a composition of baubles, overcharged with paltry ornaments . . . an unnatural assemble of objects, fantastically illuminated in broken masses; seemingly contrived to dazzle the eyes and divert the imagination of the vulgar'.[138] Yet the pleasure garden could also be regarded more positively, as evidence of a healthy intermixture of ranks that ensured the notional stability of English society. Such perceptions allowed Vauxhall to survive well into the Romantic period, offering a form of recreational nostalgia through which the supposed social harmony of a pre-revolutionary era could be re-enacted in microcosm.[139]

Indeed, by the early nineteenth century, London offered myriad forms of communal entertainment and instruction, through which the city's population came to experience itself as an urban mass marked by complex patterns of social identity and difference. Panoramas, theatres, museums, shows, and lectures – the world of metropolitan 'curiosity' – all offered

routes to cultural enfranchisement; but they could also function in a
more exclusionary manner, organizing and disciplining the uncontainable
social multiplicity of the capital.[140] As Gillian Russell's chapter shows,
Keats's experience as a play-goer – both in London and in the provinces –
offers a vital insight into his literary and social self-fashioning; the
'pervasive theatricality of his efforts to construct himself as a professional
writer' reflects at once the hybridized socio-economic composition of the
Romantic theatre and the liminal cultural identity of the 'Cockney' poet.
But Keats's experience also reflects the broader role played by the London
theatre of this period in making the social body of the people visible
to itself as a stratified audience for commodified metropolitan culture.
The privileged role of the patent theatres did much to maintain the
hierarchical divisions of the city's cultural life, yet resistance to elite
control of dramatic representation led to the growth of 'illegitimate'
theatre and a profusion of popular dramatic forms such as burlesque, farce,
ballad opera, melodrama, and pantomime. From the brilliant, vulgar
machismo of Edmund Kean to the illegitimate productions of Shakespearean works mounted by minor theatres, the cultural transgressions of
the Romantic theatre 'merged imperceptibly with discourses of popular
representation and dissent in the political sphere'.[141]

For Romantic essayists such as Leigh Hunt and Charles Lamb, the
nation's capital offered a theatricalized *tableau vivant* of popular manners.
Romantic urban reportage rediscovered London through the eyes of the
'Cockney', a type of petit-bourgeois *flâneur* whose uncertain class identity
enabled an easy movement between 'ups' and 'downs', yielding the rich
catalogue of cadgers, swells, and bucks to be found in the pages of Pierce
Egan's phenomenally successful work of comic anthropology, *Life in
London*.[142] A comparable sense of social diversity can be found in Benjamin Robert Haydon's *The Mock Election*, discussed here by Gregory
Dart in connection with Haydon's visual rendering of the debtors' prison
at King's Bench as a site of social liminality and masquerade, a microcosm of the 'real life' of contemporary London. In Haydon's subsequent
painting *Punch, or May Day*, the spectacle of the town assumes a similarly
beguiling aspect, while continuing to suggest the threat of subterfuge and
imposture. The uncontainable multiplicity of urban life entrances the
viewer of Haydon's *Punch*, a work as irresistibly (and perhaps danger-
ously) captivating as the puppet show depicted within the painting. Yet
the nineteenth-century crowd could also elicit a more sublime response: a
'combined sense of awe and anxiety' in which the endless subdivisions of
tribe and class give way to a totalizing vision of the city as 'one of the

great giant representatives of mankind, with a huge beating heart', in Leigh Hunt's words – or what Hazlitt describes as 'that vast denomination, the *People*, of which we see a tenth part moving daily before us'.[143] The city thus becomes a site for confronting the broader representational problem of 'the people'. The 'unity in multiplicity' characteristic of the Romantic symbol finds expression here in the search for a common identity within the swell of bodies, 'Here, there, and everywhere, a weary throng, / The comers and the goers face to face – / Face after face'.[144]

Wordsworth's struggle, in these lines from *The Prelude*, to divine a redemptive meaning within the 'anarchy and din' of Bartholomew Fair, also registers the attenuated survival of what Vic Gatrell calls a 'plebeian carnivalesque' of revelry and ritual at the heart of the metropolis, sustained in large part by the rural migrants who made up much of the city's population.[145] Indeed, before long, the ballad sellers and blind beggars of the town would be fetishized as part of a vanishing urban culture, in much the same way as their rural counterparts. John Thomas Smith's *Vagabondiana* (1817) offered just such a picturesque gallery of mendicant life: its engravings include hawkers of 'half-penny ballads' and 'penny religious tracts', street-crossing sweepers, bone-pickers, and 'grubbers', and 'that lower order of street-musicians, who so frequently distract the harmonious ear with their droning bag-pipes, screaming clarionets, and crazy harps'.[146] Despite its evident distaste for the city's lowlife, and expressions of support for the newly founded Society for the Suppression of Mendicity, *Vagabondiana* is prefaced with an antiquarian history of begging by Francis Douce, and evinces a certain melancholy regret at its supposed decline. The representation of plebeian suffering assumes here the character of 'salvage ethnography'. As Sam Smiles points out, *Vagabondiana* is one of many contemporary attempts to catalogue classes and occupations through pictorial representation, and thus 'to organize society into coherence' at a time of rapid economic and social change.[147] *Vagabondiana*'s gallery of representative types might then constitute a visual counterpart of the statistical surveys through which contemporaries attempted to classify and organize the body of the people – although Smith's text remains unusually susceptible to the temptations of nostalgic sentiment and anecdotal, picturesque particularity (Figure 1.2).[148]

The same contradictions find recurrent literary expression in this period, most directly perhaps in Charles Lamb's 'A Complaint of the Decay of Beggars in the Metropolis', which appeared five years later, in 1822. The essay decries the progress of 'societarian reformation' of the kind praised by Smith in the preface to *Vagabondiana*, and mounts a Wordsworthian

Fig. 1.2 The urban abjection of the itinerant ballad singer: a 'particularly picturesque . . . blind chaunter of the old ballads of "There was a wealthy lawyer", or "O Brave Nell" . . . This man accompanied his voice by playing upon a catgut string drawn over a bladder, and tied at both ends of a mop-stick; but the boys continually perplexing him by pricking his bladder, and a pampered prodigal having, with a sword, let out all his wind, he fortunately hit upon a mode of equally charming the ear, by substituting a tin tea-cannister.' John Thomas Smith, *Vagabondiana* (London, 1817), p. 45. Reproduced by permission of the Syndics of Cambridge University Library.

defence of the beggar's 'common humanity . . . a dignity springing from the very depth of their desolation'. Yet Lamb's tone also betrays a distinctly parodic edge, not least in its insistent objectification of the beggar as a picturesque 'emblem':

No corner of a street is complete without them. They are as indispensable as the Ballad Singer; and in their picturesque attire as ornamental as the Signs of old London. They were the standing morals, emblems, mementos, dial-mottos, the spital sermons, the books for children, the salutary checks and pauses to the high and rushing tide of greasy citizenry—[149]

The beggar's physical presence here, as so often in Wordsworth, forces into consciousness not just the common humanity of the 'greasy citizenry', but also the broader representational challenge of the plebeian body, a challenge that is registered as forcibly in the streets of Smithfield as in the rural lanes of Cumberland.

FROM 'THE PEOPLE' TO 'THE MASSES'

In many respects, the fabric of early modern popular culture proved highly resistant to the manifold forces of 'modernization'. Nevertheless, the nineteenth century witnessed a fundamental transformation in the structure of cultural production and consumption, a process which has often been described as the rise of 'mass' culture.[150] The progress of urbanization and political reform undoubtedly quickened contemporary awareness of these changes; but they were also crucially tied to rising levels of market-oriented consumption, developing communications networks, and technological innovations such as stereotyping and the steam-driven printing press. When *Chambers Edinburgh Journal* was launched in 1832, its proprietors possessed both the means, and the market, to sell 30,000 copies weekly by the third issue.[151] The great nineteenth-century capitalization of popular culture was clearly welcomed by entrepreneurial publishers such as the Chambers brothers and their English rival, Charles Knight; yet it was a prospect that also provoked widespread trepidation. Writing in 1836 upon the 'growing insignificance of the individual in the mass', John Stuart Mill traced an intimate relationship between this process and the contemporary explosion of popular publishing.[152] Fifty years later, Mill's observations had become a commonplace, as Matthew Arnold acknowledged: 'We are often told that an era is opening in which we are to see multitudes of a common sort of readers, and masses of a common sort of literature.'[153] The 'common sort of reader' retains a distinct cultural authority for Arnold, identifying the nation's vernacular canon as, in some sense, an emergent property of communal tradition or shared 'humanity'. Yet that same canon was simultaneously to be raised as a bulwark against mass culture, securing the educated reader from the vulgarizing incursions of the 'common sort of literature'.

William Hone's 'every-day' canon, as it emerges from Mina Gorji's discussion below, offers a proleptic challenge to such tendencies, from the historical brink of the Victorian culture industry. Hone's writings yield a dehierarchized and democratic conception of literary tradition, richly interwoven with popular custom, historical incident, and anecdote. Comparable attitudes appear to have marked the reading habits of the Victorian working classes, which evince a degree of independence and (at times) idiosyncrasy belying more reductive, homogenizing treatments of the 'common reader'.[154] Indeed, while elite hostility to 'the masses' frequently played on the threat of deadening cultural uniformity, it was also, at least in part, a product of contemporary socio-economic dislocation, 'an operationally protean social order' in Peter Bailey's words, in which class identities proliferated and interpenetrated with unsettling ease. The binary distinction between the 'vulgar' and the 'polite', through which Georgian society habitually understood itself, would appear increasingly arbitrary and anachronistic, as the consumption patterns of the 'respectable' working classes shaded into the broadening strata of lower-middle-class life.[155]

Such developments would have indirect but powerful consequences for an emergent critical discourse on Romanticism itself. As Philip Connell's chapter suggests, Victorian attempts to canonize William Wordsworth as a 'poet of the people' inherited many of the contradictions and tensions implicit in Wordsworth's own 1815 'Essay'. However, later nineteenth-century critics were also forced to reconcile the poet's appeals to 'the People, philosophically characterised' with the more contingent question of his selective 'popularity' within Victorian literary culture. This uncanny and unsettling return of the people, empirically characterized, radically undercut the poet's earlier, self-serving idealization of his audience. Yet it could also be regarded as a restaging of that more complex and uncertain scene of encounter, between polite observer and plebeian subject, which remains such a fundamental and recurrent element of Wordsworth's poetic imagination.

For Raymond Williams, 'there are in fact no masses, there are only ways of seeing people as masses'.[156] The same caveat, we have suggested, could be applied to the historically anterior concept of 'the people'. There is, indeed, a complex and as yet obscure historical trajectory linking the 'discovery' or 'invention' of the people in the later eighteenth century and the equally vexing discovery of 'mass' civilization by Victorian cultural critics – a trajectory that continued to define the 'social mission' of English Studies within the twentieth-century academy.[157] The Victorians already possessed an emergent consciousness of the Romantic era itself as a distinctive epoch: 'the burst of creative activity in our literature, through the first quarter of this century', in Arnold's words.[158] That imaginative energy might seem to offer a preservative against the undifferentiated, commodified tastes of the masses. But, as the chapters in this volume set out to show, the 'creative activity' of Romanticism also drew strength from the multifarious culture of the people, in ways that continue to challenge and inspire today.

NOTES

1 William Hazlitt, 'What is the People?', in P. P. Howe (ed.), *Complete Works*, 21 vols. (London: Dent, 1930–4), vol. VII, p. 259.
2 Jean-Jacques Rousseau, *Lettre à d'Alembert sur les Spectacles* (1758), ed. Michel Launay (Paris: Garnier-Flammarion, 1967), p. 234. Translated by Gregory Dart, and quoted in *Rousseau, Robespierre and English Romanticism* (Cambridge: Cambridge University Press, 1999), p. 110.
3 Morag Shiach, *Discourse on Popular Culture: Class, Gender, and History in Cultural Analysis, 1730 to the Present* (Cambridge: Polity Press, 1989), p. 31; Dart, *Rousseau*, pp. 224–8.
4 William Wordsworth and Samuel Taylor Coleridge, *The Lyrical Ballads*, ed. R. L. Brett and A. R. Jones, 2nd edition (London and New York: Routledge, 1991), pp. 241, 245. Despite the poetry's frequent focus on plebeian female subjects, from 'Ruth' and 'The Mad Mother' to 'The Solitary Reaper', Wordsworth's Preface is consistent in its adherence to the generic masculine.
5 John Guillory, *Cultural Capital: The Problem of Literary Canon Formation* (Chicago, Ill.: Chicago University Press, 1993), p. 126.
6 Wordsworth and Coleridge, *Lyrical Ballads*, p. 249.
7 Nigel Leask, 'Burns, Wordsworth and the Politics of Vernacular Poetry', in Peter de Bolla, Nigel Leask and David Simpson (eds.), *Land, Nation and Culture, 1740–1840: Thinking the Republic of Taste* (Basingstoke: Palgrave Macmillan, 2005), pp. 202–22; Paul Brewster, 'The Influence of the Popular Ballad on Wordsworth's Poetry', *Studies in Philology* 35 (1938), 588–612; Scott McEathron, 'Wordsworth, *Lyrical Ballads* and the Problem of Peasant Poetry', *Nineteenth-Century Literature* 54:1 (June 1999), 1–26.
8 William Wordsworth, *Selected Prose*, ed. with intro. by John Hayden (Harmondsworth: Penguin, 1988), p. 311.
9 Jon Klancher, *The Making of English Reading Audiences, 1790–1832* (Madison, Wisc.: University of Wisconsin Press, 1987), p. 139.

10 *Ibid.*

11 Samuel Taylor Coleridge, *Biographia Literaria*, ed. Nigel Leask (London: Everyman, 1997), p. 209.

12 *Ibid.*, p. 194.

13 *Ibid.*, p. 210.

14 Wordsworth, *Selected Prose*, p. 411.

15 *OED*, 'Popular'.

16 Wordsworth, *Selected Prose*, p. 412.

17 *Ibid.*, p. 413.

18 Pierre Bourdieu, *The Field of Cultural Production*, trans. Richard Nice, ed. with intro. by Randal Johnson (Cambridge: Polity, 1993), pp. 29–73. On the 'culture industry', see Theodor Adorno and Max Horkheimer, *Dialectic of Enlightenment* (1944), trans. John Cumming (London: Verso, 1979), pp. 120–67; the concept retains some purchase, notwithstanding the authors' more reductive and disempowering treatment of 'the masses'.

19 Niall Ó Ciosáin, *Print and Popular Culture in Ireland, 1750–1850* (Basingstoke: Macmillan, 1997); see also J. G. A. Pocock, *The Discovery of Islands: Essays in British History* (Cambridge: Cambridge University Press, 2005); John Kerrigan, *Archipelagic English: Literature, History, and Politics, 1603–1707* (Oxford: Oxford University Press, 2008).

20 Edward Said, *Orientalism* (London: Routledge and Kegan Paul, 1978).

21 Peter Burke, *Popular Culture in Early Modern Europe* (1978), rev. reprint (Aldershot: Scolar, 1994), p. xi. Further page references will be given in the text.

22 Peter Burke, 'The Discovery of Popular Culture', in Raphael Samuel (ed.), *People's History and Socialist Thought* (London: Routledge and Kegan Paul, 1981), p. 218.

23 On the problems with a 'two-tier' model, see also J. M. Goldby and A. W. Purdue, *The Civilisation of the Crowd: Popular Culture in England 1750–1900* (London: Batsford, 1984), p. 30.

24 Dianne Dugaw, 'The Popular Marketing of "Old Ballads": The Ballad Revival and Eighteenth-Century Antiquarianism Reconsidered', *Eighteenth-Century Studies* 21:1 (Fall 1987), 84–5.

25 Quoted in Paul Keen, *The Crisis of Literature in the 1790s: Print Culture and the Public Sphere* (Cambridge: Cambridge University Press, 1999), p. 151.

26 Raymond Williams, *The Country and the City* (London: Hogarth Press, 1993), pp. 60–7.

27 E. P. Thompson, *Customs in Common* (London: Merlin Press, 1991). See also Eileen Yeo and Stephen Yeo (eds.), *Popular Culture and Class Conflict 1590–1914: Explorations in the History of Labour and Leisure* (Sussex: Harvester, 1981).

28 Tim Harris (ed.), *Popular Culture in England, c.1500–1850* (Houndmills: Macmillan, 1995), p. 10.

29 Terry Eagleton, *The Function of Criticism: From the Spectator to Post-Structuralism* (London: Verso, 1984), pp. 14–15; Jürgen Habermas, *The Structural Transformation of the Public Sphere: An Inquiry into a Category of Bourgeois Society*, trans. Thomas Burger (Cambridge: Polity, 1989).

30 Keen, *Crisis of Literature*, pp. 170, 145.

31 Mikhail Bakhtin, *Rabelais and His World*, trans. Helene Iswolsky (Bloomington: Indiana University Press, 1984), p. 19.

32 Stuart Gillespie and Neil Rhodes (eds.), *Shakespeare and Elizabethan Popular Culture* (London: Arden Shakespeare, 2006), pp. 5, 6.

33 *Ibid.*, p. 5. See Bob Bushaway, *By Rite: Custom, Ceremony and Community, 1700–1880* (London: Junction, 1982). Nevertheless, the literary ideal of carnival is an important presence in the poetry of the eighteenth-century Scottish vernacular revival. See Allan H. MacLaine (ed.), *The Christis Kirk Tradition: Scots Poems of Folk Festivity* (Glasgow: ASLS, 1996).

34 Peter Stallybrass and Allon White, *The Politics and Poetics of Transgression* (London: Methuen, 1986), p. 107.

35 *Ibid.*, pp. 107, 99.

36 *Ibid.*, p. 124.

37 Roger Chartier, 'Culture as Appropriation: Popular Cultural Uses in Early Modern France', in Steven L. Kaplan (ed.), *Understanding Popular Culture* (New York and Amsterdam: Mouton Publishers, 1984), pp. 229–54 (p. 231).

38 *Ibid.*, p. 233.

39 Michel de Certeau, *The Practice of Everyday Life*, trans. Steven Rendell (Berkeley and London: University of California Press, 1984), p. 172.

40 Emma Griffin, 'Popular Culture in Industrializing England', *Historical Journal* 45 (2002), 619–35.

41 Harris, *Popular Culture*, p. 23.

42 For Goldby and Purdue see note 23, above. For a critique of this view in relation to contemporary discourse, see Simon Frith, 'The Good, the Bad, and the Indifferent: Defending Popular Culture from Populists', *Diacritics* 21:4 (Winter 1991), 101–15.

43 John Mullan and Christopher Reid (eds.), *Eighteenth-Century Popular Culture: A Selection* (Oxford: Oxford University Press, 2000), p. 19.

44 Raphael Samuel, *Theatres of Memory, Volume 1: Past and Present in Contemporary Culture* (London: Verso, 1994).

45 John Brand, *Observations on Popular Antiquities: Including the Whole of Mr Bourne's Antiquitates Vulgares* (Newcastle upon Tyne, 1777), p. iv.

46 *Ibid.*

47 *Ibid.*, p. xvi.

48 *Ibid.*, p. vi. Brand's project was continued by Joseph Strutt in his popular *Sports and Pastimes of the People of England* (1801).

49 Brand, *Observations*, p. ix.

50 Marilyn Butler, 'Antiquarianism (Popular)', in Iain McCalman (ed.), *An Oxford Companion to the Romantic Age: British Culture 1776–1832* (Oxford: Oxford University Press, 1999), p. 329.

51 Joseph Ritson, *Observations on the Three First Volumes of the History of English Poetry* (London, 1782) and 'A Historical Essay on the Origin and Progress of National Song', in *A Select Collection of English Songs*, 3 vols. (London, 1783); Philip Connell, 'British Identities and the Politics of Ancient

Poetry in Later Eighteenth-Century England', *Historical Journal* 49 (2006), 161–92 (181, 184).

52 Quoted in Marilyn Butler (ed.), *Burke, Paine, Godwin, and the Revolution Controversy* (Cambridge: Cambridge University Press, 1984), pp. 203–5 (p. 204).

53 Butler, 'Antiquarianism (Popular)', pp. 335–8.

54 Mark Salber Phillips, *Society and Sentiment: Genres of Historical Writing in Britain, 1740–1820* (Princeton: Princeton University Press, 2000), p. 151.

55 Robert Burns, *Poems and Songs of Robert Burns*, ed. James Kinsley, 3 vols. (Oxford: Clarendon Press, 1968), vol. 1, p. 494.

56 Quoted in Raymond Williams, *Keywords* (London: Fontana, 1988), p. 136.

57 Morag Shiach, *Discourse on Popular Culture*, pp. 108, 113.

58 *Ibid.* See Leask's chapter in the present volume.

59 De Certeau, *Practice of Everyday Life*, p. 132. See also David Vincent, *Literacy and Popular Culture: England, 1750–1914* (Cambridge: Cambridge University Press, 1989); Adam Fox, *Oral and Literate Culture in England 1500–1700* (Oxford: Clarendon Press, 2000).

60 Quoted in Howard Gaskill (ed.), *The Poems of Ossian, and Related Works*, intro. by Fiona Stafford (Edinburgh: Edinburgh University Press, 1996), p. 5.

61 Nick Groom, *The Making of Percy's Reliques* (Oxford: Clarendon Press, 1999), pp. 76, 92.

62 Jonathan Barry, 'Literacy and Literature in Popular Culture: Reading and Writing in Historical Perspective', in Harris (ed.), *Popular Culture*, p. 75.

63 *Ibid.*, p. 82.

64 Patricia Anderson, *The Printed Image and the Transformation of Popular Culture, 1790–1860* (Oxford: Clarendon Press, 1991), p. 17.

65 Ó Ciosáin, *Print and Popular Culture*, p. 186.

66 Albert B. Friedman, *The Ballad Revival: Studies in the Influence of Popular on Sophisticated Poetry* (Chicago, Ill.: Chicago University Press, 1961), p. 6.

67 Robert S. Thomson, *The Development of the Broadside Ballad and Its Influence upon the Transmission of English Folksongs* (unpublished PhD thesis, University of Cambridge, 1974), p. 23.

68 Dugaw, 'Popular Marketing', 75.

69 Leslie Shepard, *The History of Street Literature* (Newton Abbot: David and Charles, 1973), pp. 72, 30.

70 Susan Pedersen, 'Hannah More Meets Simple Simon: Tracts, Chapbooks and Popular Culture in Late Eighteenth-Century England', *Journal of British Studies* 25 (1986), 99; W. B. Stephens, 'Literacy in England, Scotland and Wales, 1500–1900', *History of Education Quarterly* 30 (1990), 545–71. Irish figures for the eighteenth century are hard to estimate, although the 1841 estimate of 47 per cent readership is reliable. Ó Ciosáin comments on the 'remarkably' high level of English literacy in largely rural Ireland which in 1800 was still predominately Irish speaking, so that 'this literacy was being achieved in a new language' (*Print and Popular Culture*, p. 33).

71 Ó Ciosáin, *Print and Popular Culture*, p. 163.

72 *Ibid.*, pp. 53, 56.
73 Dugaw, 'Popular Marketing', 84.
74 Barry, 'Literacy and Literature', p. 84.
75 Edward J. Cowan and Mike Paterson (eds.), *Folk in Print: Scotland's Chapbook Heritage, 1750–1850* (Edinburgh: John Donald, 2007), p. 20.
76 Dugaw, 'Popular Marketing', 88.
77 Thomson, 'Broadside Ballad', p. 96.
78 Ann Wierda Rowland, ' "The false nourice sang": Childhood, Child Murder, and the Formalism of the Scottish Ballad Revival', in Leith Davis, Ian Duncan, and Janet Sorensen (eds.), *Scotland and the Borders of Romanticism* (Cambridge: Cambridge University Press, 2004), p. 226; see also Dianne Dugaw, 'Women and Popular Culture: Gender, Cultural Dynamics, and Popular Prints', in Vivien Jones (ed.), *Women and Literature in Britain 1700–1800* (Cambridge: Cambridge University Press, 2000), pp. 263–84.
79 Barry, 'Literacy and Literature', p. 82.
80 Deborah Symonds, *Weep Not for Me: Ballads and Infanticide in Early Modern Scotland* (University Park, Penn.: Pennsylvania State University Press, 1997), p. 37; see also Dianne Dugaw, *Warrior Women and Popular Balladry, 1650–1850* (Cambridge: Cambridge University Press, 1989).
81 William St Clair, *The Reading Nation in the Romantic Period* (Cambridge: Cambridge University Press, 2004), p. 348.
82 *Ibid.*, pp. 349–50.
83 Quoted in George Deacon, *John Clare and the Folk Tradition* (London: Francis Boutle, 2002), p. 45.
84 Ruth Finnegan, *Oral Poetry: Its Nature, Significance, and Social Context* (Cambridge: Cambridge University Press, 1977), p. 160.
85 Thomson, 'Broadside Ballad', p. 180.
86 See Deacon, *John Clare*, p. 51; Anderson, *Printed Image*, p. 21.
87 Robert Jamieson, *Popular Ballads and Songs* (Edinburgh, 1806), p. 117.
88 See Cowan and Paterson (eds.), *Folk in Print*, pp. 46–9; Shepard, *Street Literature*, pp. 81–106.
89 R. A. Houston, *Scottish Literacy and Scottish Identity: Illiteracy and Society in Scotland and Northern England, 1600–1800* (Cambridge: Cambridge University Press, 1985). For the divergent attitudes to pedlars in Ireland see Ó Ciosáin, *Print and Popular Culture*, pp. 61–71.
90 See Flemming G. Andersen, 'From Tradition to Print: Ballads on Broadsides', in F. G. Andersen, O. Holzapfel and T. Pettit (eds.), *The Ballad as Narrative* (Odense: Odense University Press, 1982), pp. 39–58 (p. 44).
91 *Ibid.*, p. 47.
92 Dianne Dugaw, 'Anglo-American Folksong Reconsidered: The Interface of Oral and Written Forms', *Western Folklore* 43:2 (April 1984), 83–103 (88).
93 James Hogg, 'Reminiscences of Former Days', in *Altrive Tales*, ed. Gillian Hughes (Edinburgh: Edinburgh University Press, 2005), p. 61.
94 Shepard, *Street Literature*, p. 70; Dugaw, 'Anglo-American Folksong', 88.

95 William Roberts, *Memoirs of the Life and Correspondence of Mrs Hannah More*, 4 vols. (London, 1834), vol. II, p. 458 (More to Zachary Macaulay, January 1796).

96 Miles Taylor, 'John Bull and the Iconography of Public Opinion in England, *c.* 1712–1929', *Past and Present* 134 (1992), 93–128; John Brewer, *The Common People and Politics 1750–1790s* (Cambridge: Chadwyck-Healey, 1986); Tamara L. Hunt, *Defining John Bull: Political Caricature and National Identity in Georgian England* (Aldershot: Ashgate, 2003), pp. 143–69.

97 Kathleen Wilson, *The Sense of the People: Politics, Culture and Imperialism in England, 1715–1785* (Cambridge: Cambridge University Press, 1995), p. 21.

98 *Ibid.*; see also Nicholas Rogers, *Crowds, Culture, and Politics in Georgian Britain* (Oxford: Clarendon Press, 1998); John Brewer, 'Theatre and Counter-Theatre in Georgian Politics: The Mock Elections at Garrat', *Radical History Review* 22 (1979–80), 7–40, and 'Commercialization and Politics', in John Brewer, J. H. Plumb, and Neil McKendrick, *The Birth of a Consumer Society: The Commercialization of Eighteenth-Century England* (London: Hutchinson, 1983), pp. 197–262.

99 See William Donaldson, *The Jacobite Song: Political Myth and National Identity* (Aberdeen: Aberdeen University Press, 1988), pp. 49–71, 90–108; Murray Pittock, *Poetry and Jacobite Politics in Eighteenth-Century Britain and Ireland* (Cambridge: Cambridge University Press, 1994), pp. 223–42.

100 Jim Smyth, *The Men of No Property: Irish Radicals and Popular Politics in the Late Eighteenth Century* (Basingstoke: Macmillan, 1992); C. H. E. Philpin (ed.), *Nationalism and Popular Protest in Ireland* (Cambridge: Cambridge University Press, 1987).

101 Anderson, *Printed Image*, p. 8.

102 H. T. Dickinson, *The Politics of the People in Eighteenth-Century Britain* (Basingstoke: Macmillan, 1994), pp. 255–86; David Eastwood, 'Patriotism and the English State in the 1790s', in Mark Philp (ed.), *The French Revolution and British Popular Politics* (Cambridge: Cambridge University Press, 1991), pp. 146–68.

103 [Hannah More], *Village Politics. Addressed to all the Mechanics, Journeymen, and Day Labourers, in Great Britain. By Will Chip, a Country Carpenter*, 2nd edition (London, 1792), p. 18.

104 On Ireland, see Ó Ciosáin, *Print and Popular Culture*, p. 138. For the comparable efforts of George Miller of Haddington in Scotland, publisher of *Cheap Tracts* (1802–4) and the *Cheap Magazine* (1813), see Cowan and Paterson, *Folk in Print*, pp. 33–4.

105 Pedersen, 'Hannah More', 88.

106 Joanna Innes, 'Politics and Morals: The Reformation of Manners Movement in Later Eighteenth-Century England', in Eckhart Hellmuth (ed.), *The Transformation of Political Culture: England and Germany in the Late Eighteenth Century* (Oxford: Oxford University Press, 1990), pp. 57–118.

107 Robert W. Malcolmson, *Popular Recreations in English Society 1700–1850* (Cambridge: Cambridge University Press, 1973), pp. 118–57; but see also Hugh Cunningham, *Leisure in the Industrial Revolution, c. 1780–c. 1880* (London: Croom Helm, 1980).

108 Henry Thornton, 'Cheap Repository for Moral & Religious Publications', in *Cheap Repository Tracts, Published during the Year 1795* (London, n.d. [1797]); Sheila O'Connell, *The Popular Print in England 1550–1850* (London: British Museum, 1999), pp. 66–128.

109 Anderson, *Printed Image*, p. 38.

110 Pedersen, 'Hannah More', 103.

111 Ó Ciosáin, *Print and Popular Culture*, p. 133.

112 Samuel Taylor Coleridge, *Collected Letters of Samuel Taylor Coleridge*, ed. Earl Leslie Griggs, 6 vols. (Oxford: Clarendon Press, 1956–71), vol. III, p. 410.

113 Keen, *Crisis of Literature*, p. 159.

114 Penny Fielding, *Writing and Orality: Nationality, Culture, and Nineteenth-Century Scottish Fiction* (Oxford: Clarendon Press, 1996), p. 34.

115 Quoted in *The Evangelical Magazine* 3 (1795), 288–9.

116 Quoted in Deacon, *John Clare*, p. 35; from Peterborough MS A45, p. 5.

117 *Ibid.*

118 'Proceedings of the People', *Black Dwarf* 3 (24 February 1819), 114. On the counter-public sphere in this period, see Kevin Gilmartin, *Print Politics: The Press and Radical Opposition in Early Nineteenth-Century England* (Cambridge: Cambridge University Press, 1996).

119 Samuel Taylor Coleridge, *The Friend*, ed. Barbara E. Rooke, 2 vols. (London and Princeton: Routledge and Princeton University Press, 1969), vol. II, p. 86.

120 Dror Wahrman, 'Public Opinion, Violence and the Limits of Consti-tutional Politics', in James Vernon (ed.), *Re-reading the Constitution: New Narratives in the Political History of England's Long Nineteenth Century* (Cambridge: Cambridge University Press, 1996), pp. 83–122.

121 Percy Bysshe Shelley, *The Letters of Percy Bysshe Shelley*, ed. Frederick L. Jones, 2 vols. (Oxford: Clarendon Press, 1964), vol. II, p. 191.

122 Samuel Taylor Coleridge, *On the Constitution of Church and State*, ed. John Colmer (London: Routledge, and Princeton, N. J.: Princeton University Press, 1976), pp. 42–3.

123 Ian Dyck, *William Cobbett and Rural Popular Culture* (Cambridge: Cambridge University Press, 1992); see also Alun Hawkins and C. Ian Dyck, ' "The Time's Alteration": Popular Ballads, Rural Radicalism and William Cobbett', *History Workshop Journal* 23 (1987), 20–38.

124 John Barrell, *The Dark Side of the Landscape: The Rural Poor in English Painting, 1730–1840* (Cambridge: Cambridge University Press, 1980); 'Cottage Politics', in Barrell, *The Spirit of Despotism: Invasions of Privacy in the 1790s* (Oxford: Oxford University Press, 2006), pp. 210–46.

125 Iain McCalman, *Radical Underworld: Prophets, Revolutionaries, and Porno-graphers in London, 1795–1840* (Oxford: Clarendon Press, 1993), p. 211.

126 Robert Southey, *Wat Tyler; A Dramatic Poem. A New Edition. With a Preface, suitable to Recent Circumstances* (London, 1817), p. 18.

127 Neil Fraistat, 'Illegitimate Shelley: Radical Piracy and the Textual Edition as Cultural Performance', *Publications of the Modern Language Association of America* 109 (1994), 415; St Clair, *Reading Nation*, pp. 311–34, 676–91.

128 [William Hone], *'Don John', or Don Juan Unmasked*, 2nd edition (London, 1819), p. 7; Ben Wilson, *The Laughter of Triumph: William Hone and the Fight for the Free Press* (London: Faber, 2005), pp. 281–4.

129 William Hone, *The Table Book* (London, 1827), col. 4 (quotation); *The Every-Day Book; or, Everlasting Calendar of Popular Amusements*, 2 vols. (London, 1826–7).

130 Butler, 'Antiquarianism (Popular)', p. 335.

131 P. J. Corfield, *The Impact of English Towns* (Oxford: Oxford University Press, 1982), p. 9; T. M. Devine, *The Scottish Nation 1700–2000* (London: Allen Lane, 1999), pp. 152–69.

132 Martin Daunton, *Progress and Poverty: An Economic and Social History of Britain 1700–1850* (Oxford: Oxford University Press, 1995), pp. 413–15. See also Peter Clark, 'Migrants in the City: The Process of Social Adaptation in English Towns 1500–1800', in Peter Clark and David Souden (eds.), *Migration and Society in Early Modern England* (London: Hutchinson, 1987), pp. 267–91.

133 See for example Bushaway, *By Rite*.

134 Rosemary Sweet, *The Writing of Urban Histories in Eighteenth-Century England* (Oxford: Clarendon Press, 1997), p. 257.

135 Peter Borsay, *The English Urban Renaissance: Culture and Society in the Provincial Town 1660–1770* (Oxford: Clarendon Press, 1989), pp. 285–96, and 'All the Town's a Stage: Urban Ritual and Ceremony, 1600–1800', in Peter Clark (ed.), *The Transformation of English Provincial Towns, 1600–1800* (London: Hutchinson, 1984), pp. 228–56.

136 Borsay, *Urban Renaissance*, p. 286; on the limitations of popular/polite binarism, see also his 'Introduction' to Borsay (ed.), *The Eighteenth-Century Town: A Reader in English Urban History 1688–1820* (London: Longman, 1990), pp. 34–5.

137 Roy Porter, *London: A Social History* (London: Penguin, 1996), p. 131.

138 Tobias Smollett, *The Expedition of Humphrey Clinker*, 3 vols. (London, 1771), vol. 1, pp. 186–7.

139 Jonathan Conlin, 'Vauxhall Revisited: The Afterlife of a London Pleasure Garden, 1770–1859', *Journal of British Studies* 45 (2006), 718–43.

140 Richard D. Altick, *The Shows of London* (Cambridge, Mass.: Harvard University Press, 1978); John Brewer, 'Sensibility and the Urban Panorama', *Huntington Library Quarterly* 70 (2007), 229–49; Nigel Leask, *Curiosity and the Aesthetics of Travel Writing 1770–1840* (Oxford: Oxford University Press, 2002), pp. 152–6, 299–314.

141 Jane Moody, *Illegitimate Theatre in London, 1770–1840* (Cambridge: Cambridge University Press, 2000), p. 146; see also Jonathan Bate, *Shakespearean Constitutions: Politics, Theatre, Criticism 1730–1830* (Oxford: Clarendon Press,

1989); Gillian Russell, *The Theatres of War: Performance, Politics, and Society, 1793–1815* (Cambridge: Cambridge University Press, 1995); David Worrall, *Theatric Revolution: Drama, Censorship, and Romantic Period Subcultures 1773–1832* (Oxford: Oxford University Press, 2006).

142 Pierce Egan, *Life in London* (London, 1821); see Gregory Dart, '"Flash Style": Pierce Egan and Literary London 1820–28', *History Workshop Journal* 51 (2001), 180–205.

143 Leigh Hunt, *Table-Talk* (London, 1882), p. 263; William Hazlitt, 'On Londoners and Country People' (1823), in *Complete Works*, vol. XII, p. 77; Mark Harrison, *Crowds and History: Mass Phenomena in English Towns, 1790–1835* (Cambridge: Cambridge University Press, 1988), p. 169.

144 William Wordsworth, *The Prelude* (1805), Book VII, lines 171–3, in *The Prelude: 1799, 1805, 1850*, ed. Jonathan Wordsworth *et al.* (New York: Norton, 1979).

145 *Ibid.*, line 660; V. A. C. Gatrell, *City of Laughter: Sex and Satire in Fight-eenth-Century London* (London. Atlantic, 2006), pp. 194–201.

146 John Thomas Smith, *Vagabondiana; or, Anecdotes of Mendicant Wanderers through the Streets of London* (London, 1817), pp. 45–6; see also T. L. Busby, *Costume of the Lower Orders of London* (London, n.d. [1820]).

147 Sam Smiles, *Eye Witness: Artists and Visual Documentation in Britain 1770–1830* (Aldershot: Ashgate, 2000), p. 108; see also Lucy Peltz, 'Aestheticizing the Ancestral City: Antiquarianism, Topography and the Representation of London in the Long Eighteenth Century', in Dana Arnold (ed.), *The Metropolis and its Image: Constructing Identities for London, c. 1750–1950* (Oxford: Blackwell, 1999), pp. 6–28.

148 Michael J. Cullen, *The Statistical Movement in Early Victorian Britain: The Foundations of Empirical Social Research* (Hassocks: Harvester, 1975); Mary Poovey, *Making a Social Body: British Cultural Formation 1830–1864* (Chicago, Ill.: University of Chicago Press, 1995).

149 Charles Lamb, 'A Complaint of the Decay of Beggars in the Metropolis', in *The Works of Charles and Mary Lamb*, ed. E. V. Lucas, 7 vols. (London: Methuen, 1903–5), vol. II, pp. 114–16.

150 See Leo Lowenthal, *Literature and Mass Culture* (New Brunswick: Transaction, 1984), pp. 153–65; Anderson, *Printed Image*, pp. 9–11, 192–8; Asa Briggs, 'The Language of "Mass" and "Masses" in Nineteenth-Century England', in D. E. Martin and D. Rubinstein (eds.), *Ideology and the Labour Movement* (London: Croom Helm, 1979), pp. 62–83.

151 Anderson, *Printed Image*, pp. 192–8; Cowan and Paterson, *Folk in Print*, pp. 36–7.

152 John Stuart Mill, 'Civilization', in *Collected Works*, ed. J. M. Robson *et al.*, 33 vols. (Toronto: University of Toronto Press, 1981–91), vol. XVIII, p. 134.

153 Matthew Arnold, 'The Study of Poetry' (1880), in *Complete Prose*, ed. R. H. Super, 11 vols. (Ann Arbor: University of Michigan Press, 1960–77), vol. III, p. 262.

154 See Jonathan Rose's survey of autodidact culture, *The Intellectual Life of the British Working Classes* (New Haven, Conn.: Yale University Press, 2001); and Richard D. Altick's older but still valuable study, *The English Common Reader: A Social History of the Mass Reading Public, 1800–1900* (Chicago: University of Chicago Press, 1957).

155 Peter Bailey, *Popular Culture and Performance in the Victorian City* (Cambridge: Cambridge University Press, 1998), p. 42.

156 Raymond Williams, *Culture and Society 1780–1950* (London: Chatto and Windus, 1958), p. 300.

157 Chris Baldick, *The Social Mission of English Criticism, 1848–1932* (Oxford: Clarendon Press, 1983).

158 Matthew Arnold, 'The Function of Criticism at the Present Time' (1864), in *Complete Prose*, vol. III, p. 262.

PART II

Ballad poetry and popular song

CHAPTER 2

'A degrading species of Alchymy':
ballad poetics, oral tradition,
and the meanings of popular culture

Nigel Leask

> The scandal of the ballad is in its very revival: the production of a
> ghost, freed of a history that scholarship will take on as its duty to
> supply.[1]

In the 'Essay on the Ancient Minstrels in England' which prefaced his 1765
Reliques of Ancient English Poetry, Thomas Percy distinguished between
two kinds of ballads:

> The old Minstrel-ballads are in the northern dialect, abound with antique words
> and phrases, are extremely incorrect, and run into the utmost licence of metre;
> they have also a romantic wildness, and are in the true spirit of chivalry. – The
> other sort are written in exacter measure, have a low or subordinate correctness,
> sometimes bordering on the insipid, yet often well adapted to the pathetic; these
> are generally in the southern dialect, exhibit a more modern phraseology, and are
> commonly descriptive of more modern manners.[2]

Although neither Percy nor his successors made much effort to distinguish
the ballad as a 'short narrative poem' from the pastoral song or lyric, in
this passage he establishes a series of binaries between northern/southern,
antique/modern, incorrect/correct, licentious/regular, chivalric/urbane,
wild/insipid. Notably absent here is any opposition between orally and
textually transmitted ballads: although Percy conjectured an oral provenance for 'old Minstrel-ballads' he specified that the originals were
irrecoverable, so nearly all the specimens published in the *Reliques* were
gleaned from later printed and manuscript sources. We'll see that in this
respect Percy was typical of his age, although the citation of oral sources
would grow in frequency, if not legitimacy, in the decades that followed.[3]
In the pejorative sense intended by Percy, ballads in modern 'southern
dialect' (for which read 'urban' broadsides) are associated with contemporary popular culture, insofar as they were circulated for commercial
profit, their cheapness making them accessible to a broad spectrum of

lower-class purchasers. In contrast, Percy's 'old Minstrel-ballads' assume, if not a securely 'literary' status, then at least an aesthetic quality of 'romantic wildness', taking their place in what Bourdieu denominates an 'autonomous' position within the literary field, compared to the 'heteronomy' of commercial stall ballads.[4]

Nearly a century and a half later, we find an updated version of Percy's distinction still flourishing in an 1895 article on balladry in the *Universal Cyclopaedia* by Francis James Child. Child was a Harvard professor and ballad scholar, whose monumental five-volume *English and Scottish Popular Ballads* (1882–98) completed the work of consecration and canonization of which Percy's *Reliques* had been the first faltering step.[5] Child insisted that 'the popular ballad is not originally the product of the lower orders of the people': although he hinted at a courtly pedigree, he claimed that ballads had their rise in an indeterminate past preceding the rise of class society. Only in the process of popular transmission, however, do ancient ballads begin to 'smell of the groom . . . or suggest the broom', and he was accordingly pessimistic about collecting from oral sources (vol. v, p. 764).[6] Child dismissed 'vulgar' or broadside ballads printed from the sixteenth century onwards, as 'products of a low kind of *art*, and most of them are, from a literary point of view, thoroughly despicable and worthless' (vol. v, p. 757). We see here the outlines of a critical genealogy stretching from Percy to Child, even if (in striking contrast to Percy) Child's best material has been gleaned, albeit at second hand, from 'the mouths of unlearned people' (vol. v, p. 759). It's notable that most of the oral sources recorded in Child's collection were women, and despite the active role of middle- and gentry-class women as sources or mediators, the editors of cited published collections were uniformly men.[7] It's also noteworthy that Child preferred to risk the ambivalence of the word 'popular' in the title of his collection, rather than the recently stabilized term 'folk', and that despite his interest in ballads brought to his native Boston by Irish immigrants, he excluded Ireland as a source for his ballads.

Wordsworth's claims for the 'language of low and rustic life' as a model for poetry in the 1800 Preface to *Lyrical Ballads* is Romantic theory's best-known mediation of popular culture. Yet the ballad poetics surveyed in this chapter embody a more elaborate construction of the popular which deserves to be better known by students of British Romanticism: the reason they are not is largely the result of the history of disciplinary formation. Although the Gottingen-trained Child was in 1876 elected to the first Chair of English Literature at Harvard (replacing the older chair of Rhetoric), and had published an edition of Spenser and an important study of the language of Chaucer and Gower, the subsequent importance of his *English and Scottish Popular Ballads* lay in the field of folklore rather than in literary studies, a disciplinary distinction still institutionalized within the US academy (vol. 1, pp. xxiii–xxxi).

Although there have been important scholarly border crossings between the two disciplines (notably Albert Friedman's 1961 *The Ballad Revival*, and more recently the work of Susan Stewart and Nick Groom),[8] a fetishized distinction between the oral and the written long disguised the deep roots of Romantic consanguinity which link them. Stewart proposes that 'modern literary scholarship, with its task of genealogy – the establishment of paternity and lines of influence – and its role in the legislation of originality and authenticity, depended upon the articulation of a "folk" literature that "literature" was not',[9] In this chapter I shall examine the transition from Percy's discrimination between ancient Minstrel ballads and modern broadsides, axiomatic to ballad editing in the period 1765–1830, and a related discrimination between orally and textually transmitted material which was superimposed upon it in the later period, along the lines of a disciplinary distinction between literary and folklore studies. At stake are questions concerning the role of popular culture in the construction of an emergent British literary canon, as well as of class, gender, and national identities, questions of central importance to contemporary discussions of Romanticism.

Both these binary distinctions are closely connected to the gendering of cultural production. Earlier song collections like Allan Ramsay's *Tea-Table Miscellany* (1724) elevated street songs to the parlour table under the sign of a feminized 'politeness', often marrying new English lyrics with old Scottish melodies in the service of a unified, post-1707 'British' aesthetic. As Peggy, heroine of Ramsay's pastoral drama *The Gentle Shepherd* (1725), puts it, 'I'll sing you ane, the *newest* that I ha'e' (the very reverse of a *reliquary* of 'old ballads') [my italics].[10] Percy's privileging of the 'Minstrel' ballad directly challenges Ramsay's apotheosis of 'femininity', 'modernity', and 'politeness' in the name of a masculine 'antiquity' and 'sublimity', making common cause with his friend Thomas Warton's reappraisal of the earlier English canon in his *History of English Poetry* (1774–81). Jonathan Brody Kramnick proposes that 'once politeness is seen as too common and too modern, too much like conversation as such, critics discover an abstruse, quasi-Latinate vernacular in older, canonical English'. Negotiating a formative tension between aesthetic and historicist criticism, scholars like Percy and Warton discovered an energizing obscurity in the form and content of 'old ballads' which approached the Burkean sublime, decomposing a polite culture of effeminate taste; for 'the idea that sublime obscurity dwells in folk culture hints at the high-cultural appropriation of antique common forms'.[11]

Percy was here insisting too much. Dianne Dugaw has shown that the eighteenth-century ballad revival wasn't limited to 'sophisticated' readers, but that middle- and lowbrow purchasers of chapbooks and broadsides from William and Cluer Dicey's London-based warehouse also 'wanted their ballads "antique": collected together and couched in a retrospective framework of dates, sources, analogues, and learned commentary'.[12] This of course questions the 'bi-polar' model of the relation between elite and popular culture discussed in the introduction, supporting the notion of overlapping frames of appropriation. William St Clair argues that the boundary of 'the reading nation' needs to be conceived in the light of copyright legislation, which was just as binding on popular as on elite publishing. For St Clair, the archaic fare on offer in eighteenth-century British chapbooks and broadsides wasn't so much the result of any nostalgic readerly demand for 'antique' (he prefers the term 'obsolete') ballads and tales, but rather 'the effect of an unregulated private monopoly from the first invention of a new product in the sixteenth century, through increasing cartelisation, to near total monopoly'.[13] To support his case, he argues that as soon as the monopoly in the supply of popular print was lifted around 1800, aspiring plebeian readers jettisoned the tradition of *Bevis of Southampton* and *Guy of Warwick* 'without regret', leaving it to polite poets like Wordsworth to bewail the loss of the old imaginative world 'Of Jack the Giant Killer, Robin Hood / And Sabra in the forest with St George!'[14]

St Clair makes the point that Percy's *Reliques* was itself originally intended by the owners of the ballad warehouse to be a successor to the earlier, 1723–4 *Collection of Old Ballads* in maintaining copyright control.[15] To this end Percy was given the run of the Dicey stock, so it isn't surprising that of the 180 pieces published in the *Reliques*, more than 60 were also circulating on Dicey broadsides in 1765.[16] But Percy harboured nobler ambitions, and his rescuing of an old folio manuscript of seventeenth-century ballads from being burnt as fuel by his housemaid (a manuscript which he deliberately withheld from public view) enabled him to claim a more venerable antiquity for many of his pieces, as well as licensing his creative 'polishing and mending' of old material. In a fulsome dedication to the Countess of Northumberland, Percy 'gift wrapped' his volume along the lines of the new aesthetics of the sublime. The ballads are the 'rude songs of ancient Minstrels'; 'not ... labours of art, but ... effusions of nature, showing the first efforts of ancient genius, and exhibiting the customs and opinions of remote ages; of ages that had been almost lost to memory, had not the gallant deeds of your illustrious ancestors preserved them from oblivion'.[17] The large number of songs and ballads associated with Shakespeare and Renaissance pastorals appealed to the historicizing inclinations of the Warton circle, in search of the deep contexts of English poets like Chaucer, Spenser, and Shakespeare.[18]

Nick Groom has underlined the contrast between the decorous, scholarly redaction of Percy's *Reliques* and the actual contents of many of the ballads included, which 'welter in gore: the bloodiness of death and dismemberment incarnadines the entire three volumes, and if occasionally watered by humour or levity, it is more often deepened by a colossal amorality'.[19] Ann Wierda Rowland acutely notes that 'the impressive scholarly apparatus that the ballad revival bequeaths to British literature is, in fact, a way of *not* reading or responding to the contents of popular literature'.[20] This exactly describes Percy's editorial strategy in his 'Essay on the Ancient Minstrels', which balances an insistence on the ballads' historical and geographical 'remoteness' from metropolitan modernity with the continuity of national tradition. 'Most of the old heroic ballads in this collection', he wrote, were composed by minstrels who sang them 'to the harp at the houses of the great'.[21] Percy's minstrels hailed from the north of England or southern Scotland (he included a substantial number of Scottish ballads contributed by Lord Hailes), explained by the fact that 'the northern countries, as being most distant, would preserve their ancient manners longest, and of course the old poetry, in which those manners are peculiarly described' (vol. 1, p. liii).

Given his contempt for the contemporary 'singers of old ballads' populating the street corners, markets, and fairs of eighteenth-century Britain, Percy had no need to apologize for the print and manuscript sources of his material (vol. 1, p. xlviii). But as Groom has argued, he also reacted against the strongly disputed claims made by Macpherson's *Ossian* for the orality of Celtic poetry, which had survived intact through millennia of bardic tradition without any recourse to writing.[22] Granted, minstrel ballads were originally orally performed, but 'as the old Minstrels gradually wore out, a new race of Ballad-writers succeeded, an inferior sort of minor poets, who wrote narrative songs merely for the press' (vol. 1, pp. liii–liv).[23] Anxious to avoid the sceptical storm that greeted Macpherson's claims, Percy represented the black-letter sources of *Reliques* as antiquarian *objects* (his title evoking a *reliquary* containing sacred fragments) which, unlike Macpherson's evanescent productions, wouldn't simply blow away when exposed to scholarly scrutiny. The *Ossian* debacle certainly was not the end of this association between Scotland and a 'feminized' oral tradition, even if Scottish editors like Pinkerton, Jamieson, and Motherwell had little sympathy with bardic nationalism of the Ossianic stamp.[24]

Just as Warton's *History* represented the Norman Conquest as a harbinger of aristocratic chivalry and romance, thereby opposing a radical discourse of the 'Norman Yoke', Percy's minstrels embodied a desirably aristocratic point of origin for English literature in the confluence of Saxon and Norman culture. Philip Connell questions some aspects of Groom's influential view that the 'Essay on the Ancient Minstrels' established a 'gothic' genealogy for English culture, to meet the Celtic challenge of the Ossianic 1760s. Connell underlines Percy's political links with the Earl of Bute, Scottish prime minister of Great Britain and dedicatee of *Ossian*, as well as his inclusion of Scottish ballads, arguing that the 'Essay' constructs a common cultural inheritance for both England and Lowland Scotland. Rather than flying the flag for either English or Scottish cultural nationalism, in Percy's hands the ballad revival was dedicated to the post-1707 Unionist project of promoting 'a more diverse and inclusive understanding of English literature, as a vehicle for ideological containment of linguistic, ethnic, and national difference within an expanding imperial state'.[25] Despite his long residence in Ireland as Bishop of Dromore, and his active involvement in the Irish Society of Antiquaries, Percy would include no Irish ballads in later editions of *Reliques*.[26] After Percy, and notwithstanding the latter's concentration on English material, the future of the ballad revival was predominately Scottish, a fact that is perhaps difficult to explain solely in terms of Groom's argument.[27]

In 1779 the Scottish antiquary, forger, and Celtophobe John Pinkerton sent Percy a copy of 'a Scots Song I have lately recovered' entitled 'Where Helen lies', which he hoped could be included in the next edition of *Reliques* (it wasn't).[28] Taking licence from Percy's 'mending and polishing', Pinkerton included a liberal dose of his own forged texts in his 1781 collection *Scottish Tragic Ballads*.[29] Subsequently, in a bid for literary respectability, he confessed in *Antient Scotish Poems* (1786) that he had himself forged the second part of 'Hardyknute' (he apologized for being 'taken in' by the first part, written by Lady Elizabeth Wardlaw in 1719), the 'Laird of Woodhouselie', half of 'Binnorie', the 'Death of Menteith', and all of 'Where Helen lies' except the first three lines 'which he heard a lady recite'.[30]

The poetry in the 1786 volume was transcribed from the 'respectable' Maitland MS held in Magdalene College, Cambridge.

Although David Herd's 1776 *Ancient and Modern Scottish Songs* drew on oral sources, albeit without acknowledging the fact, and provided a valuable resource to subsequent collectors and 'improvers' like Robert Burns, James Johnson, and Walter Scott, Herd was light on editorial commentary.[31] In contrast, S. B. Hustvedt describes Pinkerton's 'Dissertation on the Oral Tradition of Poetry' (prefaced to the 1781 volume) as 'the first connected discussion of ballad technique'.[32] Pinkerton here sketched the formal mnemonic devices characteristic of bardic or minstrel poetry, with illustrations from Homer, Ossian, 'Hardyknute' (he cited his own forged verses), 'Child Maurice', and the alliterative poetry of Middle English and Scots. He sought to refute Dr Johnson's criticism that memory-based oral transmission over a long *durée* was an impossibility in pre-literate societies by demonstrating 'the utility of the Oral Transmission of Poetry, in that barbarous state of society which necessarily precedes the invention of letters'.[33] Pinkerton proposed that an 'authentic' minstrel tradition had been transmitted from time immemorial without ever being committed to print: 'the frequent returns of the same sentences and descriptions expressed in the very same words . . . served as landmarks, in the view of which the [reciter's] memory travelled secure over the intervening spaces' (p. xx).

Although Pinkerton argued that 'in proportion as Literature advanced in the world Oral Tradition disappeared' (p. xv), he suggested (against Percy) that its vestigial existence explains why 'the most noble productions of former periods have been preserved in the memory of a succession of admirers, and have had the good fortune to arrive at our times pure and uncorrupted' (p. xxvii). In arguing for the survival of ancient ballads in contemporary oral tradition, he acknowledged that plebeian singers best served as *involuntary* transmitters. For example, in underlining the authenticity of 'Hardyknute', he drew on personal experience that 'the common people of Lanarkshire . . . can repeat scraps of both the parts'. Given that the ballad was 'so fraught with the science of ancient manners', it was inconceivable that his labouring-class singers could have invented it, any more than a 'mere woman' like Lady Wardlaw (p. 106). As revealed by his proto-formalist approach to the ballad text, ancient formulae and burdens embody an antique 'nobility' all but inaccessible to their modern plebeian or female transmitters. Disconcertingly, we find the earliest articulation of a 'scientific' theory of oral tradition employed as an alibi for Pinkerton's own ballad forgeries. Seen from a sceptical perspective, insight into the 'formulaic' structure of ballad verse produces better 'impositions', by avoiding some of the traps of stylistic anachronism evident in the 'distressed' verse of Wardlaw, Macpherson, or Chatterton.

For Sir Walter Scott's generation Pinkerton's fame as an antiquary rested largely on his attempt to construct a non-Celtic genealogy for Scottish literature, as presented in his 'Essay on the Origin of Scotish Poetry' (appended to *Antient Scotish Poems*, 1786) and *Dissertation on the Origin and Progress of the Scythians or Goths* (1787).[34] On the flimsiest of evidence, he insisted that the Scots language was a more ancient 'gothic' language than English, given that it had descended from an earlier Scandinavian tongue called 'Pictish' which had arrived in north Britain before the Anglo-Saxons had crossed over the North Sea. By contrast, Celtic 'is of all savage languages the most confused . . . for the Celts were so inferior a people, being to the Scythae as a negro to an European, that as all history shews, to see them, was to conquer them'.[35] As Colin Kidd has demonstrated, in Pinkerton's historiography, reinforced and illustrated by his ballad theory, 'the emergence of Celts and Goths, or Teutons, as racial categories served to blur the differences between Scots Lowlanders and the English nation, and to sharpen differences between Highlanders and Lowlanders within the Scottish nation', as well as drive a wedge between the Scots and Gaelic Irish.[36] Although Scottish song collections often fly the flag of cultural nationalism, particularly in relation to the rich heritage of Jacobite song, to claim that the ballad revival was a blow struck against 'English hegemony' is to ignore the strongly Unionist ideology supporting the work of Pinkerton and others.[37]

Pinkerton's subsequent notoriety as a ballad forger was in large part owing to the Northumbrian antiquary, radical, and eccentric Joseph Ritson, who attacked Percy and Pinkerton with equal and unsparing fury. In his 'Historical Essay on National Song', Ritson insisted that Percy's 'English' minstrels were in fact Norman, and that the real English variety were by Elizabethan times legally designated 'rogues, vagabonds, and sturdy beggars' who could sing but not write, so 'whatever their songs may have been, they seem to have perished along with them'.[38] The materials collected in the *Reliques*, he added, 'bear the strongest intrinsic marks of a very modern date'.[39] As the many broadsides published in his *Northumberland Garland* (1793) and *Scotish Song* (1794) attest, Ritson went against the grain of the general ballad theory of the long eighteenth century in his genuine affection for contemporary popular culture, both printed and oral, especially song performance. Not surprising then that he preferred a modern broadside like 'Children in the Wood' to a 'minstrel' ballad like 'Little Musgrave and Lady Barnard'.[40] Ritson also struck at the roots of Pinkerton's ballad theory, arguing that 'with respect to vulgar poetry, preserved by tradition, it is almost impossible to discriminate the ancient from the modern, the true from the false'.[41] In fact he had little respect for oral transmission because as 'the purest strain become polluted by the foulness of its channel, [it] may in turn be degraded to the vilest jargon. Tradition in short, is a species of alchemy which converts gold to lead.'[42] If Chaucer's *Canterbury Tales* had been orally transmitted, not a single word of the original poetry would have survived (p. lxxxii).

In his 'Historical Essay on Scotish Song', Ritson defended the Celtic provenance of Scottish culture against Pinkerton's 'Pictish' theory (p. xiv), and mischievously proposed that the majority of Scottish songs and ballads were of recent origin, the work of 'obscure or anonymous authors, of shepherds and milkmaids' rather than ancient minstrels (p. lxxix). Taking a further dig at Pinkerton, who had boasted that Scottish women had too much 'sense of decency and propriety to commence authors',[43] he indicated the strong creative contribution made by eighteenth-century Scottish women poets to the ballad canon, including Lady Wardlaw and Lady Grisell Baillie (p. lxxvii). Finally, he implied that fetishizing oral tradition in the style of Pinkerton (or indeed Macpherson) was often a cover for forgery: had Pinkerton 'used the same freedom in any private business . . . he would have been set in the pillory' (p. lxxv). Taking revenge for having to apologize for his English birth in the preface to his *Scotish Song*, he suggested that the question 'why the Scotish literati should be more particularly addicted to literary imposture than those of any other country, might be a curious subject of investigation for the Royal Society' (pp. lxx, lxi). Despite this national animus, Robert Burns acknowledged his profound indebtedness to Ritson's essay in freeing an evergreen Scottish song tradition from the dead hand of antiquarian editors.[44]

Although Scott's *Minstrelsy of the Scottish Border* (1802–3) is the most celebrated ballad collection of the Romantic period, it rather timidly aspired 'to imitate the plan and style of Bishop Percy, observing only more strict fidelity concerning my originals'.[45] Scott domesticated Percy's theory of minstrel composition via medieval Border minstrels like 'Thomas the Rhymer', and fulsomely dedicated his book to his patron the Duke of Buccleuch. Taking issue with Pinkerton's 'Pictish' theory of Scottish origins, he restored a Celtic genealogy to Scottish culture, which he regarded as a harmonious melding of Celtic and Saxon.[46] Scott's original introduction to *The Minstrelsy* was intended to be 'rather of a historical than a literary nature' (vol. 1, p. 5), presenting a detailed context for the ballads in the social and political history of the Scottish Borders. As we saw, Percy had singled out the Borders as the classic ground of the British ballad tradition. Scott concurred, 'install[ing] the "Border" chronotope of a dynamic liminality rather than an imperial dead centre, the space-time of an historical modernity that ... looks backward in order to move forwards'.[47] Ballads were the product of 'habits of intimacy betwixt the Borderers of both kingdoms, notwithstanding their mutual hostility and reciprocal depredations ... there was little difference between the Northumbrian and the border Scottish' (vol. 1, pp. 168–9).

In 1834 James Hogg recalled his mother Margaret Laidlaw's angry outburst to Scott, during one of the latter's ballad collecting 'raids' in Ettrick in the early 1800s: 'There was never ane o' my songs prentit till ye prentit them yourself, an' ye hade spoilt them a'thegither. They war made for singing, an' no for reading; and they're nouther right spelled nor right setten down.'[48] According to Valentina Bold, Margaret Laidlaw's celebrated 'put-down' is most probably a 'vigorous anecdote from a great story teller' (i.e. Hogg himself), grumbling about three decades of Scott's editorial practice.[49] Bold shows in some detail that Hogg family ballads like 'The dowy houms o' Yarrow' and 'Old Maitland' were indeed neither 'right spelled nor right setten down' in *The Minstrelsy*, given Scott's alterations, cuts, and poeticisms, forcing source material into line with the romantic and chivalric lineaments of contemporary literary taste.[50]

Hogg's anecdote does however accurately reflect Scott's low opinion of oral transmission. In the introduction to *The Minstrelsy*, he lamented the scarcity of surviving manuscripts, insisting that, on account of the unreliability of 'popular poetry', 'it is the frail chance of recovering some old manuscript, which can alone gratify our curiosity regarding the earlier efforts of the Border Muse'. Having failed to locate sixteenth- and seventeenth-century collections mentioned by 'the learned Mr Ritson', he apologized that 'the Editor has been obliged to draw his material chiefly from oral tradition' (vol. 1, pp. 222, 222–3). (Apparently only one item collected in *The Minstrelsy* was taken by Scott directly 'from recitation'.[51]) Although he did derive a rich body of material at second hand from the Hogg family and other Border singers, as well as from the manuscript repertoire of Anna Gordon Brown of Falkland, Scott here downplays the fact that he also drew liberally on the Herd MSS, the Glenriddell MS, and other written and printed sources.[52]

Nevertheless, whereas Percy legitimized his refashionings with reference to the 'Folio manuscript', Scott often invokes oral sources to authenticate material, despite this distaste for oral transmission. Of the *Minstrelsy's* version of 'The Battle of Otterburn' (which differs from those published by Percy and Herd), he wrote: 'fortunately two copies have since been obtained from the recitation of old persons residing at the head of Ettrick Forest, by which the story is brought out, and completed in a manner much more correspondent to the true history' (vol. 1, p. 351).[53] (In contrast to the polite Mrs Brown, Scott's vulgar informants aren't here dignified with names.) But like Percy, Scott was happy to give a broad hint that he had 'patched and mended' traditional material; as in the case of 'Kinmont Willie', of which he wrote, 'the ballad is preserved, by tradition, on the West Borders, but much mangled by reciters; so that some conjectural emendations have been absolutely necessary to render it intelligible' (vol. 11, p. 50).

Part of the difficulty in assessing Scott's practice as a ballad editor lies in the nature of this 'composite technique', which he later regretted in an 1824 letter to William Motherwell:

I think I did wrong myself in endeavouring to make the best possible set of an ancient ballad out of several copies obtained from different quarters, and that, in many respects, if I improved the poetry, I spoiled the simplicity of the old song ... perhaps, it is as well to keep [different versions] separate, as giving in their original state a more accurate idea of our ancient poetry, which is the point most important in such collections.[54]

Like Percy, Scott was a *belle-lettrist* before he was a ballad scholar: receiving numerous versions of ballads from Anna Brown, James Hogg, John Leyden, William Tytler, and others, he polished, refined, and 'completed' fragmentary variants to produce 'Historical' and 'Romantic' texts which would appeal to contemporary literary taste. Like the consummate 'reconditioning' of old songs by Robert Burns, Scott 'got away with it' because, as Friedman points out, he was so 'close to the ballad tradition' itself that his 'changes and interpolations blend smoothly with the authentic portions of the text'.[55] But Scott was also closer to literary fashion than most ballad editors. As he admitted in his 1830 *Essay on Imitations of the Ancient Ballad*, his enthusiasm had in any case been kindled by the German imitation ballads of Burger and their 'Englishing' by William Taylor and Mathew Lewis, and he elsewhere sought a more 'literary' genealogy by proposing that ballads were abridgements of earlier metrical romances.[56] In a note to the *Lay of the Last Minstrel* (1805), the first of

a stream of hugely successful 'medieval' romances which flowed from
Scott's pen over the next decade, he described how he had come under
the spell of the variegated octosyllabic couplet and the metrical magic
of Coleridge's *Christabel*, at a time when the imitation ballad had lapsed
from fashion, and its measure 'become hackneyed and sickening, from
its being the accompaniment of every grinding hand-organ'.[57] As Friedman notes, for the aspiring poet, 'the metrical romances were rich in the
colourful, evocative language and in the details, ceremony, and chivalric
circumstances that the ballads so woefully lacked'.[58]

William Motherwell's 'Historical Introduction' to *Minstrelsy: Ancient
and Modern* (1827) in many ways anticipates the new 'disciplinary' approach that reached its apogee in the work of F. J. Child. Two recent
monographs entirely dedicated to Motherwell, by William McCarthy and
Mary Ellen Brown, rightly emphasize his influence on modern folklore
studies, although his contribution also needs to be contextualized in
relation to earlier ballad poetics, particularly the largely unacknowledged influence of Pinkerton.[59] Motherwell was in many respects an
unattractive character, a misogynist Orangeman who energetically
resisted the tide of political reform in Scotland in the 1820s and 30s as a
trooper in the Renfrew Yeomanry, while making a living as editor of the
conservative *Paisley Advertiser* and *Glasgow Courier*. Sharing the Norse/
Gothic enthusiasm of Pinkerton, Scott, and Jamieson, his original poems
'imaginatively evoked the Scandinavian presence in Scotland' and rhap-
sodized the masculine virtues of warfare.[60] The warrior narrator of 'The
Sword Chant of Thorstein Raudi', for example, apostrophizes his mighty
blade: 'In some battle-field, / Where armour is ringing, / And noble
blood springing, / And cloven, yawn helmet, / Stout hauberk and shield. /
DEATH GIVER! I kiss thee.'[61]

Motherwell's importance lies in his recuperating of the value of oral
transmission, preferring to turn his scorn on the editorial practice of
'mending and patching' old ballads, recently taken to new extremes in the
songs forged by 'Honest Allan' Cunningham for *Songs of Scotland* (1825).
Motherwell thundered:

The tear and wear of three centuries will do less mischief to the text of an old
ballad among the vulgar, than one short hour will effect, if in the possession of
some sprightly and accomplished editor of the present day, who may choose to
impose on himself the thankless and uncalled for labour of piecing and patching
up its imperfections, polishing its asperities, correcting its mistakes, embellishing
its naked details, purging it of impurities, and of trimming it from top to toe
with tailor-like fastidiousness and nicety, so as to be made fit for the press.[62]

Not only did these 'manufacturers of antique gems' 'poison the sources of history' (p. ix), but their editorial practice was likened to a form of perverted or deviant masculinity, as in his evocation of Allan Cunningham as a necrophiliac 'ransack[ing] the tomb, and rifl[ing] the calm beauty of the mute and unresisting dead' (pp. xcvi–xcvii).

Motherwell exemplifies the idealizing and conservative strain of Romantic popular culture discussed in the introduction, holding that 'primitive forms of speech, particularly idiomatick expressions and antique phrases' survived best among the common people, whose poverty and lack of education retarded the effects of modernization (p. iii). In common with Scott and Jamieson, he saw his work as a form of salvage ethnography, because traditional virtues were rapidly succumbing to 'paltry philosophers, political quacks, and illuminated dreams on Economick and Moral Science' (p. cii). The oral tradition of Scottish balladry was a repository of the traditional wisdom of the peasantry (in language anticipating Thomas Carlyle), 'an actual embodiment of their Universal mind, and of its intellectual and moral tendencies' (p. v). Because print culture was a paramount vehicle for modernity (particularly of the 'steam intellect' variety), oral tradition safeguarded the ancient ballads from contamination: ballads must accordingly 'be gathered from the lips of "the spinsters and knitters in the sun, who use to chaunt [them]"' (p. ii).

Despite the *volkische* idiom evident in this reference to the 'Universal mind' of the peasantry, Motherwell uncritically accepted the 'minstrel theory' with hardly a glimpse at the emergent 'communalist' explanation of folk composition associated with the German school, later developed in the writings of Andrew Lang, in Durkheim's group consciousness, or in Levy-Bruhl's theory of the primitive mind.[63] Pursuing a stiffened version of Scott's idealization of chivalry, Motherwell promoted the medieval ballad chronotope associated with his precursor for transparently ideological reasons, given that ballads derive from 'a state of society, comparatively rude, in which the distinctions of rank are few, but deeply marked. [Their personages] ... move in the higher classes, which is another proof of their antiquity, and places them anterior to those circumstances, that overthrew the institutions of chivalry, and sapped the foundations of feudal aristocracy' (p. xxv). Always eager to proselytize in favour of the humble ballad, with its appeal to 'an unsophisticated and manly taste' (p. iv), he challenged Scott and other antiquaries by affording it chronological priority over the metrical romance (p. xxxii). In order to defend the ballads from Ritson's sceptical 'poetic archaiology [*sic*]', which denied antiquity to the Scottish ballad corpus, he went to

unprecedented lengths to produce internal evidence of the deep antiquity
of ballads, for example calculating that in the year 1228 the Feast of the
Assumption (15 August) fell on a Monday, in order to 'date' 'Sir Patrick
Spens' to the thirteenth century (p. xliv).

While believing that the ballad traditions of England and Scotland were
largely shared, the fact that chivalry endured longer in Scotland ensured
the later survival of minstrelsy, and helped explain Scotland's particularly
rich endowment (p. xxxvi). 'If England exhibits ancient manuscripts
in which these ballads are contained, Scotland proves immemorial possession of them, by oral transmission even to the present time' (p. xxxix).
Percy had traced a line of descent from Saxon and Celtic bards to
medieval minstrels, but the Celtophobe Motherwell followed Pinkerton
in erecting a *cordon sanitaire* to separate them. In fact Motherwell's
loathing for Celtic bards is evident in his enthusiastic description of their
proscription from early modern Scotland: 'a vagabond, thief, counter-
feiter, limmer, and bard were synonymous'; and he reported that in
Renfrewshire the term 'bardy' still signified 'impudent, rude, uncivil,
forward, or quarrelsome' (p. xxxvii). Motherwell sought to isolate the old
Scottish ballads from the wares of contemporary Irish ballad singers currently arriving in large numbers in the Presbyterian bastion of his native
southwestern Scotland.

Nevertheless Motherwell's theory of oral transmission set new standards for the scholarly recognition of the 'traditional ballad'. He differed
from Scott's practice in *The Minstrelsy* in presenting his ballads 'in the
very garb in which they are remembered and known', rather than producing ideal or composite texts (p. v). Despite differences of region and
dialect, he discerned 'certain common-places which seem an integrant
portion of the original mechanism of all our ancient ballads, and the
presence of which forms one of their most peculiar and distinctive char-
acteristicks, as contrasted with the modern ballad' (p. vi). From Pinkerton
he had learned that the commonplace was a mnemonic aid, fundamental
to the survival of a traditional narrative structure in oral transmission;
the ballad narrator's 'ever agreeing in describing certain actions in one
uniform way – their identity of language, epithet, and expression, in
numerous scenes where the least resemblance of incident occurs' (p. xix).

Thus, for instance, when a fate-determining letter or message is
received by the protagonist (as by Sir Patrick Spens in the eponymous
ballad) 'the saut tear blinds his e'e' (p. xxi); or else 'the expression of
wiping [a sword] on the sleeve, drying on the grass, and slaiting o'er the
strae, always occur in such ballads as indicated a dubious and protracted

and somewhat unequal combat' (p. xxiii). These commonplaces are a kind of 'brachigraphy' or shorthand, completely alien to the compositional habits of the 'modern versifier' (p. xxii). The ballad refrain or 'burthen' had a similar role in assisting the memory of the singer, and Motherwell hypothesized that ballad refrains such as 'derry down, down, hey derry down' (p. xix) were the fossilized fragments of still more ancient lyrics originally sung to the same tune, 'to which the Ramsays and Cunninghams of those times had fitted new words for the nonce' (p. xxiv).

Motherwell insisted that commonplaces and burthens, unlike other elements of diction, allusion, and style, were resistant to normal historical mutation. They 'serve as land marks, and helps to the memory of the reciter, while they secure the stream of the narrative from being broken or interrupted by the innovation of time, and the mutations of language' (p. xi). Recent interest in Motherwell amongst American folklorists is based on the hypothesis that he was the unacknowledged (and unconscious) originator of a version of the 'oral-formulaic theory' of ballad transmission based on the research of Alfred Lord and Milman Parry, in which the singer not only *remembers* but 'recreates [the traditional ballad] . . . by moulding the story in the shaping dies, verbal and architectonic, of his tradition'.[64] Such performative creativity (perhaps with a nod to the Italian *improvvisatore* who fascinated Romantic poets) is certainly implied in Motherwell's account of the ballad formula as 'a kind of ground-work, on which the poem could be raised. With such commonplaces indelibly fixed in this memory, the minstrel could with ease to himself, and with the rapidity of extemporaneous delivery, rapidly model any event which came under his cognizance into song' (p. xxiii).

Even more important for modern folklorists is the evidence of Motherwell's extensive field collecting preserved in his Manuscript and Notebook (including over twenty-two ballads and fragments from Agnes Lyle, a Kilbarchan weaver), both of which were copied by Child and used as a major source for *English and Scottish Popular Ballads*. McCarthy and Brown both focus on Motherwell's emergent practice and theory (in that order) of field collecting, the former claiming Agnes Lyle as a skilled practitioner of oral-formulaic performance. The Manuscript is taken to provide evidence of Motherwell's shift from a text-based interest in ballad 'paradigms' to their variants, collecting oral performances and itemizing the repertoire of individual performers, some seventy-five of whom are referred to by name in his papers.[65]

Nonetheless, some caution is required here. Compared to the elaborate poetics of 'trinary, binary and annular patterning', Motherwell's application is limited and his theory somewhat vague, despite his salutary emphasis on the importance of melody in ballad performance. Far from anticipating structuralist analysis, he resorts to a *belle-lettristic* notion of literary 'tact' in supposing an 'intuitive and auxiliary sense' which can distinguish the traces of 'National Minstrelsy' from the modern copy, through sensitivity to the 'aureate terms' of commonplace and burthen (p. xii). Most important, his notion of the distinctive features of a traditional ballad is still beholden to Percy's seminal distinction (which he quotes approvingly), rather than to empirical insights into oral variants gathered in the field.

Moreover, despite his concern to inventorize sources in his notebooks, Motherwell's attitude to his plebeian female informants (many of them as ancient as the 'manly' feudal ballads which they perform) is strangely facetious. At one point he warns the male collector 'I have unfortunately for myself, once or twice notably affronted certain aged virgins, by impertinent dubitations touching the veracity of their songs', warning that such scepticism is guaranteed to seal 'the lips of every venerable sybil in the land' (p. xxxvii). The women's ignorant credulity serves to guarantee the purity of their transmission. Motherwell nonetheless showed himself fully aware of the currency of printed ballads in Scottish working-class households (p. xlvii) and distinguished the broadside format of 'ballads intended for being sung through the streets' from the chapbook format characteristic of those 'vended through the country by the worshipful fraternity of Flying Stationers' (p. xlii). The headnotes to the ballads in his collection, in tune with those of his predecessors, list manuscript and print sources more often than oral performance. Despite this awareness, there is unsurprisingly no attempt to theorize the constant interaction between printed and oral ballads.[66]

Although there is some justice in the view of Motherwell as a major harbinger of modern ballad scholarship, he is really a transitional figure whose roots lie deep within the long eighteenth-century and Romantic tradition surveyed in this chapter. When Sir Walter Scott wrote his important 'Essay on Popular Poetry' in 1830 in reply to Motherwell's essay published five years before, he decisively rejected the latter's oral theory. Adapting Ritson's metaphor, he described the popular transmission of ballads, whether oral or printed, as 'a degrading species of Alchymy', and likened its effects to the rubbing of a coin which 'by passing from hand to hand, loses in circulation all the finer marks of the impress'.[67] Evident here is the elder Scott's distaste for the ballad as poetic form, and his rejection of Motherwell's special pleading for its distinctive stylistic features of formulae and repetition: 'the least acquaintance with the subject will recall a great number of commonplace verses, which each ballad-maker has unceremoniously appropriated to himself; thereby greatly facilitating his own task, and at the same time degrading his art by his slovenly use of over-scutched phrases' (vol. 1, p. 17). Scott's metaphor here associates the ballad with the vulgar and female world of the kitchen sink, a far cry from Motherwell's bid to attempt to lend scholarly respectability to the 'aureate terms' of oral tradition.

By 1830 Scott saw the 'romantic ballad' as a degraded form of metrical romance, the 'historical ballad' (where it survived) as a mere auxiliary to better-attested historical sources (vol. 1, p. 40). In conclusion we might say that, although the oral ballad poetics initiated by Pinkerton and refined by Motherwell were well established by the end of the Romantic period, they were far from initiating acceptance of traditional ballads as popular performance, and had the effect of buttressing rather than undermining Percy's antiquarian theory of minstrel origins. Seen in the light of Scott's authoritative judgement, the poetics of oral transmission hardly represent a dominant 'Romantic' discourse of balladry. It may be the case, as Maureen McLane has recently claimed, that by 1803 the practice of 'dated transcription' of oral performances had passed a Foucauldian 'threshold of epistemologization' to 'become part of that singular mode of cultural inquiry, balladeering'.[68] But as this chapter has argued, Romantic ballad theory (as opposed to the *practice* of Ritson, Burns, or Hogg) showed a stubborn resistance to a feminized oral tradition and to contemporary popular performance. Even in Motherwell's pioneering remarks on orality, we can see many surviving features of Percy's distinction mobilized to provide a last-ditch defence of a distinctively anti-popular feudal ideal against contemporary demotic culture. And as my brief remarks on Child have demonstrated, the distinction initiated by Percy and developed during the Romantic decades would contribute in important ways to the widening distinction of 'folk' from 'popular' culture in the course of the following century.

NOTES

My thanks to Leith Davis, Suzanne Gilbert, Kirsteen McCue, and Phil Connell for their help and expertise in the preparation of this chapter.

1 Susan Stewart, *Crimes of Writing: Problems in the Containment of Representation* (New York and Oxford: Oxford University Press, 1991), p. 108.
2 Thomas Percy, *Reliques of Ancient English Poetry*, 3 vols. (Dublin, 1766), vol. 1, p. lxix.

3 See Flemming G. Andersen, 'Oral Tradition in England in the Eighteenth Century', in F. G. Andersen, O. Holzapfel, and T. Pettit (eds.), *The Ballad as Narrative* (Odense: Odense University Press, 1982), pp. 59–70; Maureen McLane, 'Dating Orality, Thinking Balladry: Of Milkmaids and Minstrels in 1771', *Eighteenth Century: Theory and Interpretation* 47:2–3 (Summer–Fall 2006), 131–49.

4 Pierre Bourdieu, 'The Field of Cultural Production, or, The Economic World Reversed', in Bourdieu, *The Field of Cultural Production*, ed. Randal Johnson, trans. Richard Nice (Cambridge: Polity Press, 1993), pp. 29–73.

5 Francis James Child, *The English and Scottish Popular Ballads*, 5 vols. (New York: Dover Publications, 1965). Subsequent references are in parentheses in the text. Volume v includes a précis of Child's encyclopaedia article, his only 'theoretical' reflection on ballad editing.

6 See Dave Harker, *Fakesong: The Manufacture of British 'Folksong' from 1700 to the Present Day* (Milton Keynes: Open University Press, 1985), p. 113 and pp. 101–20 on Child in general.

7 Gleaned from the collections of Scott, Jamieson, Motherwell, Buchan, *et al.* See Deborah Symonds, *Weep Not for Me: Women, Ballads, and Infanticide in Early Modern Scotland* (University Park, Penn.: Pennsylvania State University Press, 1997), p. 11.

8 Albert B. Friedman, *The Ballad Revival: Studies in the Influence of Popular on Sophisticated Poetry* (Chicago and London: Chicago University Press, 1961). For Groom, see note 26 below. See also the special ballad issue of *Eighteenth Century: Theory and Interpretation* 47:2–3 (Summer–Fall 2006).

9 Stewart, *Crimes of Writing*, p. 103.

10 Steve Newman, 'The Scots Songs of Allan Ramsay: "Lyric" Transformation, Popular Culture, and the Boundaries of the Scottish Enlightenment', *Modern Language Quarterly* 63:3 (September 2002), 289.

11 Jonathan Brody Kramnick, *Making the English Canon: Print Capitalism and the Cultural Past, 1700–1770* (Cambridge: Cambridge University Press, 1998), pp. 43, 77.

12 Dianne Dugaw, 'The Popular Marketing of "Old Ballads": The Ballad Revival and Eighteenth-Century Antiquarianism Reconsidered', *Eighteenth-Century Studies* 21:1 (Fall 1987), 74–5.

13 William St Clair, *The Reading Nation in the Romantic Period* (Cambridge: Cambridge University Press, 2004), p. 350.

14 *Ibid.*, p. 346. Paula McDowell responds that only one 'particular section of the popular print marketplace that had been copyrighted [such as Dicey's stock of reprints] was monopolized . . . Other printers did continue to print popular broadside ballads that were never registered (and so never part of any "monopoly").' 'The Manufacture and Lingua-Facture of Ballad Making: Broadside Ballads in Long Eighteenth-Century Ballad Discourse', *Eighteenth Century: Theory and Interpretation* 47:2–3 (Summer–Fall 2006), 174n.4.

15 St Clair, *Reading Nation*, p. 345.

16 Dugaw, 'Popular Marketing', 83.

17 Percy, *Reliques* (1766), vol. 1, p. ii. He alludes to the Countess's descent from the Percy celebrated in 'Chevy Chase', fortuitously enough a namesake of the editor himself.

18 See Steve Newman, *Ballad Collecting, Lyric and the Canon: The Call of the Popular from the Restoration to the New Criticism* (Philadelphia: University of Pennsylvania Press, 2007), pp. 97–135.

19 Nick Groom, *The Making of Percy's 'Reliques'* (Oxford: Clarendon Press, 1999), p. 45.

20 Ann Wierda Rowland, ' "The false nourice sang": Childhood, Child Murder, and the Formalism of the Scottish Ballad Revival', in Leith Davis, Ian Duncan, and Janet Sorensen (eds.), *Scotland and the Borders of Romanticism* (Cambridge: Cambridge University Press, 2004), p. 227.

21 Quoting from the extended text of the 'Essay' published in *Reliques of Ancient English Poetry*, 4th edn, 3 vols. (London, 1794), vol. 1, p. xxiii. Subsequent references are to this edition and in parentheses in the text.

22 Groom, *Percy's 'Reliques'*, pp. 75–82. See introduction to this volume, pp. 17–18.

23 Stewart argues that 'the minstrel origins theory legitimates . . . the professional status of the bard/author. It legitimates the notion of a national literature and its corollary genesis in the naturalized category of feudalism, poses the security and fixed identity of patronage against the flux and anonymity of the literary marketplace' (*Crimes of Writing*, p. 114).

24 See Penny Fielding, *Writing and Orality: Nationality, Culture and Nineteenth-Century Scottish Fiction* (Oxford: Clarendon Press, 1996).

25 Phil Connell, 'British Identities and the Politics of Ancient Poetry in later Eighteenth-Century England', *Historical Journal* 49:1 (2006), 189.

26 Nick Groom, ' "The Purest English": Ballads and the English Literary Dialect', *Eighteenth Century: Theory and Interpretation* 47:2–3 (Summer–Fall 2006), 182. This despite his patronage of Charlotte Brooke, discussed by Leith Davis in her chapter in the present volume.

27 According to the findings of the Glasgow SCRAN project, 216 of Child's 305 ballads are 'Scottish' on the basis of theme or information (editor's introduction to Edward Cowan (ed.), *The Ballad in Scottish History* (East Lothian: Tuckwell Press, 2000), p. 15n.4).

28 Pinkerton also sent the forged second part of 'Hardyknute'. See *The Percy Letters: The Correspondence of Thomas Percy and John Pinkerton*, ed. Harriet Harvey Wood (New Haven and London: Yale University Press, 1985), pp. 18–21.

29 John Pinkerton, *Scottish Tragic Ballads* (London, 1781). This was prefaced by two dissertations 'On the Oral Tradition of Poetry' and 'On the Tragic Ballad'. Pinkerton followed this up with *Select Scotish Ballads* (London, 1783) which contained mainly pastoral and comic songs.

30 [Anon.], *Antient Scotish Poems, Never Before in Print. But now published from the MS Collection of Sir Richard Maitland. . .*, 2 vols. (London, 1786), vol. 1, p. cxxviii.

31 David Herd, *Ancient and Modern Scottish Songs, Heroic Ballads, etc., collected by David Herd*, 2 vols. (1776; rpt Edinburgh and London: Scottish Academic Press, 1973), incorporating an earlier collection of 1769. See Harker, *Fakesong*, p. 29.

32 S. B. Hustvedt, *Ballad Criticism in Scandinavia and Great Britain during the Eighteenth Century* (New York and London: Oxford University Press, 1916), p. 248.

33 Pinkerton, *Scottish Tragic Ballads*, p. x. Subsequent references are in parentheses in the text.

34 Jonathan Oldbuck in Scott's *The Antiquary* is a convinced Pinkertonian.

35 John Pinkerton, *A Dissertation on the Origin and Progress of the Scythians or Goths* (London, 1787), pp. 102, 123.

36 Colin Kidd, 'Race, Theology and Revival: Scots Philology and its Contexts in the Age of Pinkerton and Jamieson', *Scottish Studies Review* 3:2 (Autumn 2002), 22.

37 I pass over Jacobite song here as it has been well served by other critics. See William Donaldson, *The Jacobite Song: Political Myth and National Identity* (Aberdeen: Aberdeen University Press, 1988) and Murray Pittock, *Poetry and Jacobite Politics in Eighteenth-Century Britain and Ireland* (Cambridge: Cambridge University Press, 1994).

38 Joseph Ritson, 'An Historical Essay on the Origin and Progress of National Song', in *A Select Collection of English Songs* (1783), 2nd edition with notes by Thomas Parks, 3 vols. (London, 1813), vol. 1, pp. i–xcviii, lxviii. (The first part of this actually quotes from Percy's 'Essay'.) Many of the cuts were engraved by William Blake.

39 *Ibid.*, p. lxxvi.

40 See Friedman, *Ballad Revival*, p. 238.

41 Ritson, *English Songs*, vol. 1, p. lxxxi.

42 Joseph Ritson, 'An Historical Essay on Scotish Song', in *Scotish Song in Two Volumes* (London: Joseph Johnson, 1794), vol. 1, p. lxxxi (subsequent page numbers are in parentheses in the text). In fact to the extent that alchemy depended on courtly patronage in the late middle ages, it bears a closer link to minstrelsy than to oral tradition. Thanks to Simon Schaffer for this observation.

43 John Pinkerton, *Select Scottish Ballads* (London, 1783), p. xv.

44 Robert Burns, *Letters of Robert Burns*, ed. J. Lancey Ferguson and G. Ross Roy, 2 vols. (Oxford: Clarendon Press, 1985), vol. 11, p. 318. In his *Commonplace Book 1783–5*, ed. with intro. by Raymond Lamont Brown (Wakefield: S. R. Publishers Ltd, 1969), Burns praises the 'glorious old Bards' who have authored 'ancient fragments', but signs off as 'a poor rustic Bard' who continues the 'anonymous tradition' (p. 49).

45 Walter Scott, *Minstrelsy of the Scottish Border, consisting of Historical and Romantic Ballads*, ed. J. G. Lockhart (1833), vols. 1–1V of *The Poetical Works of Sir Walter Scott*, 12 vols. (Edinburgh: Adam and Charles Black, 1861), vol. 1V, p. 77. Henceforth in parentheses in the text.

46 Leith Davis, *Acts of Union: Scotland and the Literary Negotiation of the British Nation 1707–1830* (Stanford, Calif.: Stanford University Press, 1998), pp. 158–61.

47 Editors' introduction to Davis *et al.* (eds.), *Scotland and the Borders of Romanticism*, p. 13. See also Susan Oliver, *Scott, Byron and the Poetics of Cultural Encounter* (Basingstoke: Palgrave Macmillan, 2005), pp. 19–68.

48 Quoted in Valentina Bold, ' "Nouther right spelled nor right setten down": Scott, Child and the Hogg Family Ballads', in Cowan (ed.), *The Ballad in Scottish History*, pp. 116–41 (p. 117). The passage is from Hogg's *Familiar Anecdotes of Sir Walter Scott* (1834).

49 Bold, ' "Nouther right spelled" ', p. 117.

50 *Ibid.*, esp. p. 125.

51 Harker, *Fakesong*, p. 58.

52 For Brown, see Norman Buchan, *The Ballad and the Folk* (East Lothian: Tuckwell Press, 1997), pp. 66–73.

53 Child was sceptical of Scott's claim for the 'Scottish' Otterburn. See Child, *Popular Ballads*, vol. III, p. 293.

54 Quoted from the original MS by Mary Ellen Brown, *William Motherwell's Cultural Politics* (Lexington: University Press of Kentucky, 2001), p. 82. Scott's letter clearly influenced Motherwell's editorial practice, establishing a principle later adopted by Child.

55 Friedman, *Ballad Revival*, p. 243.

56 See S. B. Hustvedt's discussion in *Ballad Books and Ballad Men* (Cambridge, Mass.: Harvard University Press, 1930), pp. 38–40.

57 Walter Scott, *Poetical Works of Sir Walter Scott*, ed. J. Logie Robertson (London, 1913), pp. 51–2.

58 Friedman, *Ballad Revival*, p. 296.

59 William Bernard McCarthy, *The Ballad Matrix: Personality, Milieu, and the Oral Tradition* (Bloomington and Indianapolis: Indiana University Press, 1990); Mary Ellen Brown, see note 54.

60 Brown, *Motherwell's Cultural Politics*, p. 64.

61 *Ibid.*, p. 66.

62 William Motherwell, *Minstrelsy: Ancient and Modern, with an Historical Introduction and Notes* (Glasgow: John Wylie, 1827), p. iv. Henceforth in parentheses in the text.

63 Friedman, *Ballad Revival*, pp. 247–50.

64 Buchan, *The Ballad and the Folk*, p. 58.

65 McCarthy, *Ballad Matrix*, p. 36; see Brown, *Motherwell's Cultural Politics*, Appendix 1, for list. Brown is however sceptical of some of McCarthy's claims.

66 See Robert S. Thomson, 'The Development of the Broadside Ballad and Its Influence Upon the Transmission of English Folksongs', unpublished PhD thesis, University of Cambridge (1974).

67 Scott, *Minstrelsy*, vol. 1, p. 22. Henceforth in parentheses in the text.

68 McLane, 'Dating Orality', 139.

CHAPTER 3

Refiguring the popular in Charlotte Brooke's
Reliques of Irish Poetry

Leith Davis

In 'A Discipline in Shifting Perspective: Why We Need Irish Studies', James Chandler raises the 'question of what Irish Studies might mean in and for today's university'.[1] He suggests that a consideration of Ireland in relation to issues in English literature and culture provides both 'an elevation of perspective, a shift of scale that allows one to extend a horizon and thus to bring parallel histories into relation with one another', and, at times, a 'reversal of critical perspective'.[2] Chandler's intervention, though valuable in its advocacy of a 'four nations' approach, is limited by its image of Irish Studies fitting linearly – either as extension or reversal – into a conventional scholarly perspective on English literary studies. Rather, with its strange shifting and triangulated conflations of self, self/other, and other, Ireland operates variously both to support and to challenge the dominant paradigms of critical inquiry on which our understanding of the discipline of British literature – and, indeed, of Britain itself – is based.[3]

An exploration of popular culture in the Romantic era from an Irish perspective, for example, presents more than just an 'extension' or 'reversal' of the views on the subject. It also presents a significantly different relationship between the popular and the elite than that offered by Peter Burke and subsequent commentators. In *Popular Culture in Early Modern Europe*, Burke defines the popular as that which belongs to 'the non-elite, the "subordinate classes" as Gramsci called them'.[4] He argues that popular and elite culture became more and more polarized in Europe so that, in the eighteenth century, elite interest in popular culture manifested itself as a 'discovery of the people'.[5] But in Ireland, the conquests in the twelfth century and colonial plantations in the sixteenth and seventeenth centuries resulted in a different configuration.[6] Richard Kearney asks the following question in relation to Ireland: 'who exactly are the people? Are they *a* people, *the* people, or peoples?'[7] It is equally pertinent to enquire, 'Who exactly are the *elite*?', as in both waves of colonialism 'non-elite' status was

conferred on the entire native population, although the previously existing elites continued to exercise some power, both symbolic and economic.[8]
For its part, the Protestant population was marginalized from the perspective of English metropolitan culture, and after the plantation under
James VI Protestants were divided from within into Anglican, Presbyterian,
and Dissenting communities, the latter two of which were legally disen-
franchised in the eighteenth century. The distinction between popular and
elite groups, then, while fluid in any context, was particularly fraught in
Ireland.

Moreover, while colonial conquest imposed an artificial and more violent process of polarization between elite and dominant groups on Ireland,
it arguably also introduced what can be seen as more of a self-conscious
awareness of the political uses of culture.[9] Although much discussion of
popular culture in the Romantic era dates 'the rush to publish the national
archive of ballad and song' to the latter half of the eighteenth century,
in fact an interest in using the 'reliques' of the past to reflect on present
conditions can be seen earlier than this in Ireland and Scotland.[10] The
strategic representation of the past and 'the people' was well understood
by a Catholic population anxious to repeal the harsh penal laws and an
Anglo-Irish population concerned both to assert their cultural affiliation
with the country in which their families had settled and to obtain greater
economic and political independence from England while still maintaining their cultural connection with the metropolis. As the publication of
Dermod O'Connor's translation of Geoffrey Keating's *The General History
of Ireland* (1723), Jonathan Swift's translation of Hugh MacGauran's
'Pléaráca na Ruarcach' (1735), and the Neales' *A Colection* [sic] *of the most
Celebrated Irish Tunes* (1724) attest, the identification and publication of the
'national archive' for writers in Ireland was bound up variously with
attempts to assert native Irish identity, to call into question English political
hegemony, and to appeal to English metropolitan culture.[11] When the first
substantial translation of Gaelic poetry into English, Charlotte Brooke's
Reliques of Irish Poetry, appeared in 1789, it followed a good half-century
or more of these different interests competing for the use of Irish culture,
and, to a certain extent, represents a combination of all of them.[12] While
Brooke's work may be partially connected to a more general European
'discovery of the people' at the end of the eighteenth century, a close
examination of the *Reliques* also suggests the anomalies that characterize the
relationship between elite and popular culture in Romantic-era Ireland.[13]

The *Reliques* consists of '*Heroic Poems, Odes, Elegies, and Songs Translated
into English Verse*', accompanied by copious '*Explanatory and Historical*'

notes which reference Brooke's contemporaries Charles O'Conor, Sylvester O'Halloran, General Charles Vallancey, and Joseph Cooper Walker.[14] With its poems on Finn and Ossian, the work is, in many ways, designed to counter Macpherson's claims for the Scottish origins of Ossianic poetry.[15] Brooke demonstrates a desire to avoid the controversy that dogged Macpherson, however, as she includes the '*Originals in the Irish Character*'. In addition to refuting Macpherson's assertions regarding the history of Scottish poetry, the *Reliques* also responds to the history of English poetry found in the three-volume *Reliques of Ancient English Poetry* (1765) by Bishop Percy. Percy was a mentor of Brooke's, and, although she pays homage to him in the title and the subject of her work, her *Reliques* also rewrite the relationship between popular and elite culture that Percy depicts.[16]

In the Preface to his *Reliques of Ancient English Poetry*, Percy draws the reader's attention to the material which makes up the bulk of his collection, some two hundred 'poems, songs and metrical romances' which he found in a folio manuscript. He notes his initial reluctance to publish the poems, as they 'are of great simplicity, and seem to have been meerly [*sic*] written *for the people*'.[17] But Percy justifies his decision to bring the poems 'to the attention of the public' by suggesting that they are works of historical significance: they can be used to 'shew the gradation of our language, exhibit the progress of popular opinions, display the peculiar manners and customs of former ages, or throw light on our earlier classical poets'. In fact, Percy constructs a genealogy for the *Reliques* that sees them not as specimens of popular poetry, but as traces of an illustrious court tradition. He suggests that the poems are 'select remains of our ancient English Bards and Minstrels, an order of men who were once greatly respected by our ancestors' (vol. 1, p. ix). According to Percy, the 'Saxon ancestors' of the English held bards 'in the highest reverence'. When the Saxons converted to Christianity, however, their 'rude admiration' for the bards 'began to abate, and poetry was no longer a peculiar profession' (vol. 1, p. xv). Instead, a class of minstrels developed who were only slightly less revered than their ancestors. The minstrels wrote poetry similar to that of the great bards and sang 'at the houses of the great' (vol. 1, p. xvi). The end of the era of minstrels was accomplished not by an act of faith but by an act of parliament, as, toward the end of the fifteenth century, a statute was passed by which 'Minstrels, wandering "abroad" were included among "rogues, vagabonds, and sturdy beggars"' (vol. 1, p. xxi). The minstrels were in turn succeeded by 'a new race of ballad-writers' (vol. 1, p. xxii).[18]

The poems in the *Reliques of Irish Poetry*, like those in the *Reliques of Ancient English Poetry*, are presented as the work of a venerated bardic order at a time when poetry was 'the vital soul of the nation'.[19] Brooke asserts that 'All Irish Histories, Chronicles and Poems, concur in the testimony of the high respect in which the office of the Bard, and the favours of the Muse, were formerly held in this kingdom' (p. 81). As was the case with the poetry of Percy's English bards, the poetry of the Irish bards was intimately connected with their religion and political organization. Kings were both rulers and poets: 'Irish history informs us, that those of their Monarchs or Chiefs who, besides the accustomed patronage of science and song, were *themselves* possessed of the gifts of the muse, obtained, on that account, from their Fileas, and from their countrymen in general, a distinguished portion of honor, respect and celebrity' (p. 174).

But whereas Percy represents the poetry of the English bardic order deteriorating over time as it slips into the hands of the populace, Brooke presents 'antient' Irish poetry as continuing in a relatively static manner down to the present day. In the *Historical Memoirs of the Irish Bards* (1786), Brooke's mentor, Joseph Cooper Walker, had written what was basically a prose elegy for Irish culture, implying that the golden age of Ireland had been disrupted by the invasion of the English.[20] In the Preface to her own work, Brooke concurs that little of the older Irish poetry, that which is often considered the best, is preserved: 'few of those compositions of those ages that were famed, in Irish annals, for the *light of song*, are to be obtained by the most diligent research' (p. iv). The majority of the poems that are still available, she suggests, 'were written during the middle ages; periods when the genius of Ireland was in its wane, "Yet still, not lost / All its original brightness"' (p. v). Yet, qualifying this Miltonic image of Irish poetry fading during its fall from grace, Brooke suggests 'On the contrary' that 'many of the productions of [the middle ages] breathe the true spirit of poetry' (p. v). The translations that she provides in the body of the *Reliques* are peppered with footnotes pointing out to the reader the 'true spirit of poetry' that is evident in these poems. In her footnote to 'Magnus', for example, Brooke notes: 'How beautifully pathetic is the close of this poem! Surely every reader of sensibility must sympathize with a situation so melancholy, and so very feelingly described' (p. 65n). In his *Reliques*, Percy feels compelled to apologize for presenting to the public poems that are rude and rough: 'In a polished age, like the present, I am sensible that many of these reliques of antiquity will require great allowances to be made for them' (vol. 1, p. x). Brooke indicates no such need for apology. The Irish 'productions', she suggests, abound 'with numberless beauties' (p. 73n) and can stand up to the demands of 'every *candid reader*' (p. 140).

For Percy, the deterioration of English poetry from the elite to the popular level is associated with a change in the medium through which it is disseminated. The English minstrels, in the spirit of their ancestors, the Scandinavian bards, presented their poetry orally, singing 'verses to the harp, of their own composing' (vol. 1, p. xv). Even their imperfect descendants, the 'old strolling' minstrels, were removed from the institutions of the marketplace: they 'composed their rhimes to be sung to their harps, and . . . looked no farther than for present applause, and present subsistence' (vol. 1, p. xi). However, their uncouth successors, the 'new race of ballad-writers', were firmly entrenched in the venality of commodity culture, writing 'narrative songs meerly [*sic*] for the press' (vol. 1, p. xxii). English poetry slouches from the spirit of the word to the character on the page.

Whereas Percy represents the descent of English poetry from elite songs performed at the court to ballads 'meerly [*sic*] written for the people' (vol. 1, p. ix), Brooke's trajectory for Irish poetry takes a different shape. For Brooke, Irish poetry, too, originated in a courtly tradition and ended up in the hands of the people. But Brooke revises Percy's media genealogy, bypassing the corruptions that accompany work for 'the press', as the Irish poems are passed along through the oral tradition. Brooke herself learned about the Irish poems from listening to one of her father's labourers. As Walker writes, 'in her infancy, she often heard him read to a rustic audience in her father's fields. The bold imagery, and marvellous air of these poems, so captivated her youthful fancy, that they remained for some years strongly impressed on her memory.'[21] Walker's account of Brooke's experience is echoed in the description Brooke supplies in the *Reliques* of Cormac Common's oral relationship to the Irish poems: '*by frequent recitation*, [the poems] *became strongly impressed upon his memory*' (p. 215). Where print impressions threaten to corrupt, 'impressions on memory' are capable of preserving the essence of the originals.

Brooke suggests that the 'antient' elite poetry continues to play a role in contemporary popular Irish literary efforts. The 'antient' Irish poems, Brooke indicates, have been carried along from one generation to the next with little change: 'With the beauties of these singular compositions, every Irish reader, of every age, must have been eager to acquaint himself; and when acquainted with them, to communicate to others the knowledge, and the pleasure they afforded him' (p. 140). The 'genius' of the ancient poetry is still visible in the work of 'modern' poets. Beginning

with 'Heroic Poems' from the middle ages and ending with 'Songs' by the
harpers and composers Turlough Carolan and Patrick Linden, Brooke's
Reliques presents elite Irish poems from past centuries blending seam-
lessly with those written by Gaelic commoners in Brooke's own time.
Eighteenth-century works like M'Cabe's 'Elegy on the Death of Carolan'
recall earlier works like 'The Lamentation of Cucullin over the Body of
his Son Conloch'. A footnote from the last translated work, 'The Maid
from the Valley' by Linden, draws attention to the connection between
this song and the first poem of the collection: 'See the poem of *Conloch*'
(p. 260n), suggesting the way that earlier works inform more recent
compositions. If Percy's 'obsolete poems' serve as antiquarian objects that
shed light on the historic elite past, Brooke's *Reliques* are living materials
which continue to circulate among non-elite groups.

Brooke's avowed concern in the *Reliques* is to rescue the reputation of
the Irish from 'modern prejudice' by asserting that they had a culture of
'cultivated genius' when 'the rest of Europe was nearly sunk in barbarism'
(p. vii). By suggesting that the elite traditions are still a vital part of Gaelic
culture, she presents contemporary Irish society as reflective of a tradition
of 'refinement' (p. vii) and worthy of being introduced to 'our noble
neighbour of Britain' (p. vii). But Brooke's efforts on this front also serve
another purpose, as she represents the Anglo-Irish elite as the logical and
necessary successors of the Gaelic elite.[22] Brooke's descriptions of the
collection of the poetry suggest how, in Walker's phrase, 'impressions on
memory' constitute embodied transactions. She notes that the second
poem in the section on 'Elegies' in the *Reliques*, for example, was '*taken
down from the dictation of a young woman, in the county of* Mayo, *by*
Mr. O'Flanagan, *who was struck with the tender and beautiful simplicity
which it breathes*' (p. 199). The 'striking' suggests a physical link in the
process of transferring Ireland's Gaelic past to the present. In the footnotes
of Brooke's *Reliques*, the people are figured as the medium connecting
the old with the new elite.

Brooke's original poem, the 'Tale of Mäon', which is 'subjoined' to the
Reliques, suggests a different configuration, however. Percy had included
'a few modern attempts' to 'atone for the rudeness of the more obsolete
poems' (vol. I, p. x). But Brooke's 'modern attempt' aims not to differentiate itself from but to ally itself with the earlier poetry, as Brooke
represents herself as a modern equivalent of the ancient Gaelic bards.
The 'Tale of Mäon' serves as proof of the strength of the 'impression' that
Irish poetry has had not just on Brooke's 'memory', but on her imagination. Brooke notes that she had 'no original' for the 'TALE which is

annexed to this volume'; however, 'the story . . . is not my own' (p. viii), but rather is taken from *'the ancient history of* Ireland' as *'related by* Keating, O'Halloran, Warner, &c.' (p. 323). Her variation on the 'Tale of Mäon', though, differs in important ways from the accounts of her predecessors. History, suggests Brooke, 'Left half untold the tale' (p. 332), and the poem is intended to fill in the blanks.

Significantly, the tale concerns an illegitimate conquest, the usurpation of Mäon's father, Laoghaire Lork, monarch of Ireland, by his brother Cobthach. Thanks to the bard Craftinè, Mäon escapes from the assault and eventually flees to Gallia (France) to train in arms. Fired by the patriotic poetry of his beloved, the Irish Moriat, and helped by the forces of Gallia, Mäon returns to Ireland to regain his rightful throne. Brooke's recreated tale bears an uncanny resemblance to the original moment of English conquest, when Diarmait Mac Murchada was ousted and sought help in his feud against the High King Tairrdelbach mac Ruaidrí Ua Conchobair from Henry II of England. In the 'Tale of Mäon', however, the external nation, instead of declaring its own conquest of Ireland, retreats to allow the Irish to continue with their own political affairs – and their personal relationships; the daughter of the King of Gaul, Aidé, renounces her interest in Mäon when she learns of the existence of Moriat.

The colonial conquest that 'Mäon' does suggest occurs not in the tale itself, but in the 'Introduction', and takes the more insidious form of cultural appropriation, as Brooke represents her narrator becoming the legitimate mouthpiece for 'The message of the Muse' (p. 325) of Ireland. The narrator describes her initial reluctance to attempt writing about such an illustrious topic in case she incurs 'critic scorn' (p. 326). She is subsequently urged to take up the 'glorious task' (p. 327) by a visitation from the 'Irish Muse', who appears to have been suffering of late:

> "Long, her neglected harp unstrung,
> "With glooms encircl'd round;
> "Long o'er its silent form she hung
> "Nor gave her soul to sound. (p. 328)

The Muse appears to her in the form of Craftinè, the bard who protected Mäon in the tale, and urges her to take up the cause:

> "Rous'd from her trance, again to reign,
> "And re-assert her fame,
> "She comes, and deigns thy humble strain
> "The herald of her claim. (p. 328)

The narrator is finally convinced to undertake to tell Mäon's story by Craftinè's exhortation for her to consider the tale as a 'gift' to her friends and patrons, Mr and Mrs Trant (p. 329). They are, suggests the bard, a 'Pair' who are 'by Genius lov'd, / By every Muse inspir'd' and who have 'approv'd' Brooke's 'unpractis'd strains' and 'fir'd' her 'ambition', and so will prove suitable recipients of the tale (p. 328).[23]

It is here that Brooke's representation of Irish poetry breaks open to further reveal the pressures of the colonial situation, for the same 'Dominick Trant, Esq.' whom Brooke praises for his 'judgment and taste' and thanks for his 'assistance and advice' (p. ix) penned an anti-Catholic pamphlet in 1787, the same year in which Brooke commenced work on her *Reliques*. *Considerations on the Present Disturbances in the Province of Munster*, which targets the Rightboy movement, an agrarian protest against the payment of tithes, went through three printings in its first year of publication.[24] Trant received money for the publication of his pamphlet from Dr Richard Woodward, who, in his *Present State of the Church of Ireland*, denounced the Rightboy protests as evidence of 'Catholic disloyalty and an argument against any further reform of the Penal Laws'.[25] In his description of the disturbances, Trant offers a significantly different view of the relationship between elite and popular groups than that suggested by Brooke.

Brooke's *Reliques* represents a literally harmonious relationship between the Catholic peasantry and the Anglo-Irish elite effected through the medium of oral poetry. Trant, in contrast, describes a different kind of 'impression' that the native Irish population make: 'houses burnt, corn in flames, honest and unoffending men buried alive, and some of our unsuspecting and unguarded fellow subjects dragged from their beds and butchered in cool blood'.[26] He notes the 'fond hope' of those involved in the disturbance:

to level all those distinctions which have ever been established in all states, and, by a sort of Agrarian law, to reduce the nobility of the land, the ecclesiastical establishment, the opulent representatives of the property of this kingdom in its parliament, and every other proprietor of land and possessor of personal wealth, to a degrading subjection to the will of the lowest order of the state, the mere popish peasantry of this country. (p. 6)

In Trant's view, 'the people' are a *'deluded and ignorant multitude'* eagerly awaiting their chance to overthrow the elite (p. 10).

In his *Considerations*, Trant suggests the fundamental difference that exists between the elite and plebeian populations, one that turns not on status, but on religion. Like Edmund Burke in his *Reflection on the Revolution in France* (published three years later), Trant praises the British constitution's ability to guarantee a citizen's right to life, liberty, and property 'in a manner unknown to citizens of other nations' (p. 1). For Trant, the civil constitution is a reflection of the ecclesiastical constitution: 'who is there so ignorant as not to know that the political constitution of a country has an intimate connection with its national church?' (p. 7). The 'freedoms' of the British constitution are associated specifically with Protestantism: 'civil liberty' was 'the natural attendant' on the 'bright star of the Reformation', and the 'political constitution of England was strengthened and improved' (p. 8). Because 'the manners, morals, habits and opinions of the people are framed and moulded by the nature of their creeds', Trant argues, the Catholic population is not, by nature, 'framed' for liberty (p. 7). As long as they remain Catholic, they must remain subordinate. What becomes clear in Trant's account is that the granting of 'civil liberty' to some individuals depends on the denial of those liberties to others (p. 8).

Trant's pamphlet paints an image of an Ireland on the verge of civil war if measures are not taken to put down the present rising: 'The disturbances which *now more immediately* affect the *province of Munster*, ... threaten, *in their consequence*, to involve the *whole kingdom*' (p. 3). He calls for the 'total suppression' (p. 56) of the present uprising and suggests a number of different ways in which landlords and magistrates can unite against the present-day 'armed invaders' (p. 56) to uphold those laws 'without which their possessions, their honours, and all those distinctions in life which separate them from the dregs of the people, must be swept away into the gulph of universal ruin' (p. 57). In particular, he puts his hope in the figure of the 'TRUE PATRIOT LEGISLATOR' who will emerge in times of peace, describing the measures which this legislator must take in order to ensure that rebellion does not occur again. Chief among the duties of this 'TRUE PATRIOT LEGISLATOR' is to 'establish the arts of cultured life thro' every corner of the island' (p. 60).

Brooke's *Reliques* works to fulfil this mandate. By focusing on the 'arts of cultured life' of the Gaelic population of pre-Catholic Ireland, the *Reliques* shifts attention away from the political struggles between Catholics and Protestants in the present, and provides a safe focus for Catholic interest in the tales of the past. But the 'Tale of Mäon', coming at the end of the *Reliques*, suggests the ultimate 'ends' of Brooke's project, for whereas the rest of the *Reliques* presents the descent of poetry from elite to popular then back to the elite in a harmonious blend, 'Mäon' represents the seamless passing of the elite Gaelic poetic tradition to the Anglo-Irish imagination without a popular intermediary. In the 'Tale of Mäon', the medium of the message of Irish poetry is not the Gaelic people, but Brooke's own authorial persona. The people are bypassed, and poetry based on Gaelic history becomes a 'gift' to be 'bestowed' (p. 329) on one elite member by another:

> Go then to thy accomplish'd friends;
> The Muse commands thee go;
> Bear them the grateful gift she sends,
> 'Tis all she can bestow.
>
> Bear them the pride of ancient days;
> Truth, science, virtue, fame;
> The lover's faith, the poet's praise,
> The patriotic flame! (p. 329)

In Chandler's terms of reference, an examination of the *Reliques* represents an extension of the horizon of British popular culture, as we see Brooke's work in relation to the representation of popular culture in Percy's *Reliques*. While Brooke upholds many of Percy's claims about poetry, she also rewrites them for an Irish context, in particular revising Percy's genealogy of poetry descending from the elite to the populace. At the same time, a consideration of the *Reliques* also suggests a reversal of the horizon of British popular culture, as, reading Brooke's work in relation to the published opinions of her mentor, Dominick Trant, we see what is at stake in the representation of 'the people' singing their songs to be copied down by the elite in the midst of the violence of unevenly applied 'civil liberties'.

But a consideration of Brooke's *Reliques* in relation to Trant's *Considerations* also suggests discontinuities in the horizon of popular and elite culture in Ireland. Stuart Hall identifies an attempt to 'disorganise and reorganise popular culture' and 'to enclose and confine its definitions and forms within a more inclusive range of dominant forms' in the later eighteenth century.[27] This struggle was not just more 'uneven and unequal' in Ireland, as I have suggested, but also productive of some unexpected results, as popular and elite cultures continually interrupt and destabilize each other in a colonial context. Trant's own case represents the slipperiness of the categories of popular and elite culture in Ireland. As Amyas Griffith notes in his 'Letter to Dominick Trant', Trant was born into a Catholic family and was himself originally a practising Catholic: 'Your father, mother, and all your ancestors, were all excellent *holy* ROMAN CATHOLICS: – You *yourself*, in your early days ... went to mass.'[28] Trant converted to Protestantism, however, in order to study and practise law, as

Catholics were unable to practise at the bar under the penal laws. As his
Considerations suggests, he took his elevation to an elite position very
seriously, to the extent of attempting to warn the reading public about
those of the elite whose allegiances were misdirected toward 'the mere
popish peasantry of this country' (p. 6). Trant shot the Protestant Sir John
Colthurst, a supporter of the Rightboy movement, in a duel arising from
the publication of the *Considerations*. The fact that Colthurst supported a
popular movement to promote 'Agrarian law' and that he inspired a street
ballad, 'The Elegy of Sir J. Colthurst', further suggests the anomalies in
the categories of elite and popular in Ireland.[29]

In a subsequent republication of Brooke's work, we see a different kind
of anomaly, an example of popular culture attempting to 'disorganise and
reorganise' elite representations. In 1795, the first Gaelic-language magazine, *Bolg an tSolaír* ['bag of goods' or 'miscellany'], appeared, including
'the famous fenian poem THE CHASE', 'Elegy on the Death of Carolan',
and 'a collection of choice IRISH SONGS, translated by Miss Brooke'.[30]
The editor of the magazine, Patrick Lynch, was a teacher of Gaelic in
Belfast and a member of the United Irishmen, a group aiming to unite
the disparate factions in Ireland in the common cause of an Irish republic.
Bolg an tSolaír was printed at the office of the *Northern Star*, the official
newspaper of the United Irishmen of Ulster, and the paper was also used
to advertise the magazine.[31]

Lynch shares with Brooke a desire to revise negative stereotypes of the
Irish by focusing on the fact that Ireland was once 'the seat of the muses,
from times of the remotest antiquity' (*Bolg an tSolaír*, p. 9). He, too,
praises Gaelic as the language most fit to express 'the feelings of the heart'
(*ibid.*) and suggests, as Brooke does in her footnotes, that the Gaelic
poetry became the property of the common people. He notes the existence of a number of Irish manuscripts 'lying dormant and unheeded', and
comments that forty years previously 'they were read, and listened to with
pleasure, even by the common people; there was scarce any neighbourhood wherein there was not some Irish scholar to be found, who could
entertain his neighbours, by reading some ancient poems or stories of the
achievements of their heroic ancestors' (p. 10). But while Brooke presents
the elite Gaelic poetry as either descending to the common population
only to be re-presented in English form for an English-speaking elite or,
as in the 'Tale of Mäon', passed on directly to her compatriots in a new
creative form, Lynch attempts to renew popular interest in the poems in
their original form and in the Gaelic language itself. Along with the
poems and translations by Brooke that Lynch includes in *Bolg an tSolaír*,

he also prints a Gaelic grammar, a short dictionary, and a series of educational dialogues. Where Brooke only gestures toward the actual 'beauties' of the language, concentrating her efforts instead on 'clothing the thoughts of our Irish muse in a language with which [the English-speaking reading public] are familiar', Lynch's project is to teach the Irish to read Gaelic: 'It is chiefly with a view to prevent in some measure the total neglect, and to diffuse the beauties of this ancient and once-admired language, that the following compilation is offered to the public.'[32] Instead of 'gifting' the 'pride of ancient days' to a new elite, Lynch uses Brooke's translations to 'bestow' the Gaelic texts on a popular literate audience in order to promote a non-sectarian society based on the 'Rights of Man'.[33]

Three years after the publication of the *Bolg an tSolair*, Ireland erupted in a bloody civil war. In the aftermath of the war and the subsequent Act of Union joining Britain and Ireland, the *Reliques* and Brooke herself were seemingly forgotten. An 1816 republication of the *Reliques* followed close on the heels of the formation of the Gaelic League in 1808, but the editor, Aaron Crossley Seymour, was more concerned with presenting Brooke as a model of daughterly piety than as a translator and author in her own right.[34] The 1 September 1832 edition of the *Dublin Penny Journal* attempts to bring Brooke back to the attention of the reading public, noting, 'There are few writers, male or female, to whom we think Ireland owes a greater debt of gratitude than to Miss Charlotte Brooke', and expressing an 'anxious desire to see her genius more fully appreciated'.[35] Despite the waning of her reputation, however, the legacy of Brooke's work can be seen in the burgeoning interest in two other genres in the early nineteenth century. In her attempt to 'introduce' the 'British muse' to her 'elder sister in this isle' and in her copious use of footnotes explaining Irish customs and culture, Brooke anticipates the impulse and form behind the national tale. And in her declaration that there is 'no other musick in the world so calculated to make its way directly to the heart' as Irish music, Brooke heralds a new vogue in Irish song.[36] In the years following the Union, skilful mediators like Sydney Owenson and Thomas Moore would use these genres to further the cause of the people of Ireland whom Brooke both elevated and elided.

NOTES

1 James Chandler, 'A Discipline in Shifting Perspective: Why We Need Irish Studies', *Field Day Review* 2 (2006), 19.
2 *Ibid.*, 21, 26.

3 For varying perspectives on Ireland and the effects of colonialism, see David Cairns and Shaun Richards, *Writing Ireland: Colonialism, Nationalism, and Culture* (Manchester: Manchester University Press; New York: St Martin's Press, 1988); Seamus Deane, *Strange Country: Modernity and Nationhood in Irish Writing since 1790* (Oxford: Clarendon Press, 1997); Declan Kiberd, *Inventing Ireland: The Literature of the Modern Nation* (Cambridge, Mass.: Harvard University Press, 1995); Terry Eagleton, Frederic Jameson, and Edward Said (eds.), *Nationalism, Colonialism, and Literature* (Minneapolis: University of Minnesota Press, 1990); Luke Gibbons, *Transformations in Irish Culture* (Notre Dame, Ind.: University of Notre Dame Press, 1996); David Lloyd, *Anomalous States: Irish Writing and the Post-Colonial Moment* (Durham, Ind.: Duke University Press, 1993) and *Ireland after History* (Notre Dame, Ind.: University of Notre Dame Press, 1999).

4 Peter Burke, *Popular Culture in Early Modern Europe*, rev. reprint (Aldershot: Scolar Press, 1994), p. xi.

5 See Burke, *Popular Culture*, Chapter 1.

6 Sean Connolly and Kevin Whelan both discuss the relationship between popular and elite in Ireland. My introductory remarks are indebted to their more lengthy explorations. Connolly, ' "Ag Déanamh Commanding": Elite Responses to Popular Culture, 1660–1850', in James Donnelly and Kerby Miller (eds.), *Irish Popular Culture* (Dublin: Irish Academic Press, 1998), pp. 1–29 and Whelan, *The Tree of Liberty: Radicalism, Catholicism and the Construction of Irish Identity 1760–1830* (Cork: Cork University Press, 1996). In the 'Introduction' to *Irish Popular Culture*, Donnelly substitutes the idea of oral-based and print-based for popular and elite traditions (pp. xi–xxxi). See also Niall Ó Ciosáin, *Print and Popular Culture in Ireland, 1750–1850* (Basingstoke: Macmillan, 1997).

7 Richard Kearney, *Postnationalist Ireland: Literature, Culture, Philosophy* (London: Routledge, 1997), p. 2.

8 In the centuries following the twelfth-century conquest, the conquering elite adopted many of the customs and culture of their Gaelic counterparts, as Edmund Spenser noted to his chagrin in *A Vewe of the Present State of Irelande*. The brutal Cromwellian suppressions and the enforcement of the penal laws in the eighteenth century resulted in the extended disenfranchisement and dispossession of both the original Gaelic and Hiberno-Norman elite. See Whelan, *Tree of Liberty*, for further discussion regarding the role of the dispossessed Catholic population in the wake of the penal laws.

9 See Gibbons, *Transformations in Irish Culture*, and Lloyd, *Anomalous States* and *Ireland after History*.

10 Marilyn Butler, 'Antiquarianism (Popular)', in Iain McCalman (ed.), *An Oxford Companion to the Romantic Age: British Culture 1776–1832* (Oxford: Oxford University Press, 1999), p. 335. For the Scottish case, see, for example, James Watson, *A Choice Collection of Comic and Serious Scots Poems*, 3 vols. (Edinburgh: James Watson, 1706–11); Elizabeth Wardlaw, *Hardyknute: A Fragment of an old Heroick Ballad* (Edinburgh: James Watson, 1719); and

Allan Ramsay, *The Ever Green: Being a Collection of Scots Poems Wrote by the Ingenious before 1600* (Edinburgh: Thomas Ruddiman, 1724) and *The Tea-Table Miscellany* (Edinburgh: Thomas Ruddiman, 1724). See also Katie Trumpener on the political uses of the figure of the bard in Ireland and Scotland (*Bardic Nationalism: The Romantic Novel and the British Empire* (Princeton: Princeton University Press, 1997)).

11 See Geoffrey Keating, *The General History of Ireland*, trans. Dermod O'Connor (London, 1723); Jonathan Swift, 'The Description of an Irish-Feast, translated almost literally out of the Original Irish', in *Miscellanies, in Prose and Verse. Volume the fifth* (London: printed for Charles Davis, 1735), pp. 14–18; and John and William Neale, *A Colection* [sic] *of the most Celebrated Irish Tunes* (Dublin, 1724). Also included in Swift's volume are poems relating to his persona of the Drapier and to the affair of Wood's half-pence: 'Drapier's Hill', 'Verses on the upright Judge, who condemned the Drapier's Printer', 'On *Wood*, the Ironmonger', and 'Wood, *An Insect*'.

12 Charles Henry Wilson had produced an earlier collection of translations which does not seem to have attracted the attention that Brooke's work did.

13 By the end of the eighteenth century, Ireland was still stinging from the bloody conflicts and dispossessions of the Williamite wars, and its Catholic population was burdened by the Penal Laws. A major victory for the Protestant Ascendancy was gained in 1782 with the establishment of a separate Irish parliament under Henry Grattan, and concessions to Catholics began to be made, but Catholic relief was still a long way away.

14 See Charles O'Conor, *Dissertations on the History of Ireland* (Dublin, 1753); Sylvester O'Halloran, *A General History of Ireland*, 2 vols. (London: A. Hamilton, 1778); Charles Vallancey, *A Vindication of the Ancient History of Ireland* (Dublin: Luke White, 1786); and Joseph Cooper Walker, *Historical Memoirs of the Irish Bards* (London, 1786).

15 Although Brooke doesn't directly engage with the debate, she does include a reference in Irish script to the Irish poems of Ossian: 'A Oisín, as binn linn do sgéala [O, Oisín / We are charmed by your stories'] (Charlotte Brooke, *Reliques of Irish Poetry Consisting of Heroic Poems, Odes, Elegies, and Songs Translated into English Verse with Notes Explanatory and Historical; and the Originals in the Irish Character. To Which is Subjoined An Irish Tale By Miss Brooke* (Dublin: George Bonham, 1789), title page). See Mícheál MacCraith, 'Charlotte Brooke and James MacPherson', *Litteraria Pragensia: Studies in Literature and Culture* 10:20 (2000), 5–17.

16 Burke suggests that Percy 'did not think ballads had anything to do with the people, but rather that they were composed by minstrels enjoying a high status at medieval courts' (*Popular Culture*, p. 5). What is interesting about Percy's work for the purposes of my argument, however, is how he constructs the descent of the ballads from the court to the people and how Brooke refigures this devolution.

17 Thomas Percy, *Reliques of Ancient English Poetry: Consisting of Old Heroic Ballads, Songs, and Other Pieces of Our Earlier Poets*, 3 vols. (London: J. Dodsley,

1765), vol. 1, p. ix. My italics. Subsequent references are in parentheses in the text.

18 Percy's representation of the popular English (and Scottish) songs and ballads as descended from the court fuelled the criticism of commentators like Joseph Ritson. See Nigel Leask's chapter above, pp. 58–9.

19 Brooke, *Reliques of Irish Poetry*, p. iv. Hereafter referred to in parentheses in the text.

20 For a fuller discussion of Walker, see my *Music, Postcolonialism and Gender: The Construction of Irish National Identity, 1724–1874* (Notre Dame: University of Notre Dame Press, 2005), Chapter 2.

21 Walker, *Historical Memoirs*, pp. 41–2. Charles Henry Wilson's description in his 1804 *Brookiana* of the history of the composition of the *Reliques* builds on this image: 'As she learned the Irish language, she was often charmed to find many beauties in the songs, even of the unlettered bards in that tongue. At first she only intended to collect a little nosegay of these poetical flowers. The peasants were so pleased with this intelligence, that they waited on her with all the scattered verses that memory could collect' (C. H. Wilson, *Brookiana*, 2 vols. (London: Richard Phillips, 1804), vol. II, p. 211).

22 Ó Ciosáin contends that 'Antiquarian and literary interests among land-owners were . . . a way of establishing links with the old order and achieving a status based on antiquity of title' (*Print and Popular Culture*, p. 172). Joep Leerssen, too, suggests that '[t]he adoption and central canonization of a Gaelic cultural affiliation and a Gaelic-oriented historical self-awareness . . . was to remain central to the Anglo-Irish sense of national identity' (*Mere Irish and Fíor-Ghael: Studies in the Idea of Irish Nationality, Its Development and Literary Expression Prior to the Nineteenth Century* (Notre Dame: Notre Dame University Press, 1986), p. 376).

23 According to the list of subscribers' names in the *Reliques*, the Trants subscribed for six copies each.

24 Land used for grazing was exempt from tithes, while potatoes were tithed. Munster, with its high proportion of cottiers growing potatoes for subsistence, was the centre of protest against such tithes. See Maurice Bric, 'Priests, Parsons and Politics: The Rightboy Protest in County Cork 1785–1788', *Past and Present* 100 (1983), 100–23.

25 *Ibid.*, 119.

26 Dominick Trant, *Considerations on the Present Disturbances in the Province of Munster, Their Causes, Extent, Probable Consequences and Remedies* (Dublin, 1787), p. 5. Subsequent references are in parentheses in the text.

27 Stuart Hall, 'Notes on Deconstructing the Popular', in Raphael Samuel (ed.), *People's History and Socialist Theory* (London: Routledge, 1981), p. 233.

28 Amyas Griffith, *Miscellaneous Tracts* (Dublin: James Mehain, 1788), pp. 82–3.

29 'The Elegy of Sir J. Colthurst', in *Hush the Mouse Off of the Hob* (Dublin, 1788). Bric details how the Rightboy protests were connected with the 1783 elections in Cork during which Sir John Colthurst ran as an Independent ('Priests, Parsons and Politics', 101).

30 *Bolg an tSolair: A Reprint of the Gaelic Magazine of the United Irishmen*, ed. Brendan Clifford and Pat Muldowney (Belfast: Athol Books, 1999), p. 1. Subsequent references are in parentheses in the text.

31 Because of the exceptionally high literacy rate in Ulster, the *Star* reached approximately 40,000 readers (Whelan, *Tree of Liberty*, p. 66). The *Northern Star* also printed *Paddy's Resource*, a radical songbook of the United Irishmen.

32 Brooke, *Reliques of Irish Poetry*, p. vii; *Bolg an tSolair*, p. 11.

33 Brooke, *Reliques of Irish Poetry*, p. 329. Kevin Whelan notes how an increase in print propaganda 'washed through English-speaking Ireland in the 1790s', promoting a more vernacular kind of political discourse, diminishing 'the authority of print culture', and creating new genres that were intelligible by those who could not read (*Tree of Liberty*, pp. 71–2). Lynch's attempt to educate a United Ireland in the 'beauties' of Irish texts went no further, however. The offices of the *Northern Star* were destroyed in 1797 by government military forces, and the following year witnessed the uprising and violent repression of the United Irish forces. Lynch himself was arrested during the 1803 insurrection and freed only upon appearing as Crown witness against Thomas Russell.

34 Charlotte Brooke, *Reliques of Irish Poetry . . . To Which is Prefixed A Memoir of Her Life and Writings by Aaron Crossley Seymour* (Dublin: J. Christie, 1816).

35 *Dublin Penny Journal* (1 September 1832), 74.

36 Brooke, *Reliques of Irish Poetry*, p. 233.

CHAPTER 4

'An individual flowering on a common stem': melody, performance, and national song

Kirsteen McCue

The title of this chapter is taken from one of Ralph Vaughan Williams's essays, 'The Evolution of Folk-song', first published in 1934:

> So you see the individual has his share in the creation of the folk-song and the race has its share. If I may venture to give my own definition of a folk-song I should call it 'an individual flowering on a common stem'. We folk-song collectors are often asked 'what is the origin' of a particular tune or 'how old it is'. There is no answer to either of these questions; there is no original version of any particular tune; any given tune has hundreds of origins. Nor can we say how old it is; in one sense any particular tune is as old as the beginnings of music, in another sense it is born afresh with the singer of today who sang it. Sometimes we are laughed at: the scoffer says, 'I expect that is not an old tune at all, the old man who sang it to you invented it himself'. Quite possibly to a certain extent he did. It is not the age but the nature of the tune which makes it a folk-song.[1]

These comments might relate closely to the exploration of folk or popular song collecting in periods other than his own. Articulating the 'nature' of folk-song is a difficult business and, as Vaughan Williams comments, tracing a single source for any such song can seem a misguided enterprise. By the 1930s, due to its wide dissemination (both orally and in printed form), especially within theatrical, concert, and middle-class domestic environments, not to mention the creative efforts of composers like Vaughan Williams himself, folk-song had become a widely accepted musical genre which was no longer 'the exclusive property of the peasant' but had 'come into line with the composed music of which they [folk-songs] are supposed to be the antithesis'.[2] In another essay in the same collection, entitled 'Should Music be National?', Vaughan Williams focuses on the close connections between the local and the universal – the artists who are inspired firstly by their own environment, but who ultimately speak to everyone. Along the way, as they passed from generation to generation and migrated across national borders, songs collected from local areas were mixed with songs from new, often foreign localities and were frequently transformed by the priorities of performers, collectors, and publishers. If Vaughan Williams's theory is credible then regardless of these transformations there was still something of 'the race' about these songs. Lyrics might establish a local or national connection by geographical reference, names, or use of local dialect. And the sound of a song might still contain something of its local or national roots in the modes or 'national scales' on which its melody was based. Vaughan Williams notes, in the above quotation, that songs are 'born afresh with the singer of today' and he clearly believes that it is the tune or melody which marks a song as coming from a folk or popular source. Carl Dahlhaus, writing just a few years before him, referred to these modal folk melodies as containing something of a national 'geist' or 'spirit of nationhood' which survived any transformations they might have undergone.[3]

As discussed in the introduction to this volume, the 'discovery of the people' in the eighteenth and early nineteenth centuries found a particularly powerful vehicle in the collection and dissemination of popular song. Peter Burke's theory that such song culture aided the smaller nations on the European periphery in the process of 'national liberation' is one which provides an interesting context for exploring the many song collections of Scotland, Ireland, and Wales during this period, for such publications often expressed their nationality whilst, at the same time, reinforcing notions of Britishness.[4] The process of collecting and publishing popular song in the Romantic period reveals what might best be described as a natural ebbing and flowing between oral and printed cultures, illustrating a confident interaction between Burke's 'great' and 'little' traditions. There is no existing oral archive (unlike Vaughan Williams and his contemporaries working with their wax cylinders); there is simply the testimony of collectors, writers, and editors. In contrast to these written forms of mediation, song, whether ethereal or printed, is based on the sonic and aural medium of melody. The importance of appreciating the sound of songs is therefore crucial. The success, and thus contemporary popularity, of certain songs often relied on the qualities of the tune to which the lyrics were written and/or sung, on the timbre of the voice which sang them, on the atmosphere generated by a particular performance, or indeed on the promotional prowess of an individual performer – in other words on the oral transmission of the songs themselves.[5]

Songs which appeared in print as lyrics alone did not completely divorce themselves from their melodic partner. Although Celeste Langan has suggested that around 1800 poetic orality as a medium dies on account of the triumph of print, this is not necessarily the case with printed song.[6] Nick Groom has noted that even the printed ballad or song lyric, missing its musical component, still created a 'soundscape' or 'phonic world' all of its own – by its known historical relation to a melody, by its word choice or the rhythms and sounds of its refrain.[7] Moreover, songs published in the long eighteenth century did frequently appear with titles of airs or melodies alongside and, more importantly still, often with musical notation.[8] Created for performance in small spaces, primarily for the drawing rooms of the burgeoning middle class (especially its young women) and for amateur performance, these newly published and polished versions of 'traditional' or 'popular' songs allowed the middle classes to role-play their way into a romanticized peasant culture. Orality was double-edged in Georgian Britain – for published song both presented the voice of its alleged peasant roots, and gave breath to the fashionable voice of the more well-to-do foster parents. Melody – because of its oral/aural virtues (it required only ears and no literary skills) – was arguably the essential social adhesive of a newly enlightened society, apparently transcending class and bringing together all men and women of the region and/ or nation.[9]

The process by which demotic (or popular) song tradition becomes national song is one still requiring a great deal of exploration, though Thomas Crawford's pioneering *Society and the Lyric* does suggest that the fashion for, and number of, peculiarly 'Scottish' song publications prior to 1780 might establish Scotland as one of the first European nations to exemplify this process.[10] Most British song collections of this period are primarily identified by nation/region rather than by their 'popular' provenance, although the latter is presupposed in the former: thus, 'Scottish Songs' (or 'Highland Songs', 'Galloway Songs', etc.), 'English Songs', 'Irish Songs', or 'Welsh Songs'. But, as the editors of this volume note in their introduction, the notion of 'popular song' is ambiguous, denoting both 'the people' as the inhabitants of traditional rural societies who supposedly create these songs as part of an uneducated and oral culture, and also, by the early nineteenth century, a growing public of consumers deriving pleasure from a printed song culture (also often in performance), and offering the prospect of substantial commercial success to song publishers.

The importance of melody and performance to song collectors and writers of the period is well attested. Robert Burns, regarded by many then and now to be, alongside Thomas Moore, the finest song writer of the period, had a hand in presenting some 373 songs, most of which were published between his Edinburgh visit in 1787 and his death in 1796. Burns tells of the childhood influence of his mother's singing,[11] and of the thrill of hearing the sound of the voice of his first love, his harvesting partner Nelly Kilpatrick, who inspired his first poetic creation:

Indeed I did not well know myself, why I liked so much to loiter behind with her, when returning in the evening from our labors; why the tones of her voice made my heartstrings thrill like an Eolian harp; . . . Among her other love-inspiring qualifications, she sung sweetly; and 'twas her favorite reel to which I attempted giving an embodied vehicle in rhyme.[12]

Emily Lyle's work on this song – 'O Once I lov'd a bonnie lass' – has identified the tune as 'I am a man unmarried', a popular tune which had already appeared in several Scottish chapbooks with a variety of different lyrics, and a variant of a melody also found in collections of English and Irish tunes.[13] This demonstrates that the popularity of contemporary song tunes was promoted both orally and in print, as well as supporting Thomas Crawford's proposal that 'song culture was at this time an all-British one'.[14]

Burns is said to have had a dreadful voice and, according to his sister, he was an indifferent fiddler.[15] But his musical expertise is evident in his correspondence with George Thomson, his second song editor, where he makes frequent and detailed reference to the characteristics of particular melodies and sometimes includes melodic notation.[16] Moreover his famous description, in his letter of early September 1793 to Thomson, in which he describes in detail how he writes a song lyric – 'untill I am compleat master of a tune, in my own singing, (such as it is) I never can compose for it' – challenges any existing anecdotal evidence. In this description he also notes that as he composes he needs to keep moving rhythmically, 'swinging, at intervals, on the hind-legs of my elbow-chair, by way of calling forth my own critical strictures, as my pen goes on'.[17] Burns's deep understanding of and interest in melody is also illustrated several times in his *Commonplace Book*, where he talks of the creative processes and thoughts behind many of his songs. One of his entries for September 1785 explains the process of intimately 'southing' the tune – gently whistling it – as 'the readiest way to catch the inspiration and raise the Bard into that glorious enthusiasm so strongly characteristic of our old Scotch Poetry'.[18] In another entry of the same month Burns ponders on 'a degree of wild irregularity' in many of the old songs and fragments he hears sung by the people around him. He also notes that this irregularity is connected to 'a redundancy of syllables with respect to that exactness of accent & measure that the English Poetry requires, but which glides in, most melodiously with the respective tunes to which they are set'.[19] He illustrates this by comparing the Scots song 'The Mill, Mill O' – which reads badly, but sounds wonderful sung – with 'To Fanny fair I could impart' in Robert Bremner's collection of 'Scotch Songs', which reads beautifully, but sounds 'flat & spiritless' when sung.[20] Burns knew that, in performance, the success of certain songs with the public clearly had as much to do with the nature of the 'air' as it did with the power of the lyric – it required a compound of both elements.

Other key song writers of the period were also accomplished performers. The young John Clare was surrounded by singing, both by his parents and by the local gypsy community: his love of local Northampton song resulted in his becoming one of the first English song collectors. He recalled that he 'used to spend the long evenings with my father & mother & heard them by accident hum over scraps of the following old melodies which I have collected & put into their present form'.[21] And that his father 'could sing or recite above a hundred' ballads and had 'a tolerable good voice, & was often calld [*sic*] upon to sing at those convivials of bacchanalian merry makings'.[22] Clare learnt the fiddle from one of his gypsy friends and enjoyed performing local dance tunes himself. As Jonathan Bate notes, two of Clare's 'most beautiful' creations are his music books, in which he notated over 250 tunes.[23] The fiddle was also the key to melody for James Hogg, whose sometimes unreliable 'Memoir of the Author's Life' includes entertaining stories of his youthful efforts to teach himself the fiddle, and to learn to play the tunes of songs he had heard at local gatherings. Hogg notes that he bought his first fiddle at the age of fourteen and that, if he was not too tired after a day shepherding, he 'generally spent an hour or two every night in sawing over my favourite old Scottish tunes'.[24] This activity no doubt resulted in his writing melodies for many of his own songs, several of which he famously performed himself.

Burns's upbringing in rural Ayrshire, like that of John Clare and James Hogg, gave him an understanding of traditional song that was to his huge advantage as a song writer. While certainly both Burns and Hogg enjoyed the posing and posturing required by their respective literati (and many of their song adaptations or new songs embody these very qualities), neither could deny the rural realities of their birth, nor their skills and experiences as ploughman and shepherd. And, as is also true of Clare, this meant that they provided a direct line to the traditional rural popular culture much sought after by contemporary editors and publishers. It's arguably the case that their prowess in collecting, adapting, and then writing new songs was enabled by the extent to which, as mentioned in the introduction to this volume, they were 'participant observers' of that popular culture. Nevertheless, Burns, Hogg, and Clare were avid readers of printed song collections too. To contemporary readers, epithets such as 'heaven taught ploughman', 'Ettrick Shepherd', and 'Northampton Peasant', touted by publishers and patrons, signified innate artistic development, natural rather than acquired genius. But, as is evident in many of Burns's finest songs, learning from a print culture could also be a profitable and legitimate exercise, albeit one that had moved sideways from the apparent purity of first-hand orality.

Although most collectors and song writers of the Romantic period were male, many cited female sources for their songs. Wales's 'last bard', Edward Williams (Iolo Morganwg), was inspired, like Burns and Hogg, by his mother's voice ('My mother sang agreeably'), but he noted that she learned her songs from a book entitled *The Vocal Miscellany* and it was the powerful combination of learning and performing that encouraged her son to think about his own poetic and lyrical skills.[25] Williams's background was modest, being the eldest son of a stonemason, but his mother had received her education through the patronage of wealthier relatives. The Irish poet and song writer Thomas Moore's earliest musical memories are reminiscent of those of Williams. His love of melody seems to have originated in the family drawing-room through a combination of his own natural childhood ability for picking out tunes on the harpsichord and his mother's love of songs. Apparently her discovery of his beautiful voice led to his performing 'party pieces' at social gatherings from an early age, some of them songs by Charles Dibdin, hailed as the hero of the new mode of national song. And Moore's skill as singer/performer was to stay with him, later identified and promoted by the Power brothers, publishers of his *Irish Melodies*. Moore's discovery of Irish tunes, to which he would write those famous lyrics, was connected to his friendships with United Irishmen Edward Hudson and Robert Emmet at Trinity, when they were students there in the 1790s, and was inspired by Hudson's abilities as a keen flautist and Moore's fascination with recently published ancient Irish tunes collected by Edward Bunting.[26] But clearly each of the writers mentioned was initially inspired by maternal performance, indicating an important affective link between mother and song and the origins of national identity. Moreover each of them was also aware of the power of melody and the ultimate success of a song relying on a fine performance, whatever the environment.

THE CASE OF GEORGE THOMSON'S COLLECTIONS
OF 'NATIONAL AIRS'

The Edinburgh song editor George Thomson is most famous for his connections with Burns, Haydn, and Beethoven, even though his project involved detailed collaboration with upwards of thirty contemporary literary men and women, and some six major European composers.[27] Thomson has attracted little scholarly interest, but he provides a fascinating case study of the song collector and editor working in Britain in the early 1800s.[28] His publishing career began with *A Select Collection of Original Scot[t]ish Airs*, in sets of 25 songs in the 1790s, but ultimately his Scottish collection – which wasn't completed until the mid 1840s – included 6 volumes comprising some 300 songs.[29] Capitalizing on his early success, by the early 1800s Thomson had already begun to think about publishing both a Welsh collection and a set of Irish songs. It is worth noting that Thomson was unusual in this respect, as most editors concentrated on collections which focused on one area (i.e. Scottish, Irish, or Welsh) or which provided a mixture of songs from all three and with English songs in addition. Thomson's *A Select Collection of Original Welsh Airs* appeared in three volumes of fifty songs each in 1809, 1811, and 1817 respectively, and *A Select Collection of Original Irish Airs* then appeared in two volumes also containing fifty songs each in 1814 and 1816. He had plans to produce a collection of songs from a wide variety of other nations, though he never completed this project, and while English tunes crept into the other collections he never produced a separate publication of English songs.

Thomson was partly inspired by what he believed to be the lacklustre volumes of his competitors, but his initial stimulation was performance-based.[30] Firstly, he had been brought up in the northeast of Scotland, an area which was a hotbed of musical activity. Several key fiddlers and collectors, including James Oswald (1710–69), William Marshall (1748–1833), and David Herd (1732–1810), hailed from this area, and Thomson himself learned to play the fiddle there as a child.[31] When he moved to Edinburgh in the mid 1770s to work as a civil servant, his musical interests were expanded to include the Gentlemen's Concerts organized and promoted by the relatively new Edinburgh Musical Society.[32] The performance of Scots songs, long in vogue on the London concert platform, by the visiting Italian castrato Ferdinando Tenducci and Alice Bacchelli, the wife of Edinburgh-based Italian musician Domenico Corri, were legend.[33] Tenducci's singing of these national songs was held in such reverence that he was forgiven for being 'foreign' in the then contemporary heated debate over the 'authenticity' of such performances. William Tytler, after stating quite clearly in his 'Dissertation on the Scottish Music' that Scots songs could only be sung by a Scottish voice, was willing to make an exception for Tenducci because of his skills as a performer and his prepossessing 'genius for the pathetic'.[34] Thomson explained that Tenducci and Signora Corri:

so delighted every hearer that in the most crowded room not a whisper was to be heard, so entirely did they rivet the attention and admiration of the audience. Tenducci's singing was full of passion, feeling, and taste, and, what we hear very rarely from singers, his articulation of the words was no less perfect than his expression of the music.[35]

Tenducci's rendition of Scottish songs, more than anything else, struck a note with Thomson, who even presented a list of the songs in his account: 'Lochaber no more', 'The Braes of Bellenden', 'I'll never leave thee', and 'Roslin Castle'.[36] The singer's 'expressive simplicity', and the 'intensity of interest' which he displayed 'by his impassioned manner, and by his clear enunciation of the words',[37] Thomson said later, 'inoculated [*sic*] me for Scottish song'.[38] This 'injection' of passion for the foreign renditions of his native song is a fine illustration of the agency of an individual performer in promoting particular songs. But Thomson's choice of the term 'inoculation' might also suggest some degree of initial discomfort with the spectacle of national song being rendered by a foreign voice, as it were uprooted from its native soil. Like other song collectors of the period, Thomson possessed the antiquarian's sense that his role was to collect, protect, enhance, and better promote his native songs, and ultimately to 'improve' their musical and lyrical components. Consequently Thomson set out to commission the best of new European composers – Pleyel, Kozeluch, Haydn, Beethoven, Carl Maria von Weber, and Hummel – to provide 'symphonies & accompaniments' for these Scottish songs, and later for his Welsh and Irish collections. The symphonies acted as little instrumental introductions and conclusions framing the song proper, which usually had slightly simpler accompaniments. These were set for the piano-forte and its forerunner the early forte-piano, violin, violoncello, and sometimes the wooden or German flute.

Thomson aimed at the lucrative new middle-class domestic music market (chiefly composed of young women amateurs) – in Nicholas Temperley's words still an 'ill-defined and fluctuating entity' at this time – but he also expected his songs to appeal to professional performers.[39] Temperley notes that the language of songs in publications aimed at the polite, female end of the market removed 'all the distinguishing marks of working-class song: no dialects, no vulgarity, no low humour'.[40] But this didn't mean that national song collections in the period were willing to dispense with local words and phrases, and particular national musical characteristics, despite their 'alternative' anglicizing lyrics. Thomson's Scottish collection usually provided an alternative lyric in English for every Scottish air with a first-choice lyric in Scots, in order to make his work accessible to a wider British public.

Thomson's volumes, while sharing similarities with those of his Edinburgh-Italian rivals Pietro Urbani and Domenico Corri, were much more technically sophisticated than the simpler Scottish settings provided by Robert Bremner or James Johnson. As far as Thomson was concerned such sophisticated settings of simple songs enhanced the best qualities of these national airs and helped to introduce them to a new audience previously ignorant of the richness of their national musical repositories. Often accused of making a travesty of traditional material, of committing some heinous sin by commissioning work from foreign composers who had no idea of the intrinsic 'national' qualities of the tunes they were setting, Thomson only sought to heighten the public's awareness of its indigenous music, and to educate amateur musicians in the performance of their 'ancestral' songs and melodies. Musical embellishment of such airs – and the foreign influences often incorporated in them – was the subject of heightened aesthetic deliberation at the time. The fascination with music as an expressive art, a form capable of both imitating and exciting emotion, is well known. If Jean-Jacques Rousseau's definition of 'Natural (Naturel)' in the *Dictionnaire de Musique* of 1767 is taken as exemplary, then the voice provides the most natural form of music, shown to best effect when performing a melody that is 'effortless, sweet, graceful, and uncomplicated'.[41] This opinion was wholeheartedly echoed throughout many essays on music, including those by James Beattie, Charles Avison, and Oliver Goldsmith, and is found in prefaces to song collections by Herd, Ritson, Tytler, and many others. Popular melodies or airs, be they Scottish, English, Irish, or Welsh, epitomized this simplicity, and thus represented a much sought-after purity. Thomson noted that he had 'visited distant parts of the country, to collect on the spot what he could not obtain by means of Correspondents; invariably preferring that set or copy of every Melody which seemed the most simple and beautiful, whether he found it in print, or in manuscript, or got it from a voice, or an instrument'.[42] In Thomson's opinion the best singers required no accompaniment, but most needed the support of a setting which also enhanced the listener's pleasure.

This notion of 'purity' was clearly of great importance. Thomson's preface to his first volume of *Scottish Airs* from the early 1800s onwards noted that he had set out to 'procure the Airs in their best form'.[43] But he also believed that such melodies participated in a living tradition, and had often 'been preserved, we know not how long, by oral tradition, and thus were liable to changes before being collected'. Thomson explains the process of selection in quite some detail:

It is certain, however, that in the progress of Airs to modern times, they have in some parts been delicately moulded by judicious Singers, into a more simple and pleasing form than that given to them by the early Publishers. If any one doubts it, let him compare the Airs in the Orpheus Caledonius, with the same Airs in this work. In selecting the Airs, the Editor not only consulted every Collection, old and new, comparing the same Airs in each, but availed himself of the communications of such intelligent friends as he knew to have been much conversant with their native music.[44]

As with the collecting of popular lyrics and ballads, there was evidently an evolutionary process in the selection of melodies, the sources of which ranged from oral rendition to personally scribbled manuscripts or published sources, all of which seemed to hold the same level of importance. Thomson's description strikes a chord with Dahlhaus's belief that the 'romantics clung to a divided notion of folk song'.[45] On one hand they followed a driving ambition to find a direct line to the past and to the purest forms, and this is certainly illustrated by Thomson's attempts to include real harpers' melodies in his Welsh collections. On the other hand, as Dahlhaus notes, such collectors also wanted to '"romanticize" and "poeticize" their own age'.[46] It was possible for the new composers and 'recasters' to write in the style of these old melodies, to work simply by imitating the original tunes, and as far as they were concerned this newly forged melody, if it was so closely based on an older, 'original' tune, was still 'authentic'. Quoting from Ferdinand Hand's *Aesthetik der Tonkunst* (1841), Dahlhaus explains: 'by taking traditional melodies as their starting point they preserve that peculiarity of spirit that continues to thrive inbred in the Folk until altered or spoilt by alien influences'.[47] The 'spirit' or melodic 'geist', it could be argued, is retained regardless of the amendments and changes made by the adapter. Dahlhaus states that it is virtually impossible to know whether folk melodies which appear in print at this time are 'real' or not. But Thomson and his contemporaries – Ritson and Tytler included – state that antiquity can be distinguished 'internally' by the experienced ear. Thomson's 'Dissertation on the National Melodies of Scotland', which he published in the first volume of his octavo edition in 1825, discusses in depth (as does Tytler's 'Dissertation') the characteristics of the national scale:

The truth, in short, is, that there is but one series of sounds in the national scale, upon which every ancient Scottish air is constructed, whatever may be its varieties either by mode or of character. This *national scale* is the modern diatonic scale, divested of the *fourth* and *seventh* . . . In saying, that an air is constructed upon a certain scale, it is meant that the melody is strictly confined to the notes of that scale, though they may be taken in any order, or carried upwards or downwards to any extent. Our primitive musicians might wander up and down the scale, forming such successions of notes, and dwelling or stopping on such parts of the scale that pleased them; but they could no more introduce minuter divisions of the scale, or sounds not comprehended in it, than a musician of the present day could introduce sounds not to be found in the scale to which his ear has been accustomed.[48]

He went so far as to mark the 'truly antique' airs in the index of melodies included in some of his volumes. Yet later in his 'Dissertation' he noted how easy it was to 'fake' such melodies, and even provided a simple 'Do it yourself' guide to the composition of a Scots air:

it is very possible for a modern composer, who is acquainted with the peculiar character of our melodies, to imitate them very exactly. Thus, the 'Banks and Braes of Bonny Doon' was composed by a gentleman of Edinburgh, who had been jocularly told that a Scottish air could be produced by merely running the fingers over the black keys of a piano-forte, which give precisely the progression of the national scale.[49]

While this tune worked successfully by adhering to the pentatonic scale, Thomson did note that even if such new tunes are 'often pretty', they are still detectable because they contain notes which 'do not belong to the national scale'.[50] The purity and authenticity of airs was a key focus, though some editors, like R. H. Cromek, believed that the process of reworking the traditional songs of Galloway and putting them into printed form was itself a process of purification, for he refers to Burns as an artist who 'purified and washed from their olden stains many of the most exquisite [lyrics] of past ages'.[51]

Discovering the popular songs of the past in order to 'romanticize' them for the present is clearly to the fore when Thomson comes to deal with songs from Ireland and Wales, geographic and cultural areas relatively foreign to him as a Scot, although perhaps less so as a 'North Briton'. The idea for an Irish Collection was first suggested by Burns in 1793,[52] and Thomson was happy to note the similarities between the melodies of the Scots and the Irish, a comparison already suggested by

Joseph Ritson in *A Select Collection of English Songs* (1783). The argument that Scottish melodies derived from Irish originals had been proposed by Thomas Campbell in his *Philosophical Survey of the South of Ireland* (1777), but Ritson rejected it. Thomson's preface concerns itself most closely with Beethoven's arrangements and Thomson chooses to rely on other dissertations (those already published by Joseph Cooper Walker, Edward Bunting, and Thomas Moore), rather than offer any historical account of Irish music himself. He does choose, like Moore, to include several of the melodies recently notated by Edward Bunting at the 1782 Belfast Harp Festival which, as Leith Davis notes, was supposed to revive interest in the ancient harping tradition of Ireland.[53] The revival and continuation of the Welsh bardic competitions or Eisteddfods fuelled the same fire as the Belfast Festival, at once celebrating the past and ensuring that this peculiarly local tradition became a focus for modern perform-ance and for national feeling. The Eisteddfod was revived from the early 1700s, and, as Prys Morgan explains, it took on an altogether new level of importance from the 1780s.[54]

As in other contemporary musical collections, Thomson took a free hand in adapting traditional material. Apparently original oral forms – such as the *penillion telyn* or short epigrammatic stanzas which could be and were adapted by singers and harpers to a wide range of harp melodies – were used as the basis of something new. Thomson discussed the necessity of simplifying what were traditionally instrumental and often improvisatory melodies, '*in order to make Songs of them*'.[55] His Welsh collection adhered closely to the melodic content of those by harpers John Parry (*A Selection of Welsh Melodies With Appropriate English Words*, 1809) and Edward Jones (*Musical Relicks of the Welsh Bards*, 1800) – Parry's collection appearing during the same year as Thomson's first Welsh volume. In contrast to his Irish collection, and with a nod to Percy and Charlotte Brooke, Thomson chose to provide a prefatory dissertation 'Of the Welsh Bards and Minstrels'. While much of his Scottish and Irish material had come from printed sources, the Welsh landscape and its living musicians seemed to lure Thomson in person and, inspired by Pennant's tour in the early 1770s, Thomson took off to visit the mountains and 'to hear the Airs played by the best Harpers, to collate and correct the manuscripts he received, and to glean such Airs as his correspondents had omitted to gather'.[56] As in the case of his Scottish experience, he was finding variants of melodies with the same titles in different printed sources and 'manuscripts transmitted to him'.[57] But here in Wales Thomson was acutely aware of oral transmission: 'In the lapse of time, accidental

derivations, or supposed improvements, are gradually introduced; and in
different counties, even in different parts of the country, the same Air is
found more or less varied; every performer asserting, however, that his own
is the correct and genuine copy!'[58] As with his publication of alternative
English lyrics for Scottish songs, Thomson's editorial policies clearly reveal
unionist sympathies, even though his collections sought to promote the
distinctive national cultures of Britain's 'Celtic fringes'. His constant
efforts to avoid offending a 'British' clientele through the editing of his
Scottish songs, and his failure to provide a dissertation on Irish music,
might also be seen in this light. So it is perhaps surprising that in his Welsh
collection he makes a bolder political statement by insisting on giving the
titles of the melodies in Welsh and noting in the preface that it was
impossible to find English verses in Wales, for the Welsh refused to sing in
the tongue of their 'inveterate enemies'. With the help of a local circle of
Welsh writers – led by Richard Llwyd (1752–1835) and including Thomas
Griffith (dates unknown) and two clergymen, Revd James Grahame (1765–
1811) and Revd George Warrington (dates unknown) – Thomson also
commissioned his stalwart lyrical collaborators William Smyth, Anne
Grant, Amelia Opie, Joanna Baillie, Walter Scott, Alexander Boswell,
William Roscoe, and others, to furnish his Welsh melodies. Edward
Williams (Iolo Morganwg) contributed some lyrics, though it is highly
possible that the songs by the ancient bard Dafydd ap Gwilym, proudly
presented by Thomson as true bardic productions, were Morganwg's
forgeries.[59]

   The case of George Thomson's collections of Scottish, Irish, and
particularly Welsh songs illustrates clearly that, by the 1810s, 'national
song' was evolving rapidly in both oral and printed environments. Like
many of the most important song writers of the period, Thomson happily
collated materials from a variety of oral and printed sources which he
amalgamated and transformed with the help of both musicians and
writers. Like Burns, Hogg, Clare, or Moore, the role of melody was
crucially important to him as a collector and editor and was usually the
starting point for creating songs afresh, as Vaughan Williams was later to
suggest. Despite the transformations which we have seen traditional
melodies undergoing in the hands of Thomson and his collaborators, he
increasingly insisted on the purity, authenticity, and distinctive ethnic
characteristics of his melodies (in their use of modality and 'national
scales') as well as their provenance in oral tradition. Fundamentally, again
reflecting the practices of song writers and collectors like Burns, Hogg,
Clare, and Moore, Thomson's collections were initially inspired by, and

ultimately intended for, performance – so that he at once captured an older oral tradition and sought to refashion it for a polite nineteenth-century musical public. While the stem, in Vaughan Williams's description, had now sprouted many new shoots, and the plant sported a more romantic and exotic blossom,[60] it remained rooted in its native soil, evoking the oral tradition of a vanishing rural past.

NOTES

1 Ralph Vaughan Williams, *National Music and Other Essays* (Oxford: Oxford University Press, 1963), pp. 32–3. I should like to offer particular thanks to Nigel Leask and Leith Davis for their involvement in the 'evolution' of this chapter. Also to Pamela Perkins, Gerard Carruthers, Rhona Brown, and Marjorie Rycroft who engaged in fruitful discussion.

2 Williams, *National Music*, p. 38.

3 Carl Dahlhaus, *Ninteenth-Century Music*, trans. J. Bradford Robinson (Berkeley: University of California Press, 1989), p. 111. This text was first published in 1928. See also the introduction to this volume, and Nigel Leask's chapter, for a discussion of the Romantic conception of 'medieval minstrelsy' which underpinned the work of many editors of that period, and which complicates any simple narrative of the Herderian notion of collective creation so important to Vaughan Williams and his contemporaries.

4 Peter Burke, *Popular Culture in Early Modern Europe*, rev. edn (Aldershot: Scolar Press, 1994), p. 12. See Chapter 1, 'The Discovery of the People', pp. 3–22.

5 See Dianne Dugaw's recent essay 'On the "Darling Songs" of Poets, Scholars and Singers: An Introduction', *Eighteenth Century: Theory and Interpretation* 47:2–3 (Summer–Fall 2006), 97.

6 See Celeste Langan, 'Understanding Media in 1805: Audiovisual Hallucination in *The Lay of the Last Minstrel*', *Studies in Romanticism* 40 (March 2001), 49–70.

7 See Nick Groom, '"The purest English": Ballads and the English Literary Dialect', *Eighteenth Century: Theory and Interpretation* 47:2–3 (Summer–Fall 2006), 179–202 (179, 180).

8 See Celeste Langan, 'Scotch Drink & Irish Harps: Mediations of the National Air', in Phyllis Weliver (ed.), *The Figure of Music in Nineteenth-Century British Poetry* (Aldershot: Ashgate, 2005), pp. 25–49. Langan states that 'the naming of the air or "tune" foregrounds the text as an act of *mediation* – the transmission of one (oral-acoustic) medium by another (print-visual) medium'. She also notes that 'the "air" thus referenced seems to haunt, or hover slightly beyond, the printed page' (p. 30). Indeed it might be argued that this 'reference' to an air does create a mysterious sound world, which has a quite separate set of connotations for the person reading the lyric.

9 Further discussion of this theory can be found in Thomas Crawford's *Society and the Lyric: A Study of the Song Culture of Eighteenth-Century Scotland* (Edinburgh: Scottish Academic Press, 1979). See also Steve Newman, 'The Scots Songs of

Allan Ramsay: "Lyrick" Transformation, Popular Culture, and the Boundaries of the Scottish Enlightenment', *Modern Language Quarterly* 63:3 (September 2002), 277–314. Newman's work on Allan Ramsay's songs substantiates Crawford's thesis and also discusses the power of melody to stimulate 'feeling' and sentiment, and thus its key importance during the Enlightenment.

10 For Crawford see preceding note.

11 Burns's famous 'autobiographical letter' to Dr John Moore (August 1787) in *The Letters of Robert Burns*, ed. De Lancey Ferguson and Ross Roy, 2nd edition, 2 vols. (Oxford: Clarendon Press, 1985), vol. 1, p. 135 (Letter 125).

12 *Ibid.*, p. 137.

13 See Emily Lyle, ' "Thus began with me Love and Poesy": Burns's First Song and "I am a man unmarried" ', in Kenneth Simpson (ed.), *Love & Liberty: Robert Burns: A Bicentenary Celebration* (East Lothian: Tuckwell Press, 1997), pp. 334–40.

14 Crawford, *Society and the Lyric*, p. 6.

15 See David Daiches, *Robert Burns* (Edinburgh: Spurbooks, 1981), p. 43, and James Mackay, *Burns: A Biography of Robert Burns* (Edinburgh: Mainstream, 1992), p. 79.

16 Thomson began corresponding with Burns in 1792. Prior to this Burns had worked closely with Edinburgh publisher James Johnson on his *Scots Musical Museum* which was ultimately to contain 6 volumes of 600 songs published between 1787 and 1803. Donald A. Low claims that some 220 of these songs were written, collected, or adapted by Burns (*The Scots Musical Museum*, ed. D. A. Low, 2 vols. (Aldershot: Scolar Press, 1991)). This is a facsimile of the first editions of the six volumes.

17 Burns, *Letters*, vol. 11 (1790–6), pp. 239–48 (Letter 586); p. 242.

18 Robert Burns, *Robert Burns's Commonplace Book 1783–1785*, ed. David Daiches (Sussex: Centaur Press, 1965), p. 41.

19 *Ibid.*, pp. 38, 37.

20 *Ibid.*, p. 37.

21 Quoted in George Deacon, *John Clare and the Folk Tradition* (London: Francis Bootle Publishers, 2002), p. 24. Deacon notes this quote is from Clare's Northampton MS 18.

22 *Ibid.*, p. 25. Here Deacon quotes from Northampton MS 14, p. 3.

23 See Jonathan Bate, *John Clare: A Biography* (London: Picador, 2003), pp. 94–5.

24 See 'Memoir of the Author's Life' in James Hogg, *Altrive Tales*, Stirling/South Carolina Research edition of *The Collected Works of James Hogg* (Edinburgh: Edinburgh University Press, 2005), pp. 14–17. *Altrive Tales* was first published in 1832 – there were earlier versions of his 'Memoir' which first appeared with *The Mountain Bard* in 1807 and 1821 (*Collected Works*, p. 14). Hogg's entertaining head notes for each song he chose to include in his final collection *Songs by the Ettrick Shepherd* in 1831 identify many of them as having melodies which he wrote himself. Other head notes talk of his talents as a singer of his own songs.

25 See Mary-Ann Constantine, *The Truth against the World: Iolo Morganwg and Romantic Forgery* (Cardiff: University of Wales Press, 2007), p. 45. Mary-Ann Constantine quotes here from Williams's *Poems, Lyric and Pastoral*, 2 vols. (London, 1794). She notes that *The Vocal Miscellany* first appeared in 1733 but was reprinted throughout the century. The quote is: 'My mother sang agreeably, and I understood that she learned her songs from this book, which made me so very desirous of learning it. This I did in a short time, and hence I doubt not, my original turn for poetry.'

26 See L. A. G. Strong, *The Minstrel Boy: A Portrait of Tom Moore* (London: Hodder and Stoughton, 1937), pp. 17–18. For the most recent informative work on Moore see Leith Davis, *Music, Postcolonialism and Gender: The Construction of Irish National Identity, 1724–1874* (Notre Dame: University of Notre Dame Press, 2006). Davis's fascinating study covers both Bunting and Moore in detail – see Chapters 4 and 6.

27 Thomson has received consistently bad press in Burns scholarship over issues of payment, and for publishing Burns's songs with posthumous alterations to existing lyrics or to different choices of tune.

28 See K. C. McCue, 'George Thomson (1757–1851): His Collections of National Airs in their Scottish Cultural Context', unpublished PhD thesis, Oxford University (1993). See also James Cuthbert Hadden, *George Thomson, The Friend of Burns: His Life and Correspondence* (London: John C. Nimmo, 1898).

29 The bibliography of Thomson's Scottish collection is one of the most complex in publishing history of this period. See Kirsteen McCue, ' "The most intricate bibliographical enigma": Understanding George Thomson (1757–1851) and his Collections of National Airs', in Richard Turbet (ed.), *Music Librarianship in the United Kingdom* (Aldershot: Ashgate, 2003), pp. 99–120. See also Cecil Hopkinson and C. B. Oldman, 'Thomson's Collections of National Song', *Transactions of the Edinburgh Bibliographical Society* 2:1 (1940), 3–64 and 3:2 (1954), 123–4.

30 See the Preface to George Thomson, *A Select Collection of Original Scotish Airs*, first set (London: Preston, 1793). Thomson noted here that many collections were 'liable to particular objections'; that several omitted 'many charming airs'; and that 'every collection that has yet been published, is exceptionable with respect to the poetry'. The first four Thomson publications in the 1790s were called 'sets' and included twenty-five songs each. From 1801 they were termed 'volumes' and included fifty songs each. Much of the material in the first four 'sets' was incorporated in the first issues of volumes I and II in 1801.

31 Oswald and Marshall's tunes were of great importance to Burns, who used them to inspire his lyrics.

32 See Jenny Burchell, *Polite or Commercial Concerts? Concert Management and Orchestral Repertoire in Edinburgh, Bath, Oxford, Manchester, and Newcastle, 1730–1799* (New York and London: Garland, 1996).

33 See Roger Fiske, *Scotland in Music: A European Enthusiasm* (Cambridge: Cambridge University Press, 1982). Fiske's first chapter looks at the London vogue of the 'Scotch Song' from the beginning of the eighteenth century.

34 William Tytler, 'Dissertation on the Scottish Music', in *Transactions of the Society of Antiquaries of Scotland* (Edinburgh and London, 1792), pp. 495–6.

35 J. Wilson, *The Land of Burns: A Series of Landscapes and Portraits Illustrative of the Life and Writings of the Scottish Poet* (Edinburgh, 1840), p. 39. Thomson wrote an autobiographical account for Wilson's volume, pp. 38–42. See also Hadden, *George Thomson*, p. 20.

36 Robert Chambers, *Traditions of Edinburgh*, new edition (Edinburgh and London, 1868), p. 277. Thomson supplied Chambers with an account of the social and musical gatherings at 'St Cecilia's Hall' which was built, by subscription, by the Edinburgh Musical Society in 1762.

37 *Ibid.*

38 Hadden, *George Thomson*, p. 21.

39 Nicholas Temperley, 'Ballroom and Drawing-Room Music', in Nicholas Temperley (ed.), *The Romantic Age 1800–1914* (London: Athlone Press, 1981), p. 116. Charles Rosen has noted that 'The distinction between orchestral style and chamber style, or music for the general public and music for amateurs to play privately, was never absolutely clear cut' (*The Classical Style* (London: Faber and Faber, 1984), p. 45).

40 Temperley, 'Ballroom and Drawing-Room Music', p. 119.

41 The *Dictionnaire* was published first in Geneva in 1767 and in Paris the following year. For extracts see James Day and Peter le Huray (eds.), *Music and Aesthetics in the Eighteenth and Early-Nineteenth Centuries* (Cambridge: Cambridge University Press, 1987), pp. 66–94; this quotation p. 89.

42 George Thomson, *Thomson's Collection of the Songs of Burns, Sir Walter Scott Bart, And other eminent Lyric Poets Ancient and Modern united to The Select Melodies of Scotland and of Ireland and Wales with Symphonies and Accompaniments for the Piano Forte by Pleyel, Haydn, Beethoven &c. the whole composed by George Thomson F.A.S. Edinburgh in Six Volumes* (London: Preston/Hurst Robinson, 1825), vol. 1, p. i. Thomson produced his first five-volume octavo set entitled *The Select Melodies of Scotland, Interspersed with those of Ireland and Wales* in 1822–3. He then produced a sixth volume in 1825 and retitled the work *Thomson's Collection . . .* The first five volumes of these two sets are virtually identical in content. He continued to release issues of these volumes until the late 1830s, but the content is identical to those in the earlier volumes. Hopkinson and Oldman believe he used the same plates.

43 *Ibid.*

44 This is the Preface from a copy of George Thomson, *A Select Collection of Original Scottish Airs for the Voice. With Introductory & Concluding Symphonies & Accompaniments for the Piano Forte, Violin & Violoncello By Pleyel, Kozeluch & Haydn. With Select & Characteristic Verses both Scottish and English adapted to the Airs, including upwards of One Hundred New Songs by*

BURNS, 2 vols. (London: T. Preston, 1817), vol. 1. The colophon is dated 1817, but this preface may have appeared with other volumes too. See McCue, ' "The most intricate bibliographical enigma" '. William Thomson's *Orpheus Caledonius* was published in London in 1725 and was reissued in 1733. It was arguably the most important collection of Scottish songs to appear in Britain in the early eighteenth century, of lasting significance to musicians, songwriters, collectors, and editors from then until the mid nineteenth century. Thomson was a London-based Scottish music publisher and many of the songs he included in this publication were taken directly from Allan Ramsay's contemporaneous *Tea-Table Miscellany* (from 1724). Ramsay did not collaborate with Thomson on his project and was bitter towards him for including his songs without permission.

45 Dahlhaus, *Nineteenth-Century Music*, p. 110.

46 *Ibid.*

47 *Ibid.*

48 George Thomson, 'Dissertation on the National Melodies of Scotland', in *Thomson's Collection of the Songs of Burns*, vol. 1, p. 3.

49 *Ibid.*, p. 11. Thomson was most probably here quoting Burns from a letter to Thomson by the poet in November 1794. Burns tells Thomson that Stephen Clarke, the Edinburgh musician who worked closely with Burns on Johnson's *Scots Musical Museum*, has recounted a similar story about 'the black keys of the harpsichord'. See Burns, *Letters*, vol. 11 (1790–6), p. 325 (Letter 646).

50 *Ibid.*

51 R. H. Cromek, *Remains of Nithsdale and Galloway Song: with Historical and Traditional Notices relative to the Manners and Customs of the Peasantry* (London, 1810), p. i.

52 Burns, *Letters*, vol. 11 (1790–6), p. 252 (Letter 588). In this letter dated September 1793 Burns wrote: 'Since you are so fond of Irish music, what say you to twenty five of them in an additional Number?'

53 Davis, *Music, Postcolonialism and Gender*, p. 95. Leith Davis places the festival firmly in its political context, for this festival and its foregrounding of the harp further enhanced the emblem of the harp recently adopted by the United Irishmen, and it also coincided with a celebration they arranged to celebrate the fall of the Bastille three years previously. Davis follows the evolution of Bunting's collection through the nineteenth century, where it appeared in new guises as the decades passed.

54 Prys Morgan, 'The Hunt for the Welsh Past in the Romantic Period', in Eric Hobsbawm and Terence Ranger (eds.), *The Invention of Tradition* (Cambridge: Cambridge University Press, 1983), pp. 43–100. The section on the Eisteddfod is cited at pp. 56–62.

55 George Thomson, *A Select Collection of Original Welsh Airs* (London and Edinburgh: Preston and Thomson, 1811), p. 1. Thomson's italics.

56 *Ibid.* See also Marjorie E. Rycroft, 'Haydn's Welsh Songs: George Thomson's Musical and Literary Sources', in S. Harper and W. Thomas (eds.), *Bearers of*

Song, Welsh Music Studies 7 (Cardiff: University of Wales Press, 2007), pp. 92–133.

57 Thomson, *Welsh Airs*, p. 1.

58 *Ibid.*

59 See Constantine, *The Truth against the World*, pp. 27–41.

60 Simon McVeigh notes the vogue for things Chinese and Turkish in London musical entertainment during the late 1700s and early 1800s, and that 'Welsh laments or Scottish pibroch' were also regarded as having this fashionable 'foreign colouring': see *Concert Life in London from Mozart to Haydn* (Cambridge: Cambridge University Press, 1993), pp. 114–15.

PART III

Politics and the people

CHAPTER 5

Rus in urbe

John Barrell

THE DISTRESSED MECHANIC

For loyal Britons, January 1795 was probably the lowest point of the war with the new republic of France. Holland was falling to the French army, the war in northeastern Europe was effectively lost, and the alliance of kings against the French Republic was crumbling. The bitter weather, which had frozen the rivers of the low countries and left Holland without her natural defences, was also threatening severe scarcity at home, the effects of which would be exacerbated by high wartime taxes, economic depression, and unemployment. As this complex crisis was coming to a head, a letter appeared in the periodical *Politics for the People*, addressed to its editor, Daniel Isaac Eaton. It was sent from the east London suburb of Hoxton, a place of weavers, furniture-makers, and other traders badly affected by the depression, and was signed by 'A Distressed Mechanic'. This is a fascinating letter: it lies at the heart of what I want to say in this chapter, and I shall need to quote a substantial part of it, starting with its references to the Scottish martyrs sentenced to be transported to Botany Bay in 1793 and 1794, and to the 'acquitted felons', campaigners for universal manhood suffrage, who had just been found not guilty of High Treason in London in late 1794.

When men are dragged to dungeons, and banished their native country, or left at the mercy of unjust Power, because they possess minds capable of sympathizing with their miserable countrymen; because they have wisdom to discern the causes, and are honest enough to discover the evils, that, if persisted in, will, ere long, involve in its ruin not only the weak and defenceless, but the men who, through the suffocating stench of inequality, are deprived of that public spirit which can alone produce salvation for a fruitful, though a land mourning for the greatest of all blessings, Public Liberty, where can we hide, and not hear the voice of Sensibility expressing itself in the language of this little selected piece[?][1]

The syntax of all this is very unorthodox, its inaccuracy no doubt partly an effect of the distress, the passion, the enthusiasm with which this mechanic deplores the repression of the mid 1790s, partly perhaps left uncorrected to function as a sign of that enthusiasm, too precipitate to go back and correct its utterances. Nevertheless its meaning is clear enough, that in a land enslaved by men without public virtue, the complaints of sensibility are heard everywhere. At this point Sensibility itself speaks, in the form first of an apostrophe to the blessings of Public Liberty, and then of a lament for her passing:

– O Liberty! Thou enlivener of life, thou solace of our toils, thou patron of arts, thou encourager of industry, thou spring of opulence, thou something more than life, beyond the reach of fancy to describe, all hail! It is thou that beamest the sunshine in the Patriot's breast; it is thou that sweetenest the toil of the labouring mechanic! Thou dost inspire the ploughman with his jocund mirth; and thou tunest the merry milk-maid's song! Thou canst make the desart smile, and the barren rock to sing for joy; by thy sacred protection the poorest peasant is secure under the roof of his defenceless cot, whilst Oppression, at a distance, gnashes with her teeth, but dares not show her iron rod, and Power, like the raging billows, dashes its bounds with indignation, but cannot overpass them.[2]

I want briefly to notice here, that when the voice of Sensibility speaks through the pen of this Hoxton mechanic, the mode it chooses is pastoral, and pastoral at its most self-consciously literary, with echoes of Shakespeare's songs perhaps, or Milton's 'L'Allegro', or Izaak Walton's *Compleat Angler*, or Gray's 'Elegy', where ploughmen are also 'jocund', a word virtually unused in the eighteenth century except in pastoral poetry where it is used everywhere. This pastoral becomes something else again, however, when the voice of Sensibility goes on to lament the passing of the liberty that turns hard labour into idyllic leisure.

But where thou art not, how changed the scene! How tasteless! How irksome labour! How languid industry! Where is the beauteous rose, the gaudy tulip, the sweet-scented jessamine? Where the purple grape, the luscious peach, the glowing nectarine? Wherefore smile not the valleys with their beauteous verdure, nor sing for joy with their golden harvest? – All are withered by the scorching sun of lawless Power! – Where thou art not, what place so sacred as to be secure. Or who can say, this is my own? This is the language only of the place where thou delightest to dwell. But as soon as thou spreadest thy wings to some more pleasing clime, Power walks abroad with haughty strides, and tramples upon the weak; whilst Oppression, with its heavy hand, bows down the unwilling neck to the yoke![3]

The linking of Liberty and Property, and the notion that Plenty, in the shape of golden harvests, and often coupled with Peace, is the gift of liberty, and pre-eminently of British Liberty – by 1795 these had been commonplace for nearly a hundred years. But what flight of fancy led this mechanic to suggest that liberty was so especially bountiful as to favour the growth of the grape, peach, and nectarine? Such fruits, when grown at all in Britain, were to be found on the south-facing garden walls of the rich: they often failed to ripen, and when they were ripe they did not keep; they were luxury fruits, and their cultivation was probably favoured by a good measure of the inequality that the passage associates with tyranny.

Of course I'm taking the lines much too literally; but it is precisely to the point that the voice of Sensibility is here as remote from the daily experience and concerns of Hoxton mechanics as peaches and nectarines were from the sooty market-gardens on Hoxton's eastern fringe. These exotic fruits, along with the 'sweet-scented jessamine' and the 'gaudy tulip', have been imported into the world of *Politics for the People* from the tradition of polite pastoral with its predilection for the flora of the Mediterranean: the 'purple grape' will be found in *Comus*, in the garden of Eden as described in *Paradise Lost*, and in a dozen and more eighteenth-century poems by Thomas Blacklock, Richard Blackmore, Walter Harte, Richard Jago, Edward Young, and so on; the 'luscious peach' has been scrumped from James Beattie's translation of Virgil's second pastoral, and the 'glowing nectarine' from a poem by Henry Pye, poet laureate.[4] It was finding these fruits mixed in with the more domestic ingredients of Eaton's 'salmagundy for swine', as he subtitled the periodical, that started the train of thought set out in this chapter ...

RADICAL PERIODICALS

... which is an attempt to talk about pastoral and the voice of sensibility in what we term, though as will become clear I do not like the term, 'plebeian' radical periodicals of the mid 1790s: in Daniel Isaac Eaton's two periodicals *Politics for the People* and *The Philanthropist*, in Thomas Spence's *Pig's Meat*, in John Thelwall's *Tribune*, in Benjamin Crosby's *Register of the Times*, and in the *Moral and Political Magazine* of the London Corresponding Society. These periodicals are not easy to discuss, however, and before I begin I need to build some elaborate defences to protect myself from the risks of generalizing about them. To begin with, though we think of them as 'plebeian' periodicals, published cheaply for an audience primarily of London shopkeepers, artisans, clerks, and so on, they are very different from each other. Thus when Eaton renamed *Hog's Wash, Politics for the People*, he may have thought of himself as repositioning the periodical a little upmarket, either in search of a new readership, or acknowledging the relative literary sophistication of the readers he already had, or both. The same may have been true when *Politics for the People* was replaced by *The Philanthropist*, but then again perhaps not, as Eaton priced it at 1d compared with 2d for its predecessor. Both periodicals are as he calls them salmagundies, made up of very mixed ingredients usually by contemporary authors. Like Eaton with *Hog's Wash*, the original title of *Politics for the People*, Spence offers *Pig's Meat*, his mixture of excerpts from Whig political classics and more recent political writings, to a readership Burke would have identified as a 'swinish multitude'. *The Register of the Times*, a news digest offering short articles on current affairs, is a more complex case: over its two-year run, Crosby, who wore his political convictions more casually than Eaton or Spence, tirelessly searched for readers by changing the length and frequency of its issues, its price, its contents, and even its politics, from cautiously liberal to radical to loyalist and finally to Foxite Whig before killing it off a few months into 1796. *The Tribune*, edited and largely written by Thelwall, seems, by its format and the length of its articles, to be aiming to unite a relatively sophisticated plebeian audience with a hoped-for polite middle-class readership. The *Moral and Political Magazine* appears to be aimed at the serious, rational, reading wing of the LCS, with fewer songs and less satire and sentiment than Eaton's periodicals, for example.

Perhaps the main problem in discussing all these periodicals with the exception of *The Tribune* and *Pig's Meat* is that for the most part we have little idea of where the contents come from or who they are by. Some items are attributed, most are not; some appear to have been written for the periodical in which they appear, others are borrowed from other publications, sometimes with, sometimes without, acknowledgement. This uncertainty about provenance causes a particular difficulty with regard to the poetry published in these volumes, which is where the voice of sensibility is chiefly to be heard, and which is probably mainly written by authors considerably more polite than the readership of the periodicals. It is at least as difficult to identify the origins of many of the political songs printed in the periodicals as of the poems, but this seems less of a hindrance to criticism, because the songs appear to belong to a collective culture of jovial political sociability in which individual authorship seems of no particular account: they are sung, or imagined to be sung, at LCS divisional meetings, celebration-dinners, at tavern-clubs and free-and-easys. They express ideas and feelings supposed to be widely shared, and are the reason, therefore, why those who sing them have associated together. Poems of sensibility, however, often arouse a curiosity about their authorship as songs do not, because they often invite us to understand them as monologues spoken by a lone individual, saying in poetry what he or she cannot say in company or in public. Many of the sentimental pastorals in the plebeian periodicals allude to Gray's 'Elegy' (which Spence reprints entire in the second volume of *Pig's Meat*[5]), the paradigmatic example of a poetry we think of as the expression of newly valued and largely middle-class notions of privacy and interiority. It is not at all clear what we should make of such sentimental pastorals once they are transplanted into periodicals that are dedicated to fostering a collective radical popular culture.

PASTORAL AND UTOPIANISM

There is, unsurprisingly enough, a familiar and straightforward use of pastoral in these periodicals to give expression to a utopian political programme. Thomas Spence associated his own utopianism with Oliver Goldsmith's *The Deserted Village*, and he reprinted a long extract from Goldsmith's poem in the first volume of *Pig's Meat*.[6] It seems not to have been until the 1790s that the subversive potential of the poem came to be understood. It described an imagined village, Auburn, which had enjoyed a golden age ambiguously situated in the author's youth or prior to the Norman Conquest. This golden age had been destroyed by commerce, 'by trade's unfeeling train',[7] more specifically by a rich nabob returned from India who has driven away the inhabitants and destroyed the village in the process of landscaping his park. What trade had driven away, along with the villagers themselves, was not however the usual golden age of English pastoral, characterized by a paternalist moral economy and the fake equality of jovial masters and cheerfully loyal employees. Auburn's history had been truly exceptional, it seems; it had had no manor-house, no hall, no great estate: it had been a place of true economic equality where 'every rood of ground maintained its man' (line 58). The villagers were freeholders; they paid rent to no landlord, so that 'light labour' was sufficient to furnish them with the necessaries of life (line 59), and they had no desire for the luxuries. The poem became a model for the land reform promoted by Spence, who believing that land had been distributed thus in the past believed it could be so again in the future. One of the farthing tokens he made, partly as propaganda, mainly to sell to collectors, displayed a design borrowed from Spence's fellow-Geordie Thomas Bewick, a ruined village on the obverse, the trees dead, the cottages ruined, with the legend taken from Goldsmith, 'One only master grasps the whole domain' (line 39). On the reverse the design most frequently found shows a shepherd reclining beneath a tree, his light labour done and his living assured under Spence's plan.[8]

The villagers driven out of Auburn by the imparkment of their farmland were represented as leaving, many of them, for an uncertain and frightening future as emigrants to the New World, but several later poems designed as answers to or continuations of Goldsmith's poem imagined that they found in America a pastoral utopia. Two of the pastorals in the plebeian periodicals do something similar. 'The Prospect of Emigration' in *Politics for the People*, originally published in the *Cambridge Intelligencer*, was written by John Towell Rutt, an early member of the polite association of reformers known as the Society for Constitutional Information, and a learned dissenting drug-merchant who had inherited a substantial business.[9] The poem lamented the oppression and corruption of Britain, and the violent justice that had sentenced Muir and Palmer to transportation, and imagined an escape from what he called 'Europe's servile coast' to the land 'beyond the western wave'. There, as once in Auburn, they would be under the protection of God, and in the shadow of no great house:

> Nor o'er those meads shall frown th'embattled dome,
>   Rear'd by some haughty Tyrant of the soil,
> But Independence glad the peasant's home,
>   And Plenty recompense his willing toil.
>
> There all the children of one bounteous Sire,
>   In friendship join, on Nature's equal plan,
> To virtue's true nobility aspire,
>   And boast alike the *dignity of Man*.[10]

In *The Philanthropist* Eaton published a similar poem entitled 'An Ode to Kentucky, by an Emigrant' who promises those who will strike off their 'European fetters' a new life in a landscape apparently empty and belonging to no one, where fragrant flowers, like the violet in Gray's 'Elegy', waste their sweetness on the desert air. It is a land 'Whose rich production will supply each want; / Whose ample resources, with little toil, / Will crown their labours, and their cares beguile'. Kentucky, the emigrant tells us, is not only without great houses and grasping landlords: there are no taxes, no kings, no game laws, no primogeniture, no parsons, no tythes, no bishops, no politicians – in particular no Pitt, no Burke, no Windham, no Dundas; there are no nabobs, no state pensioners, no spies, no informers, and there are no prostitutes because there are no royal princes to employ them.[11]

PASTORAL, CRIMPING, AND PRESSING

Alongside this utopian strand of pastoral in the periodicals, deriving mainly from Goldsmith, is an elegiac strain which takes as its main inspiration the elegy 'written in a country churchyard' by Thomas Gray. This elegiac quasi-pastoral is the commonest kind in the periodicals and to me the most puzzling, for as we shall see, in an effort to maximize its sentimental charge, it assumes an account of rural life which appears to be incompatible with the political programme of the reform movement.

Among the advantages of Kentucky over Britain, according to the poem I have just glanced at, was that in the New World there were: 'No harden'd crimps in government employ, / To steal your children, or your youths decoy'.[12] For Londoners of the plebeian classes, the potential readers of these periodicals almost all of whom would have been living east of the West End, probably the most visible, certainly the most powerful effects of the war during the mid 1790s were the crimping riots that raged through the capital sometimes for days at a time. 'Crimping' was the practice of kidnapping men and forcibly enlisting them in the army, or of getting them drunk, sometimes with the encouragement of prostitutes, and either swearing them in when they were in no condition to know what they were doing, or telling them they had enlisted when they had no memory of the previous night's doings. In August 1794 a riot began at a Charing Cross crimping house following the suicide of George Howe, a reluctant recruit imprisoned there, and for four days the worst street violence since the Gordon Riots spread all over inner London, as far east as Whitechapel, as far north as Clerkenwell. Fires were raised, crimping houses were pulled down, and later one of the rioters was hanged. More crimping riots followed through the early months of 1795, and in July of that year another supposed crimping house was attacked in Charing Cross. This time the riots spread west, causing the Prime Minister William Pitt to flee Downing Street, and south of the river to St George's Fields. Two of the rioters were trampled to death by the cavalry, many others were injured, and the soldier who had first identified the crimping house – though it probably was not one – was hanged.[13]

Eaton responded to these events by publishing a pamphlet, claiming to be written by a soldier, on what it called 'the pernicious custom of recruiting by crimps', and a closet drama by the pseudonymous 'Henry

Martin Saunders' entitled *The Crimps, or the Death of Poor Howe*, in which the events leading up to Howe's suicide are dramatized. The play makes a good job of setting the crimping houses within the environment of late eighteenth-century London, contrasting the sleaziness and brutality of the crimps with Howe's naive confidence in the safety of London's streets. While the crimps are beating up a former sailor wounded at the battle of the Glorious First of June and pressing him into the army, Howe, a proud loyalist and anti-reformer, is reassuring his mother 'That London is a place of liberty, And just security'. Perhaps in former times there were crimps, he concedes, but ministers now are not tyrants; now 'The *great* men are the *good.*' Only in the countryside, benighted as it is, are 'tales ... Of blood-bowl allies, and of ruffian gangs' still believed.[14]

In response to the repeated disturbances over recruitment in London, the plebeian periodicals become much exercised by fraudulent or forcible enlistment, which is probably the most recurrent theme of their poetry. It seems to be impossible, however, for them to address the domestic tragedies brought about by crimps and press-gangs with a due measure of sensibility except in the mode of elegiac pastoral in a rural setting, even though the large-scale organized crimping of the kind that gave rise to the London riots, and that was so present to the minds of their readers, was necessarily an urban affair. These sentimental pastorals in the popular periodicals – and there are examples in all of them apart from *The Tribune* – all tell more or less the same tale. A young man, either about to be married or already so and the father of young children, is torn from his family and his humble but comfortable cottage to serve in the army or navy. If he is the narrator, he is expecting to die; if the tale is told in the third person, he is already dead, and his partner has often died too, of a broken heart. The poem 'The Wrongs of Poverty' in *Politics for the People* is a poem in the stanza of Gray's 'Elegy', again by John Towell Rutt, and again borrowed from the *Cambridge Intelligencer*. In imagining the effects at home of a soldier's absence and imminent death it attaches itself to the tradition of sentimental pastoral by close verbal echoes of the 'Elegy', in which the death of the father of a family is imagined by imagining an evening ritual outside the cottage door which happens – the phrase is like a death-knell – 'no more'. This is Rutt's version:

> No more at eve my pratt'ling babes repair,
> To greet their Sire, his daily labour done:
> But now, defrauded of a father's care,
> Some niggard hand may deal the scanty boon.[15]

A similar vision of a pastoral landscape, which, following the enlistment of the father of a family, is pastoral 'no more', is conjured up by an anonymous poet writing in the same elegiac stanza for *The Register of the Times*:

> Scenes, which were cover'd once with golden store,
>   Where smiling plenty fill'd her copious horn,
> Neglected lie; for plenty is no more,
>   And mourning rustics view the scene forlorn.
> Once sounds of gladness came from ev'ry plain;
>
>   Once sweet contentment o'er the vallies spread; –
> The wife now mourns her distant husband slain,
>   And sees her children droop for want of bread.[16]

Same story, same stanza in the *Moral and Political Magazine*, where a poem entitled 'A War Elegy' tells the story of Henry, a young swain tricked by the sharp practice of a recruiting-party into leaving his peaceful hamlet and his sweetheart Jemima on the very morning of their wedding day. Jemima hears nothing of him for a year, and at last the news reaches her that he has been shot to pieces in battle. She dies of a broken heart.[17] Yet another version appeared in *Pig's Meat*, this time about a sailor called 'Palemon', named after the pastoral swain in Thomson's *Seasons*, no doubt, rather than the knight in the *Canterbury Tales*. He is a very rural sailor, for whom the Britain he has left is a place of hills and plains, not streets and alleys; he has spent a long voyage anticipating his reunion with the pastorally named Chloe, but just as he is about to reach Britain he is taken off his merchant ship by a press-gang, and within a few stanzas has died.[18] There is a pastoral song on crimping, 'The British Soldier's Reflection', in *The Philanthropist*, written from the suburb of New Brentford, just west of London. It announces itself as a parody of Charles Dibdin's well-known patriotic song 'The Jolly Young Waterman',[19] and to that waterman's jovial contentment it opposes the sentimental pathos of a man 'trepann'd' and 'torn' from his 'happy cottage', his plough, his milking cow, and his 'faithful loving wife': this is not a song for a free-and-easy. As it nears its end, the soldier realizes that troops recruited by crimping have no chance against Frenchmen armed with 'REASON' and 'FREEDOM', and that he will never see his wife and village again.[20]

Other pastoral treatments of recruiting and the press-gang in *Politics for the People* are in the form of short prose tales. 'A Tale of the Times' opens with a rustic couple, Richard and Harriet, walking 'arm in arm over the flowery meadows. They were going to milk the cows, and pleased themselves with talking on the theme of love.' That this is a 'pure and harmless love', as the tale assures us, seems to be guaranteed by the character of scene itself, where 'the mild beams of the evening sun shone upon the spires of the village church'. Richard tells Harriet of the delightful pleasures that await them after their marriage, when they will sit at evening outside their cottage with their children playing about them. It required little imagination to picture the scene, which had already been imagined for him by numerous cheap popular prints of rural ease and innocence.[21] Into this rural paradise, however, comes a recruiting-sergeant promising glory, honour, and riches to all who enlist. Richard proposes to go 'a very little time to the wars' and to return with enough money to set the pair of them up in comfort. Harriet reminds him that he would be killing men who might share his own dreams of family happiness, but Richard, unwilling to be thought a coward, accepts the fatal shilling, and is marched off to the wars against France, where he soon forgets that in fighting for glory he is fighting against Liberty. He is horrifically wounded and dies, and, when she hears of his death, Harriet goes mad and drowns herself. 'This picture', the tale assures us, 'is daily exhibited in our villages', where 'the dearest *rights of man* are burst asunder'.[22]

A companion tale, ironically titled 'British Liberty', tells of the doomed pastoral love of William and Nancy, the archetypal sailor and his sweetheart of eighteenth-century songs. It opens with Nancy sitting outside her father's cottage, longing for William to return from the sea. He too, like Richard, had planned a single, short absence, a voyage to the East Indies, intending to return rich and to marry Nancy. Suddenly William appears and the enraptured lovers embrace. Just as suddenly a press-gang enters, seizes William, and drags him away 'like a sheep to the slaughter'. He is killed on the 'Glorious First of June', and two weeks after hearing of his death, Nancy dies too. 'Ye who pity the fate of William and Nancy, know', the tale continues, 'that this kingdom affords daily instances of the most cruel barbarity', visited upon the fathers and sons of families by crimps and press-gangs, the agents of 'a *few Tyrants*, who are wallowing in luxury'.[23]

RADICAL REPRESENTATIONS OF RURAL LIFE

In the last chapter of my book *The Spirit of Despotism*, I examined the cottage as a motif in the wartime propaganda of the 1790s. I suggested that loyalist propaganda, with the obvious exception of Hannah More's tracts, was as determined as it had been before the war that cottage scenery should depict an idealized version of the rural poor as thoroughly domesticated and, despite the high taxation and high prices of wartime, in full enjoyment of the blessings of peace, the rewards of domestic virtue, and the protection of the law. Thus represented, it was imagined that the individual cottage family could stand for the collective identity of the whole nation, supposedly united in the belief that Happy Britannia, a land of loyalty, freedom, plenty, and piety, was fighting a just and necessary war against atheist, republican, and poverty-stricken France. Loyalist poets, I attempted to show, described rural life as entirely unchanged by war, or by anything – as serenely and timelessly the same, the same, the same. In the poetry of the opponents of the war with France, on the other hand, by Charlotte Smith, Joseph Cottle, Robert Merry, Mary Robinson, Coleridge, Wordsworth, Southey, and others, the cottage was shown as ruined or abandoned or a place of misery and poverty, sometimes following the enlistment and perhaps the death of the father of the family, sometimes simply through the effects of wartime taxation and wartime prices on the standard of living of the poor. I was mostly concerned with anti-war poems by polite authors, and to the implicit question, why were they so preoccupied with representing the war in terms of a ruined pastoral landscape, it seemed sufficient to return the answer that such writers saw in the cottage the place of all places in Britain where the effects of the war, and of the corrupt despotism that caused it, were most visible and in their most unvarnished form. The unspoken corollary of this view, in many if not all of these poems, was that if only the war could be brought to an end the countryside would recover the jocund pastoral character it had formerly enjoyed.[24]

I am not sure that answer is full enough, however, when such poems appear in Eaton's and other periodicals aimed at plebeian readers in London. For I persist in finding it odd that, with the exception of *The Tribune* and, for the most part, *Pig's Meat*, the periodicals were so willing to represent social problems that were at least as visible and as keenly felt in the metropolis as in the countryside by stories of self-consciously literary swains and their sweethearts whose lives, before the recruiting parties and press-gangs invaded their villages, had been apparently every bit as idyllic as loyalist poetry claimed they still were. I am not imagining that the readers of the plebeian periodicals were not capable of recognizing the pastoral convention used in the crimping pastorals as a convention. The conventions of pastoral were as familiar even to the illiterate as they were to the highly educated; popular songs frequently represented the countryside in terms of the same conventions, and yet cannot have succeeded in persuading anyone that the countryside really was as idyllic as they suggested, or was so at least until whatever recent catastrophe had provoked the latest elegy. Urban members of the popular radical movement, to judge by the occasional mentions of the countryside in radical addresses and manifestos, no doubt thought of the countryside as a place, whatever its attractions, of extreme deprivation, where the poor, impoverished by tythes and grasping landlords and menaced by the game laws, lived without security of employment or security of tenure.[25] Their condition would be ameliorated, of course, by the ending of the war, but the permanent injustices they suffered could be put right only by universal suffrage.[26]

There are certainly poems in the periodicals, at least in *Pig's Meat* and *The Tribune*, where we can find representations of rural life more in tune with the politics of the popular radical movement. Along with *The Deserted Village*, Spence reprints two other then-canonical poems of rural life. The first was a poem called 'The Beggar's Petition', written by Thomas Moss, which first appeared in 1769, but which before 1800 had been reprinted over 100 times, mostly in the numerous editions of didactic anthologies designed for children and young persons, and plainly with the idea that it taught resignation to heaven's will along with a warily benevolent attitude to the poor. The beggar appears to be soliciting charity from the owner of a magnificent country house, and explains how he has fallen on hard times: 'Heav'n sends Misfortunes,' he says, '– why should we repine?' The suffering of the poor is God's will? Spence will have none of that and none of the beggar's resignation either. He changes the line to read: 'Woes sprung from villains, should we *not* repine?' (my emphasis).[27] Moss's old man continues: 'My Cattle dy'd and blighted was my Corn.' Spence makes these acts of God into those of a villainous landlord: 'My cattle seiz'd,' he writes, 'as also was my corn.'[28] These changes he made silently, as we say, but the poem was so well known that his silence must have been audible enough. He also reprinted another much-anthologized sentimental poem of rural life, 'The Poor Man's Prayer' by W. Hayward Roberts, a schoolmaster at Eton, who first published it in 1766 under the name 'Simon Hodge, a Kentish Labourer'. This was a slightly feistier poem, about a man and his family evicted from their cottage; it is addressed to William Pitt the Elder, the Earl of Chatham, who has just become Prime Minister, and who, we are reassured, will spare time from affairs of state to relieve the imaginary sufferings of this imaginary labourer. Spence's version excised all reference to the charitable father of the present Prime Minister; changed the title from 'The Poor

Man's Prayer' to 'The Peasant's Lamentation on the Exportation of Corn'; but otherwise contented itself with heavily italicizing the key line of the narrative, 'Our *tyrant* LORD *commands us from our home.*'[29]

According to the ministerial press, when in July 1795 the crimping riots reached St George's Fields, they were led by John Thelwall, who was able to prove, however, that at the time he was holidaying with his family near Ryde on the Isle of Wight.[30] He left the island at the end of August, composing a poem at the time which he published in *The Tribune* and which, in its treatment of life in the country, is as wary as Spence of the sentimental pastoralism of the crimping poems. As so often, Thelwall assumes a heroic tone as, about to re-engage in political activism in London, he represents himself almost like a trepanned recruit, as leaving behind

> The lisping babe, whose artless smiles impart
> Joy's anxious throb to the paternal heart,
> And the soft partner, whose kind cares bestow
> Sweets to each joy, and balm to every woe.[31]

The countryside he is leaving, however, is anything but the rural paradise inhabited by Richard and Harriet and William and Nancy and Henry and Jemima. In *The Peripatetic*, published in 1793, Thelwall had represented himself as appalled by the condition of the rural poor in the villages around London.[32] As he makes clear elsewhere in *The Tribune*, he had been no less appalled by the poverty of the rural labourers on the Isle of Wight. His renewed activism will be in part on their behalf; for 'who can view', he asks,

> The peasants' starving wretchedness; the woes
> Which Labour's palid progeny enclose
> In each proud city; or the village train
> Of barefoot, ragged children, who sustain
> A vagrant life of penury and pain
> By cringing beggary, and dog the wheels
> Of passing Luxury . . .
> – Who, that has thought, such piteous scenes can view,
> Nor feel indignant ardours urge his soul
> The cause of wrongs so numerous to controul,
> At vile Corruption's o'ergorg'd throat to fly,
> And quell the fiend, or in the conflict die![33]

There is another poem in *The Tribune* written in a similar spirit by a woman described as 'A Female Citizen', who also appears to have contributed

a poem to the *Moral and Political Magazine*. Imagining the destruction
wrought in the theatre of war, the citizen describes a once-pastoral
landscape now destroyed. Where once, in the manner of the Deserted
Village before it was deserted, 'The rural sport and rustic dance was
seen, / And joy fantastic trod the neighbouring green', now

> Many a weeping peasant's left to mourn,
> His harvest trampl'd, and his hopes forlorn,
> His kindred slain, and his once happy cot, . . .
> Wrapt in devouring flames, or prostrate laid
> By frantic glory's desolating trade.

Turning to Britain, however, where no cottages have been burned or
demolished, the citizen finds no pastoral haven, only a people drooping in
their chains, and a corrupt aristocracy 'fed by the tradesman's and the
peasant's toil'.[34]

SENTIMENT AND POPULAR RADICALISM

The crimping pastorals have none of that, and it is not just the crimping
pastorals. In the *Moral and Political Magazine*, for example, are some
'Lines on the Banishment of Mr. Thomas Muir. By a young Female
Citizen', written in the liltingly melancholy stanza of William Shenstone's
'Pastoral Ballad', one of the best-loved pastoral poems of the late eighteenth century, about how forlorn are the shepherds of the once-happy
valley of the Clyde:

> No longer they crowd the gay bent,
> > Nor assemble to dance on the green:
> While the easy gay smile of content
> > No longer enlivens the scene.

This and other changes have been caused by the banishment of the young
shepherd Muir, with whom 'Bless'd Liberty' was also banished.[35]
  I have been speaking of the crimping poems in Eaton's periodicals, in
the *Moral and Political Magazine* and *The Register of the Times*, as sur-
rendering a radical account of the life of the rural poor in exchange for the
greater sentiment of elegiac pastoral, in order to immerse us more fully in
the pleasurable melancholy of elegy, the warm nostalgia of remembering
what is 'no more' and 'no longer', as if it had ever existed. But why should
the editors of these periodicals, in selecting the poems they do, be willing
to make this exchange? Why keep alive a set of conventions which by

the 1790s are widely regarded as moribund, when the political and propaganda advantages of abandoning them must have been apparent enough? Is it that they see the poetry of sentiment, and prose fiction as in Eaton's crimping and pressing tales, as offering their readers an imaginative space in which the claims of collective radical politics, though still present, are allowed to be less urgent? Where they can be addressed, as the poetry of sentiment always addresses its readers, not as members of a political movement but as the members of families, whose tears can be elicited most readily by the domestic tragedies of husbandless wives, wifeless husbands, dying parents, orphaned children? The contrast here with Thelwall's poems of the mid 1790s is particularly sharp. Thelwall evokes his family in the classical republican manner of a father who loves them to the utmost, but who if the cause requires it is willing to sacrifice even their happiness by sacrificing himself to freedom.[36] Something of the same stern republicanism animates the poet Richard 'Citizen' Lee's poem to the secretary of the LCS, Thomas Hardy, on the death of his wife Lydia when he was awaiting trial in 1794.[37] Poems such as these dramatize the conflict between familial love and civic duty, and to all but the most zealous radicals may have seemed too keen to insist that duty must always win. The crimping poems allowed them to lose the citizen in the private individual.

Or is it that they see the cultivation of sentiment as an important aspect of the political education they seek to impart? Whatever else it was, the popular radical movement of the 1790s saw itself as an educational movement. When it began, the polite Society for Constitutional Information, founded to teach men below the rank of the polite the essentials of political information and the language of political debate, was dormant. The popular radical societies took over that task, and in doing so re-awoke the energies of the SCI. The LCS in particular offered its members, in the language of the day, the opportunity to 'improve', by a course of political reading and political discussion, and the radical London periodicals were effectively a part of the same programme. The appeal of this programme, in a period before the appearance of more formal institutions for adult education, must have been very considerable – many of those who joined the LCS were not content to remain the 'plebeians' that, borrowing the terminology of E. P. Thompson, I have called them. They were men seeking to better themselves, not only intellectually but economically and probably socially as well, and despite the obvious risks of identifying themselves as radicals a striking number of them did so. We are not dealing here with the kind of working-class collectivism which regards social betterment as the goal only of class traitors: for members of the popular radical movement, social as well as intellectual improvement seem to have been understood as increasing the prestige of the members of the movement and therefore the authority with which it spoke.[38] For such a readership, an education in sentiment, in the cultivation of sensibility, may well have been as welcome and seemed as essential to their improvement as lessons in the political theory of Locke and Paine. For the possession of sensibility – perhaps especially in the sense of the ability to feel for the sufferings of others – was understood in the late eighteenth century as a mark of social as well as emotional refinement.

This is how I understand the exotic pastoralism of the Hoxton mechanic with whose effusion on liberty this chapter began. Pastoral was not the highest genre of literature but it had long been regarded as the most refined, because only by the most exquisite refinement could the base matter of rural life at its lowliest be made acceptable to an aristocratic or polite taste. If to contribute to a periodical publication was in itself a mark of an aspiring lower-class intellectual, to write and to have published a sentimental pastoral was more so, and perhaps still more so by virtue of his tasteful choice of such exotic fruit, those peaches and nectarines, as emblems of the return of liberty. Something of the same seems to be true of the Kentucky poem: its author, the 'Emigrant', may be one of Eaton's self-taught readers, for though in its long satirical section the writing is crisp and forceful, its opening pastoral hymn to the 'modern Eden' that is Kentucky is written by someone who appears to have had little formal education and probably none in the principles of verse-composition. Here are the first lines:

> HAIL modern Eden! – hail thy blooming *sweets*!
> Thy promis'd savours, and thy fragrance, greets
> My ardent wishes to salute thy *plains*,
> And plant thy *mead[ow]s* with European grains,
> Hail happy spot! That yields thy *sweets profuse*,
> To *waste* in air, or rot in morning dews
> Un*cultivate*d – unenjoy'd by Man,
> Reserv'd for latter ages in th'Almighty's plan.
> No longer let thy fertile region *waste*
> Its fruit (spontaneous fitted for the *taste*),
> But let me now thy proffer'd *sweets* caress,
> Thy rich *profusion taste*, thy *meads* possess.
> May heav'n inspire a train of honest swains,
> To emigrate, and *cultivate* thy *plains*[.][39]

It may not be so much the errors of grammar and scansion that suggest that these lines are by a relatively uneducated poet, as the constant repetition of words, here italicized by me, from the specialized vocabulary of refined pastoral: as if the more often they are repeated the more indisputably pastoral and refined the lines become. It is perhaps appropriate that the opening phrase, 'blooming sweets', is probably derived from a passage of the poet Mark Akenside which was frequently anthologized under the title, 'The Pleasures arising from a Cultivated Imagination'.[40] The phrase is poetic for fragrant flowers, or rather flowery fragrances, but understandably enough the 'Emigrant' does not seem to know that, hence his desire to 'caress' the scents of Kentucky in line 11. Compared with the racy colloquialism of the satirical section of the poem, this pastoral introduction is almost painfully halting. But such writing may tell us as much about the aspirations of many artisan radicals as do the public addresses of the London Corresponding Society to the people and the nation.[41]

NOTES

1 *Politics for the People: or, A Salmagundy for Swine*, 2 vols. (London: D. I. Eaton, 1794–5), vol. 11, pp. 392–3.
2 *Ibid.*, p. 393.
3 *Ibid.*, pp. 393–4.
4 *Comus*, line 46; *Paradise Lost* IV, line 259; James Beattie, 'The Second Pastoral. Alexis', in *Original Poems and Translations* (London: A. Millar, 1760), p. 104; Henry Pye, 'The Parsonage Improved. A Poem', in his *Poems on Various Subjects*, 2 vols. (London: John Stockdale, 1787), vol. 1, p. 175.
5 *One Pennyworth of Pig's Meat; or, Lessons for the Swinish Multitude*, 3 vols. (London: Thomas Spence, 1793–5), vol. 11, pp. 124–8.
6 *Ibid.*, vol. 1, pp. 32–6.
7 Goldsmith, *The Deserted Village*, line 63. Line numbers are given subsequently in parentheses in the text.
8 See R. Dalton and S. H. Hamer, *The Provincial Token-Coinage of the Eighteenth Century* (London: B. A. Seaby, 1967), pp. 166, 170; and David Bindman, *The Shadow of the Guillotine: Britain and the French Revolution* (London: British Museum Publications, 1989), p. 199.
9 Rutt (1760–1841), probably the most prolific contributor of poetry to the *Cambridge Intelligencer*, had been at school in Northampton with its editor, Benjamin Flower. For much information about Rutt and the *Intelligencer* I am indebted to Tim Whelan.
10 *Politics for the People*, vol. 11, p. 416.
11 *The Philanthropist* (London: D. I. Eaton, 1795) 24 (7 September 1795), 2–4.
12 *Ibid.*, 4.

13 For accounts of the crimping riots of 1794 and 1795 see John Stevenson, 'The London "Crimp" Riots of 1794', *International Review of Social History* 16 (1971), 40–58; Stevenson, *Popular Disturbances in England 1700–1780* (London and New York: Longman, 1979), esp. Chapter 8; and John Barrell, *The Spirit of Despotism: Invasions of Privacy in the 1790s* (Oxford: Oxford University Press, 2006), pp. 42–7.

14 'Henry Martin Saunders', *The Crimps, or the Death of Poor Howe: A Tragedy in One Act* (London: D. I. Eaton, 1794), p. 10.

15 *Politics for the People*, vol. ii, p. 79.

16 *The Register of the Times*, 8 vols. (London: B. Crosby, 1794–5), vol. viii, p. 77.

17 *The Moral and Political Magazine of the London Corresponding Society*, 2 vols. (London: John Ashley, for the Society, 1796–7), vol. ii, p. 45.

18 *Pig's Meat*, vol. ii, pp. 141–3.

19 Charles Dibdin, *The Songs, Chorusses, Duets, &c. in The Waterman. Or, the First of August. And in the Interlude of Plutus and Wit* (No publication details [London?, 1774?]), pp. 8–9.

20 *The Philanthropist* 17 (20 July 1795), 7–8.

21 See for example the anonymous mezzotints illustrated in my *The Spirit of Despotism*, pp. 226–7, 234.

22 *Politics for the People*, vol. ii, pp. 232–7.

23 *Ibid.*, pp. 313–15.

24 Barrell, *The Spirit of Despotism*, pp. 210–46.

25 See for example *The Report of the Committee of Constitution, of the London Corresponding Society* ([London]: Thomas Spence, [1794]), p. 3; John Thelwall, *Political Lectures. Volume the first – Part the first: Containing the Lecture on Spies and Informers* (London: D. I. Eaton and John Smith, 1795), p. 61; *Moral and Political Magazine*, vol. i, pp. 219, 312; and Edward Iliff, *A Summary of the Duties of Citizenship! Written expressly for the Members of the London Corresponding Society* (London: Richard Lee, Eaton, George Riebau, John Smith, and J. Burks, 1795), p. 9; though according to Thomas Hardy, Secretary of the LCS 1792–4, Iliff named these booksellers as the publishers of his pamphlet without permission: see Mary Thale (ed.), *Selections from the Papers of the London Corresponding Society* (Cambridge: Cambridge University Press, 1983), p. 326n.9.

26 See for example Thelwall, *The Peripatetic*, ed. Judith Thompson (Detroit: Wayne State University Press, 2001), pp. 133–40.

27 Thomas Moss, 'The Beggar', in his *Poems on Several Occasions* (Wolverhampton: G. Smart, and London: Longman, Dodsley, 1769), p. 2; *Pig's Meat*, vol. iii, p. 198. The poem was usually anthologized as 'The Beggar's Petition'.

28 Moss, *Poems*, p. 3; *Pig's Meat*, vol. iii, p. 198. These changes are similar to those made by Wordsworth as the 'Salisbury Plain Poems' developed towards their final version as 'Guilt and Sorrow', except of course that while Spence radicalizes Moss's poem, Wordsworth revises his poem away from its original radicalism. Compare in particular the lines by Moss quoted here with stanza twenty-nine of 'Salisbury Plain', in Stephen Gill (ed.), *The Salisbury Plain*

Poems of William Wordsworth (Ithaca: Cornell University Press, and Hassocks: Harvester Press, 1975), p. 29, written in 1794 when Wordsworth was still 'Citizen' Wordsworth.

29 [William Roberts], *The Poor Man's Prayer. Addressed to the Earl of Chatham. An Elegy. By Simon Hodge, a Kentish Labourer* (London: T. Payne, 1766), p. 6; *Poems by Dr. Roberts of Eton College* (London: J. Wilkie, T. Payne, *et al.*, 1774), p. 121; *Pig's Meat*, vol. III, p. 260.

30 See Barrell, *The Spirit of Despotism*, pp. 46–7.

31 John Thelwall, 'A Patriot's Feeling; or the Call of Duty. On Quitting the Isle of Wight', in Thelwall, *The Tribune*, 3 vols. (London: D. I. Eaton *et al.*, 1795), vol. II, p. 298.

32 See note 26 above.

33 Thelwall, *The Tribune*, vol. II, pp. 298–9.

34 'F. A. C.', 'Lines Written by a Female Citizen', in Thelwall, *The Tribune*, vol. III, pp. 105–6.

35 'Lines on the Banishment of Mr. Thomas Muir. By a young Female Citizen', in *Moral and Political Magazine*, vol. II, pp. 47–8.

36 See Thelwall's *Poems written in Close Confinement in the Tower and Newgate, under a Charge of High Treason* (London: J. Ridgway, H. D. Symonds and D. I. Eaton, 1795).

37 Richard Lee, *On the Death of Mrs. Hardy, Wife of Mr. Thomas Hardy, of Piccadilly; Imprisoned in the Tower for High Treason* (London: J. Smith and J. Burks, 1794).

38 For a recent analysis of the LCS as a society concerned to encourage 'civility' in its members, see Michael Davis, 'The Mob Club? The London Corresponding Society and the Politics of Civility in the 1790s', in Michael Davis and Paul Pickering (eds.), *Unrespectable Radicals? Popular Politics in the Age of Reform* (Ashgate: Aldershot and Burlington, Vt.: Ashgate, 2008), pp. 21–40. Davis sees this concern as a response to loyalist representations of the society as a 'mob' (see especially p. 26), but this may be to make the aspirations of the members of the LCS too much a mere reaction to criticism and insult.

39 *The Philanthropist* 24 (7 September 1795), 2–3.

40 Mark Akenside, *The Pleasures of the Imagination* (London: R. Dodsley, 1744), Book 3, line 572.

41 My thanks to Greg Claeys, Harriet Guest, Nigel Leask, Jon Mee, and Tim Whelan for various kinds of help to me while I was writing this chapter.

CHAPTER 6

The 'sinking down' of Jacobinism and the rise of the counter-revolutionary man of letters

Kevin Gilmartin

The murder of Prime Minister Spencer Perceval by John Bellingham in the lobby of the House of Commons on the evening of 11 May 1812 shocked loyal subjects and reinforced a sense of crisis that followed directly upon the economic disruptions of the Napoleonic wars and months of newspaper reporting about Luddite riots and industrial protest in Nottingham, Yorkshire, and Lancashire.[1] For some, there was reassurance in the discovery that the assassination was the result of a personal grievance, unconnected with any wider radical conspiracy. However, both Robert Southey and Samuel Taylor Coleridge remained convinced that this violent event represented disturbing new evidence of the fragility of established government and the reckless energy of a new generation of radical leadership and organization. Of course, neither writer had to be urged on at this late date to hostility to radical reform: the years after the resumption of war with France in May 1803 provided them with ample occasion to reconsider the hazards of republican ambition and the virtues of British constitutional government. Yet the distressed conditions of 1812, and the particular circumstances under which reports of the assassination circulated back and forth through both their public and private lives, ensured that the alarming spirit of political resistance that seemed to erupt in violence in the lobby of the House of Commons would be cast in the distinctive form of conspiratorial popular resentment, which both men refused to recognize from their own past radical experience.

To be sure, the radical parliamentary reform movement that emerged in the early nineteenth century did involve new forms of argument and organization. E. P. Thompson has contrasted the 'English Jacobins' of the 1790s, committed to Paine and to open organization, with the 'pugnacious piecemeal' movement of the early nineteenth century, defined less by ideological principle than by a belligerent tone of opposition to corrupt government.[2] While the 'Gagging Acts' of 1795 and the later Combination Acts set enduring limits on public assembly and political criticism, radicals in the early nineteenth century found rhetorical and tactical ways around these restrictions. The circulation of William Cobbett's *Political Register* and other cheap radical weeklies became a feature of national organization, joining political leaders like Cobbett and Sir Francis Burdett with reading audiences through popular habits of shared reading and discussion in clubs, debating societies, taverns, and public houses.[3]

Periodical appeals to 'the people' and to opinion outside parliament helped reinforce democratic aspiration. Whether this indicated the emergence of a specifically working-class political consciousness has been the subject of controversy. Since Thompson's contention that the working class was 'present at its own making', others have suggested instead that radical protest in these years was more concerned with distinctions between the represented and unrepresented, or the productive and the unproductive, than with any economic division between labour and capital.[4] Yet whatever the development in class consciousness, it is clear that radicalism was being transformed in its social composition. As James Epstein has observed, post-war reform activism 'was decidedly more working-class in its composition than the movement of the 1790s had been, as radicalism's center of gravity shifted toward the manufacturing districts of the North'.[5] At the same time, identities further up the social scale were also subject to political pressure. Dror Wahrman has mapped a dialectical process by which radical and conservative claims upon 'public opinion' in the early nineteenth century shaped conceptions of the middle class, with advocates on both sides seeking to appropriate the middling ranks by eliminating political moderation. 'The social middle was now brought up and sought after by those who *denied* a political middle, precisely for this reason: whichever of the opposing political camps could demonstrate that the "middle class" was joining its ranks, would have thus proved itself to be speaking for "the people".' Ominous political events reinforced the sharpening of class language, and Wahrman points especially to the Peterloo Massacre of 1819 as a kind of watershed in the process by which the middle class was distinguished from the lower orders.[6]

There were good reasons then why those alarmed by the revival of radical protest in the early nineteenth century felt that it required some new estimation, hinging upon the 'popular' character of the movement, and upon a powerful but elusive relationship between the political consciousness of ordinary subjects and social practices of reading and public assembly. The response of the Lake School conservatives allows us to see how popular radical mobilization was made to seem evidence of political degeneration, with no real claim upon popular feeling. It also suggests how the forms of literary authority being imperfectly knit together by conservative intellectuals like Southey and Coleridge were compelled to shadow even as they repudiated the vulgar countenance of radical protest.

Remorse for Jacobin youth was certainly at work here, as Southey and Coleridge asserted their own increasingly resolute defence of established powers by reducing radical expression to a sub-political form of aggression. This was a case of innocence by dissociation, and it helped bring into focus the enduring Romantic image of the English Jacobin in the 1790s as a misguided but essentially well-meaning visionary. Yet whatever the distortions involved, there is no reason to doubt the profound shock that gripped both men upon first news of Perceval's assassination. 'I was turned numb, & then sick, & then into a convulsive state of weeping on the first Tidings just as if Perceval had been my near & personal Friend,' Coleridge wrote to Southey the following day. Deferring an announced series of lectures on drama at Willis's Rooms, he instead offered his journalistic services at the Fleet Street office of the *Courier*, a newspaper that was by now firmly ministerial, and through its proprietor T. G. Street actually in receipt of Treasury payments.[7] The resulting 14 May notice in the *Courier* opened with an expression of 'astonishment and horror at this atrocious assassination', and then set a reverential portrait of Perceval's virtues against Napoleon's sinister imperial designs. Yet even as Coleridge rose to a melodramatic vision of the 'glorified spirit' of the dead minister, 'already perhaps pleading before the Throne of his Maker for his murderer, and his slanderers', he pleaded against clemency for the 'incendiary publications' that supposedly urged on the fanatical deed. The notice closed with a warning that commemorative retrospection was inadequate to a revolutionary situation: 'For his memory the sound of mourning and regretful love suffices! But our country demands the voice of alarm and warning.'[8]

Writing in turn from Keswick to his friend the civil servant Grosvenor Bedford, Southey relayed Coleridge's shocking report about public rejoicing in a London public house upon news of the murder, and recalled his own similar bouts of weeping. The warning voice Coleridge invoked was already well established in Southey's prose. 'Did I not speak to you with ominous truth upon this subject in one of my last hasty letters?' he enquired of Bedford. 'This country is upon the brink of the most dreadful of all conceivable states – an insurrection of the poor against the rich.' This judgement was sufficiently harrowing that Southey felt obliged to disavow the fears of an 'aguish politician', appealing to his own recent contributions to the *Edinburgh Annual Register* and to an economic analysis of the social consequence of manufacturing that went back to his 1807 *Letters from England, by Don Manuel Espriella.* 'Things are in that state at this time that nothing but the army preserves us: it is the single plank between us and the red sea of an English Jacquerie, – a Bellum Servile.'[9]

The *Letters from England* had indeed marked an important stage in Southey's political development and, according to Wahrman, in the development of Britain's political languages of class. Recording the fictional Espriella's experiences in England in 1802 and 1803, the *Letters* were composed by Southey from 1803 to 1807, years that he and Coleridge both considered crucial for remedying the divisions of the 1790s and forging a national consensus in support of the war against Napoleon. Wahrman shows how, by casting impoverished industrial labourers in the role of a new insurrectionary lower class, Southey's account contributed to a 'taming' of the middle class. A class whose 'effective edge' had in the 1790s been 'directed upwards, against the ruling elite and the government, ... was now redirected downwards' against the insurrectionary poor: repositioned in this way, the middle class appeared now '*in defence of the present social and political order*'.[10] By insisting in his letter to Bedford that revolutionary desire did not result from 'grievous oppression', but was instead 'prepared by the inevitable tendency of the manufacturing system, and hastened on by the folly of a besotted faction' (*LRS*, p. 196), Southey outlined the themes that came to dominate his public writing over the course of the next two decades.

It is worth considering how an alarmist response to the death of Perceval unfolded within a private correspondence calculated to extend outward through print expression and public authority. It was precisely to mobilize the pen of Southey as journalist and as correspondent with men in power that Coleridge first related his harrowing descent into 'the Tap room of a large Public House' (*CL*, vol. III, p. 410) near his rooms off Oxford Street, where the murder of the Prime Minister was felt to be welcome news. In comparing William Wordsworth's similarly shocked but more distanced response to the assassination, the biographer Richard Holmes has assigned Coleridge's underworld experience to a concerted reportorial interest in a still unfolding public tragedy: 'Coleridge, all of his journalistic instincts aroused, hurried out to the streets to see for himself.'[11] Southey interestingly anticipated this impression when he relayed to Bedford what his friend had 'heard in a pot-house into which he went on the night of the murder, not more to quench his thirst than for the purpose of hearing what the populace would say' (*LRS*, p. 196).

Yet in his letter, Coleridge suggests that his presence in the public house was in fact a matter of thirst, occasioned by the rigours of a pedestrian journey to the *Courier* offices. At the same time, he certainly framed the import of the experience in terms of his alarm over popular unrest. A usual Coleridgean ambiguity about matters of intention was perhaps compounded here by the fact that the death of Perceval coincided with his imperfect reconciliation with William Wordsworth, after a break in their friendship over Wordsworth's supposed disparagement of his personal habits, including reports that the poet had accused him 'of running into debt at little Pot-houses for Gin'.[12]

In this case personal and public anxieties were not far apart. The more sharply class-inflected sense of political division that radical protest was opening up for many elite observers was manifestly expressed in a shifting social geography of drink. Iain McCalman has shown how older eighteenth-century institutional arrangements for public drinking – alehouses for the common people, and taverns and inns for prosperous patrons – were rapidly transformed in the Romantic period by commercial as well as social and political pressures. Loyalist movements targeted metropolitan alehouses in particular as sites of seditious reading and communication, while evangelically inspired moral reformers attacked alehouse intemperance along with gaming, brawling, impiety, and sexual licence. A more intensively capitalized brewing industry assisted market fragmentation as well as the trend towards respectability, with some in the middle class withdrawing in favour of domestic entertainment. Taverns and alehouses evolved into the internally demarcated public houses of the nineteenth century, with saloon bars for genteel drinking and separate taprooms for the working orders.[13] Of course this spatial reordering was an uneven development, and terminology remained variable. Where Coleridge situated his experience in 'the Tap room of a large Public House', Southey wrote more pejoratively of a 'pot-house', and both men continued to some extent to write loosely about taprooms, pothouses, alehouses, and taverns as sites for subversive popular assembly.[14] In any case, the more telling *negative* point about the episode and its fallout has less to do with Coleridge's reluctance to enter such a place than with the hostile construction of the political public house as an irredeemably vulgar and subversive social space – a repository for political energies that had to be disavowed because they could not be rehabilitated or excused. The thesis about a 'sinking down of Jacobinism' that I am exploring in this chapter was presented by the parties involved as an observation about the historical development of political opinion since the 1790s, and in this sense it had some sociological truth, given the increasingly working-class character of the radical reform movement. Yet such a thesis is no less revealing as a synchronic register of the way elite anxieties about radical protest in the early nineteenth century led to a concerted reworking of popular cultural space in order to demarcate and contain the threat of subversion.

While by no means elaborately circumstantial, the relation of the tap-room experience to Southey stands out in the correspondence of a writer increasingly committed to advancing ideas and principles over matters of fact:

On my return from the Courier, where I had been to offer my services if I could do any thing for them on this occasion, I was faint from the Heat & much Walking – & took that opportunity of going into the Tap room of a large Public House frequented about 1 o/clock by the lower Orders – . It was really shocking – Nothing but exultation – Burdett's Health drank with a Clatter of Pots – & a Sentiment given to at least 50 men & women – May Burdett soon be the man to have Sway over us! – These were the very words. 'This is the beginning' – 'more of these damned Scoundrels must go the same way – & then poor people may live' – 'Every man might maintain his family decent & comfortable if the money were not picked out of our pockets by them damned Placemen' – 'God is above the Devil, *I* say – & down to Hell with Him & all his Brood, the Minister Men & Parliament Fellows' – 'They won't hear Burdett – No! he is a Christian Man & speaks for the Poor' – &c &c – I do not think, I have altered a word. – (*CL*, vol. III, p. 410)

The impressionistic relation of 'the very words' is meant to disclose raw evidence of disaffection, and in this sense there is something of the spy about Coleridge's reportage. Yet the fragmenting of conversation moves in two directions at once. On the one hand, political expression is dis-solved, chiming only with the meaningless 'Clatter of Pots', so as to deny the possibility of dialogue or deliberation within the plebeian domain of a large public house. By contrast, Coleridge was himself involved in deli-berate political exchange with Southey and a radiating network of further correspondents and readers, and there was appropriative violence in his refashioning of the shards of verbal protest as evidence of sedition.

On the other hand, reducing plebeian communication to fitful out-bursts of resentment conceals even as it discloses a crucial form of poli-tical transmission. Coleridge framed the episode with an appeal to Southey to take up the case against sunken Jacobinism, and with a sense of outrage at the way plebeian audiences were passively incorporating the arguments of a new generation of radical leaders:

I write now to urge you, if it be in your power, to give one day or two of your time to write something in your impressive way, on that theme which no one, I meet, seem[s] to feel as they ought to do – and of which I [find] scarcely any, but ourselves, that estimate according to its true gigantic magnitude – I mean, the sinking down of Jacobinism below the middle & tolerably educated Classes into the Readers & all-swallowing Auditors in Tap-rooms &c, of the Statesman, Examiner, Cobbet, &c – I have ascertained that throughout the great manufacturing Counties Whitbread's, Burdett's, & Waithman's Speeches, and the leading Articles of the Statesman & the Examiner, are printed in Ballad Form, & sold at a halfpenny & a Penny each – (*CL*, vol. iii, p. 410)

A faithful rendering of the experience lay in disintegrated utterances because these betrayed the transmitted idioms of radical journalists and orators: 'them damned Placemen', 'Minister Men & Parliament Fellows', 'They won't hear Burdett'. Here, Coleridge certainly distorts popular radical culture. To reconstruct events differently, we need only consider James Epstein's brilliant account of the symbolically complex role of dining and toasting in early nineteenth-century radical reassertions of the 'right to move within public space'.[15]

   Yet such a critique should acknowledge how closely Coleridge's representational strategy was calculated to deny what might otherwise have been witnessed, the subversive process by which informal and decentralized habits of tavern sociability became vectors for efficient political communication across a whole range of critical differences the reform movement had to bridge: between orality and literacy, between gentlemen radical leaders and popular audiences, between metropolitan centres and provincial or rural peripheries, between the experience of economic dispossession and the claim upon political representation. Coleridge's condescending reportage reduces a credible bid for political representation into a delegitimating case of the poor having learned to let other sinister leaders speak on their behalf. In this sense, his taproom remained an ambiguous representational space, at once contained and uncontainable. Stumbled upon accidentally, it narrowly enclosed within its walls the seditious opinions it disclosed, even as it scandalously opened out upon the 'great manufacturing Counties' of the north and wider networks of popular radical expression and association.

   Whether an acknowledgement of Coleridge's own thirst hinted perversely at a connection between the spy and the spied upon is far from clear. But argument was certainly sustained in the way the same physical need that brought the reporter to the taproom was made to account for both the higher cognitive and lower bodily functions of ordinary patrons. It was as 'all-swallowing Auditors' of secondhand press slogans that disaffected labourers became taproom politicians. The intentional structure of this 'shocking' encounter lies not so much in the dash and ampersand that ambiguously connect Coleridge's departure from the *Courier* office with his arrival in the taproom, but rather in the framing sequence of transmissions by which a faithful verbal record of alarming developments in popular sentiment, themselves derived from the radical press, get picked up and directed back through a countervailing network (Southey, Bedford, the *Courier*, the *Quarterly Review*) for securing established powers. While Southey sometimes bristled under Coleridge's hand, in this case the instigation to write was evident in his later work for the *Quarterly*, and more immediately in his letter to Bedford, which proposed a revival of loyalist associations and a system of honours to secure troop loyalty, and urged as well the further transmission of the letter's contents to such well-connected men as William Gifford and John Charles Herries.

The epistolary appeal from the public house to Southey's pen revealed the way in which loyalist transmission mirrored its shadowy radical antitypes. After all, if Coleridge's praise for Southey as Britain's leading 'popular essayist' was partly condescending, what made him appropriate for this occasion was precisely the capacity to reach and move loyal readers in something like the way Cobbett moved radical readers.[16] Antithesis was reinforced and complicated by a sense of shared radical past. Presumably, 'scarcely any, but ourselves' could appreciate 'the sinking down of Jacobinism' because others had not personally experienced the different nature of Jacobinism in the 1790s. As a way of framing a vividly recent encounter, this retrospective gesture was at once alarmist and ironic, since it transected the present tension between plebeian radical celebration and elite loyalist alarm with a historical narrative of social degeneration running from the 1790s down through to 1812. Of course one of the ironies about Coleridge's effort to dispossess ordinary subjects of their radical opinions, and to distinguish elite Jacobinism from its present sunken condition, was that the case for vulgarization was – far more than Coleridge was prepared to allow – a recapitulation of earlier political contests, most notoriously in the endless reworking of Burke's 'swinish multitude'.[17]

In the two decades after Perceval's assassination Southey took up the case for Jacobin degeneration, notably in December 1812 in the most ambitious and programmatic of his early *Quarterly Review* essays.

Nominally a review of Patrick Colquhoun's *Treatise on Indigence* (1806), the essay was meant, as Southey explained in a letter to his brother Henry, to alert complacent authorities to the threat of insurrection. 'To-morrow I go, tooth and nail, to the *Quarterly*, for the purpose, if possible, of making our men in power see the imminent danger in which our throats are at this moment from the Luddites' (*LRS*, p. 202). Even by his own uncompromising standards this was an alarmist piece of writing, haunted by the violent death of the Prime Minister and by news of agricultural distress and Luddite rioting. Its implicit criticism of government inaction led Gifford to moderate the tone by cutting key passages, including a paragraph that closed sensationally upon a precise verbal echo of Southey's warning in the letter to Bedford about 'a *Jacquerie*, a *bellum servile*'.[18] The passage was not restored until the essay was reprinted, under the title 'On the State of the Poor', in the two-volume collection of 1832, *Essays, Moral and Political*. By then Southey was aware, as indeed he was when he set about 'tooth and nail' in June 1812, that Perceval's assassination was the work of a deranged individual. But he took little comfort from this knowledge, and still less did he consider it a diminishment of the insurrectionary threat. On the contrary, he maintained that Coleridge's experience evinced a revolutionary situation regardless of Bellingham's condition. In the sense that his argument concerned language and imagination rather than the violence as such, it recalled the legal principle of constructive treason, according to which it was a crime to 'compass or imagine' the death of the king.[19] A political assassination had according to Southey taken place *in effect*, and *after the fact*, when 'the pot-house politicians of London who have for years past been sucking in the venom and virulence of the demagogue journalists with their daily potations' took it upon themselves to welcome the death of the Prime Minister. 'They ratified the murder; they made it their own act and deed, and even contracted in it a degree of guilt which did not attach to the perpetrator' (*EMP*, vol. 1, p. 137). This inflammatory logic restored the initial sense of crisis by converting a misguided act of personal retribution back into seditious conspiracy.

Although Gifford let stand the argument for political responsibility 'contracted' after the fact, he obscured the rationale by omitting a previous passage that alluded directly to Coleridge's taproom experience:

Before it had been suspected, or could possibly be known, that the assassin was in a state of mind which rendered him as much an object of compassion as of horror, he became the favourite of the mob, as if he had been their friend, their champion, their self-devoted hero and deliverer. Attempts were made to rescue him, as he was conveyed to prison, by the chance rabble collected on the way;

and at those public-houses which are frequented by the lower orders about town, scenes were witnessed not to be remembered without shuddering. Healths were drunk, accompanied with ferocious exultation for what had been done, and more ferocious anticipation of what, it was hoped, was soon to follow. The imagination of a dramatist could conceive no fitter prelude to the most dreadful tragedy of popular madness. (*EMP*, vol. 1, p. 137)

In Coleridge's letter, the series of intentions that conducted the writer from his planned lectures on drama to the *Courier* office and then the public house gave way, under the shock of popular exultation, to a more fragmentary impressionism. By contrast, Southey's case for constructive assassination sustained a terrifying narrative sequence. A 'ferocious exult-ation for what had been done' was joined with a still more 'ferocious anticipation of what, it was hoped, was soon to follow', through all the familiar gothic machinery of assassination and mob violence, villainy and heroism, imprisonment and deliverance, compassion and horror. This sensationalism remained a hallmark of his prose in the decades to come, and he revisited taverns and factories as plebeian 'scenes' of a terrible revolutionary energy. Like the 'dramatist' whose imagination was imagined here, his own counter-revolutionary imagination was well served by social spaces that were at once contained and uncontainable, the reservoir for 'ferocious' popular expectations on the verge of exploding into violence.

The case for constructive assassination reinforced prophetic authorial claims first intimated in the letter to Bedford, as Southey's essay recom-mended the 'foresight' of two paragraphs from his pseudonymous 1807 *Letters from England* on the relation between manufacturing and social disorder (*EMP*, vol. 1, pp. 117–18). The assassin Bellingham became the instrumental hinge in an extraordinary sequence by which Southey-Espriella anticipated an event that the radicalized London populace then contracted as political conspiracy after the fact. Where Bellingham became the instrument of darker political forces because of his insanity, Southey came to argue with increasing tenacity that the populace was instrumentalized by factory labour, in ways that reinforced many of Coleridge's assumptions about what happened in the radicalized public house. Adam Smith's *Wealth of Nations* made man 'a manufacturing animal', denied the capacity for virtue or reflection, and reduced to 'the gain which can be extracted from him, the *quantum of lucration* of which he can be made the instrument' (*EMP*, vol. 1, pp. 111–12). What political economists and factory owners emptied, radical journalists and orators filled. In the complex narrative of constructive sedition, political agency finally seemed to lie with the seditious demagogues who cynically exploited the discontent of the industrial labourer – and left Southey the periodical prophet of insurrection to shadow their instigation.

This line of argument converged on the public house, now paired with the factory as scene of subversive transmission: 'these are the topics which are received in the pot-house, and discussed over the loom and the lathe' (*EMP*, vol. 1, p. 121). And it required Coleridge's principle of Jacobin degeneration:

If at any former time the mob were inflamed with sedition, they were a headless multitude, bound together only by the momentary union of blind passion; they are now an organized association, with their sections, their secret committees, and their treasury. These are fearful circumstances, even if temporary distress were the only cause of the existing spirit of insubordination. But in addition to this, there is to be taken into the account of danger the alarming fact, which few have noticed, and of the importance of which fewer still are aware, that Jacobinism, having almost totally disappeared from the educated classes, has sunk down into the mob; so that, since the year 1793, our internal state has in this respect undergone as great a change as our foreign relations, and a far more perilous one. (*EMP*, vol. 1, pp. 125–6)

Though he explicitly disavowed Barruel and the conspiracy theories of the 1790s, Southey supported his case for revolutionary crisis with a sketch of the co-ordinated effect of four typical writers. Though 'utterly unconnected' with one another, and actuated by a range of motives (faction, malevolence, poverty, and ill-humour), they managed to 'co-operate as effectually together to one direct end as if they were bound by oaths and sacraments, and that end is as directly the overthrow of their country as if all four were the salaried instruments of France' (*EMP*, vol. 1, pp. 119–20). It was this effort to convey the very real threat of revolution 'as if' that returned Southey's counter-revolutionary imagination to the public house as scene for assembly by proxy in a conspiracy whose principal members need never have met together.

If a political theory of 'the sinking down of Jacobinism' was more reminiscent of earlier attitudes about radical vulgarity than either Coleridge or Southey acknowledged, the same can be said of the identification of taverns and public houses as vectors for radical transmission. This association went back to the political upheavals of the seventeenth century, and intensified again in the period of the American and French Revolutions.[20] No less an authority on the first wave of anti-Jacobinism than John Reeves's *Association for Preserving Liberty and Property against Republicans and Levellers* had set its sights on radical assembly in public houses, even as its own London committee met at and reported from the Crown and Anchor Tavern. A resolution of 4 December 1792 on the 'great mischief ... effected in this country by the circulation of Newspapers filled with *disloyalty and sedition*' urged 'all good Subjects', but particularly 'Keepers of Inns, Taverns, or Coffee-houses', to 'discontinue and discourage the use and circulation of all such disloyal and seditious Newspapers'.[21] Loyalist innkeepers agreed to ban Jacobins from their premises, and warning notices appeared on taverns and public houses.[22] Justices of the Peace were alert to the threat, and their efforts to combat it raised many of the same issues later pursued by Southey and Coleridge: tavern transmission of print, the vulnerability of the ignorant and the poor, the organization of radical protest in clubs and societies, and the eruption of discontent in fitful acts of violence.[23]

Yet it is clear too that Southey and Coleridge responded to emerging differences in popular radical culture, in ways that were consistent with shifting attitudes among elites. Historians of British radicalism have traced the way an increasingly plebeian radical movement was shaped reciprocally by the tendency for polite society to retreat from the unruly public spaces of the tavern and coffee house to the private home.[24] For Southey and Coleridge in 1812, the political public house was a more alien and uniformly dangerous place than it had been for Reeves and his fellow Crown and Anchor associates in 1793. Peter Burke has advanced a thesis about 'the withdrawal of the upper classes' to describe how throughout Europe a popular culture that had in 1500 been 'everyone's culture' came by around 1800 to be abandoned by elites and to belong more exclusively 'to the lower classes'.[25] Of course Burke describes a series of intermittent developments, without any one decisive break. What Southey and Coleridge underscore is the way plebeian radical protest in Britain conditioned elite perceptions about popular culture, so that politicized domains of ordinary recreation came to seem irretrievably corrupted. 'For the labouring man,' Southey wrote in 1818, 'the ale-house is now a place of pure unmingled evil' (*EMP*, vol. 11, p. 120).

By contrast, the loyalist pamphleteering of the 1790s tended not to consider the plebeian tavern beyond reclamation. William Jones's broadsheet series of 'John Bull' letters, brought out in 1792 and 1793 under loyalist Association auspices, was typical in this regard. In one tract, Thomas Bull recalled an itinerant subversive who 'thrust himself in amongst us at a Public house', talking 'at a high Rate about French Liberty'. He is readily talked down, and his packet of '*Tom Pain's* Books' would have been burned if he had been foolish enough to produce them.[26] In another, the French sympathizer Dick Spendall is similarly given 'a good dressing' by

John Bull and an 'honest ploughman'. The two loyalists then retire with their neighbours to a local tavern where they 'got a Pot of Beer, sung God save the King! and drank God bless him! and a health to the Constitution of Good Old *England*'.[27] The proposition in these pseudo-popular tracts that radical discourse was an alien French intrusion reinforced a sense that indigenous popular spaces were not hopelessly compromised from within. Indeed, convivial assembly and popular song in the public house help inoculate contented subjects from ideological contagion. My point here is not to deny that the world of John and Thomas Bull was a grotesque fantasy, but to suggest that the fantasy remained credible among elites anxious to soothe popular discontent. The public house had not yet become Southey's 'place of pure unmingled evil'.

Hannah More's evangelical publications provide a distinct but equally revealing point of comparison. More was certainly aware of the dangers of the radical public house, and as early as *Village Politics* (1793) she addressed the danger that the Paineite Tim Standish posed to a club of working men at the Rose and Crown Tavern. Yet while the later Cheap Repository tracts (1795–8) remained alert to this supposedly new and alien challenge, they were at the same time calculated to combat the long-standing and indigenous threat to popular subordination posed by unruly popular culture.[28] Again and again, taverns and alehouses such as Checquers in *The Cottage Cook* and the Black Bear and Red Lion in *The History of Tom White* conveyed the dangers of drunkenness, lost wages, card-playing, gambling, fighting, swearing, impiety, and loose company.[29] Yet even as More heightened the evils of tavern life she did not abandon its victims, but rather sought to narrate the process by which they could be reclaimed through a moral reform movement that sustained close custodial relations between the subordinate poor and the activist middle class. Tom White begins his narrative life as a young coachman who falls from virtuous habits into tavern vice and impiety, but he winds up becoming the wealthy Farmer White who joins his wife and the local vicar in managing and directing the neighbourhood poor. Throughout the tale, he actively participates in his own moral and spiritual regeneration, and follows his creator Hannah More in replacing the popular recreations that nearly destroyed him with invented pious habits of Saturday reading and community psalm-singing.

Neither Southey nor Coleridge stooped to the kind of 'vulgar conservative' expression advanced by the Cheap Repository and the loyalist Association.[30] Southey had his chance in late 1816 when he was invited to London by the Liverpool administration to take on a new periodical in support of the government, but he wound up declining the overture.[31] Coleridge went so far as to announce that the two Lay Sermons of 1816 and 1817, addressing 'the higher classes' and 'the higher and middle classes', would be supplemented by a third Lay Sermon to 'the Lower and Labouring Classes of Society'. But this final volume made no appearance beyond an advertisement on the back wrapper of *The Statesman's Manual*.[32] Epstein has suggested an intriguing analogy between the code of the duel and tavern 'challenges and counter-challenges to drink particular toasts or to stand by one's words and allegiances'.[33] In declining whatever such challenge may have lurked in the taproom on the day of Perceval's murder, Coleridge betrayed his constitutional conviction that 'the lower Orders' did not possess political convictions meriting representation and address.

The response Coleridge seems to have preferred – listen and learn, correspond and converse with like-minded friends, but leave intervention to other authorities – is reminiscent not so much of Reeves and More as of the anti-Jacobin fiction that flourished in the decade between the repressive legislation of the late 1790s and the revival of radical fortunes from around 1808. I have written elsewhere about the way Thomas Harrall's 1805 novel *Scenes of Life*, in narrating a more riotous and satirical version of Coleridge's underworld excursion, extricated its hero Sir Frederic Stanley from a radical debating society of the 1790s so he could develop a critical perspective on Jacobinism within the framework of domestic conversation.[34] The novel anticipated Coleridge's theory of Jacobin sinking by justifying this logic of withdrawal with a historical sketch of the 'dreadfully degenerated' condition of eighteenth-century urban civic culture.[35] Though Southey and Coleridge did not follow anti-Jacobin narrative romance in assigning elite and middle-class critical faculties to the home, they agreed with the underlying principle that civic enterprise was inadequate to the threat of revolution. Southey's initial call in his letter to Bedford for revived loyalist association was later submerged in his demand for state initiative in both popular education and legal repression. Coleridge's theory of the clerisy can be understood as an attempt to suppress the forms of education and acculturation that had taken shape within the deformalized framework of the political public sphere over the course of the eighteenth century, and return them instead to the more closely managed framework of a parish clergy supplemented by national schools.

In picking up Coleridge's taproom report and developing it in the *Quarterly* alongside a critique of manufacturing, Southey highlighted the formative challenge that a new generation of 'pot-house politicians' presented for a new generation of counter-revolutionary public writers. To begin with, he rejected the extrinsic claim that 'the anarchist writers are in the pay of France' (*EMP*, vol. 1, p. 131). The radical public house was a vector for indigenous political forces – Sir Francis Burdett and Henry Hunt, the *Political Register* and the *Examiner*. Yet the resistance of these indigenous forces to internal tavern correction was the fault of a manufacturing system which had ravaged the embedded popular culture that Hannah More wanted to correct, and that Southey was more willing to idealize in its pre-industrial form. The rural peasantry represented for him habits of piety, deference, and contentment that had been obliterated among a rapidly expanding urban proletariat. 'On the State of the Poor' presented a rustic idyll of 'the natural and softening impressions' of religion in the village world of the 'peasant', so that it could then sketch the horrifying process by which these natural virtues tended to 'wither away' under industrial conditions that gathered men together 'in herds from distant parts': 'The town manufacturer is removed from all these gentle and genial influences; he has no love for his birth-place or his dwelling-place, and cares nothing for the soil in which he strikes no root. One source of patriotism is thus destroyed; for, in the multitude, patriotism grows out of local attachments' (*EMP*, vol. 1, pp. 112–13). If this echoes Burke's conception of the 'little platoon we belong to in society' as the first link in a series of patriotic affections, what was distinctive in Southey was the extent to which industrial labour subverted natural loyalty.[36] There is evidence too of widening class differences in Southey's suggestion that only 'the multitude' properly derived their patriotism from 'local attachments'.

As a site for the conservative imagination of radical sociability, then, the pothouse was both vulgarized and mechanized: it became a place for those who had no place and no sense of personal belonging, and whose affiliations and connections were wholly formed for them by the radical press. Where Hannah More promulgated competing forms of acculturation, Southey witnessed a terrifying void. In this sense, new industrial debasement reinforced old popular dissipation. 'It is notorious that the manners of the people in manufacturing districts are peculiarly dissolute. Saint Monday is the only saint in the journeyman's kalendar; and there are many places where one of the working days of the week is regularly set apart for drunkenness, like a Sabbath of irreligion' (*EMP*, vol. 1, p. 117). And because human social terms no longer seemed to apply, the figure of the worker was bestialized in Southey's prose, becoming a 'manufacturing animal' gathered together in 'herds'. There was a direct challenge here to radical discourse, where the rise of public opinion was expressed through portentous print representations of the emerging collective human body of the people. And there was a sense too that evangelical strategies of charitable remediation were inadequate, as Southey's proposals for national education under church auspices indicated the enhanced role of the State in his social vision.[37]

Coleridge continued to explore the political consequences of Jacobin degeneration in his own later public writing. Two years after the Perceval obituary, in the autumn and winter of 1814, the *Courier* published his series of six letters 'To Mr. Justice Fletcher', occasioned by what he considered the insufficiently alarmist terms in which Judge William Fletcher had challenged inflammatory newspaper reports about conspiracy and unrest in Wexford. Although the letters responded to events in Ireland, they contained what Coleridge later termed 'no exaggerated picture of the predominance of Jacobinism' in England as well (*CL*, vol. IV, p. 565). From the outset, such a picture was disturbingly obscure. The sheer versatility of subversion seemed to resist literary representation as well as political containment: 'Many and strangely various are the shapes which the spirit of Jacobinism can assume' (*EOT*, vol. II, p. 383). It was from this terrifying impression, meant in part to account for the ability of a Wexford Justice to overlook a threat just outside his door, that Coleridge worked towards his own version of Southey's theory of seditious organization without conspiratorial design.

If subversion assumed clearer proportions over the course of the Fletcher letters, the imperfect trend towards embodiment followed less from individual or collective calculation than from the very principle of dispersed association. What alarmed Coleridge was 'the passion and contagion of club government', fermenting through 'the great mass of the people', and advanced by a sinister radical leadership:

I cannot regard, without apprehension, the present numberless societies and combinations of the mechanics and lower craftsmen of every description, interlapidated and cemented as they all are, each in the club of his own trade: and all these several clubs forming, as they actually do form, so many contiguous vaults and magazines of one immense fortress, moated and *law-proof*; all the parts of which mutually support and command each other, and all communicating by well contrived passages and galleries, with one common and central chamber, the close Divan of their elective Commanders in Chief. (*EOT*, vol. II, p. 392)[38]

Fifteen years after declaring Jacobinism not dead but in a 'state of suspended animation' (*EOT*, vol. 1, p. 86), Coleridge observed its reanimation in this sublime architecture of a degenerate eighteenth-century associational world.[39] And the 'huge and living fabric' of the radical reform movement was not merely Jacobinism revived, but 'the most formidable, the most intensely *jacobinical* phaenomenon that has ever appeared in Great Britain' (*EOT*, vol. 11, pp. 392–3), outstripping the United Irishmen or the London Corresponding Society of the 1790s. Ironically, the unity in diversity that Coleridge observed was directly conditioned by the terms of repressive legislation. As Iain McCalman has shown, by outlawing large public meetings and requiring licences for lecture halls, the Seditious Meeting Act of 1795 had proven effective against substantial forums for radical debate, but it left smaller clubs and informal public house assemblies beyond the scope of control.[40]

What Southey and Coleridge discovered in the radicalized taverns and taprooms of the early nineteenth century was a form of political aspiration that seemed to fall so far beyond the boundaries of the political nation that it could not be rehabilitated or reformed. In treating popular assembly and conversation as hopelessly compromised by sedition and debased by manufacturing, they contributed to the political dimensions of a wider process by which elites and the middle classes increasingly distanced themselves from the spaces and habits of popular culture. At the same time, in choosing to stigmatize radical reform by identifying it with Jacobin subversion, they raised associations that involved their own earlier political identity and experience. If these associations served finally to reinforce rather than mitigate their attack on radical reform, this was partly because the networks of personal correspondence and public expression they were knitting together on behalf of established powers were so closely, if negatively, aligned with the radical networks they were determined to combat. In Coleridge's clerisy, and in Southey's related alignments with established institutions, we witness an effort to escape the antinomies of the 1790s and construct a permanent foundation for stabilizing forms of public writing. This was itself a complicated gesture: to reject some of the merely crisis-oriented loyalist interventions of the 1790s was to bid for the enduring role of the conservative public intellectual, and also to recognize that subversion had become an intractable problem.[41] In this sense, the early nineteenth-century rise of the conservative public writer required as its antithetical premise not only the sinking down of the Jacobinism of the 1790s, but also the corresponding rise of more enduring forms of popular political protest.

NOTES

1 For the assassination and public alarm, see Denis Gray, *Spencer Perceval: The Evangelical Prime Minister, 1762–1812* (Manchester: Manchester University Press, 1963), pp. 455–60. For a study of the assassination and trial in relation to the law and insanity, see Kathleen S. Goddard, 'A Case of Injustice? The Trial of John Bellingham', *American Journal of Legal History* 46 (2004), 1–25.

2 E. P. Thompson, *The Making of the English Working Class* (New York: Vintage Books, 1966), pp. 459, 466.

3 I have discussed the organizational role of the press in *Print Politics: The Press and Radical Opposition in Early Nineteenth-Century England* (Cambridge: Cambridge University Press, 1996), pp. 65–113.

4 Thompson, *Making of the English Working Class*, p. 15. For one influential revision of class-based conceptions, see Gareth Stedman Jones, *Languages of Class: Studies in English Working Class History, 1832–1982* (Cambridge: Cambridge University Press, 1983), pp. 104–7.

5 James A. Epstein, *Radical Expression: Political Language, Ritual, and Symbol in England, 1790–1850* (Oxford and New York: Oxford University Press, 1994), pp. 151–2.

6 Dror Wahrman, *Imagining the Middle Class: The Political Representation of Class in Britain, c. 1780–1840* (Cambridge: Cambridge University Press, 1995), pp. 190, 196, 200–1.

7 Samuel Taylor Coleridge, *Collected Letters of Samuel Taylor Coleridge*, ed. Earl Leslie Griggs, 6 vols. (Oxford: Clarendon Press, 1956–71), vol. III, pp. 409–10. Further references to this edition will be included in the text, with the abbreviation *CL*. For Coleridge and the politics of the *Courier*, see *Essays on His Times*, ed. David V. Erdman, 3 vols. (Princeton, N.J.: Princeton University Press, and London: Routledge and Kegan Paul, 1978), especially vol. 1: pp. cxxx–cxxiv, cxli–cxliii, cxlviii–clvi.

8 Coleridge, *Essays on His Times*, ed. Erdman, vol. 11, pp. 347–9. Further references to this edition will be included in the text, with the abbreviation *EOT*.

9 Robert Southey, *Letters of Robert Southey*, ed. Maurice H. Fitzgerald (London: Henry Frowde, 1912), p. 196. Further references to this edition will be included in the text, with the abbreviation *LRS*.

10 Wahrman, *Imagining the Middle Class*, pp. 169–71.

11 Richard Holmes, *Coleridge: Darker Reflections, 1804–1834* (New York: Pantheon Books, 1998), p. 308.

12 Quoted in Holmes, *Coleridge: Darker Reflections*, p. 214. For the quarrel and reconciliation, see Coleridge, *Collected Letters*, vol. III, pp. 296–7, 403–7, and Holmes, *Coleridge: Darker Reflections*, pp. 211–15, 291–2, 298–307.

13 *An Oxford Companion to the Romantic Age: British Culture, 1776–1832*, ed. Iain McCalman *et al.* (Oxford: Oxford University Press, 1999), s.v. 'taverns and alehouses'. For the internal architecture of the public house, see Paul Jennings, *The Public House in Bradford, 1770–1970* (Keele: Keele University Press, 1995), pp. 25–37, 119–21.

14 For developments in terminology, see Jennings, *Public House*, p. 19.

15 Epstein, *Radical Expression*, p. 151.

16 Samuel Taylor Coleridge, *Biographia Literaria*, ed. James Engell and W. Jackson Bate, 2 vols. (Princeton, N. J.: Princeton University Press, 1983), vol. 1, p. 63.

17 For a history of the phrase, see Don Herzog, *Poisoning the Minds of the Lower Orders* (Princeton: Princeton University Press, 1998), pp. 505–45.

18 Southey, *Essays, Moral and Political*, 2 vols. (London: John Murray, 1832), vol. 1, p. 138. Further references to this edition will be included in the text, with the abbreviation *EMP*.

19 For the role of this principle in the 1790s, see John Barrell, *Imagining the King's Death: Figurative Treason, Fantasies of Regicide, 1793–1796* (Oxford: Oxford University Press, 2000).

20 For the seventeenth century, see Peter Clark, 'The Alehouse and Alternative Society', in Donald Pennington and Keith Thomas (eds.), *Puritans and Revolutionaries* (Oxford: Clarendon Press, 1978), pp. 47–72, and for the period of the American Revolution, see Iain McCalman, *Radical Underworld: Prophets, Revolutionaries and Pornographers in London, 1795–1840* (Oxford: Clarendon Press, 1993), p. 113, and John Money, 'Taverns, Coffee Houses and Clubs: Local Politics and Popular Articulacy in the Birmingham Area, in the Age of the American Revolution', *Historical Journal* 14 (1971), 15–47.

21 Association for Preserving Liberty and Property against Republicans and Levellers, *Association Papers* (London, 1793), Part I: *Proceedings of the Association*, No. 1:12.

22 See Epstein, *Radical Expression*, pp. 150–1, and Peter Clark, *The English Alehouse: A Social History, 1200–1830* (New York: Longman, 1983), pp. 324–5.

23 See for example the *Notice to the Inn-Holders and Ale-House-Keepers in the Hundred of Mutford and Lothingland in the said County of Suffolk*, not paginated. British Library shelfmark 648.c.26.(11).

24 See James Epstein, ' "Equality and No King": Sociability and Sedition: The Case of John Frost', in Gillian Russell and Clara Tuite (eds.), *Romantic Sociability: Social Networks and Literary Culture in Britain, 1770–1840* (Cambridge: Cambridge University Press, 2002), pp. 56–8.

25 Peter Burke, *Popular Culture in Early Modern Europe*, rev. edn (Aldershot: Scolar Press, 1994), p. 270.

26 [William Jones], *One Penny-worth More, or, A Second Letter from Thomas Bull to His Brother John* (London, 1792).

27 [William Jones], *John Bull in Answer to His Brother Thomas* (London, [1792?]).

28 For an account of these tracts that shifts attention from Jacobinism to unruly popular culture, see Susan Pedersen, 'Hannah More Meets Simple Simon: Tracts, Chapbooks, and Popular Culture in Late Eighteenth-Century England', *Journal of British Studies* 25 (1986), 84–113.

29 *The Cottage Cook; or, Mrs. Jones's Cheap Dishes* (1797), and *History of Tom White the Postilion* (1795).

30 The term is from Mark Philp, 'Vulgar Conservatism, 1792–3', *English Historical Review* 110 (1995), 42–59.

31 See Mark Storey, *Robert Southey: A Life* (Oxford: Oxford University Press, 1997), p. 250.

32 See Samuel Taylor Coleridge, *Lay Sermons*, ed. R. J. White, vol. VI of *The Collected Works of Samuel Taylor Coleridge* (Princeton: Princeton University Press, 1972), p. xxxi, and n. 5.

33 Epstein, ' "Equality and No King" ', pp. 47–8.

34 Kevin Gilmartin, *Writing against Revolution: Literary Conservatism in Britain, 1790–1832* (Cambridge: Cambridge University Press, 2007), pp. 175–96.

35 Thomas Harrall, *Scenes of Life*, 3 vols. (London, 1805), vol. I, pp. 175–6.

36 Edmund Burke, *Reflections on the Revolution in France*, in *The Writings and Speeches of Edmund Burke*, ed. Paul Langford *et al.*, 9 vols. (Oxford: Clarendon Press, 1981–), vol. VIII, pp. 97–8.

37 See David Eastwood, 'Robert Southey and the Intellectual Origins of Romantic Conservatism', *English Historical Review* 104 (1989), 320.

38 Coleridge's treatment of radicalism as dangerous in its form and formlessness recalls loyalist anxieties about the London Corresponding Society in the 1790s. See John Barrell, 'London and the London Corresponding Society', in James Chandler and Kevin Gilmartin (eds.), *Romantic Metropolis: The Urban Scene of British Culture, 1780–1840* (Cambridge: Cambridge University Press, 2005), pp. 102–8.

39 I take the term 'associational world' from Peter Clark, *British Clubs and Societies, 1580–1800: The Origins of an Associational World* (Oxford: Clarendon Press, 2000).

40 McCalman, *Radical Underworld*, pp. 21–2, 114–15, 243n.60.

41 I have argued this point more broadly in the final chapter of *Writing against Revolution*.

CHAPTER 7

Shelley's Mask of Anarchy *and the visual iconography of female distress*

Ian Haywood

It would not be an exaggeration to say that, at least in its intention, Shelley's *Mask of Anarchy* has the most impeccably 'popular' credentials of all canonical Romantic poems. The poem was a product of the resurgent radical movement of the late Regency period which returned 'the people' to the centre of political debate. Moreover, the content and form of the poem are conspicuously democratic. As everyone knows, the *Mask* was Shelley's outraged response to the Peterloo 'massacre' of August 1819 in which a peaceful mass demonstration for political reform was charged by mounted cavalry. Such unprovoked violence seemed to confirm the enduring radical analysis of British politics as a binary opposition between the forces of Old Corruption (the aristocratic elite) and the 'people' (the unrepresented majority).[1] From his self-imposed exile in Italy, the galvanized Shelley planned to publish 'A little volume of *popular songs* wholly political, & destined to awaken & direct the imagination of the reformers',[2] an 'exoteric' or public collection of verse in which the *Mask* would have undoubtedly been the centrepiece.[3]

Determined to make his mark, Shelley wrote like a virtual demagogue, wielding the rhetorical artillery of sensationalism and melodrama. Taking his lead from the biblical and allegorical imagination of radical poetry, he created a fantastical, apocalyptic narrative of class war in which Peterloo is transformed into a redemptive encounter between the deathly Anarchy and the heroic British people who have supernatural intervention on their side. Also taking a cue from the radical press, which by 1819 had grown into a formidable political force,[4] Shelley made the second half of the poem fiercely didactic: having 'awakened' his readers, he now 'directed' them towards proto-socialist reforms. It is this aspect of the poem which has created most problems for critics and raised doubts about the extent to which Shelley succeeded in his role as an acknowledged poetical legislator. The poem's manifesto for peaceful reforms seems to be aimed primarily at the polite radical reader who has access to the political establishment, but the poem also instructs its readers to rise up 'in unvanquishable number', an inflammatory exhortation directed at the 'popular impatience' of the 'vanquished' masses of Peterloo.[5] This inconsistency could be a classic case of Romantic ambivalence about popular intelligence and popular politics which echoes Coleridge and Godwin's attacks on radical demagoguery in the 1790s, or Coleridge's failure to produce a third *Lay Sermon* addressed to the lower classes,[6] but it is equally possible that Shelley was putting his own poetic theories into practice by expressing the spirit of the age.[7] The poem's apparently confusing prescriptions for mass action actually reveal the tensions which existed within radical discourse between constitutionalism and more revolutionary tendencies: as Mark Philp notes, radicalism was a 'broadly popular rather than a class form'.[8] This awareness of the 'cross-class' composition of the 'people' meant that Shelley refused to fully endorse the Peterloo 'myth' which, as we shall see, depicted the people as the abject victims of Old Corruption. Though he exploits this imagery, Shelley also inverts it and presents powerful and memorable images of popular resistance. Remarkably, considering that women are the quintessential victims of Peterloo, he makes female agency the basis of political opposition. In order to achieve this feminized triumph, Shelley turned to another valuable resource of popular culture, the caricature tradition.

In this chapter I want to focus on an undervalued aspect of *Mask*'s interaction with contemporary popular culture which I believe plays a key role in Shelley's mission to 'awaken and direct the *imagination* of the reformers' (my emphasis): the poem's use of allegorized female agency. I want to claim that the poem's remarkable foregrounding of female political action utilizes a long tradition of popular iconography which flourished in visual caricature and which reached a new peak of cultural authority in the Peterloo controversy. In the popular radical imagination, the Peterloo massacre of 16 August 1819 was constructed from the beginning as a gendered confrontation between brutal, unprovoked, unpatriotic State violence and defenceless, feminized victims. George Cruikshank's well-known caricature print *Massacre at St Peter's, or Britons Strike Home!!!* (Figure 7.1) gave dramatic visual expression to public opinion by placing an imploring woman and child at the centre of the scene of carnage.[9]

The propaganda appeal of such imagery relied on its contradictory representation of the people: defined by injustice and defeat, their abjection is actually a moral victory and an irrefutable argument for the justness of their cause. The feminization of suffering adds sentimental authority to the scene and makes a direct appeal to the (predominantly

Fig. 7.1 George Cruikshank, *Massacre at St Peter's, or Britons Strike Home!!!* (Thomas Tegg, 1819). Copyright Trustees of the British Museum.

male) readers' or viewers' chivalrous instincts. As I shall show, Shelley makes substantial use of this tried and tested trope of distress in his poem, but he also spectacularly inverts the trope and puts female agency at the centre of the narrative. Though it takes allegorical form, Shelley's response is therefore an accurate reflection of the feminist strain within popular politics at this time, and it is undoubtedly aimed, at least in part, at female readers.[10] In the poem, the challenge to the power of the tyrannical Anarchy takes the form of three powerful but perplexingly indistinct allegorical female figures: the 'maniac maid' Hope (a representative of non-violent direct action); the ethereal and maternal 'Earth' (the poem's demagogue who espouses a proto-socialist manifesto); and the inspirational 'Shape'. Although the gender of the latter two figures is not specified explicitly in the poem, the critical consensus is that these spiritual entities exhibit predominantly feminine characteristics.[11] Paradoxically it is precisely the allegorical vagueness of these three figures which enhances rather than weakens their symbolic political agency by soaking up allusions and associations from the longer caricature tradition.[12]

CARICATURE AND POPULAR CULTURE

Of all the visual forms in the Romantic period, caricature or graphic satire has a strong claim to be regarded as a 'popular' form, provided that (as I argue below) we define that word in a distinctively eighteenth-century way. Unlike painting or sculpture, which relied on attracting a restricted number of viewers to a fixed point of display, the caricature print was an essentially reproductive medium with its roots in print culture. The cultural appeal and function of caricature was much more like that of newspapers, periodicals, advertising, and political propaganda. The aim was to make an immediate impact on public opinion through a visceral mixture of playful symbolism and (frequently devastating) political allusion. As David Bindman notes:

from the end of the fifteenth century to the mid-nineteenth century, prints in a certain sense controlled the ways in which the world was made visible to all but the few who had access to paintings and drawings, or to ceremonial forms of representation.

Bindman adds that printmaking was 'at its height' during the Romantic period and that 'graphic satire, or caricature', was 'the most successful of all branches of printmaking in the late eighteenth century'.[13] The clearest evidence of caricature's ability to 'control the ways in which the world was made visible' is the success of the caricature publishers who sponsored Gillray, Rowlandson, the Cruikshanks, Richard Newton, and many other graphic artists in the Romantic period. It was in the printshops of Hannah Humphrey, Rudolph Ackermann, Samuel William Fores, William Holland, and other caricature publishers that the most vivid and dramatic expressions of Romanticism's popular iconographic imagination were generated. It was not just the interior of these shops which attracted a socially diverse audience; the printshop window was such a popular venue for viewing images that it became a satirical 'conversation piece' in its own right. It is unsurprising that these social and cultural features of caricature seemed impressively egalitarian to outsiders: one German tourist went so far as to call printshops the 'real galleries' of the nation.[14] Available statistics for sales and circulation are impressive. In the Romantic period at least twenty thousand caricatures were published, an average of one per day. Gillray alone produced over one thousand prints, averaging two per week at his peak in the late 1790s.[15] Print runs were usually in the low hundreds but could be as high as two thousand. Though only the middle and upper classes could afford to pay the average price of one shilling for a black and white print (hand-coloured versions were much more expensive), the fact that prints could also be borrowed for the evening means that many more people saw prints than purchased them. The lower classes were certainly excluded from buying or renting prints, but the evidence of the (admittedly satirical) printshop window scenes is that plebeian spectators brushed shoulders with their genteel counterparts on the crowded pavement.

Clearly, the carnivalesque qualities of Romantic-period visual satire exerted a strong cross-class appeal which embraced many ranks in society from the prosperous artisan to the aristocrat. But as I shall show, many examples of the 'popular' print drew on the imagery and content of the 'fine' arts. Caricature is symptomatic of the wider condition of popular culture at this time. As Iain McCalman has argued, it is misleading to see eighteenth-century popular culture as synonymous with an 'authentic' plebeian culture which was suppressed by the combined force of political repression, moral reform, and commercialism: 'conventional bipolar divisions between elite and popular, polite and vulgar, or pre-industrial and modern, tend to elide the considerable degree of cultural appropriation and exchange that took place among different social groupings'.[16] For Vic Gatrell, caricature was a prime location for such cultural miscegenation.[17] It would be a mistake, therefore, to apply Bourdieu's influential theory of the politically regulatory function of culture to the promiscuous world of caricature. Bourdieu's idea that 'art and cultural consumption are predisposed . . . to fulfil a social function of legitimating social differences' has only a marginal bearing on caricature's popularity.[18] Caricature prints have also been neglected in Habermas's equally influential theory of the public sphere. Habermas's narrative of the rise of public opinion in the eighteenth century overlooks the power of caricature to rival or complement the press in the production of 'critical publicity'.[19] This kind of theoretical and critical neglect has also obscured the fact that caricature's popularity eroded gender as well as social differences. All the printshop window scenes show women enjoying the variety of visual wares on display. Far from being the means of 'legitimating social differences', therefore, caricature's excessively populist, anti-authoritarian, and egalitarian credentials may have ensured that it became one of the Romantic period's most carnivalesque cultural forms, capable of generating a profound influence on the iconographic and radical imagination. For reasons that have yet to be fully explained, visual satire was not regarded as a serious threat by the authorities, and this freedom from prosecution ensured that a popular symbolic and allegorical imagination prospered throughout the Romantic period. The aim of the rest of this chapter is to consider the extent to which the *Mask*'s representation of female agency is deeply embedded within this broader tradition of popular iconography.[20]

HOPE

Shelley's Hope is a 'maniac maid', a hybrid symbol of self-sacrifice and resistance, and a figure which is clearly based on the trampled women who were at the visual and moral centre of the popular iconography of Peterloo.[21] The radical press lost no time in foregrounding this trope in both reportage and poetry.[22] Just a few weeks after the massacre, Thomas Wooler's *Black Dwarf*, one of the most widely read radical periodicals of this period, published a poem called 'The Peterloo Man'. As well as being one of the first literary texts to coin the term Peterloo, the poem launched a blisteringly sarcastic attack on the patriotic soldier who shows his mettle (and metal) by attacking innocent women and children:

> How brave were the heroes, what muse can relate;
> On the breast of its mother, he bade the babe bleed!
> And the mother herself would in vain shun the fate,
> That awaited her under the hoofs of his steed.
> Stained deep with their gore, how he dashed along,
> Of banditti the first, since fell murder began;

How tremble the feeble among the sacred throng,
When they hear the fierce shout of the Peterloo Man![23]

The modest reference to martyrdom ('sacred throng') anticipates Shelley's full-blooded vision of apocalyptic terror in the figure of the 'fell' rider Anarchy. It is also worth noting that the 'sacred throng' of martyred innocents includes both men and women. As Scrivener notes, the trope of powerlessness feminized both the male and female victims of Peterloo. In Hone and Cruikshank's *The Man in the Moon* (1820), for example, the curtailment of freedom of expression is sensationally represented by the depiction of soldiers forcing their bayonets into the mouths of working-class men. For Scrivener, the trope of humiliating sexualized violence debunked the paternalist ideology of the State and exposed it as the equivalent of a 'bad father'.[24] There is no denying the force of these images, but it is also important to note that such images of oral rape and sexual humiliation were not unusual in caricature and were a familiar part of the radical allegorical lexicon, though this did not lessen their ability to shock.[25] By widening the frame of iconographical references both synchronically and diachronically, it also becomes apparent that oedipal betrayal is only one of the tropes evoked in the Peterloo myth. The central image of the trampled multitude evoked three distinct visual traditions of massacre which operated at all levels of culture from the high to the low: the Triumph of Death from the biblical Apocalypse; the military atrocity; and the urban riot. The ground of Peterloo, in other words, was an iconographical crowded field.

The Apocalypse is the most conspicuous visual source for *Mask*. The tyrant Anarchy is explicitly likened to the Pale Rider of Revelation 6:8:

Last came Anarchy: he rode
On a white horse, splashed with blood;
He was pale even to the lips,
Like Death in the Apocalypse.[26]

This Pale Rider was a popular subject for Romantic artists and many contemporary readers of Shelley's poem would recall the terrifying skeletal horsemen depicted by John Hamilton Mortimer and Benjamin West.[27] Mortimer's *Death on a Pale Horse* was first exhibited at the Society of Arts in 1775 and became widely known through an engraving published in 1784, the year after Benjamin West exhibited his version of the same scene at the Royal Academy (West went on to paint two other versions in 1796 and 1815–17). Both artists foreground melodramatically prostrate and supplicating women: as the poem puts it, 'see the Tyrant's crew / Ride over your wives and you' (lines 190–1). As Bindman notes, Romanticism's 'English Apocalypse' was a complex and controversial theme which foregrounded the sentimental trope of the slaughter of innocent victims but also carried revolutionary connotations of the divine overthrow of earthly power.[28] The Apocalypse attracted radical artists and poets like West, Mortimer, and William Blake (who declines to show trampled victims under the horse's hooves, perhaps to enhance the scene's revolutionary potential), while its satirical possibilities were exploited by caricaturists like Gillray, whose *Presages of the Millenium* (1795) shows a skeletal Pitt on a white horse charging down his political opponents. The Peterloo 'myth' (which Shelley both drew on and contributed to) can be regarded as an appropriation of the English Apocalypse in which the trampled multitude function simultaneously as sufferers of unwarranted violence and omens of sublime justice. In the apocalyptic narrative of the Bible and in the related popular iconography of the Triumph (or Dance) of Death, social and political rank are no protection against Death's dart. In *Mask* Shelley shows his debt to both the sublime high culture of West and Blake and the satirical popular culture of Gillray by turning the retributive millenarian logic of this divine moment of reckoning against its fiendish agents:

> And Anarchy, the ghastly birth,
> Lay dead upon the earth –
> The Horse of Death tameless as wind
> Fled, and with his hoofs did grind
> To dust, the murderers thronged behind. (lines 130–4)

This strategic adoption of apocalyptic imagery could be one explanation for the poem's omission of collective revolutionary violence. In the popular allegorical imagination, the immense injustice of Peterloo required nothing less than 'divine' intervention. As we shall see, Shelley's turn to female agency for such an intervention was fully in line with the wider popular iconographical response to Peterloo and the ensuing political crisis.

Yet Shelley's figure of Hope does not fit neatly into the iconographical conventions of the English Apocalypse. Though she is Anarchy's most conspicuous victim, we should not forget that she throws herself under the pale rider's hooves voluntarily. This action is completely alien to the symbolic and ideological composition of the trampled apocalyptic multitude. Hope is a hybrid figure: though she 'looked more like Despair' (line 88) she is also a 'maniac maid' (line 86) of resistance. Shelley's innovation is to fuse the quintessential female victim of sublime Terror with a very different figure from Romantic popular culture: the grotesque, comic, or plebeian political woman. From this fusion emerges a completely new female agency: non-violent direct action.[29] This strategy may seem risky, as Shelley's use of the troubling word 'maniac' seems to collude with anti-Jacobin stereotypes of political women. These stereotypes were still in active use in 1819 in conservative attacks on the large numbers of women who were active in the reform movement. In 1818, *Black Dwarf* published a poetical exchange between a satirical anti-feminist called 'Roderick Random' and a defender of women's rights. In 'Ode to the Ladies on Their Alleged Rights', 'Roderick Random' mocks both the existing political establishment exemplified in the figure of the voluptuary Prince Regent and the idea of women's participation in the masculine public sphere of politics:

> Our gracious Regent too, whose relish
> Is fond of all that can embellish,
> We'll find his taste exactly suited:
> When from the proud bed-chamber rout,
> *Lady-like lords* are all kicked out,
> And *lordly ladies* substituted.

In the rebuttal poem, 'Rights of Women', there is a militant assertion of women's right to participate in the political public sphere:

> Though the *rule of the sex* you so amply pourtray
> O'er the milder dominion of life:
> We had rather, believe me, our characters play
> In the national drama of strife.[30]

Within one year, this 'national drama of strife' was to be played out on the literal and symbolic field of Peterloo. Contemporary reports of the incident make clear that a conspicuous semiotic feature of Peterloo was the gendering of the crowd. The presence of Female Reform Associations was noted by many observers including John Tyas, the reporter for *The Times*:

A club of Female Reformers, amounting in numbers, according to our calculations, 150, came from Oldham; and another, not quite so numerous, from Royton. The first bore a white silk banner, by far the most elegant displayed during the day, inscribed 'Major Cartwright's Bill, Annual Parliaments, Universal Suffrage, and Vote by Ballot'. The females of Royton bore two red flags, the one inscribed 'Let us die like men, and not sold like slaves'; the other 'Annual Parliaments and Universal Suffrage'.[31]

Peterloo was therefore a highly visible expression of women's participation in politics. The focus on women as the iconic victims of the Peterloo massacre occludes the fact that they were also its most progressive political symbols. The orderly and dignified ranks of Female Reform clubs defied anti-feminist stereotypes which since the eighteenth century had depicted political women as grotesquely unfeminine. The politically inconsistent Cruikshank, for example, pilloried the women of the reform movement in several caricatures in 1819. *Reform among Females* shows four women on a platform addressing a crowd composed mainly of other women. The credibility of the women founders in a series of visual sexual jokes which includes bulging breasts, the sexually provocative way in which one of the women is grasping a pole on top of which is a cap of Liberty, and the sexual flirtatiousness of the female audience. *The Belle-Alliance, or The Female Reformers of Blackburn* is just as crude, showing grotesque plebeian men and women battling for possession of the platform. A 'maniac' plebeian political woman also figures prominently in Cruikshank's *The Radical's Arms*. Rehashing anti-Jacobin imagery, Cruikshank shows a bloody guillotine flanked by two grotesque figures: on the left, a drunken, leering, and hatchet-wielding man, on the right a menacing, gin-soaked woman. Clearly, Cruikshank was more comfortable with the idea of women as victims rather than as the agents of politics.

Seen within the context of such caricature images, Shelley's decision to make Hope a 'maniac' was a dangerous manoeuvre, as it ran the risk of reinforcing conservative propaganda. The most likely reason for this aesthetic gamble was that Shelley wanted to absorb negative stereotypes into his sensational construction of an entirely new type of political female agency. Though Hope is clearly an allegorical figure (her father is an embittered and ailing 'Time'), there is a touch of realism about her plight. This could be the reason that Hope's cry 'Misery, oh, Misery!' (line 97) echoes the desperate lament of another Romantic victim, the infanticidal Martha Ray of Wordsworth's *The Thorn* (1798). The crucial difference between the two women is that Shelley's heroine is not a passive sufferer. Deprived of other means of agency, she can still use her body as a political weapon. The word 'maniac' connotes desperation and determination in equal measure. Hope's decision to throw herself 'Right before the horses' feet' (line 99) is a spectacular appropriation of the stereotypical unnaturalness, irrationality, and fecklessness of female political agency. Through her 'maniac' fall, Hope becomes an innovative figure of vanguard political intervention and the role model for the poem's innovative philosophy of non-violent direct action.

Placing Shelley's Hope in relation to Cruikshank's anti-feminist caricatures has shown that the 'maniac' maid is a figure forged out of

Fig. 7.2 James Gillray, *The Butchers of Freedom* (London: H. H. Humphrey, 1788). Copyright Trustees of the British Museum.

a combative and knowing engagement with the caricature tradition. In the next section of this chapter I want to deepen this analysis by bringing into the discussion a much wider range of pictorial allusion. The embeddedness of Shelley's allegory within popular iconographic traditions becomes even more evident as we turn to the other two dominant pictographic sources for images of the trampled multitude, the military atrocity and the urban disorder.

The vignette of the violated mother and child was a centrepiece of textual descriptions of military atrocities in the Romantic period, and was a key trope in anti-war writing.[32] To choose just one example which Shelley surely knew, Leigh Hunt's 'Ode for the Spring of 1814' uses the image of the distressed mother and child to express relief that the war with Napoleon was over:

> No more the widow bleeds
> To see the babe that feeds
> At her dear breast with sudden-stopping moan;
> But while his earnest task he plies,
> Smiles in his grave uplifted eyes,
> Gath'ring his little hand into her own,
> And feels that in the world she shall not be alone.[33]

But an even more potent source of images of the trampled multitude was the scene of urban disorder. The visual power of the riot derives from the way it superimposes the violent sensationalism of both the apocalyptic conquest and the military atrocity onto a familiar setting. In a very obvious way the urban disorder was the most direct iconographic antecedent of the Manchester Massacre, so it is no surprise to discover a strong resemblance between Cruikshank's *Britons Strike Home!!!* and Gillray's 1788 print *The Butchers of Freedom* (Figure 7.2).

Perhaps influenced by Rubens's *Massacre of the Innocents*, Gillray's caricature confirms the centrality of female distress in the depiction of mass slaughter. It is almost certain that Cruikshank borrowed directly from the image, as the central configuration of the supplicating mother and child is transposed with very little alteration into *Britons Strike Home!!!*. *The Butchers of Freedom* is also a remarkable inversion of anti-Jacobin stereotypes of revolutionary violence which would become Gillray's forte in the 1790s. It is particularly ironic that one of the 'butchers' about to strike the forlorn woman is Edmund Burke, who at this time was still allied to the Foxite Whigs. Within just two years of the appearance of this lampoon, Burke's *Reflections on the Revolution in France* (1790) produced probably the most famous portrayal of female distress in Romantic political writing: the invasion of Queen Marie-Antoinette's royal bedchamber by blood-thirsty *sans-culottes*.[34] In this sensational quasi-rape scene, which James T. Boulton has called the 'rhetorical and philosophical centrepoint' of Burke's text, there is a collision between the two extremes of femininity: the idealized, elevated body of the queen and the 'horrid yells, and shrilling screams, and frantic dances, and infamous contumelies, and all the unutterable abominations of the furies of hell, in the abused shape of the vilest of women'.[35] Burke's furious Jacobin women made a deep and lasting impression on the popular imagination and helped to perpetuate the stereotypical association between female political agency, vulgarity, madness, and violent revolution. The real offence of Burke's *poissards* was symbolic: the 'vilest of women' disregarded the queen's royal body, the sacrosanct emblem of the French nation. By quoting Gillray's *Butchers of Freedom*, it is possible that Cruikshank was intentionally drawing on an older iconographic tradition of social disorder in which the emblematic roles are reversed and it is the body of the plebeian woman which stands for moral virtue and social order.

The sentimental and naturalistic portrayal of female suffering in *Butchers of Freedom* also refutes Diana Donald's thesis that Georgian caricature had no visual language for the 'pathos' or 'righteous indignation' of a 'civilian massacre'. Donald's thesis is that the civilian suffering of Peterloo forced artists to turn to older traditions such as history painting and the biblical Apocalypse in order to find 'general prototypes for the raised supplicating hands and gestures of despair, the tragic mothers and infants and the brutal riders of the Peterloo prints'.[36] Though it is certainly the case that lower-class suffering is often depicted as grotesque in popular caricature (and this includes the facially elongated victims who are on the margins of *Britons Strike Home!!!*), *Butchers of Freedom* is a powerful reminder that naturalism and allegory could work together to achieve what Marcus Wood calls 'dynamic tension' and 'enrichment'.[37] If we accept that allegory and realism combine to 'enrich' popular political iconography, it is possible to imagine Shelley's Hope as simultaneously a political symbol and a heightened version of an actual female reformer. As Anne Janowitz notes, the 'central intention' of the *Mask* is to 'literalise figures' in order to imitate the effect of an actual mass meeting in which politics is simultaneously real and symbolic.[38]

Regency caricaturists like Cruikshank could also turn to Gillray for ambiguous images of militant plebeian women. In an earlier caricature with the teasing title *The Liberty of the Subject* (1779), Gillray shows two plebeian women attacking a naval press-gang. While this resistance is clearly heroic, the radicalism of the action is undermined by the grotesque facial features of the women and the displacement of the mother–child vignette onto a genteel onlooker. Gillray's ambiguous representation of assertive lower-class women was not an isolated case at this time. Just one year later, a caricature entitled *Britannia Protected from the Terrors of an Invasion* (1780) shows Britannia being defended by a burly fishwife and a Medusa-like 'scold' who is breathing fire and repelling the personifications of Spain, France, and America. The print is an intriguing combination of patriotic and anti-Jacobin stereotypes *avant la lettre*.

All these images may have been influenced by the real-life 'maniac maid' Margaret Nicholson, who tried to assassinate George III in July 1786. Instead of being hanged, drawn, and quartered, Nicholson was certified insane and spent the rest of her life in Bedlam. Though she has now been forgotten, Nicholson's 'maniac' regicidal reputation carried considerable subversive and carnivalesque authority in the Romantic period. Thomas Rowlandson's 1793 caricature *A Peep into Bethlehem* shows Nicholson hovering over the seated figures of Burke and Peter Pindar (John Wolcot) in a parody of the famous scene of Satan, Sin, and Death from *Paradise Lost*. Moreover, one of Shelley's first publications was the satirically entitled *Posthumous Fragments of Margaret Nicholson* (self-published in 1810), a collection of fiery radical poems which anticipates *Mask of Anarchy* in a number of striking ways.[39] One poem depicts the destructive power of war in the form of an allegorical procession; another called 'The Spectral Horseman' shows a figure resembling Death stalking the country on a 'white courser' (line 28). In both its themes and its forms, *Posthumous Fragments of Margaret Nicholson* provides compelling evidence that the popular political culture of the late eighteenth century provided Shelley with imaginative resources from the outset of his poetical career.

SHAPE

The next allegorical agency in *Mask of Anarchy* is a mysterious 'Shape' which appears immediately after Hope's intervention and which grows quickly from 'A mist, a light, an image' (line 103) into a colossal winged spirit 'arrayed in mail' (line 110). 'Shape' is allegorically unfixed but is obviously associated with liberty, inspiration, reason, and revolutionary action. Immediately after the line 'Thoughts sprung where'er that step did fall' (line 125), the 'prostrated multitude' raise their heads and see that Anarchy has been bloodily vanquished (line 126). Though 'Shape' is an ungendered form, its close association with Hope and the fact that its

Minerva-like 'helm' sports an image of Venus ('A planet, like the Morning's' (line 115)) provide strong grounds for ascribing a female gender to the phantom. Another reason for feminizing 'Shape' emerges when we consider the evolution of this phantom in Shelley's poetry. Its first appearance occurs at the end of Shelley's withering 1817 pamphlet on the death of Princess Charlotte, *'We Pity the Plumage, but Forget the Dying Bird'; An Address to the People on the Death of Princess Charlotte*. The hyperbolic national mourning for Charlotte was vilified by radicals as a diversion of public attention away from the execution of the Pentridge rebels Brandreth, Ludlum, and Turner.[40] In this pamphlet, Shelley reversed the loyalist construction of Charlotte's death by giving equal weight to the two events. Shelley also took the radical critique one step further by ending the pamphlet with a parody of the most spectacular feature of the glorification of Charlotte's death, her apotheosis. In both official memorials and popular prints, Charlotte was depicted as a quasi-divine figure. Lieutenant P. R. Read's *Apotheosis of Her Royal Highness Princess Charlotte Augusta of Wales* (1818) shows Charlotte ascending into the heavens from a pseudo-classical sarcophagus. Her tomb is flanked by the mourning figures of Britannia on one side and Faith, Hope, and Charity on the other. A less extravagant version of this scene was used for J. and M. Wyatt's official burial monument in St George's Chapel, Windsor (1821), in which the ascending Charlotte is assisted by two angels. A more populist approach was taken in an 1818 print which shows the skeletal arm of Death emerging from the ascending cloud, a detail which recalls the social levelling of the Dance of Death.[41] Shelley saw the opportunity to transform this hegemonic display of Paineite 'plumage' into a republican apotheosis:

Let us follow the corpse of British Liberty slowly and reverentially to its tomb; and if some glorious Phantom should appear, and make its throne of broken swords and sceptres and royal crowns trampled in the dust, let us say that the Spirit of Liberty has arisen from its grave and left all that was gross and mortal there, and kneel down and worship it as our Queen.[42]

By reviving this 'Glorious Phantom' of Liberty in 1819, Shelley elevated Peterloo into a sublime reworking of the events of 1817.[43] The 'Shape' of things to come would emerge from the national mourning for Peterloo's victims: the inspirational visionary power of the poet and the practical organization of mass political agitation would work together to liberate the 'Spirit of Liberty' from its temporary tomb.

In order to appreciate the full iconographic force of Shelley's Queen Liberty, however, we must take account of the evolution of political apotheosis in the longer caricature tradition, an evolution in which sexual politics figured prominently from the outset. The trope emerged in the 1780s with responses to the cult of the Duchess of Devonshire, the friend of Charles James Fox and the most famous political woman of her time.[44] In a pro-Duchess print called *The Apotheosis of the Dutchess* (1784), Georgiana is shown on a cloud accompanied by the bare-breasted figures of Virtue and Truth; underneath her feet is the prostrate figure of Scandal. Needless to say, this image of the Duchess as the ideal of female virtue was also lampooned. In a print called *Devonia, The Beautiful Daughter of Love and Liberty, inviting the Sons of Freedom to her Standard in Covent Garden* (1784), the Duchess and two female followers are shown cavorting with plebeian men. In the 1790s the apotheosis trope reached a peak of visual sophistication with Gillray's stunning *Apotheosis of Hoche* (1798), a parody of Michelangelo in which the ascending French general is surrounded by apocalyptic scenes of Jacobin slaughter. Despite Gillray's *tour de force*, Shelley was not deterred from imagining the radical apotheosis of Charlotte Corday in one of the *Margaret Nicholson* poems. Corday's last words anticipate the patricidal Beatrice Cenci:

> But what is sweeter to the revenger's ear
> Than the fell tyrant's last expiring yell.
> Yes! Than love's sweetest blisses 'tis more dear
> To drink the floatings of a despot's knell. (lines 109–12)

The post-war resurgence of mass radicalism made the allegorical idealization of democracy an essential target of loyalist caricature. Cruikshank's *Universal Suffrage, or the Scum Uppermost!!!* (1817) could have been an attempt to discredit Shelley's Glorious Phantom. The print shows a hydra squatting on top of a heap of constitutional fragments which resemble Shelley's 'broken swords and sceptres and royal crowns trampled in the dust'. The subtitle of the print is also significant: 'An Allegory, to demonstrate the fatal consequences of "Radical Reform" in Plain English Revolution'. Despite these incursions by conservative caricaturists, the allegorical tide was about to flow in the radical direction. What no one, including Shelley, could have foreseen in 1817 or even in 1819 was that the Queen Caroline controversy of 1820–1 would breathe spectacular new life into both Queen Liberty and the trope of the political apotheosis.[45] When Caroline died in August 1821, having failed to secure her claim to the English crown, a tribute poem appeared in *Black Dwarf*:

> Tho' denied a seat on earth,
> Due to her illustrious birth;

Crown'd on high in Court Divine,
Reigns the Royal Caroline.
With contempt she views below
Short liv'd pageantry and show;
Whilst eternal splendours shine
Round the throne of Caroline.[46]

The sentimental appeal of Caroline's death was amplified by the idea that she had finally been reunited with her daughter Charlotte. The two royal deaths formed a narrative of enforced separation and reunion which exposed the masculine callousness of the newly crowned king and his regime. Shelley must have been aware that the Caroline controversy promoted women's rights, but his anti-monarchism made it impossible for him to openly support her cause. His literary response was the full-blooded allegorical comedy *Swellfoot the Tyrant*.[47]

Within this broader iconographic field of contested images of political and monarchical apotheosis, Shelley's indistinct 'Shape' functions as a new version of Queen Liberty and a republican appropriation of the two royal apotheoses which frame the period of post-war mass agitation: Charlotte (as tragedy) and Caroline (as farce). Within the narrower bounds of the poem's narrative, 'Shape' also prepares the symbolic ground for the poem's third female allegory: a figure that can also be seen as an alternative national icon of Liberty.

EARTH

Shelley's 'Earth' is *Mask*'s presiding deity. Her address to the 'Men of England' takes up almost two-thirds of the poem and outlines a proto-socialist programme of economic and political reforms. Though she has no physical shape, her commanding position and her maternal role as 'indignant Earth / Which gave the sons of England birth' (lines 139–40) give her the allegorical credentials of a national female icon. She is the poem's equivalent of those two dominant national female icons in the Romantic period, Britannia and Liberty, figures that are so closely related that they are often interchangeable.[48] Once we position the poem in this contextual layer, Shelley's vague figure becomes supercharged with allegorical energy which revitalizes the symbolic agency of both Hope and the 'Shape'.

The most striking feature about representations of Britannia and Liberty in caricature prints is that they are often shown in situations of dire distress as well as sublime power. The caricature record shows that it is a mistake to assume that Britannia and Liberty had a fixed hegemonic role in the Romantic period. From the mid eighteenth century onwards, political crisis was often expressed through scenes of Britannia and Liberty in perilous predicaments. Conflict with America, for example, was represented by the violation or dismemberment of Britannia's body, but this theme was not unique. Images of a vulnerable, trampled, abused, and threatened Britannia recur throughout the Romantic period.[49] In a print called *The Hydra* (1780), for example, a helpless Britannia is mauled by the claws of a monstrous hydra, her discarded shield offering no protection. In Gillray's *The Genius of France Triumphant, or Britannia Petitioning for Peace* (1795), a bedraggled Britannia is on her knees offering her shield and the British crown to a French demon called 'Libertas'. Gillray's wittiest caricature on this theme was his pro-war *The Nursery, with Britannia Reposing in Peace* (1802), which shows Britannia sleeping in a cradle like a child while Fox and other radical politicians perform domestic chores around her. Radical poets were also fond of this trope. For example, a poem written by 'A Female Citizen' in the London Corresponding Society's *Moral and Political Magazine* (1796–7) shows Britain in the grip of a Shelleyan Anarchy:

> For lo! oppression's giant form is seen
> With rapid stride to pace the trembling land,
> While abject slav'ry with submissive mien
> Stoops low to kiss the terror dealing hand.[50]

The post-war years saw a spectacular revival of the feminized iconography of national crisis and threat. In response to the suspension of habeas corpus in 1817, Cruikshank produced the chillingly realistic *Liberty Suspended*. This print shows a partially naked and hooded Liberty hanging from a gallows which is built on a platform called 'British Press'. In December 1819 Cruikshank temporarily changed sides and produced his most striking Gillray-influenced caricature, *Death or Liberty! Or Britannia and the Virtues of the Constitution in Danger from the Political Libertine, Radical Reform*. The print is a re-inversion of the allegorical politics of the *Mask*. In Cruikshank's dramatic confrontation the skeletal Death figure 'Radical Reform' is shown attempting to rape a kneeling Britannia. The skeleton wears a mask (Liberty) and carries his dart slung between his legs like a menacing erect penis. He is accompanied by a train of Jacobin demons including Slavery, Starvation, and Atheism (one of the demons brandishes a copy of Paine's *The Age of Reason*). Despite this ferocious assault on the reform movement, Cruikshank's hugely popular collaborations with William Hone continued to produce many memorable images of Britannia and Liberty subjected to the violence and brutality of the State. A mock advertisement called *The New Indian Juggler* (1820) shows a manacled Britannia on her knees being forced to swallow the Duke of Wellington's sword. In *Holy Compact and Alliance*, a scene from *The Man in the Moon* (1820), Cruikshank revisits the execution scene of *Liberty Suspended* but this time shows Liberty being burned alive on a printing press while representatives of the governments of Europe (and a devil) dance round the flames. In *The Bloodhound*, from *The Political Showman – At Home!* (1821), the corpse of Britannia is mauled by a large dog which represents government surveillance and repression. The climax of this sado-masochistic tradition is probably to be found in Hone and Cruikshank's *A Slap at Slop and the Bridge-Street Gang* (1821). One scene from this mock-newspaper shows several 'Virtues of the Constitution' being tortured in a cellar by government ministers.

But caricaturists could also draw on an opposing iconographical tradition in which Britannia and Liberty are depicted as powerful, active agencies of either State or radical power. Thomas Rowlandson's loyalist *Britannia Rous'd, Or the Coalition Monsters Destroyed* (1784) shows a colossal semi-naked Britannia whirling the diminutive, Lilliputian figures of Charles James Fox and Lord North round her head. On the opposing side of the political spectrum, radical poetry harnessed the idea of a democratized, all-conquering Liberty to bolster the morale of the reform movement. An anti-war poem which appeared in Thomas Spence's periodical *Politics for the People* (1793–4) issued a solemn warning to the government:

> Tremble, ye tyrants, for your doom is seal'd!
> Tremble, ye slaves, for ye shall bite the dust;
> Triumphant Freedom, in her blood-stain'd vest,
> Despots combin'd, drags at her chariot-wheels,
> And nobly manumits a world enslav'd![51]

In the post-war period conquering Liberty once again became a focus of radical political allegory. E. J. Blandford's poem 'A Terrible Omen to Guilty Tyrants: Or, The Spirit of Liberty', which appeared in the radical periodical *Medusa* in 1819, presents Liberty as an irresistible national force:

> SPIRIT of LIBERTY, now mid'st the throng,
> In awful grandeur dost thou move along;
> From east to west, from north to south, behold
> Thy power extended, moving uncontroul'd,

Tremendous rolling through the swelling tide,
Which shall the fate of despot power deride,
With still increasing numbers in its train,
While to oppose its march all strife is in vain.[52]

Shelley could allude to this kind of sublime, all-conquering female agency without having to collude explicitly in the glorification of militancy.[53] In the *Mask*, Blandford's 'tide' of national reform appears initially as its opposite, Anarchy's diabolical procession, but Earth provides the antidote to this 'ghastly masquerade' in her call for an idealized version of the original Peterloo meeting, a 'great Assembly' of 'the fearless and the free' (lines 262–3). The political restraint of Earth's exhortation becomes apparent when we compare her intervention with the much more militant female agency depicted in popular iconography. In caricatures Britannia and Liberty are often shown in situations of heroic combat, particularly during the Caroline controversy when the feminization of politics reached a peak of 'critical publicity'.[54] The cover design for a pamphlet called *The Queen and Magna Charta, or, The Thing that John Signed. Dedicated to the Ladies of Great Britain* (1820), for example, shows Britannia holding a scroll on which is written 'To assert the Rights of Man. To avenge the Wrongs of Woman'. Hone and Cruikshank's *The Man in the Moon* contains a scene called *Of Little Books* which depicts Liberty single-handedly defending a printing press against three murderous government ministers. Richard Fores's *Firing the Great Gun, Or the Green Bag Open'd* (1820) is one of the most flamboyant and animated examples of this sub-genre of images (Figure 7.3). The scene shows Wellington firing a mortar of accusations at the serene figure of Caroline who is defended by the shield of the semi-naked figure Truth. The print is simultaneously the-atrical, comic, and spectacular.

These popular allegories of heightened radical female agency are an undervalued context for the *Mask* in particular and Romantic literature in general, but I want to end by emphasizing another aspect of these images. With a few exceptions, the majority of these allegories show the female figures assisting and protecting each other. I want to suggest that Shelley (consciously or unconsciously) took his lead from such scenes and intended his three allegorical figures to be seen as a collective agency rather than three separable acts of intervention. As many of the images cited in this chapter have demonstrated, collaborative allegorical female agency has a long history. In a print called *Britannia's Glory* (1766), for example, Britannia receives the newly titled Earl of Chatham assisted by Justice, Fame, and Minerva. At the other end of the Romantic period, Hone and

Fig. 7.3 Anon., *Firing the Great Gun, Or the Green Bag Open'd* (Richard Fores, 1820). Copyright Trustees of the British Museum.

Cruikshank's *Illumination of Queen Caroline* (1820) shows a radiant Liberty in front of a printing press; in her right hand she displays a portrait of Caroline, while her light dispels the demons of corrupt government into the shadows. If we look at this print in relation to *Mask of Anarchy*, Caroline is the equivalent of the victimized but 'serene' Hope (line 128), while the 'illuminated' figure of Liberty combines the roles of the inspirational 'Shape' and the magisterial Earth. Though Earth addresses her political manifesto to the men of England,[55] the poem also provides a compelling example of the radicalized 'communitarian female'.[56] In order to effect this transformation of the Peterloo disaster, Shelley mobilized and modified the resources of the popular caricature tradition, one of Romanticism's most underestimated cultural resources.

This chapter has argued that understanding *Mask of Anarchy*'s place within the popular culture of the Romantic period requires a fuller appreciation of the poem's wide range of popular visual allusion. More specifically, I have argued that one of the poem's most significant political innovations – its depiction of female resistance and power – drew substantially on a tradition of political caricature whose cultural authority peaked in the Peterloo years. From this perspective, the poem might truly be described as a 'popular song wholly political' which mercilessly targets the excesses of power in an allegorical language which would have been familiar to that socially diverse range of readers which constituted 'the people' in contemporary political discourse.

NOTES

1 On this topic see H. T. Dickinson, *The Politics of the People in Eighteenth-Century Britain* (Basingstoke: Macmillan, 1994).

2 Percy Bysshe Shelley, *The Letters of Percy Bysshe Shelley*, ed. Frederick L. Jones, 2 vols. (Oxford: Clarendon Press, 1964), vol. II, p. 191 (To Leigh Hunt, 1 May 1820). Though it was never published in this form, 'Popular Songs wholly political' featured a number of genres which Shelley appropriated from radical print culture including the parodic 'A New National Anthem' and the radical rallying-cry, 'Song to the Men of England'. For a discussion of these poems, see Stephen Behrendt, *Shelley and His Audiences* (Lincoln: University of Nebraska Press, 1989), pp. 192–5.

3 Shelley wrote to Leigh Hunt, 14–18 November 1819: 'You do not tell me whether you have received my lines on the Manchester affair. They are of the exoteric species and are meant not for the *Indicator*, but the *Examiner*' (*Letters*, vol. II, p. 152).

4 See Ian Haywood, *The Revolution in Popular Literature: Print, Politics and the People, 1790–1860* (Cambridge: Cambridge University Press, 2004), pp. 94–103.

5 Shelley, *Letters*, vol. ii, p. 153.

6 See Haywood, *Revolution in Popular Literature*, pp. 39–47.

7 On this aspect of Shelley's involvement in the 'hyper-active public sphere' in 1819, see James Chandler, *England in 1819: The Politics of Literary Culture and the Case of Romantic Historicism* (Chicago, Ill.: University of Chicago Press, 1998), pp. 15–22, 41–6, 79–85.

8 This aspect of radical discourse has been extensively discussed: for a useful overview, see Mark Philp, 'Revolution', in Iain McCalman (ed.), *An Oxford Companion to the Romantic Age: British Culture 1776–1832* (Oxford: Oxford University Press, 1999), pp. 17–25. See also Dror Wahrman, 'Public Opinion, Violence, and the Limits of Constitutional Politics', in James Vernon (ed.), *Re-reading the Constitution: New Narratives in the Political History of England's Long Nineteenth Century* (Cambridge: Cambridge University Press, 1996), pp. 83–122.

9 The best survey of the caricature responses to Peterloo is M. Dorothy George, *English Political Caricature 1798–1832: A Study of Opinion and Propaganda* (Oxford: Clarendon Press, 1959), pp. 179–86. See also Sally Ledger, *Dickens and the Popular Radical Tradition* (Cambridge: Cambridge University Press, 2007), Chapter 1.

10 See Helen Rogers, *Women and the People: Authority, Authorship, and the Radical Tradition in Nineteenth-Century England* (Aldershot: Ashgate, 2000), pp. 18–23.

11 Michael Scrivener, for example, identifies Britannia as one of the models for Earth (*Radical Shelley: The Philosophical Anarchism and Utopian Thought of Percy Bysshe Shelley* (Princeton, N.J.: Princeton University Press, 1982), p. 205); Susan Wolfson calls the Shape a 'miraculous epiphanic female intervention' ('Poetical Form and Political Reform: *The Mask of Anarchy* and "England in 1819"', in Neil Fraistat and Donald H. Reiman (eds.), *Shelley's Poetry and Prose* (New York: W. W. Norton and Company, 2002), p. 730).

12 I am building on the work of critics who have identified links between Shelley and Regency caricature. See Scrivener, *Radical Shelley*, pp. 196–210; Behrendt, *Shelley and His Audiences*, p. 192; Marcus Wood, *Radical Satire and Print Culture 1790–1822* (Oxford: Clarendon Press, 2004), p. 266; Steven E. Jones, *Shelley's Satire: Violence, Exhortation, and Authority* (DeKalb, Ill.: Northern Illinois University Press, 1994), Chapter 5; Ashley J. Cross, '"What a World We Make the Oppressor and the Oppressed": George Cruikshank, Percy Shelley, and the Gendering of Revolution in 1819', *English Literary History* 71:1 (2004), 167–207; Tamara Hunt, *Defining John Bull: Political Caricature and National Identity in Late Georgian England* (Aldershot: Ashgate, 2004), p. 20; Vic Gatrell, *City of Laughter: Sex and Satire in Eighteenth-Century London* (London: Atlantic Books, 2006), p. 502.

13 David Bindman, 'Prints', in McCalman (ed.), *Oxford Companion*, p. 209. See also Patricia Anderson, *The Printed Image and the Transformation of Popular Culture, 1790–1860* (Oxford: Clarendon Press, 1991), Chapter 1.

14 Cited in C. Suzanne Matheson, 'Viewing', in McCalman (ed.), *Oxford Companion*, p. 195.

15 Gatrell, *City of Laughter*, pp. 9–15, 266. See also Hunt, *Defining John Bull*, Chapter 1.

16 Iain McCalman, 'Popular Culture', in McCalman (ed.), *Oxford Companion*, p. 216. See also Peter Burke, *Popular Culture in Early Modern Europe* (1978; rev. edn, Aldershot: Scolar Press, 1994); Tim Harris, 'Problematising Popular Culture', in Tim Harris (ed.), *Popular Culture in England c. 1500–1850* (Basingstoke: Macmillan, 1995), Chapter 1; Eileen and Stephen Yeo, 'Control and Leisure versus Class and Struggle', in Eileen and Stephen Yeo (eds.), *Popular Culture and Class Conflict 1590–1914: Explorations in the History of Labour and Leisure* (Brighton: Harvester Press, 1981), pp. 128–54.

17 Gatrell, *City of Laughter*, p. 11.

18 Pierre Bourdieu, *Distinction: A Social Critique of the Judgement of Taste*, trans. Richard Nice (London: Routledge, 1994), p. 7.

19 Jürgen Habermas, *The Structural Transformation of the Public Sphere: An Inquiry into a Category of Bourgeois Society* (London: Polity Press, 1989), p. 140.

20 Theresa M. Kelley praises the 'figural power' of the *Mask* but her focus is on Anarchy's procession rather than the female allegories (*Reinventing Allegory* (Cambridge: Cambridge University Press, 1997), p. 147).

21 In addition to *Britons Strike Home!!!*, Cruikshank also produced a mock design for a Peterloo memorial, *Victory at Peterloo*, which shows a mounted cavalryman about to strike a defenceless woman with his sabre. These two figures are positioned on top of a tomb which is lined with skulls.

22 Shelley seemed to believe in the most extreme versions of the Peterloo atrocity: 'we hear that a troop of the enraged master manufacturers are let loose with sharpened swords . . . & massacre without distinction of sex or age, & cut off women's breasts and dash the heads of infants against the stones' (*Letters*, vol. 11, p. 136).

23 *Black Dwarf* 3 (1819), 659–60; in Michael Scrivener (ed.), *Poetry and Reform: Periodical Verse from the English Democratic Press 1792–1824* (Detroit, Mich.: Wayne State University Press, 1992), p. 266.

24 Scrivener, *Radical Shelley*, pp. 196–210.

25 See, for example, Richard Newton's anti-taxation print *The Inexhaustible Mine* (22 June 1797) which shows Pitt, Dundas, and the Queen extorting money from every orifice of John Bull; the scene clearly resembles a gang rape.

26 Lines 30–3. All line references are taken from Fraistat and Reiman (eds.), *Shelley's Poetry and Prose*, pp. 316–26, and are subsequently given in the text.

27 Morton D. Paley goes so far as to call the poem an 'animated cartoon' of apocalyptic imagery (*Apocalypse and Millennium in English Romantic Poetry* (Oxford: Clarendon Press, 1999), p. 243).

28 David Bindman, 'The English Apocalypse', in Frances Carey (ed.), *The Apocalypse and the Shape of Things to Come* (London: British Museum Press, 1999), pp. 208–69.

29 Jones argues illuminatingly that the intervention of Hope recalls the 'benevolent agent' of pantomime, adding another contextual layer of popular culture to the poem (*Shelley's Satire*, pp. 114–17).

30 See Scrivener (ed.), *Poetry and Reform*, pp. 257–61. As Scrivener notes, these poems 'would seem to indicate much more feminist resurgence within the reform movement than many historians have so far acknowledged' (p. 261).

31 *The Times*, 19 August 1819.

32 See Ian Haywood, *Bloody Romanticism: Spectacular Violence and the Politics of Representation 1776–1832* (Basingstoke: Palgrave, 2006), Chapters 2–4. The trope has a long history in political caricature.

33 The poem was originally published in the *Examiner* in April 1814 and subsequently included in the Preface to Hunt's anti-Napoleonic monodrama *The Descent of Liberty*, one of the sources for *Mask of Anarchy*. See *The Poetical Works of Leigh Hunt*, 3 vols. (London: Charles and James Ollier, 1819), vol. 1, p. lviii.

34 See Haywood, *Bloody Romanticism*, pp. 62–9, for an extended discussion of this scene.

35 James T. Boulton, *The Language of Politics in the Age of Wilkes and Burke* (London: Routledge and Kegan Paul, 1963), p. 98; Edmund Burke, *Reflections on the Revolution in France, and on the Proceedings in Certain Societies in London Relative to that Event*, in *The Writings and Speeches of Edmund Burke*, volume VIII, *The French Revolution 1790–94*, ed. L. G. Mitchell (Oxford: Clarendon Press, 1989), p. 122.

36 Diana Donald, *The Age of Caricature: Satirical Prints in the Age of George III* (New Haven and London: Yale University Press, 1996), pp. 188–9.

37 Wood, *Radical Satire*, p. 253. In Gatrell's words, 'satire and sensibility reacted against and lived off each other' (*City of Laughter*, p. 461).

38 Anne Janowitz, *Lyric and Labour in the Romantic Tradition* (Cambridge: Cambridge University Press, 1998), p. 103.

39 Percy Bysshe Shelley, *Posthumous Fragments of Margaret Nicholson. Being Poems found amongst the Papers of that noted Female who attempted the life of the King in 1786. Edited by John Fitzvictor*, in *The Complete Poetical Works of Percy Bysshe Shelley*, ed. Thomas Hutchinson (London: Oxford University Press, 1934), pp. 861–8. All line references are taken from this edition and are hereafter given in the text.

40 See Stephen Behrendt, *Royal Mourning and Regency Culture: Elegies and Memorials of Princess Charlotte* (Basingstoke: Macmillan, 1997), pp. 218–36.

41 See *ibid.*, pp. 192–8, for a discussion of these images.

42 [Percy Bysshe Shelley], '*We Pity the Plumage, but Forget the Dying Bird'; An Address to the People on the Death of Princess Charlotte* By the Hermit of Marlow [1817], in *The Prose Works of Percy Bysshe Shelley*, vol. 1, ed. E. B. Murray (Oxford: Clarendon Press, 1993), p. 239.

43 The 'Glorious Phantom' also appears at the end of Shelley's 'exoteric' sonnet 'England in 1819'; Queen Liberty features in another 'exoteric' poem, 'A New National Anthem'. See also Chandler, *England in 1819*, pp. 25–32.

44 See Amelia Rauser, 'The Butcher-Kissing Duchess of Devonshire: Between Caricature and Allegory in 1784', *Eighteenth-Century Studies* 36:1 (2002), 23–46.

45 See George, *English Political Caricature*, pp. 187–203, for a survey of caricature responses to the Caroline affair.

46 *Black Dwarf* 7 (1821), 348; in Scrivener, *Poetry and Reform*, pp. 273–4.

47 See Jones, *Shelley's Satire*, Chapter 6, for a detailed analysis of *Swellfoot* as a 'self-parody' of *Mask of Anarchy*. See also Samuel Gladden, 'Shelley's Agenda Writ Large: Reconsidering *Oedipus Tyrannus; or, Swellfoot the Tyrant*', in Michael Scrivener (ed.), *Reading Shelley's Interventionist Poetry, 1819–20*, Romantic Circles Praxis Series (May 2001).

48 A print called *Liberty* (1792) depicts a figure resembling Britannia in all respects except that the round shield is embossed with a solar design rather than the usual blue and red crosses. Other examples are cited below.

49 Madge Dresser regards the images of Britannia being 'variously dismembered, buggered, ridden and even flogged naked' as irredeemably misogynistic (see 'Britannia', in Raphael Samuel (ed.), *Patriotism: The Making and Unmaking of British National Identity*, vol. III, *National Fictions* (London and New York: Routledge, 1989), pp. 26–49 (p. 34)), but such a response may underestimate the viewing audience's sophistication in decoding the political tropes of images of spectacular violence: see Haywood, *Bloody Romanticism*, pp. 162–5. See also Kathleen Wilson, *This Island Race: Englishness, Empire and Gender in the Eighteenth Century* (London and New York: Routledge, 2003), p. 238n.9.

50 'Invocation to the Genius of Britain', in Scrivener (ed.), *Poetry and Reform*, pp. 129–30, lines 25–8.

51 *Politics for the People* I (Part Two), no. 8, 10–12; in Scrivener (ed.), *Poetry and Reform*, pp. 84–6.

52 Quoted in Scrivener (ed.), *Poetry and Reform*, p. 243, lines 9–16.

53 In his own *Ode to Liberty* (1820), Shelley is even more noncommittal about Liberty's intervention into British politics: 'England yet sleeps: was she not called of old' (line 181); quoted in *Complete Poetical Works*, ed. Hutchinson, p. 608.

54 See Anna Clark, 'Queen Caroline and the Sexual Politics of Popular Culture in London', *Representations* 31 (1990), 47–68.

55 Mary Shelley commented that the poem would 'make a patriot of any man' (*The Poetical Works of Percy Bysshe Shelley. Edited by Mrs Shelley*, 4 vols. (London: Edward Moxon, 1839), vol. III, p. 206).

56 Janowitz, *Lyric and Labour*, p. 104. See also Scrivener's remark that 'Earth, mother, liberty, seem to fuse into a libertarian *spiritus mundi*, a univocal symbol of both nurture and power' (*Radical Shelley*, pp. 205–6).

PART IV

The urban experience

CHAPTER 8

Popularizing the public: Robert Chambers and the rewriting of the antiquarian city

Ina Ferris

Romanticism can be seen as rooted in the problem of fully inhabiting the present. From Wordsworth's 'Lines Written Above Tintern Abbey' (wherein the poet imagines his present as a future past) to Scott's *Waverley* (whose subtitle defines the present as "'Tis Sixty Years Since'), its signature texts typically locate the present in relation to other times – retrospective, anticipatory, recursive. Such moves, generating the complicated temporality characteristic of Romantic writing, respond to the accelerated time of modernity, which famously unmoored the present and stimulated the period's multivalent investment in the past. Romanticism is saturated in memory, reconstruction, recollection, revival, all of which have attracted a great deal of critical attention in recent years. Most has been directed either to questions of national formation and consolidation or to the widespread interest in familiar modes of recollection (e.g. memoirs, biographies, diaries). Both phenomena reflect a desire to bring the past closer to home, registering the heightened interest in more intimate access to the past which followed in the wake of the new understanding of the everyday as a historical subject by the late eighteenth century.[1] Historicization of the everyday opened up and valorized the study of what we now call social or cultural history (hence bringing 'the people' into historical visibility), but it affected not only the approach to the past, bringing equally into view the present's own historicity and spotlighting the question of how it is people live in everyday historical time. Posing this question in an acute way was the site of the city or town. Despite the well-recognized, powerful mediating function of urban space as an interface situated between private and public realms and between the '*near order*' of groups and the '*far order*' of the State (as Henri Lefebvre influentially puts it), the city has not received the notice in Romantic studies accorded to the more abstract 'nation'.[2] Nor has the genre of civic history (which flourished at this time) aroused an interest comparable to that directed to the writing of national or literary history. But in this lowly (if not low) local genre the subject of everyday public life found important articulation and the matter of 'popular culture' was given a more modern shape, understood as pertaining less to a pre-modern 'folk' of carnivalesque rituals like Bartholomew Fair than to a familiar 'public' whose contours and significance were to be vigorously debated in the press for decades.

This chapter focuses on the city that threw into especially dramatic relief questions of urban space, everydayness, and public life: the Scottish capital, Edinburgh. At the height of its cultural power in the early decades of the nineteenth century, Edinburgh flourished as a centre of literary, publishing, and professional innovation second only to London itself. As Ian Duncan has shown, it successfully marketed itself as a 'capital of modern letters': 'a new kind of national capital – not a political or commercial metropolis, but a cultural and aesthetic one'.[3] To achieve this new status, he argues, Edinburgh stripped itself of the specificity of its historical and civic identity, becoming at once an abstract 'modern Athens' and a 'natural' site of sublime or picturesque beauty to underwrite a cultural nationalism that relegated markers of national identity safely to the past, so as to permit the modern nation ready entry into the present British imperial arrangement of things. But if the new capital displayed itself in this way – as it did – the question of local and historical bearings was never fully erased. Not only in the local press and local genres but in the hugely circulated Waverley Novels of Walter Scott (e.g. *Redgauntlet, Heart of Midlothian, Chronicles of the Canongate*), the question of local affiliations kept intruding as part of a broad civic concern with public spaces and their social import.

The city's physical layout made the topic inescapable. Edinburgh's striking topography, the result of its unprecedented, rapid transformation in the late eighteenth century, set a medieval Old Town and an enlightenment New Town starkly across from one another, the two 'faces' of the city visibly articulating the question of how people inhabit places and make urban spaces. If the transformation of Edinburgh, begun in the 1760s, promoted civic pride in the city's definitive entrance into modernity, confirming its emergence from an earlier 'Dark Age' of provincial backwardness and stagnation, it equally prompted civic anxiety over the loss of forms of publicness and connection enabled by the distinctive layout of the Old Town. Recalling the jolt his generation experienced in the wholesale move of the city's professional and gentry classes from the Old Town in the course of a few decades, Henry Cockburn wrote: 'It altered the style of living, obliterated local arrangements, and destroyed a thousand associations, which nothing but the still preserved names of houses and of places is left to recal [*sic*].'[4] For the generation after Cockburn, the aftershocks remained even as memories of the Old Town rapidly faded. Their vanishing impelled an obscure, impecunious young bookseller of literary ambition to seek out and start recording living memories of the 'auld town'. Robert Chambers's *Traditions of Edinburgh* (1825) rewrote civic antiquarian history as urban 'traditions', launching a new mode in urban writing, although the *Traditions* itself has remained well under the critical radar.[5] Intersecting with gentry writings in its antiquarian cast, the *Traditions* also made innovative use of the oral memory more typically associated with everyday life. The conjunction turned the civic antiquary into popular but not populist historian and (not so incidentally) laid the foundation for one of the most prolific and influential careers in cheap print publishing in the nineteenth century.

In her study of the writing of urban histories in the eighteenth century, Rosemary Sweet emphasizes the 'exponential rise in urban historiography' at the end of the century in urban centres outside London.[6] Manifesting itself in different modalities (e.g. touristic, antiquarian, chronicle), this historiography converged in reflecting a burgeoning sense of civic assurance and independence consequent on a town's move into modernity. As Peter Clark has observed: 'Towns are portrayed as centres of a new-style civilization, confident, reformed, free of the old superstitions of the past, dynamos of commercial and industrial expansion.'[7] Witness the author of *The History of Nottingham* (1815), striking the generic keynote: 'in point of manufacturing and commercial genius – in industry and useful invention, it yields preference to no town or city in the British empire; and in its progress in the fine arts it will give up the palm but to few'.[8] Modernized as they were, such towns nonetheless took pride in their 'antiquities', which enhanced civic distinction by testifying to deep historical roots on the one hand and adding aesthetic dimension to the current townscape on the other. The incorporation of antiquities in such texts underlines the increasing popularization and commercialization of antiquarianism by the end of the century when, as Sweet demonstrates, antiquaries of lower social origin began to enter the field in significant (if not massive) numbers. Their entry challenged the authority of the gentleman amateur as custodian of the nation's past, claiming study of this past on behalf of a more inclusive sense of the public. This does not mean, as Sweet observes, that antiquarianism was class neutral. But it does mean that it provided 'a language within which people from very different backgrounds could communicate and exchange information' across class lines (if not across the gender divide).[9]

Not all forms of antiquarian activity were equally hospitable, of course. County history, for instance, remained very much a gentry practice in contrast to urban history. County histories, commissioned or produced by landed gentry, were typically issued in handsome folios and quartos whose price was established in guineas; by contrast, urban histories, produced by locals from a range of backgrounds and often commissioned by printers or booksellers, appeared in smaller, cheaper formats for a few shillings. In the early eighteenth century (when few such histories were produced) the authorship was largely made up of local professionals such as lawyers and clergymen, but by the end of the century the social band had widened to include what Clark terms 'secondary or quasi-professions' such as school-mastering, land-surveying, and (in significant numbers) printing and bookselling.[10] Urban histories thus expanded the definition of who had a stake in the nation's past, bringing into play the lower reaches of the middle classes to whose self-conscious sense of being 'modern' they offered tangible expression.

Picture of Edinburgh (1806) by the printer John Stark neatly exemplifies the standard genre.[11] Despite the aesthetic promise of 'picture' in its title, the work is abstract and taxonomic, approaching the city as a quasi-scientific object of modern representation.[12] An external, impersonal survey and inventory (complete with a plan of the city), it displays Edinburgh to the reader in easily digestible entries, lists, and statistics. Taking up its position in city hall, so to speak, it concentrates exclusively on the official city, understanding it as organized and managed space. Stark includes a prefatory 'History of Edinburgh', along with a list of 'Antiquities', but in his account the city's past is simply a prelude to a progressive present, its antiquities municipal adornments. His descriptive entries lean heavily toward civil establishments (e.g. 'Political and Civil Establishments', 'Municipal Establishments', 'Banks', 'Literary Establishments', 'Charitable Institutions', and so on). Only when Stark turns to his own profession in 'Progress and Present State of Printing' does the text achieve a measure of animation. Later editions add new civic institutions (e.g. 'Jury Court', 'Insurance Companies', 'Observatory and Astronomical Institution'), under-scoring the temporality of expansion that guarantees the city's modern rationality.

In sharp contrast stands the informal, jumbled Edinburgh of Robert Chambers's *Traditions of Edinburgh*. Originally published in six paper-bound numbers for two shillings each (1824–5), 'this fortunate little work' (as Chambers termed it) proved surprisingly successful from the start. The initial print run of 300 was soon raised, and reached 2,700 for the last three numbers, after which the whole was gathered into two small volumes for publication in 1825.[13] Substantially revised new editions, along with off-shoots such as *Reekiana* (1833), continued to appear up to the death of Chambers in 1871, followed by abridgments and reissues, the latest of which was published in 1996. The *Traditions* rewrites not only the city as scientific object of representation, as in municipal histories like Stark's, but also the city of antiquarians, the repository of 'curious' objects and documents from a remote past, notably the medieval past of gothic architecture. Chambers's project is motivated by the loss of a much closer past: 'The ancient part of Edinburgh has, within the last fifty years, experienced a vicissitude scarcely credible to the present generation.'[14] So declares the opening sentence, activating the two-generation span identified by Scott in *Waverley* as the measure of Scotland's modern alteration. Unlike Stark and the writers of municipal histories, Chambers takes up his position in the informal city of the street and domestic interiors. Dividing the volumes into 'Old Houses' and 'Characters, &c.', he records local anecdotes, legends, and memories (even as he describes buildings and tracks family genealogies) to produce the city as what Michel de Certeau calls a 'haunted place'. The anecdotes of local memory, Certeau writes, animate urban places with the presence of what is now absent ('*Here*, there used to be', '*That's* where'), and they come to 'haunt' the city like 'superfluous or additional inhabitants', unsettling the flattened, rational parameters of functional definitions of urban space.[15]

Commenting on the *Traditions* some decades later in a text that derives from it, the anthropologist/ethnologist Daniel Wilson reflected on Chambers's achievement vis-à-vis earlier histories of Edinburgh, and he identified the key innovation as a function of narrative focalization: the production of a close-up, familiar view of the urban scene.[16] Referring back to the standard histories of William Maitland (*The History of Edinburgh*, 1753) and Hugo Arnot (*The History of Edinburgh*, 1779), Wilson asserts that these earlier historians had failed 'to embrace' the city: 'Both of the historians of Edinburgh seem, indeed, to have lacked that invaluable faculty of the topographer, styled by phrenologists *locality*, and the consequence is, that we are treated with a large canvass, composed in the historic vein of high art, when probably most readers would much rather have preferred a cabinet picture of the Dutch school.'[17] He regrets in particular that the spirited Arnot 'should have stalked through the purlieus of old Edinburgh, elevated on historic stilts' instead of descending to snatch from oblivion 'a thousand curious reminiscences'. The *Traditions*, however, 'struck out an entirely new path' by presenting 'old-world stories of Edinburgh' with 'occasional heightening touches from the delineator's own lively fancy'.[18] Defined by the plurality of 'traditions' (in contrast to the singularity of 'tradition'), Chambers's city comes into representation through the informal knowledge represented by the city's gossip about places, persons, and events. He himself takes a gossip's garrulous delight in telling tales, less anxious about their authenticity or authentication than about simply keeping them in circulation. He may report a 'well authenticated tradition' about a proposed property deal for seemingly worthless land ninety years ago, but he is equally interested in a more dubious 'tradition' ('somewhat at variance with the *writts and evidents*') about where the Duke of Argyll spent the night before his execution (vol. 1, pp. 75, 163). In his text details spiral, footnotes spill over, and subjects follow one another in apparently random order. What propels it is a sheer 'pleasure in recording', as Chambers testifies when observing that a particular tradition attached to where the unpopular Union was signed by the Lord Commissioners is 'only part of the truth, if a still more recondite tradition, which we have now the pleasure of recording, is to be relied upon' (vol. 1, p. 19n). This 'recondite tradition' involves a surreptitious meeting in a cellar on the High Street and an ignominious flight from town under cover of darkness. Associative, digressive, disjointed – Chambers's work proves 'irregular' like the city that is its subject. He himself invited the parallel during its serial publication when he apologized to readers for some 'irregularity' in the way he was publishing the numbers. In defence he set up an analogy between the object and the medium of representation: 'It would have been just as impossible to give the work that correctness and perfection which is required in books of another stamp, as for our ancestors in the tenth century to lay out the High Street . . . in the straight lines and uniform dimensions that have been observed in the New Town.'[19]

Aged inhabitants were the primary sources of the local memory that sustains Chambers's history. Compiled largely from material supplied by such 'informants' even if not typically presented in their own words, the *Traditions* represents an early form of oral history. Chambers does not ignore textual sources – he cites a mixed bag of histories, newspapers, letters, statistical accounts, novels, poems, and so on – but he insists that he has 'always had greater recourse to oral intelligence than to the less homely information of books' (vol. 11, p. 300). In a late preface he identifies 'aged professionals and mercantile gentlemen' as the groups on which he relied most heavily for such 'oral intelligence', noting their general surprise at his own youthfulness, 'having formed the notion that none but an old person would have thought of writing such a book'. The same preface also provides specific names whose mix of high/low, famous/ obscure underlines the mix in the text itself. The illustrious Walter Scott heads the list (Scott provided Chambers with notes and anecdotes, along with a manuscript fragment on 'The Antiquities of Edinburgh'[20]) followed by Charles Kirkpatrick Sharpe, an aristocratically inclined antiquary-gossip well known in Edinburgh at the time who, Chambers says, has now himself become, 'as it were, a tradition of Edinburgh'. Two others are mentioned: a nameless 'living lady' belonging to the generation of George III; and (in an exceptionally warm tribute) a draper named David Bridges, who had a shop in the Old Town.[21] In the work itself Chambers rarely identifies informants by name, typically relying on generic identifiers such as 'some aged neighbours', 'ancient inhabitants', 'an ancient gentleman', and so on. Some of these testify to what they remember from their youth, but others serve as relays to an even earlier generation: 'The father of our informant one day accosted the laird', 'Our informant, an old non-juring acquaintance of the deceased' (vol. 11, pp. 76, 102). Even further removed are the 'traditions' pertaining to 1745 that Chambers derived from the daughter of a waiting maid who was then in the family of the Earl of Dundonald (vol. 1, p. 111).

The *Traditions* is thus memory at second- or third-hand (Chambers's own memory rarely comes into play), setting out to transmit and transfer across a gap of generations 'memories' to which those currently on the ground have no direct access. Such transfer, as Ann Rigney argues, hinges on the 'portability' of the past, a portability that is the very condition of cultural memory as by definition a form of 'memory' outside first-hand, living memory.[22] Rigney draws particular attention to the role of literary works in the making of cultural memory – their power to make literally memorable what has been forgotten or obscured – but her more general point is that any transmission of the past inevitably enters that past into an unpredictable circuit of transmutation. For Rigney such a circuit testifies to the productive mobility of culture, a positive recycling of the past, but the flip side is a sense of the vulnerability of the past, and this sense pressed sharply in a city whose rapid change had made peculiarly apparent the fragility of local memory. As the *Edinburgh Magazine* commented in a review of the *Traditions*, the city's 'modern improvement' was daily making it more and more difficult to rescue from oblivion the kind of reminiscences and anecdotes collected by Chambers: 'the vestiges of the olden time were disappearing as fast as the lofty tenements inhabited by the veterans and worthies of the last century'.[23] Chambers's entire project is posited on the erosion of specific memories, practices, and places (from houses to forms of socialization to the fashion in door knockers). Walking through the houses of the Old Town, questioning their current inhabitants, he encounters decaying buildings and oblivious inhabitants, paying special tribute to occasional exceptions such as a blacksmith named Andrew Wilson who can provide 'particulars' of the history of the building he now occupies (vol. 1, p. 104). Intent on securing what 'particulars' he can, he continually underlines the fragility of this knowledge, as when (speaking of a right of sanctuary in the Grassmarket) he notes that 'the circumstance is now very little known in the town, and might, perhaps, have been soon forgotten altogether, but for this humble memorial' (vol. 1, p. 100n). Within a few years, he laments, 'no living witnesses shall be found to attest the tales we have told' (vol. 1, p. 313).

Chambers frames this erosion of local memory in explicit class terms, presenting it as consequent on the incursion of the lower orders into the old city after the upper orders decamped to the New Town late in the eighteenth century. 'The commercial and working classes have over-run all its stately *lands,*' he sums up at the end of the first volume, which concludes with a nostalgic evocation of the last party (held in 1819) by the last 'gentleman' to occupy a house in the old city (vol. 1, p. 313). Juxtaposition of past and present, however, does more than articulate a predictable recoil from 'the vulgar' on the part of a déclassé Chambers, traumatized by his own family's social fall following the collapse of his father's textile business.[24] What comes to dominate the *Traditions* is less the sense of a particular historical instance of urban degradation than a broader awareness of the temporality of passage that governs urban spaces in general. Keeping the present close at hand but casting it within the realm of passing things, the text presents the city as a site of constant transition and metamorphosis, a moving ground. Seeking 'vestiges' and 'traces' of former buildings, uses, and inhabitants, Chambers uncovers signs both of historical layering and ongoing change (it is no accident that he will turn into the author of the *Vestiges of the Natural History of Creation*). Thus he reports in a typical construction, 'There is not now the slightest vestige of ornamental or carved work upon the premises, excepting the remains of a Gothic pillar' (vol. 1, p. 248). To this antiquarian notion of 'vestige', however, he also gives a more immediate, sociological charge by foregrounding the remains of a past much more recent than that of 'Gothic' pillars and by focusing on human as much as material remnants. His account of the West Bow, for example, traditional home of Edinburgh's tinsmiths, underlines that it has undergone such dispersion 'within the last few years, that there are now (1824) only two tin-plate workers in the whole Bow' (vol. 1, p. 133); indeed, 'within the last few years' becomes something of a refrain to announce a continuing erosion in both material and social realms. At the same time, such erosion means that old spaces are put to new uses, and if Chambers deplores the fact that a formerly ornamented cupboard has been stripped of its ornamentation in the process of becoming a coal-hole, he is more sanguine about other shifts, as in the taking over of the deserted mansions of the aristocracy by printers and publishers such as the firm of Oliver and Boyd (vol. 1, pp. 88, 247).

What all this brings home is the material dimension of memory: the degree to which in its collective civic modality in particular it is not only a memory *of* places but a memory rooted *in* place and peculiarly dependent on it. Unlike the personal memory Wordsworth made his great poetic subject, this kind of memory (quite literally 'local' memory) does not survive dislocation. Wordsworth can carry with him to distant places and times the rejuvenating power of particular memories (his delighted stumbling on a host of daffodils, his day with Dorothy above Tintern Abbey, and so on), internalizing the memory so that it floats free of its initial external triggers. Local memory, however, is not simply shaped but sustained by the physical places in which it originated and to which it refers. Chambers's key point is that memories not only fade when removed from such places but rarely survive a change in the physical place itself. Thus when he prints a list of the inhabitants of St Andrew's Square in 1773 (a list supplied by 'a person whose memory reaches back to the year 1773') he does so, he explains, in anticipation of the disappearance of this New Town square, now being cut up into shops: 'The time is not far distant when the whole of this district shall meet with a fate similar to that which we have to record respecting the Cowgate and Canongate' (vol. 1, p. 69). At once rooted and contingent, the 'fading traces' of local memory recorded by Chambers point more generally to how social formations in urban spaces turn on the exigencies of location. It was the question of such exigency that moved into especially sharp view when the divided face of Edinburgh came into focus.

In the introductory chapter on 'Changes in the Last Hundred Years', which prefaced the 1846 revision and all later editions of the *Traditions*, Chambers summed up Edinburgh as 'a kind of double city': '*first*, an ancient and picturesque hill-built one, occupied chiefly by the humbler classes; and *second*, an elegant modern one, of much regularity of aspect, and possessed almost as exclusively by the more refined portion of society'.[25] Characterizing such social division as 'only too accordant with that tendency of our present form of civilisation to separate the high from the low', he registers a carefully worded scepticism about modern progress as the effecting of 'dissociation': 'that dissociation, in short, which would in itself run nigh to be a condemnation of all progress, if we were not allowed to suppose that better forms of civilisation are realisable'.[26] Chambers was a committed modern. Indeed, by the mid-1840s when he wrote these words he was closely linked in the public mind with the active promotion of notions of utility and improvement in the new mass media of print. But this did not rule out a concern over the diminishment of public life and social fragmentation consequent on the economic order underpinning such notions and technologies. Similar concerns had shadowed the Scottish Enlightenment's complex thinking on historical progress from the outset (one thinks, for instance, of the anxiety over the attenuation of the 'bands' of society informing Adam Ferguson's *An Essay on the History of Civil Society*), and Chambers was not alone in regarding the 'dissociation' represented by the split city as a manifestation of the problematic as much as positive consequences of modernization. When it came to the Old Town in particular, the doubled city typically generated a doubled response. Despite reiterated statements about its insalubrious and unsatisfactory character, not to mention the alacrity with which most literary men and professionals themselves moved across to New Town, the old city increasingly came to function in the civic writing of the early nineteenth century as a trope of a lost social cohesion.

At the heart of this trope stood a building: the distinctive tenement of the old city known as a *land*, rows of which were packed tightly into its narrow streets and alleys. These tall narrow structures typically housed people of different social stations on different levels of a common staircase, and this physical fact underpinned a nostalgic myth of the 'auld town' as the locus of ideal pre-modern urban community. 'In an Edinburgh *land*,' wrote Walter Scott, 'a sort of general interest united the whole inhabitants, from top to the bottom of those lofty tenements.' 'Closeness of residence' made neighbours dependent on one another, he explains, and in the wake of a mutual cooperation initially 'compelled' by a pragmatic logic there developed a properly social 'habit', which gave 'a social enjoyment to the whole system'.[27] Scott's point is echoed in text after text on the old city (well into the twentieth century), and it informs Chambers's own account in the *Traditions*: 'At the period we allude to,' he observes in the second volume of the work, 'people of all ranks lived very closely and cordially together, and the whole world were in a manner next-door neighbours' (vol. II, p. 25). Such idealization, R. A. Houston points out, depends on an inferential leap from the fact that different ranks lived in close proximity to the implication of close social relation: 'close proximity does not necessarily mean that they mixed together or even acknowledged each other's presence on the stairs or in closes and church aisles'.[28] As he rightly notes, tight quarters may in fact have solidified rather than dissolved social hierarchy and done little to forge social cohesion. All the same the sheer fact of proximity was crucial, making apparent the shaping force of spatial configuration on social experience (however such experience might ultimately be interpreted). In particular, it impressed on contemporaries the way the layout of the Old Town allowed for a level of publicness not available in the reconfigured New Town, one whose base was physical: the simple, casual familiarity that made people 'known' to one another (if not necessarily acknowledged) in the winding closes and crowded streets of the old city.

Modern cities, Richard Sennett has argued, are intent on configuring space so as to move bodies through it with as little resistance as possible, actively suppressing the tactile sense of one's material surroundings as well as the 'bodily awareness of other people' that characterized close, pre-modern urban space.[29] It is not incidental that much of the criticism of the New Town focused on the monotony of its wide streets, which served more readily as through-ways than as meeting places. Evaluating the New Town, Cockburn deplores 'the blunder of long straight lines of street', while *Blackwood's Magazine*, similarly unimpressed by its 'straight lines', welcomes the new planners of the 1820s who began to favour 'crescents and circuses, and turnings and windings'.[30] As planned forms, however, the latter too operated as rational spaces of orientation in contrast to the 'turnings and windings' of the old city whose steep streets and alleys made passage difficult and local knowledge paramount. James Hogg's evocation of the notorious Edinburgh mob in *Private Memoirs and Confessions of a Justified Sinner* (1824) makes the point. He is describing how the mob vanishes when attacked on the High Street: 'The unnumbered alleys on each side of the street had swallowed up the multitude in a few seconds; but from these they were busy reconnoitring; and, perceiving the deficiency in the number of their assailants, the rush from both sides of the street was as rapid, and as wonderful, as the disappearance of the crowd had been a few minutes before.'[31] Abruptly vanishing and reappearing, surging and retreating, the crowd at once exploits the layout of the streets and becomes a function of them.

The streets of the old city, then, produced a peculiarly tangible sense of how places shape movements and produce events, including those later incorporated into 'history'. Scott's depiction of the celebrated Porteous riot of 1736 in *The Heart of Midlothian* offers a striking example. Taking up its position from the start at the level of the physical city, the opening chapters establish the city itself as a ground (as opposed to a 'view', for instance) by placing readers in the Grassmarket, on the Bow, and alongside local characters, chattering as they walk along, giving vent to a distrust of 'Lunnon'. The Porteous event was firmly entrenched in Edinburgh lore as local resistance to the 'far order' of the English government, but Scott's narration of its triggering event – the execution of the popular smuggler Andrew Wilson by the unpopular John Porteous and his Town Guard – makes apparent the degree to which the specificity of location (the configuration of space around the scene of execution) acted as a catalyst. The narrow confines of the square and its surrounding streets not only pushed soldiers, spectators, and the condemned into tight proximity but meant that the bullets of the soldiers, who tried to fire above the crowd surrounding the scaffold, hit those of the higher classes who had stationed themselves in windows. As a result, Scott's narrator drily remarks, a certain unity was forged in the city: 'burghers' joined with the 'rabble' in response to the events, and 'considered the cause as common to all ranks'.[32] Common cause or civic community emerge here not as a substantive referring to an existing entity (a *Gemeinschaft*) but as a happenstance thrown up by contingency and rooted in a mundane level of urban physical being. This is not to deny the broader political and ideological meanings of the Porteous episode but it is to say that Scott's foregrounding of its location points to the way that public events (in the standard sense of those involving matters of the State, politics, and law) may rest on more informal configurations of public life rooted in specific places.

For Chambers in particular, the compactness of the old city helped to generate public identities that had little to do with official roles or positions. As he observes, the 'narrow limits of the streets and places of public resort' in the city meant that 'people all knew each other by sight' (vol. 1, p. 21n). To be known 'by sight' in this way was to become a figure in what he calls 'the public eye' but it was to do so as a body repeatedly encountered on the street rather than a person of authority or celebrity. The whole section on 'Characters, &c.' pivots on this kind of publicness, one that inheres in the literal recognition by fellow inhabitants that makes someone 'well known'. The 'slim, skeleton-looking figure' of the Edinburgh historian Hugo Arnot, we are told, was 'well-known to the public eye at the period' (vol. 1, p. 74), while an old Jacobite nicknamed the Daft Laird was 'well-known upon the streets of Edinburgh from thirty to sixty years ago' (vol. II, p. 71). Such figures are known because they become part of the everyday public life in the city, and the emphasis of Chambers's character sketches is on this dimension of its lived experience. Thus the entry on the eminent jurist Lord Kames consists of an anecdote about his daily encounter with '*Sinkum the Cadie*', who would 'walk alongside of his Lordship up the street to the Parliament-House' each morning to give him the day's gossip (vol. II, pp. 171–2). Most of Chambers's sketches devote marked attention to the appearance of their subjects – the shape of their bodies, their clothes, their gait – recalling that in this same period John Kay's visual caricatures were similarly memorializing the publicness of being on Edinburgh streets. A self-taught former barber, Kay generated almost a thousand portraits of the city's inhabitants in these years, selling individual prints from his small shop on the High Street. These were not reproduced in his lifetime, making his an eminently local collection (a selection published after his death in serial and volume achieved wider circulation and publicity[33]), and Kay himself was an intensely local character. Chambers invokes him at several points in the *Traditions*, crediting him as a source, but his most suggestive gloss on both his own and Kay's enterprise comes in the entry on Kay he wrote for his *Biographical Dictionary of Eminent Scotsmen*. Stressing that Kay drew a person 'as he walked the street every day', he delineates the caricaturist's achievement as 'a complete record of the public characters, of every grade and kind . . . who made a figure in Edinburgh for nearly half a century'.[34] Through such figures, both Kay and Chambers set out to record a rapidly eroding notion of 'public character' attached to the street as an informal, intermediate public space between the private spaces of domesticity and the formal public realm of civic institutions.

Chambers's own ramshackle work, similarly located somewhere between intimacy and monumentality, seeks to make itself an equivalent in discourse of such publicness, enacting authorship as an informal mediation and transmission of what passes in public, and constituting the space of reading as the impersonal yet familiar realm of the 'public eye'. Through the proximities of author/reader/representation, the *Traditions* establishes something like a public meeting place – a virtual public square – and it was in its sketches and anecdotes that Chambers developed the mode of authorship that became his hallmark. If he himself soon repudiated it and his other early antiquarian writings as 'merely a youthful amusement' to be put aside for the 'pursuit of literary objects of more extensive utility, and requiring a greater exertion of moral reflection', the informal space of knowledge he carved out in the *Traditions* was to underwrite his entire

career as public author and cheap print publisher.[35] As Robert Scholnick
has pointed out, 'the most distinctive feature' of the pioneering *Chambers's
Edinburgh Journal* was the informal essays contributed by Robert Chambers himself, while James Secord argues that the popular impact of the
Vestiges of the Natural History of Creation rested on the establishment of a
familiar relationship between narrator and reader which assumed that 'an
understanding of nature is accessible to all'.[36] What Chambers repudiated
when he launched himself into the cheap print market in the 1830s was
not his early authorial mode so much as an early authorial desire to repro-
duce what he termed the 'tangibilities' of the past.[37] Indeed, what now
assumed prominence was the basic implication of the authorial mode
honed in the *Traditions*: the commitment to making a public through
a print medium that was itself to be rendered ever more tangible and
proximate.

   Paul Magnusson argues in *Reading Public Romanticism* that the canonical Romantic poets must be restored to their 'locations' if we are to
grasp their public significance. The location he has in mind is the wider
'public discourse' of published writings that succeeded the more bounded
'public sphere' of the eighteenth century specified by Habermas.[38] But the
case of Chambers suggests that 'public Romanticism' may be understood
more widely and as fruitfully as a question of the location of the public:
where/what was it? Foregrounding everyday public life, the urban
'traditions' restored a body to the public, and in so doing they returned to
an understanding of public ground that preceded even as it sustained
the binary distinctions such as high/low governing cultural debate in
the period. The question of the public impelled a large number of the
intermediary, non-imaginative genres (typically designated 'secondary'),
and prompted some of Romanticism's signature generic innovations
such as the familiar essay and the familiar periodical linked to second-
generation practitioners like Leigh Hunt, Charles Lamb, and William
Hazlitt. Chambers's *Traditions of Edinburgh* takes its place among these,
setting out at once to recall vanishing forms of publicness and to constitute itself as an informal public space, but it locates the public neither
in political theory ('public opinion') nor in print culture ('the reading
public') but in the original ground of publicness: the city itself.

NOTES

1 See Mark Phillips, *Society and Sentiment: Genres of Historical Writing in
  Britain, 1740–1820* (Princeton, N. J.: Princeton University Press, 2000).

2 Henri Lefebvre, *Writings on Cities*, trans. and ed. Eleonore Kofman and Elizabeth Lebas (Oxford: Blackwell, 1996), p. 101. James Chandler and Kevin Gilmartin's recent collection, *Romantic Metropolis: The Urban Scene of British Culture, 1780–1840* (Cambridge: Cambridge University Press, 2005), should prompt renewed attention to the city, although the collection itself focuses heavily on the special case of London, metropolis and imperial capital.

3 Ian Duncan, *Scott's Shadow: The Novel in Romantic Edinburgh* (Princeton, N.J. and Oxford: Princeton University Press, 2007), p. 9.

4 Henry Cockburn, *Memorials of His Time* (Edinburgh, 1856), pp. 28–9.

5 The *Traditions of Edinburgh* does, however, continue to have something of an afterlife in tourist Edinburgh both directly, as in picture-books like Margeorie Mekie's *The Heart of Old Edinburgh* (Catrine, Ayrshire: Stenlake Publishing, 2004), and indirectly, as in the ubiquitous walking tours of the 'auld town'.

6 Rosemary Sweet, *The Writing of Urban Histories in Eighteenth-Century England* (Oxford: Clarendon Press, 1997), p. 10. The book includes an appendix listing urban histories up to 1820 organized by towns.

7 Peter Clark, 'Visions of the Urban Community: Antiquarians and the English City before 1800', in Derek Fraser and Anthony Sutcliffe (eds.), *The Pursuit of Urban History* (London: Edward Arnold, 1983), p. 122.

8 John Blackner, *The History of Nottingham, Embracing its Antiquities, Trade, and Manufactures, From the Earliest Authentic Records, to the Present Period* (Nottingham, 1815), p. 8.

9 Rosemary Sweet, *Antiquaries: The Discovery of the Past in Eighteenth-Century Britain* (London and New York: Hambledon and London, 2004), p. 60.

10 Clark, 'Visions of the Urban Community', p. 121.

11 Stark's full title reads: *Picture of Edinburgh: Containing a History and Description of the City, With a particular Account of Every Remarkable Object in, or Establishment Connected with, the Scottish Metropolis. Illustrated with a Plan, and Upwards of Thirty Engravings on Wood* (Edinburgh, 1806). The work was revised in 1820, and issued until at least 1840.

12 'Picturesque' views of cities abounded in the period, especially in the case of Edinburgh, but they form a genre distinct from urban history, taking their place more prominently in the aestheticization of Edinburgh to which Duncan draws attention in *Scott's Shadow*, Chapter 1.

13 Robert Chambers, *Man of Letters: The Early Life and Love Letters of Robert Chambers*, ed. C. H. Layman (Edinburgh: Edinburgh University Press, 1990), p. 101. On the publication of *Traditions of Edinburgh*, see Coleman O. Parsons, 'Serial Publication of *Traditions of Edinburgh*', *Transactions of the Bibliographical Society* 14 (September 1933), 207–11.

14 Robert Chambers, *Traditions of Edinburgh*, 2 vols. (Edinburgh, 1825), vol. 1, p. 1, hereafter referred to in parentheses in the text; its serial title was *Traditions of Edinburgh; or Sketches & Anecdotes of the City in Former Times*. My focus is the first edition of 1825. The 1846 edition, which became the basis for all subsequent editions, was heavily revised, adopting the conventional

frame of a 'walk' in the city, reordering material and altering the format so as to fit more closely the standard guidebook.

15 Michel de Certeau, *The Practice of Everyday Life*, trans. Steven Rendall (Berkeley and Los Angeles: University of California Press, 1984), pp. 108, 106.

16 Mark Phillips's work draws particular attention to the importance of variable dimensions of 'distance' in historical writing; see, for example, 'Relocating Inwardness: Historical Distance and the Transition from Enlightenment to Romantic Historiography', *PMLA* 118 (May 2003), 436–49.

17 Daniel Wilson, *Memorials of Edinburgh in the Olden Time*, 2 vols. (Edinburgh, 1848), vol. 1, p. v.

18 *Ibid.*, pp. ix, v.

19 The remarks, dated 1 November 1824, appear on the back cover of the third number; I consulted the run of numbers held in the Cowan Collection of the Edinburgh Public Library.

20 Scott's fragmentary manuscript is published in *The Letters of Sir Walter Scott and Charles Kirkpatrick Sharpe to Robert Chambers 1821–45*, printed from manuscripts and edited by C. E. S. Chambers (London: W. and R. Chambers, 1904), pp. 69–76.

21 Robert Chambers, 'Introductory Notice. 1868', *Traditions of Edinburgh*, new edition (Edinburgh and London, 1868), pp. v, vii. Chambers had dedicated the first volume of the 1825 edition to Sharpe, the second to Scott.

22 Ann Rigney, 'Portable Monuments: Literature, Cultural Memory, and the Case of Jeanie Deans', *Poetics Today* 25 (Summer 2004), 361–96.

23 'Chambers' Traditions of Edinburgh', *Edinburgh Magazine* n.s. 17 (August 1825), 130.

24 Chambers vividly describes the shock he experienced in *Man of Letters*, pp. 76–88.

25 Chambers, *Traditions of Edinburgh*, new edition, p. 8.

26 *Ibid.*

27 Walter Scott, *Provincial Antiquities and Picturesque Scenery of Scotland, with Descriptive Illustrations*, 2 vols. (London and Edinburgh, 1826), vol. 1, p. 74.

28 R. A. Houston, *Social Change in the Age of Enlightenment: Edinburgh 1660–1760* (Oxford: Clarendon Press, 1994), p. 74.

29 Richard Sennett, *Flesh and Stone: The Body and the City in Western Civilization* (New York and London: W. W. Norton, 1994), p. 18.

30 Cockburn, *Memorials of His Time*, p. 286; 'Great Fire of Edinburgh', *Blackwood's Magazine* 16 (December 1824), 707.

31 James Hogg, *The Private Memoirs and Confessions of a Justified Sinner*, ed. P. D. Garside (Edinburgh: Edinburgh University Press, 2002), p. 22.

32 Walter Scott, *The Heart of Midlothian*, ed. Claire Lamont (Oxford: Oxford University Press, 1982), p. 43.

33 *Kay's Edinburgh Portraits, Being Original Engravings of about Four Hundred Various Personages, by John Kay, Caricaturist, Engraver, and Miniature Painter* (Edinburgh, 1836). On Kay see Hilary and Mary Evans, *John Kay of Edinburgh: Barber, Miniaturist, and Social Commentator, 1742–1826* (Aberdeen:

Impulse Publications, 1973). Kay's portraits continue to circulate, and are available on the web and featured on book covers.

34 Robert Chambers, *Biographical Dictionary of Eminent Scotsmen*, rev. by Thomas Thomson, 3 vols. (London, 1875), vol. 11, p. 415.

35 Robert Chambers, *Reekiana: Minor Antiquities of Edinburgh* (Edinburgh: William and Robert Chambers, 1833), p. vii.

36 Robert J. Scholnick, '"The Fiery Cross of Knowledge": *Chambers's Edinburgh Journal*, 1832–1844', *Victorian Periodical Review* 32 (1999), 330; James A. Secord, *Victorian Sensation: The Extraordinary Publication, Reception, and Secret Authorship of the 'Vestiges of the Natural History of Creation'* (Chicago and London: University of Chicago Press, 2000), p. 99.

37 See his General Preface to *Select Writings of Robert Chambers*, 7 vols. (Edinburgh, 1847), vol. 1, p. iv.

38 Paul Magnusson, *Reading Public Romanticism* (Princeton, N. J.: Princeton University Press, 1998), Chapter 1.

CHAPTER 9

Keats, popular culture, and the sociability of theatre

Gillian Russell

In 1816 *The Times* published, as a '*jeu d'Esprit*', a parody of a Cambridge examination paper, the first question of which was the following:

1. Give a comparative sketch of the principal English Theatres, with the dates of their erection, and the names of the most eminent Candle-snuffers at each? What were the Stage-boxes? What were the offices of Prompter – Ballet-master – and Scene-shifter? In what part of the Theatre was the one-shilling Gallery? Distinguish accurately between Operas and Puppet-shews.[1]

In addition to making fun of the enduring formulas of the examination paper, the parody contrasted 'official' or privileged forms of knowledge with the mental world of the Regency young gentleman, dominated by urban trivia – the quotidian detail and local particularities of the metropolitan social scene. Among the topics covered by the examination paper of 'Utopia University' were the locations of the principal coach inns of London, the history of 'Spyring and Marsden's Lemon Acid', and the name of the Prime Minister in power when the boxer Tom Cribb defeated his arch-rival Molineaux. At the apex of this view of Regency London was the theatre: the candidate was expected to have intimate knowledge of features such as the one-shilling gallery and personalities normally invisible in theatre history such as candle-snuffers and scene-shifters. The exam paper's instruction to 'distinguish accurately between Operas and Puppet-shews', encompassing the range of theatrical entertainments in the metropolis, from the English and Italian opera houses to the booths of Bartholomew Fair, also poses a challenge to students of Romantic-period culture in the twenty-first century: is it possible to distinguish between 'high' and 'low' forms of theatre, and how might recognition of such subaltern knowledges and experiences complicate our current understanding of Romanticism?

One possible candidate for *The Times*'s examination was John Keats, for whom the social and literary circles of the metropolis, including the theatre, were an informal, even 'Utopian', university from 1815, when he moved to London to study medicine at Guy's Hospital at the age of twenty. The productions of the opera houses were beyond Keats's income, but he was a regular play-goer at the patent theatres of Covent Garden and Drury Lane, and though we have no record of his response to puppet shows it is highly likely that he was familiar with the entertainments of Bartholomew Fair and other metropolitan fairs such as those of his childhood home in Edmonton. The latter was one of the stamping grounds of the celebrated itinerant penny showman John Richardson, whose booth at Bartholomew Fair was commemorated by William Hone in 1825. Illuminated by 'fifteen hundred variegated illumination-lamps', Richardson's theatre staged a programme of melodramas, pantomimes, and panoramas for up to 1,000 people, at ticket prices ranging from 2 shillings for 'box seats' to sixpence for the 'gallery', suggesting considerable overlap with the clientele of the fixed theatres.[2] As a nursery for actors such as Edmund Kean and a resource for older performers in search of employment, Richardson's travelling show exemplifies the mobility of artists and theatre workers, capital, audiences, and product that characterizes the theatrical culture of the Regency period. This traffic complicates accounts of popular culture that define it in homogeneous terms and in binary opposition to hegemonic elite culture. Keats himself practised a form of this traffic when, on one January evening in 1818, he combined witnessing Edmund Kean as Richard III in the opulence of Drury Lane theatre with attendance at a grubby little private theatre nearby. Private theatres, Regency developments of the spouting clubs of the eighteenth century, were venues associated with taverns and drinking dens, where lower-class artisans could pay to perform in plays: as David Worrall has shown, they proliferated in this period and were linked with a reinvigorated popular radicalism after 1815.[3] Granted access behind the scenes, Keats was able to observe the performers at close hand in all their 'pothouse' glory, describing the experience as 'a great treat'.[4]

A similar catholic interest in theatre is apparent in Keats's play-going outside London: he attended a performance at the theatre in Teignmouth in Devon, at which he was 'insulted' by a member of the audience, and while on his walking tour with Charles Brown in 1818 he left his friend alone for an evening to see a company of strolling players perform in a 'Barn' in Inverary in Scotland (vol. 1, pp. 246, 336). Keats's interest in theatre, which has been extensively documented, has received sporadic attention in studies of his poetic development. Bernice Slote argued for its importance in 1958, while more recently Jonathan Mulrooney has claimed that the performance style of Edmund Kean, with its emphasis on feeling in process, was an influence on Keats's conceptualization of negative capability.[5] What has not yet been taken fully into account is the impact on Keats of theatre not just at the level of ideas but as a material, sensory, and, above all, a sociable experience, an encounter with various embodied publics that interacted with other aspects of his sociable career. Keats's account of the evening at Drury Lane and the private theatre, in its relish for the contiguity of opulence and dirt, the star performer Kean and the 'sweaty' nobodies who wished to emulate him, illustrates the appeal of Regency theatricality in its totality as a distillation of a hybridizing social body, with the Romantic writer often cast as the spectator/participant who, in mediating the spectacle of theatre sociability, is also involved in mediating and defining his/her own authorial subjectivity. As a Regency theatre-goer and subsequently canonical Romantic writer, Keats therefore offers a test case of how the categories of popular culture, theatre, and Romanticism might be conjoined: what follows is not primarily designed to illuminate Keats's life and work, but explores his exemplary role as a theatre-goer and how he in turn constructed meaning from theatre. Before returning to consider Keats, I want to outline firstly the changing cultural landscape as it affected theatre and its relationship to popular culture in the immediate post-war period, focusing in particular on the Romantic status of the strolling player.

The period beginning with the Old Price riots at Covent Garden in 1809 and ending with the Theatre Regulation Act of 1843 represents an important epoch in the history of the British theatre. The traditional view of the period as one of atrophy and decline has undergone a major revision in recent years.[6] Jane Moody, pre-eminently, has argued that the victory of the Old Price rioters in 1809 compelled the patent theatres to introduce crowd-pleasing spectacle in order to make up for the commercial loss they had sustained. This signalled the triumph of the 'illegitimate theatre', a complex hybrid of traditional modes of performance and tech-nological and artistic innovation, over the 'legitimacy' of Covent Garden and Drury Lane. The latter theatres were identified with legally privileged genres such as comedy and tragedy and above all with Shakespeare. The struggle between the legitimate and illegitimate theatre, a long-standing one going back to the Licensing Act of 1737, energized rather than debilitated early nineteenth-century theatre, Moody argues, by revealing the 'deeply political character of cultural institutions'.[7] The Theatre Regulation Act of 1843, which abolished the patent theatres' monopoly over the legitimate drama, supposedly 'freeing' the stage, actually dissipated some of that energy, ultimately recasting the distinction between legitimate and illegitimate theatres in terms of the opposition between 'art' and 'entertainment'.[8] The early nineteenth century therefore represents an important period of change in the cultural politics of theatre, in which the 'popular' theatre of the fairs was beginning to be classified and archived in projects such as Hone's *Every-Day Book* as part of the 'discovery of the people' and its disappearing traditions. However, as Jacky Bratton has argued, another, in many respects countervailing, version of 'popular theatre' was emerging, a mutant offspring of the marriage of legitimate and illegitimate theatre, exemplified by the dramatizations of Pierce Egan's phenomenally successful *Life in London* in the 1820s.[9] As a multi-media event, combining the book, visual culture, journalism, theatre, and material artefacts, *Life in London* can be said to have inaugurated nineteenth-century mass culture. Emphatically presentist rather than nostalgic or commemorative, a docu-drama of urban, particularly male, self-fashioning through sociability, the dramatizations of *Life in London* exemplified Regency theatre's bastard status – both its claim to 'high' cultural lineage and its predeliction for 'low' company. Such cultural bastardry was embodied in the figure of Edmund Kean. Coleridge's claim that watching Kean was like reading Shakespeare by 'flashes of lightning' is well known: the same critique also noted the actor's 'rapid descents from the hyper-tragic to the infra-colloquial', suggesting Kean's capacity to convey, in his acting and his star personas, a caricature of sublimity – the 'hyper-tragic' – and the chatter of the everyday, the always-already lost.[10] Coleridge's striving for polarities is itself a 'hyper' reaction to the cultural landscape of theatre post-1809, betraying an anxiety that the category of legitimacy could no longer drown out the colloquial voice. Kean is the Regency actor par excellence because as a bastard product of theatre, trained by itinerant showmen such as Richardson[11] and maintaining his connection with tavern low-lifes even when he became a star, he undid the work of Garrick and Siddons in promoting the theatre as a liberal, polite, and respectable art. He embodied the persistence of an aspect of theatrical culture which was not so readily accommodated to either the romanticizing objectification of the discourse on popular culture or the new popular theatre represented by *Life in London* – that is, the 'infra-colloquial' world of the strolling player.

Strolling players described a class of itinerant actors who performed in the metropolitan fairs, the provinces, and throughout the English-speaking world. They could range in status from respectable performers undertaking the provincial circuits during the summer months, when the metropolitan stages were closed, to anonymous theatrical vagabonds, who played in barns, tents, or in the open air.[12] The diarist John Byng described an encounter with one such troop in an account of a visit to Biggleswade in 1791: 'from idleness, or from curiosity' he witnessed a performance of *Inkle and Yarico* in a barn which he compared with Hogarth's famous engraving 'Strolling Actresses Dressing in a Barn'. Though sympathetic to the players – 'greater wretchedness is not to be seen!' – Byng deplored the drain which the company was making on local resources – 'Tho' they get little, they get all that this town can give; and that is too much by every sixpence.'[13] The provincial theatre was in the vanguard of what Peter Borsay described as the 'urban renaissance' of Georgian Britain: the building of playhouses and other associated venues of entertainment such as assembly rooms, coffee houses, and circulating libraries demonstrated the alliance of politeness and commerce in ways that furthered middling-order claims to representative status and authority.[14] This development was accelerated after 1788 when changes in the regulation of theatres in the provinces made playhouse ventures more lucrative, circumstances which were given further stimulus as a result of the leisure economy of the Revolutionary and Napoleonic wars.[15] By 1803–5, when the theatre manager and aspiring literary entrepreneur James Winston mounted a kind of census of theatres in Britain for his *Theatric Tourist*, there were at least 280 playhouses. Only 24 of these playhouses were described and illustrated in the *Theatric Tourist*, the accompanying text often consisting of a narrative of theatrical progress and refinement (and ultimately the legitimacy of theatrical/literary professionalism).[16] Winston described how the barns and tents of anonymous strollers had been superseded by the solidity of bricks and mortar and the respectability of named performers and managers. However, as Byng's account suggests, it is likely that improvements in transport, the demand for entertainment, and economic and social dislocation meant that strollers were more prevalent than ever. The culture of the 'polite' provincial theatre, as represented in the solid establishments of Bath and Manchester, had its own popular penumbra in the form of the improvised, impermanent stages of the barns and the transient appearances of the stroller.

An encounter between these two configurations of theatre in the Romantic period – the legitimate and the illegitimate, the culturally hegemonic and its other – is apparent in Charles Dibdin's *Observations on a Tour through the Whole of England*, a travel book which the playwright, theatre manager, and propagandist for loyalism published in 1802.

Dibdin describes how his 'friend', a local Devonshire magistrate, granted permission for a group of 'miserable strolling actors' to perform in 'PIXAY POOL BARN', a place associated with 'goblins and frightful objects, all which in the old DEVONSHIRE dialect, are called pixays'. In an attempt to exploit this association the actors 'got up, pantomimes, shades, concave mirrors, magic lanterns, and all the wonderful effects which have so astonished and improved the metropolis, under the title of Phantasmagoria, Spectreology, and the rest of it'.[17] The Phantasmagoria, or magic-lantern show, had only been staged for the first time in London in late 1801–2, so these Devonshire strollers were introducing their audiences to the latest metropolitan sensation.[18] However, as Dibdin reports, the locals would have none of it, forcing the troop to resort to an old stalwart of the repertory, Nicholas Rowe's she-tragedy, *Jane Shore*. Even that was unsuccessful, and 'finding themselves in a most deplorable state', the actors abandoned the theatre for another version of strolling by going for soldiers.[19]

The initial attempt by the Pixay Pool players to entertain the locals is symptomatic of how metropolitan commercialized culture in the late eighteenth century tried to capitalize on popular superstition and tradition by repackaging it as gothic spectacle. Significantly, the locals rejected this poor phantasmagoria, causing the strollers to revert to an old play, *Jane Shore*, which, while more formally conventional and legitimate, was itself a hybrid product of elite and popular traditions, the story of Jane Shore having long been a staple of ballad singers and chapmen.[20] Such criss-crossings and overlays between legitimate and illegitimate forms, provincial and metropolitan artists and audiences, superstition and commercialized 'mass' magic, highlight, once again, the redundancy of the binary model of culture for this period. What is Romantic about Dibdin's account is not only the complexity of the imbrication it describes, but also Dibdin's construction of himself as the disinterested traveller, subsuming his identity as *interested* theatre professional. As producer of a successful one-man show at his Sans Souci theatre, Dibdin was an innovator in theatrical illegitimacy who contributed to the emergence of proto-mass popular theatre in the 1820s.[21] Like Winston's *Theatric Tourist* project, Dibdin was engaged in a legitimation of the respectability of his own position as a theatre professional, by projecting the Pixay Pool players as eccentric, ethnographic curiosities, the object of the scrutiny of Dibdin's 'friend', the law.

And what of the strollers themselves? Who were these rural avant-gardists? Was their magic show sincerely intended or was it a cynical mockery of local customs? In staging their performance were they merely trying to survive, or preying on the susceptibilities of other poor people? Dibdin went on to say that strolling actors should be 'treated with the respect to which all strangers were entitled' as 'the drift of their visit is to amuse and instruct, and not to inveigle and betray'.[22] As 'drifting' strangers, strolling players represented an indeterminate category in eighteenth-century society and culture insofar as the profession was nominally open to all classes. An enduring trope of picaresque fiction was the gentleman-player's embrace of the anonymity of the stroller in a liminal act of escape or desperation. At the other end of the spectrum, however, the stroller's status and profession merged with that of the Georgian sturdy poor – the itinerant world of the 'ritual' beggar, the petty salesman or pedlar, gypsies, and fortune-tellers.[23] The strolling player therefore belonged to a social group which was a long-standing focus of interest for students of popular culture from the early modern period – the category of rogues and vagabonds, whose textual corpus ranged from Elizabethan coney-catching literature to the Newgate Calendar.[24] The legal definition of actors as rogues and vagabonds, liable to prosecution if they were deemed to be disorderly or acting outside the law, which dated from the Elizabethan period, was reaffirmed in the 1737 Licensing Act and remained in force until 1824.[25] By the early nineteenth century, however, the discursive category of rogue and vagabond was being adapted to the new circumstances of a rapidly commercializing world. The writer of *The Dens of London Exposed* of 1835, for example, promised to introduce the reader to 'a road that has never yet been trodden by the man of the pen', the 'infra-colloquial' world of St Giles's, occupied by the 'flash letter-writer and the crawling supplicant; the pretended tradesmen, who live luxuriously on the tales of others . . . the match-seller and ballad-singer, whose convenient profession unites the four lucrative callings of begging, selling, singing and stealing . . . gangs of shipwrecked sailors . . . jugglers, coiners, tramps (mechanics seeking work), *strolling players*, with all the hangers-on of fairs, races, assizes, stable-yards; besides the hosts of Irish who yearly migrate from sweet Erin to happy England, to beg, labour, and steal'.[26] The strolling player is located at the centre of this ever-mutating entrepreneurial underclass, his or her performative turn standing for the incorrigible theatricality of 'St Giles' as a whole. Nor was the theatricality of indigence confined to the metropolis: an agricultural survey of the Scottish borders from the 1790s complained that the area was 'often infested with gangs of tinkers and horners' who disdained 'the name of beggars': 'At the time of sheep-shearing, too, sturdy women, chiefly from Edinburgh and Dalkeith, provincially called *Randies*, traverse the pasture district, under pretence of gathering or asking locks of wool, and are suspected of taking more than is given them . . . Quacks, jugglers, and strolling players not unfrequently pick the pockets of the industrious . . . Nobody, who resides in the county, ever begs,' noted the writer with exasperation or disappointment.[27] Such comments illuminate the outer limits of late Georgian theatrical culture, giving us fleeting glimpses of a class of itinerant performers that was discursively uncontainable, like the traversing 'Randies' and other mobile, recalcitrant marginals.

The world of the 'poor player' in the Romantic period correlates with E. P. Thompson's view of late Georgian plebeian culture as 'picaresque'.[28] Some of the characteristic features of this culture – a 'heavy inheritance of customary definitions and expectations' (p. 7), the importance of apprenticeship and 'inter-generational transmission' (p. 7) – shaped the ethos and practices of the theatrical profession well into the nineteenth century. Plebeian culture was irrevocably altered, Thompson argues, in the great 'transformation' caused by industrialization and demographic growth. This change revolutionized what Thompson calls 'needs', in the process 'destroying the authority of customary expectations': 'this is what most demarks the "pre-industrial" or the "traditional" from the modern world', he claims (p. 14). In other words, the horizonless, picaresque mobility of plebeian culture in which there was 'little predictive notation of time' (p. 13) was gradually eclipsed by a culture of 'needs' or affects, and by a new conceptualization and practice of mobility as purposeful mobility. Thompson's comments offer an alternative way of framing cultural change in the Romantic period and the elite–popular binary. They are echoed by Celeste Langan who argues, via Rousseau and Baudrillard, that:

[the Romantic] regime of liberalism . . . entails a new valorization of mobility . . . [I]ndividual mobility, as it defines a 'liberal' society, is already conceived of differentially, as Baudrillard reminds us: as 'each individual and each group searches out his-her place in an order, all the while trying to jostle according to a personal trajectory', that place is established by 'the disparity between intentional mobility (aspirations) and real mobility (objective chances of social promotion)' . . . The *valorization* of mobility . . . is thus primarily *metaphorical*, as the expression 'upward mobility' suggests.[29]

Such conditions, Langan argues, explain the Romantic poet's idealization of the vagrant as a 'reduction and abstraction' of 'mobility and expressivity' that 'crucially elevate[s] the vagrant to the status of the poet's double'.[30]

I would suggest that another process or gesture of doubling can be observed in the long eighteenth-century writer's fascination with the strolling player, who as vagrant/artist was, if anything, more troubling to the cultural imaginary negotiating Thompson's great 'transformation'. This is a topic beyond the scope of this chapter: suffice it to say, the Romantic period is notable for a corpus of writing – fiction, plays, poems, memoirs – which suggests a preoccupation with the figure of the stroller that persisted well into the nineteenth century.[31] The strolling player became another projection or double of Romanticism's anxieties of authorship. In George Crabbe's *The Borough*, for example, Letter 12 on 'Players' comes between 'Inns' and 'The Alms-House and Trustees', as a pivotal part of Crabbe's exploration of the cultural, political, and moral geography of middle England. As a mini-commonweal and as a site of sociality, the actors and their tent theatre are emblematic of both the ideals of polite provincial culture – the aspiration towards pleasurable communality – and the inevitable embeddedness of such ideals in commerce: the performers peddle a 'Trade' which 'vends each Night the manufactur'd Man'.[32] In spite of this, the travelling theatre remains profoundly attractive as a laboratory of self-transformation: it is the (last) resort of 'Pen-spurning Clerks, and Lads contemning Trade' and of 'Youths of Wealth by Dissipation eas'd'.[33] The major part of this letter in *The Borough* consists of the story of 'Frederick Thompson', the son of a merchant who spurns upward mobility for the picaresque life of a stroller, ultimately rejecting that and degenerating into a life of vice. The final image of the poem is of Thompson falling through the cracks of liminality, dying in a building 'half-ruin'd and half-built' on the outskirts of London, 'robb'd, beaten, hungry, pain'd, diseas'd and poor'.[34] Embracing the life of a strolling player is represented as the new mobility's nightmare, a fall into abjection, betraying the drama entailed in Crabbe's own engagement with mobility and expressivity, his own 'vending' of the 'manufactur'd Man'.

How does John Keats's career as a writer and a play-goer relate to the changes in theatrical culture that I have outlined here? I want to begin by considering the tour of England, Scotland, and Ireland that he made with Charles Brown between June and August 1818. Keats described the tour as a 'prologue' to his future life, a term which he also used in his prefaces to *Endymion*. In the first preface completed in March 1818, he defended the poem as 'an endeavour rather than a thing accomplish'd; a poor prologue to what, if I live, I humbly hope to do'.[35] Critics have neglected the significance of Keats's preoccupation with the term 'prologue', interpreting it as synonymous with 'preface'. However, as any student of the stage would have been aware, the prologue (with its complementary epilogue) was an important meta-theatrical device in the Georgian theatre that not only served to frame the mainpiece tragedy or comedy, or self-consciously reflect on the theatre itself and its audiences, but was also a means of negotiating the actor's traditionally servile relationship with his or her public. The prologue was therefore a customary performance of deference, an actor's acknowledgement of his dependence on the audience's goodwill because of his legal vulnerability: its gradual disappearance in the 1820s coincides with the removal from the legitimate acting profession of the stigma of association with rogues and vagabonds.[36] Keats's use of the term and, in particular, his apology for *Endymion* as a 'poor prologue' (with its echoes of Macbeth's 'poor player') reflects the pervasive theatricality of his efforts to construct himself as a professional writer in the late 1810s, and specifically how he used that theatricality to negotiate his own 'humble' class position in Romantic literary culture. The object of the northern trip was manifold: a search for inspiration and material in the picturesque north and its people; a gesture of pilgrimage/fandom in visiting the homes of Wordsworth and Burns; a homosocial escape from what Keats described as the 'miasma' of London and of his pressing family responsibilities. By following the cultural script of disinterested picturesque travel, Keats was also auditioning for status and recognition on the stage of public culture as the producer, rather than the object, of discourse.[37]

However, the precariousness of the social performance in which Keats and Brown were engaged is illustrated by how they were viewed by the people they encountered. In a letter to his sister Fanny, Keats described how they had been '*taken for* travelling Jewellers, Razor sellers and Spectacle venders because friend Brown wears a pair' (vol. 1, p. 310, my emphasis). At the *poste restante* in Portpatrick they were mistaken for soldiers – 'the man snapp'd out "what Regiment?"' – while in Ireland two men in a 'miserable house of entertainment' between Donaghadee and Belfast thought they were Frenchmen (vol. 1, p. 321). 'Mr Abbey [Keats's guardian] says we are Don Quixotes,' wrote Keats to Fanny, '. . . tell him we are more generally taken for Pedlars' (vol. 1, p. 311), a comment which suggests the polarities shaping Keats's early career – potentially unrealizable literary ambition or descent into the anonymity of the poor man's trade. As figures of social indeterminacy, outlandish 'foreigners', Keats and Brown are comparable to the strolling players encountered by Byng and Dibdin: they were 'drifting' strangers to be regarded with curiosity and wariness. (Keats's reporting of the response to them also suggests an element of self-reflexive scrutiny of himself, a curiosity as to what he might be 'taken for'.)

It is this context which makes Keats's encounter with a group of strolling players particularly suggestive. On entering Inverary, he noticed a playbill advertising a performance: 'I went to the Barn alone where I saw the Stranger accompanied by a Bag pipe – There they went on about "interesting creaters" and "human nater" – till the Curtain fell and then Came the Bag pipe – When Mrs Haller fainted down went the Curtain and out came the Bagpipe – at the heartrending, shoemending recon-ciliation the Piper blew amain – I never read or saw this play before; not the Bag pipe, nor the wretched players themselves were little in com-parison with it – thank heaven it has been scoffed at lately almost to a fashion' (vol. 1, pp. 336–7). The play in question, *The Stranger*, was the English translation of a work by the German dramatist August von Kotzebue, first staged in London in 1798. Starring Sarah Siddons in the role of the adulterous Mrs Haller, *The Stranger* was controversial because it appeared to condone infidelity by concluding with a scene in which the errant wife is restored to her husband – the 'heartrending, shoemending' scene mentioned by Keats. The play was also notable for administering a shock to the celebrity persona of Siddons, based on her reputation for private respectability: some male commentators were appalled that she had condescended to play such a part.[38] In spite or because of this, *The Stranger* was successful, becoming an established part of the dramatic repertory. Siddons was succeeded in the role of Mrs Haller by Eliza O'Neil and although Keats claimed that the play was 'out of fashion', it continued to attract audiences to the patent theatres, *The Times* ful-minating in 1815 that this 'canonized adultery' had been responsible for the corruption of at least 50,000 theatre-goers since 1798.[39] *The Stranger* was therefore a play that was particularly associated with women, in terms of its focus on adulterous femininity, its links with the 'female muse' of the British stage, Sarah Siddons, and the apparent appeal of its senti-mentalism to female taste. At the Inverary barn this dimension of the play was complicated by the orchestration of the performance by the bagpipe, turning the play into an even purer form of melodrama in the root sense of the term – music theatre. The use of the bagpipe can also be seen as an act of appropriation, in the terms proposed by Roger Chartier; that is, an indigenous remediation of a metropolitan text, producing a hybrid cultural performance – a specifically 'Inverary' *Stranger* that was neither entirely 'popular' nor 'Scottish', nor the play that maidservants were weeping over in London.[40] In this respect the Inverary *Stranger* resembled the performance of the Pixay Pool players as described by Dibdin: both occasions exemplified an almost baffling imbrication of apparently popular and metropolitan or elite cultural traditions. Keats was drawn to the Inverary barn because, as a cultural practice, the 'strolling' taking place there reflected the precarious mobility of his own position in 1818, raising questions as to where he properly belonged in relation to the 'theatre' of culture and the meanings of his own Romantic vagrancy. In order to shore up his autonomy he constructed himself as the gentleman traveller, analogous to Dibdin or Byng, by objectifying the Inverary players as 'wretched' curiosities, specifically comic curiosities. For Fanny Keats's benefit or entertainment Keats relayed the Inverary *Stranger* as worth laughing at for both the bagpipe and the intrinsic bathos of the play's pretensions to high art. Rather than demeaning the provincial version of the play in relation to its more superior metropolitan precedent, Keats was implying that they represented different versions of the same artistic failure, thereby asserting his own capacity to transcend the distinctions of centre and periphery and occupy an aesthetic 'everywhere'.

There is a gendered dimension to this response in so far as the performance history of *The Stranger*, as I have suggested, made it a feminized text, the effects of which were reinforced in the Highlands because of the long-standing association of the category of popular culture with the category of women. Keats's account of the Inverary *Stranger* as comedy can therefore be seen as gendered, an attempt to negotiate the threat of abjection represented by both women and the popular to his nascent authorial identity. In this respect, his experience in the Inverary barn was anticipated by a previous encounter on the northern tour which had taken place during a brief visit to the north of Ireland. Somewhere in north Down, Keats and Brown came across an old woman being carried in a mockery of a sedan chair. Keats christened her 'the Duchess of Dunghill':

It is no laughing matter tho – Imagine the worst dog kennel you ever saw placed upon two poles from a mouldy fencing – In such a wretched thing sat a squalid old Woman squat like an ape half starved from a scarcity of Buiscuit in its passage from Madagascar to the cape, – with a pipe in her mouth and looking out with a round-eyed skinny lidded, inanity . . . squab and lean she sat and puff'd out the smoke while two ragged tattered Girls carried her along – What a thing would be a history of her Life and sensations. (vol. 1, pp. 321–2)

In the tattered splendour of her dirt and decay, her simian inscrutability and profound deracination, the old woman exemplifies the identification of the popular with the female grotesque and vice versa, analogous to the 'female vendor's scream' which confounds Wordsworth in the labyrinth of St Giles in Book VII of *The Prelude*.[41] The location of the female grotesque at the margins or the end of the road for Romantic vagrancy reflects the enduringly problematic position of women in studies of popular culture, as defined by Peter Burke – 'women's culture is to popular culture what popular culture is to culture as a whole' – i.e. simultaneously marginal and central, symbolic of what cannot be recuperated and yet is capable of making men poets or historians.[42] 'What a thing would be a history of her Life and sensations.' Moreover, Keats's construction of the old woman in mock-epic terms – his naming of her as a duchess and her cart as a 'sedan' – not only invokes earlier Popean discourses of popular culture but also suggests the grotesque theatricality of scandalous eighteenth-century women of fashion such as the Duchess of Kingston. The figure of the woman of fashion and her counterpart in the actress are foundational to Romantic culture, as embodiments of a feminized public culture that masculinist models of political association and ultimately Romantic literary culture had to nullify and transcend.[43] The 'Duchess of Dunghill' represents the persistence of that type in the male Romantic imaginary, combining the potency of the feminized elite with the intractability of the female vagrant or Randy. As the Siddons of shite the old woman was the ultimate female stroller, resisting both Keats and history: she was/is 'no laughing matter'.

In London, Keats's experience of a 'popular' Romantic theatre was concentrated in the figure of Edmund Kean, whose career he followed (almost obsessively), not only on account of the actor's galvanizing performances of Shakespeare but also for the cultural illegitimacy that Kean represented, his risky navigation of the highs of the hyper-tragic and the lows of the infra-colloquial. Keats's declaration in an August 1819 letter to Benjamin Bailey – 'One of my Ambitions is to make as great a revolution in modern dramatic writing as Kean has done in acting – another to upset the drawling of the blue stocking literary world' – suggests the essential theatricality of his idea of literary fame, a theatricality encompassing both the 'public' sphere of the stage and the ostensibly 'private' realm of the literary salon (vol. ii, p. 139). Both domains entailed risky acts of self-presentation which for Keats inevitably meant engaging in the imbricated performance of class and gender. His desire to 'upset' the 'drawling of the blue stocking literary world', comparable to the 'shock and awe' of Kean's celebrated Richard III, announces the dramatic entrance of his otherness in a literary public which he identifies with patrician affectation and etiolated female taste (the reference to 'blue stocking' also highlights the enduring problem for Romantic male writers of the eighteenth-century feminization of public culture, which Keats had confronted in its perverse, popular configuration in the form of the Duchess of Dunghill). As an illegitimate artist and hero of low-life libertinism, Kean offered a means for Keats to negotiate the class and gender complications of his own Romantic vagrancy. In the 'Negative Capability' letter, for example, the sociability of a group of male literary friends brings Kean to mind: 'These men say things which make one start, without making one feel, they are all alike: their manners are alike; they all know fashionables . . . They talked of Kean & his low company – Would I were with that company instead of yours said I to myself!' (vol. 1, p. 193). The imaginary 'low company' of Kean – there is no evidence that the poet ever met the actor – enables Keats to differentiate himself from the social superiority and compromised masculinity of literary society.

Kean's talismanic significance for Keats is also suggested in a September 1819 letter in which the latter bewails the actor's decision to go to America, thereby depriving him of the chance of success with *Otho the Great*. A stage hit would, Keats claims, 'lift me out of the mire. I mean the mire of a bad reputation which is continually rising against me. My name with the literary fashionables is vulgar – I am a weaver boy to them – a Tragedy would lift me out this mess' (vol. 11, p. 186). The prospect of failure on the stage of public culture, associated with the loss of Kean, disturbs the cocky assurance of Keats's threat to upset 'the drawling of the blue stocking literary world': instead Keats imagines himself demeaned as 'a weaver boy', one of the emerging industrial working class which he had encountered on the northern tour. Outside Belfast in a 'most wretched suburb' Keats had heard 'that most disgusting of all noises worse than the Bag pipe, the laugh of a Monkey, the chatter of women *solus* the scream of [a] Macaw – I mean the sound of the Shuttle – What a tremendous difficulty is the improvement of the condition of such people – I cannot conceive how a mind "with child" of Philanthropy could gra[s]p at possibility – with me it is absolute despair' (vol. 1, p. 321). Keats deploys the registers which he would also use in relation to the Duchess of Dunghill and the Inverary *Stranger* – an emphasis on the superlative 'noise' of the popular, savagery, the exotic, the 'infra-colloquialism' of women – in order to convey the shock of a newly industrializing world. He gestures towards the totalizing discourses of improvement and philanthropy as a means of coming to terms with such a change but critiques

their descriptive inadequacy – 'with me it is absolute despair'. For Keats
to describe himself as a weaver boy to the literary fashionables of London
was therefore a sign of the profound insecurities of his cultural position.[44]
The gesture combines both self-flagellation and self-promotion, acknowledging the threat of abjection in his possible identification with the
'weaver boys' of England, while at the same time standing up for such
'vulgarity' against the snobbery of the salons. More than the bagpipe or
the cackling of the Duchess of Dunghill, the sound of the shuttle was the
sound of the new mobility in which Keats himself was participating:
the weaver boy could be tragedy king and vice versa.

   Such a struggle took place not only at the level of discourse for Keats
but also in his cultural practice, specifically the intense sociability in
which he engaged between 1817 and 1820. The importance of Keats's
involvement with Leigh Hunt's and other literary and radical circles has
been established by Jeffrey Cox and Nicholas Roe: what has not yet been
fully explored is the significance of the theatre as a site of sociability for
Keats which interacted with the theatricality of the other literary publics
in which he was participating.[45] In the form of the post-1809 patent
theatres, in which the distinctions between the legitimate and illegitimate
cultural hierarchies were breaking down and Kean held sway, the London
theatre represented the culturally and politically dominant model of the
public, against which Keats could measure his status and place within
literary culture and society as a whole. The question of where one belonged
in the theatre was also a question of where one belonged in society as a
whole. The letters reveal Keats's awareness of the highly charged meanings of the spaces within and around the theatre, how negotiating your
place in the late Georgian playhouse, making your way through the
crowds outside the theatre or in the spaces surrounding the auditorium,
related to the broader drama of situating oneself within the body politic.
In a letter of January 1818, for example, he describes a convivial day spent
with Wells and Joseph Severn, lubricated with claret, during which they
talked about the theatre's '1s Gallery. I said I wondered that careful Folks
would go there for although it was but a Shilling still you had to pay
through the Nose. I saw the Peachey family in a Box at Drury one Night'
(vol. 1, p. 197). It is possible that the latter comment is referring to an old
schoolfellow of Keats, James Peachey, who became an attorney (vol. 1,
p. 197n.5). If so, his noting of his friend in a place of social prominence
and material success signified by a box is a moment of wistful recognition,
even envy. Whether Keats viewed his old friend from the distant elevation
of the one-shilling gallery is unclear, as his comment suggests that a seat

there would have been an imposition on his finances. The comment as a whole triangulates a matrix of class and gender self-consciousness and social desire, linking Keats and his friends in their 'private' homosociality, the 'careful folks' of the one-shilling gallery, and Peachey in the box who may or may not have recognized the friend of his youth.

The one-shilling gallery, particularly at half price, represented the cheapest seats in the theatre and was traditionally the domain of artisans, soldiers, and sailors, and servants such as the maidservant fans of *The Stranger*. Attempts by the management of the patent theatres to downgrade the shilling galleries in the 1790s, in the case of Covent Garden abolishing the one-shilling gallery altogether, met with considerable opposition from that 'nest of riot and noise'.[46] Knowing where the one-shilling gallery was, one of the competencies expected of the candidate for the mock Cambridge exam in 1816, therefore represented much more than casual familiarity with the London social scene: it stood for acknowledgement of at least the presence of the lower orders within the collective social body signified by and in the patent theatres, a model of the theatre public, paralleling the status of the vagabond-stroller, that was fast disappearing. We can read the talk of Keats and his friends about the one-shilling gallery through the lens of another Romantic conversation about this part of the theatre in Charles Lamb's essay 'Old China'. Bridget Elia reminisces about former days in which she and Elia would 'squeeze out our shillings-a-piece to sit' in the gallery:

You used to say that the gallery was the best place of all for enjoying a play socially . . . that the company we met there, not being in general readers of plays, were obliged to attend the more, and did attend, to what was going on, on the stage – because a word lost would have been a chasm, which it was impossible for them to fill up . . . I appeal to you, whether as a woman, I met generally with less attention and accommodation, than I have done since in more expensive situations in the house? The getting in indeed, and the crowding up those inconvenient staircases, was bad enough, – but there was still a law of civility to women recognised to quite as great an extent as we ever found in the other passages – and how a little difficulty overcome heightened the snug seat, and the play, afterwards! Now we can only pay our money, and walk in. You cannot see, you say, in the galleries now. I am sure we saw, and heard too, well enough then – but sight, and all, I think, is gone with our poverty.[47]

Lamb's essay is a kind of theatre history, marking the transition of playgoing from something that was predominantly enjoyed 'socially' to a cultural commodity enjoyed in so far as it is paid for; from an idea of the public as defined by the collectivity of the playhouse to one defined primarily as a reading public; from a culture marked by 'a law of civility' to women to one dominated by a male homosociality which has as its object the effacement of women.[48] Elia ends 'Old China' by challenging Bridget's nostalgia for their poverty: 'could the good old one shilling gallery days return' they would lose 'the well-carpeted fireside' and the 'luxurious sofa' and 'once more be struggling up those inconvenient staircases, pushed about, and squeezed, and elbowed by the poorest rabble of poor gallery scramblers'. Having reached their place in the gallery, they would be confronted with the vertiginous prospect of the theatre below them – 'I know not the fathom line that ever touched a descent so deep as I would be willing to bury more wealth in than Croesus had … to purchase it.'[49] In this alternative theatre history, Elia advises Bridget to get over it: the commodity culture of domestic affect, signified by china, books, sofas, and firesides, has become modernity's new theatre, consigning the old sociality to the realm of women and 'dreams'. Moreover, in the drama of purposeful or metaphorical mobility it is essential not to look back, otherwise you will see those 'scrambling' behind you, the 'poorest rabble' of the poor.

In talking about the one-shilling gallery with Wells and Severn, Keats, like Bridget and Elia, was talking about social change, the great 'transformation' in the meaning of 'needs' in late Georgian Britain which took place not just in a material sense but also in how people thought and felt. Keats's engagement with the theatre highlights how fraught and complicated that transformation was, particularly for men such as him whose status and ideological affinities were with the unrespectable or the illegitimate but who also needed to leave the 'theatre' of popular culture behind. In this respect, Keats's mobility in and around theatre reveals the dual significance of Romantic literary culture in benefiting from the great 'transformation', as well as registering the enormity of what was lost.

NOTES

1 *The Times* (25 January 1816).
2 William Hone, *The Every-Day Book: or, Everlasting Calendar of Popular Amusements*, 2 vols. (London: Hunt and Clarke, 1826–7), vol. 1, cols. 1182, 1183.
3 David Worrall, *Theatric Revolution: Drama, Censorship, and Romantic Period Subcultures 1773–1832* (Oxford: Oxford University Press, 2006), pp. 250–65.
4 John Keats, *The Letters of John Keats 1814–1821*, ed. Hyder Edward Rollins, 2 vols. (Cambridge: Cambridge University Press, 1958), vol. 1, p. 216, hereafter referred to in parentheses in the text.

5 Bernice Slote, *Keats and the Dramatic Principle* (Lincoln: University of Nebraska Press, 1958); Jonathan Mulrooney, 'Keats in the Company of Kean', *Studies in Romanticism* 42 (2003), 227–50. See also Harry R. Beaudry, *The English Theatre and John Keats* (Salzburg: Universität Salzburg, 1973); John Kandl, 'Plebeian Gusto, Negative Capability, and the Low Company of "Mr. Kean": Keats' Dramatic Review for *The Champion* (21 December 1817)', *Nineteenth-Century Prose* 28:2 (2001), 130–41.

6 See Jane Moody, *Illegitimate Theatre in London, 1770–1840* (Cambridge: Cambridge University Press, 2000); Jacky Bratton, *New Readings in Theatre History* (Cambridge: Cambridge University Press, 2003); Worrall, *Theatric Revolution*.

7 Moody, *Illegitimate Theatre*, p. 243.

8 Bratton, *New Readings*, p. 155; for the implications of this change for the development of theatre in the nineteenth century see Tracy C. Davis, *The Economics of the British Stage 1800–1914* (Cambridge: Cambridge University Press, 2000).

9 Bratton, *New Readings*, p. 166. See also Gregory Dart, '"Flash Style": Pierce Egan and Literary London 1820–1828', *History Workshop* 51 (2001), 181–205.

10 Samuel Taylor Coleridge, *Table Talk*, ed. Carl Woodring, 2 vols. (London: Routledge, and Princeton, N.J.: Princeton University Press, 1990), vol. II, p. 41. See Tracy C. Davis's excellent reading of Coleridge's remark in '"Reading Shakespeare by Flashes of Lightning": Challenging the Foundations of Romantic Acting Theory', *English Literary History* 62:4 (1995), 933–54.

11 H. N. Hillebrand, *Edmund Kean* (New York: AMS Press, 1966), p. 17.

12 See Sybil Rosenfeld, *Strolling Players & Drama in the Provinces, 1660–1765* (Cambridge: Cambridge University Press, 1939).

13 John Byng, *The Torrington Diaries: A Selection from the Tours of the Hon. John Byng*, ed. C. Bruyn Andrews and Fanny Andrews (London: Eyre and Spottiswoode, 1954), p. 375.

14 Peter Borsay, *The English Urban Renaissance: Culture and Society in the Provincial Town, 1660–1770* (Oxford: Clarendon Press, 1989).

15 See Jean N. Baker, 'Theatre, Law and Society in the Provinces: The Case of Sarah Baker', *Cultural and Social History – The Journal of the Social History Society* 1:2 (2004), 159–78; Gillian Russell, *The Theatres of War: Performance, Politics and Society, 1793–1815* (Oxford: Clarendon Press, 1995).

16 [James Winston], *The Theatric Tourist* (London: T. Woodfall, 1805); see also Alfred Lewis Nelson, 'James Winston's *Theatric Tourist*, A Critical Edition with a Biography and Census of Winston Material', unpublished PhD thesis, The George Washington University (1968), and Jacky Bratton's discussion of Winston as 'tribal scribe' in *New Readings*, pp. 29–33.

17 Charles Dibdin, *Observations on a Tour through the Whole of England*, 2 vols. (London: G. Goulding and John Walker, 1802), vol. II, pp. 301–2.

18 See Richard D. Altick, *The Shows of London* (Cambridge, Mass.: Harvard University Press, 1978), p. 217, and Terry Castle, 'Phantasmagoria: Spectral Technology and the Metaphorics of Modern Reverie', *Critical Inquiry* 15 (1988), 26–60.

19 Dibdin, *Observations*, vol. II, p. 304.

20 See James L. Harmer, 'Jane Shore in Literature: A Checklist', *Notes and Queries* 28 (1981), 496–507.

21 For Dibdin's career see Robert Fahrner, *The Theatre Career of Charles Dibdin the Elder (1745–1814)* (New York: Lang, 1989).

22 Dibdin, *Observations*, vol. II, p. 302.

23 For begging in general see Tim Hitchcock, 'Begging on the Streets of Eighteenth-Century London', *Journal of British Studies* 44 (2005), 478–98.

24 See Peter Burke, *Popular Culture in Early Modern Europe*, rev. reprint (Aldershot: Scolar Press, 1994); John Mullan and Christopher Reid (eds.), *Eighteenth-Century Popular Culture: A Selection* (Oxford: Oxford University Press, 2000); Ken Gelder, *Subcultures: Cultural Histories and Social Practice* (London: Routledge, 2007), pp. 5–10.

25 The legal status of actors was changed in 'An Act for the Punishment of Idle and Disorderly Persons, and Rogues and Vagabonds, in that Part of Great Britain, called England', 5 George IV cap. 83 (1824). On the history of the identification of strolling players as vagabonds see Paola Pugliatti, *Beggary and Theatre in Early Modern England* (Aldershot: Ashgate, 2003).

26 *The Dens of London Exposed* (London: the author, 1835), pp. 15, 14–15 (my emphasis).

27 Robert Douglas, *General View of the Agriculture in the Counties of Roxburgh and Selkirk* (Edinburgh: G. Nicoll, 1798), p. 218.

28 E. P. Thompson, *Customs in Common* (Harmondsworth: Penguin, 1993), p. 12. Subsequent references are in parentheses in the text.

29 Celeste Langan, *Romantic Vagrancy: Wordsworth and the Simulation of Freedom* (Cambridge: Cambridge University Press, 1995), p. 34.

30 *Ibid.*, p. 17.

31 For example, Thomas Holcroft's *Alwyn: or the Gentleman Comedian* (1780) and *The Adventures of Hugh Trevor* (1794); George Crabbe's *The Borough* (1812); John O'Keeffe's *Wild Oats: or, the Strolling Gentlemen* (1791); Charlotte Smith's 'Written for the Benefit of a Distressed Player, Detained at Bright-helmstone for Debt, November 1792', in *Elegiac Sonnets* (1797–1800); S. W. Ryley's *The Itinerant: or Memoirs of an Actor* (1808); Pierce Egan's *The Life of an Actor* (1825); Christopher Thomson's *The Autobiography of an Artisan* (1847). For bibliographies related to strolling players see Elbridge Colby, 'Strolling Players in the Eighteenth Century', *Notes and Queries* 11th series, 12 (1915), 454–7; Elbridge Colby, 'Strolling Players of the Eighteenth Century', *Notes and Queries* 12th series, 9 (1921), 168; Thornton S. Graves, 'Strolling Players in the Eighteenth Century', *Notes and Queries* 13th series, 1 (1923), 6–7; Elbridge Colby, 'A Supplement on Strollers', *PMLA* 39:3 (1924), 642–54.

32 George Crabbe, *The Complete Poetical Works*, ed. Norma Dalrymple-Champneys and Arthur Pollard, 3 vols. (Oxford: Clarendon Press, 1988), vol. I, p. 472, line 38.

33 *Ibid.*, p. 476, lines 184, 186.

34 *Ibid.*, p. 481, lines 365, 352.

35 John Keats, *The Poems of John Keats*, ed. Jack Stillinger (London: Heinemann, 1978), p. 739.

36 On the history of the prologue in the early modern theatre see Douglas Bruster and Robert Weimann, *Prologues to Shakespeare's Theatre: Performance and Liminality in Early Modern Drama* (London: Routledge, 2004); on the decline of the prologue in the 1820s see Allardyce Nicoll, *A History of Early Nineteenth Century Drama 1800–1850*, 2 vols. (Cambridge: Cambridge University Press, 1930), vol. 1, pp. 30–1.

37 On the northern tour see Carol Kyros Walker, *Walking North with Keats* (New Haven, Conn.: Yale University Press, 1992).

38 For example, James Boaden, *Memoirs of Mrs. Siddons* (1827; London: Gibbings and Company, 1893), p. 422.

39 *The Times* (17 April 1815).

40 Roger Chartier, 'Culture as Appropriation: Popular Cultural Uses in Early Modern France', in Steven L. Kaplan (ed.), *Understanding Popular Culture: Europe from the Middle Ages to the Nineteenth Century* (Berlin and New York: Mouton, 1984), pp. 229–53.

41 William Wordsworth, *The Prelude: A Parallel Text*, ed. J.C. Maxwell (Harmondsworth: Penguin, 1971), p. 260, line 182 (1805–6). See also Peter Stallybrass and Allon White, *The Politics and Poetics of Transgression* (London: Methuen, 1986), esp. Chapter 2.

42 Burke, *Popular Culture*, p. 49.

43 See Gillian Russell, *Women, Sociability and Theatre in Georgian London* (Cambridge: Cambridge University Press, 2007).

44 See also a letter written 24 September 1819, a few days after the one in which he described himself as a 'weaver boy' (dated 17 September 1819), making an analogy between the 'trade' of performative punning and weavers who had recently gone on strike in Manchester: 'As for Pun-making I wish it was as good a trade as pin-making – there is very little business of that sort going on now. We struck for wages like the manchester wevers [*sic*] – but to no purpose' (Keats, *Letters*, vol. 11, p. 214).

45 Jeffrey N. Cox, *Poetry and Politics in the Cockney School: Keats, Shelley, Hunt and their Circle* (Cambridge: Cambridge University Press, 1998); Nicholas Roe, *John Keats and the Culture of Dissent* (Oxford: Clarendon Press, 1997).

46 *The Times* (17 September 1792).

47 Charles Lamb, *Elia: and, the Last Essays of Elia*, ed. Jonathan Bate (Oxford: World's Classics, 1987), pp. 283, 284.

48 I adapt Julie Carlson's claim that 'the homosociality of romantic men' is preserved by 'effacing the power of women' from Shakespeare, the public stage, and ultimately 'the illusion of England': see *In the Theatre of Romanticism: Coleridge, Nationalism, Women* (Cambridge: Cambridge University Press, 1994), p. 20.

49 Lamb, *Elia*, pp. 286, 287.

CHAPTER 10

A world within walls: Haydon, The Mock Election, and 1820s debtors' prisons

Gregory Dart

In June 1827 Benjamin Robert Haydon was imprisoned for debt in the King's Bench Prison in Southwark. It was not the first time Haydon had been behind bars, but on this occasion it gave rise to one of his most successful canvases, a comic genre piece called *The Mock Election* (Figure 10.1). The picture was inspired by a real event that took place during his stay. Donning bedsheets, curtain rings, mopsticks, and ribbons a number of the debtors had spent days staging a political masquerade in the main yard of the prison, and sparked off a jocular riot as a result.

Haydon was released from the Bench at the end of July,[1] but he was back again within a fortnight, sketching faces for a picture, 'a sort of Beggar's Opera', as he put it, 'a Polly and Macheath affair' to commemorate the event.[2] Completed during the autumn of that year, *The Mock Election* was first exhibited at the Egyptian Hall, Piccadilly, in January 1828, with Haydon offering a typically fulsome account of the genesis of the painting in his catalogue description:

To the last day of my life I shall ever remember the impression I received – baronets and bankers; authors and merchants; painters and poets, dandies of rank in silk and velvet, and dandies of no rank in rags and tatters; idiotism and insanity; poverty and affliction, all mingled in indiscriminate merriment, with a spiked wall, twenty feet high, above their heads![3]

What Haydon liked above all about the King's Bench Prison was that it appeared to present 'real life' – life at its most various and vivid – frozen in a frame. 'The world itself is a queer *mélange*,' wrote one veteran of the prison many years later, 'and in the [King's] Bench you have its most salient points, its most striking features, the most prominent of human faults, passions, vices, and virtues, concentrated in a small space convenient for contemplation by those who are fond of studying the world.'[4] Debtors' prison, as many writers of the 1820s agreed, was a place in which class society was framed as a spectacle, with each class placed in theatrical

Fig. 10.1 B. R. Haydon, *The Mock Election* (1828). Courtesy of the Royal Collection, Buckingham Palace.

proximity to its neighbours. But it was also a space that exposed imposture and performance, a space in which faces were at their most legible and types at their most transparent. It was a touchstone of modern metropolitan life. So much so, indeed, that in Egan and Cruikshank's celebrated metropolitan travelogue of 1821, *Life in London*, and in its numerous imitations and theatrical adaptations, the debtors' prison always had a central function as the ultimate hiding-place of the 'real'.

It was this modish enthusiasm that overtook Haydon in 1827. So enthused was he by the Hogarthian nature of his project, that within a few days of release he was out in the West End looking at the satirist's work. Characteristically though he came away less than impressed, considering that 'occasionally [Hogarth] bordered on caricature'.[5] To him the great strength of the King's Bench as a subject was that, precisely because 'real life' seemed to present itself more expressively there, the painter could draw out his moral without needing to exaggerate:

August 26. What a set of heads I shall have in this extraordinary picture! . . . What a set of beings are assembled in that extraordinary Place – that temple of Idleness and debauchery. Good God! When you walk amongst them you get amongst faces that are all marked by some decided expression, quite different from the people you meet in the street.[6]

It should be no surprise, then, that all of the characters in *The Mock Election* were based on real people, and drawn from the life.[7] The main action of the painting depicts the Lord High Sheriff of the King's Bench Prison, his officers, and several electors all preparing to elect an MP to voice the prisoners' grievances in the House of Commons. Taking the central group first, Haydon introduces us to the pivotal figure of the Sheriff, who is begging the candidate on the left, a red-ribboned Tory, not to fight with his Whig rivals. Appropriately enough, given the strong links between Toryism and violent sports in this period, the angry candidate is being egged on by Harry Holt the pugilist, who was well known in Regency London as 'the Cicero of the Ring'.[8] The gentleman who took the part of the angry candidate was, Haydon tells us, a man called Meredith, a navy lieutenant of considerable fortune in Ireland, who behaved that day as if he really did see a dazzling political career ahead of him. 'The belief was real,' the painter noted in his diary, '. . . he thought the Election genuine and at the conclusion of every speech promised to fight up to his knees in blood for the rights of his fellow prisoners.'[9] Opposite him, dressed in a yellow turban and quilt, is his main rival, the MP for Penrith from 1824–6, one Robert Stanton, a has-been to the Irishman's presumptuous wanna-be. 'Stanton died in a mad-house', Haydon wrote, in the margin of his own copy of the catalogue description, 'he became after spending £80,000 a clerk to Charles Pearson, saved money, became mad & died'.[10] This figure was the moving spring in the whole masquerade, the painter writes in his *Explanation*, inviting us to note the expression of 'sarcastic mischief' that played across his face throughout (p. 6). Between the Lord High Sheriff and the candidate in the quilt is the third candidate, a man called Birch, who like Stanton is sporting the Whig colours of blue and buff.

Immediately below the Sheriff is the head poll-clerk swearing in the three citizens before their vote. The three voters are holding a bit of deal, the first being 'a dandy of the first fashion just imprisoned', Haydon tells us, 'with a fifty-guinea pipe in his right hand, a diamond ring on his finger, dressed in a yellow silk dressing gown, velvet cap and red morocco slippers'. To the left of him stands 'an exquisite, who has been imprisoned three years, smoking a threepenny cigar, with a hole at his elbow, and his toes on the ground'. And the third elector is 'one of those characters of middle age and careless dissipation, visible in all scenes of this description, dressed in a blue jacket and green cap'. To the right of the dandy is another poll-clerk, entering the names of the electors. Above the clerk is the assessor, 'suppressing a laugh', and finally, to the right of the assessor is a short red-nosed man, another fake official, dressed in the red curtain of his room and proudly sporting his mace of office (p. 6).

The Mock Election presents a vivid picture of dandies both high and low, fresh and faded, of political aspirants and political failures, of metropolitan performers of every kind, all unexpectedly levelled by debt and imprisonment. It takes the burlesque spirit of an image such as Robert Cruikshank's 1825 graphic satire of King's Bench prisoners giving a lawyer the bumps and subjects it to a closer analysis (Figure 10.2).[11]

And such is the brilliant exposure of Cockney self-delusion in the painting that one cannot help but be reminded of Haydon's friend Hazlitt's 1823 essay 'On Londoners and Country People':

A real Cockney is the poorest creature in the world, the most literal, the most mechanical, and yet he too lives in a world of romance – a fairy-land of his own. He is a citizen of London; and this abstraction leads his imagination the finest dance in the world . . . his person swells out and expands into *ideal* importance and borrowed magnitude.[12]

The figures to the left of this colourful main group comprise a good, plain family in affliction, respectable people for whom all this facetiousness is

Surrey Collegians giving a Lift to a Limb of the Law.

Fig. 10.2 Robert Cruikshank, 'Surrey Collegians giving a Lift to a Limb of the Law (Banco Regis, or King's Bench)', *The English Spy* (London: Sherwood Jones and Co., 1825). Author's own collection.

folly. They are mostly dressed in black. There is a wife, 'devoted, melting, clinging to her husband', and her eldest boy, 'with all the gaiety of a child', cheering the voters. The father and mother are in mourning for the loss of their second boy, for 'troubles never come in single files', Haydon says, 'but whole battalions' (p. 8). Behind is the old nurse sobbing over a new baby, while the husband, virtuous and in trouble, is contemplating the merry electors with pain. In his hand he holds a paper which says: 'Debt £26, 10s. *paid* – costs £157, 14s. *unpaid*. Treachery, Squeeze and Co., *Thieves' Inn*'. Behind this group, Haydon tells us, is a group of electors with flags and trumpets, and all the bustle of an election. On one flag is written 'The Liberty of the Subject'; on the other, 'No Bailliffs'. The Bench's spiked wall and state house complete the background (p. 8).

The final group, two men and a woman, have a sunnier, more Mediterranean look, and are dressed mainly in white. The man sitting at the table is, Haydon tells us, a well-born soldier, who distinguished himself in Spain, and then was imprisoned for running away with a ward in Chancery. 'Embarrassment followed,' says Haydon, 'and nine years of confinement have rendered him reckless and melancholy.' 'He was one of the most tremendous heads I ever saw in nature,' the artist continues, 'something between Byron and Bonaparte.'

It was affecting to see his pale determined face and athletic form amongst the laughing afflicted, without a smile! Without an emotion! Indifferent to the humour about him, contemptuously above joining the burlesque. He seemed like a fallen angel, meditating on the absurdities of humanity! (p. 7)

Haydon then describes how he has finished off the portrait by putting this hero at his ease, talking with a companion, while champagne bottles, a dice-box, dice, cards, and a racket-bat and ball on the ground testify to the manner in which he has been spending his time. In the painter's own copy of the catalogue description there is a little pencil annotation identifying this man as 'Campbell, nephew of Sir Neil', and indeed there was a Major Campbell who spent fourteen years in the King's Bench prison during this period – a man who appears in Pierce Egan's *Book of Sports* as one of the finest racket players in the country.[13] Leaning over him is an 'interesting girl' who has apparently become attached to him 'in his reverses' (p. 7) – a figure who, like many of Haydon's women, bears a striking resemblance to his own wife, the long-suffering Mary Hyman.

To the Victorians, Benjamin Robert Haydon was seen as a pitiful figure, a man of high ambition, reckless expense, and a blustering belief in his own genius, who had spent a lifetime trying to convert other people to this conviction, while all the while driving both himself and his family ever more deeply into debt.[14] In 1846, with his finances in intractable disarray, he finally reached the end of his tether, committing suicide in his studio at No. 14 Burwood Place, Edgware Road. Seven years later, Tom Taylor published extracts of Haydon's extraordinary diaries, and his reputation grew as one of the most colourful failures of the nineteenth century. In January 1828, however, his fortunes looked to be improving. Not only was he out of prison, *The Mock Election* was getting favourable reviews in the press, more favourable certainly than he was to receive in later years, and shortly after its exhibition in Piccadilly it was bought by King George IV for 500 guineas.[15] The irony here is that *The Mock Election* and its sequels *Chairing the Member* and *Punch, or May Day* weren't really in Haydon's preferred style of painting. He always saw himself as a history painter, in the heroic tradition, not a comic genre painter like Rowlandson or Hogarth. His preferred mode was painting enormous canvases, with no expense spared, over a long period of time; certainly these were the conditions in which he produced his grandest works, *The Judgment of Solomon* (1814), *Christ's Entry into Jerusalem* (1821), and *The Resurrection of Lazarus* (1823). Hence *The Mock Election* was, for Haydon, rather like his brief term in the King's Bench, a temporary sojourn into a more vulgar Cockney realm – and yet it was among his most successful efforts.

A number of friends had rallied round Haydon in the summer of 1827 and helped secure his release from prison. Of these, by far the most energetic was J. G. Lockhart, who ten years earlier had been the anonymous author of the famous 'Cockney School' attacks in *Blackwood's Magazine*. Lockhart's main targets in those days had been the London liberals Leigh Hunt, the so-called 'King of the Cockneys', Keats, and Hazlitt. But he had also found time for a few casual swipes at their close friend Haydon, whom he had dubbed 'The Cockney Raphael'. When Lockhart met Haydon in Edinburgh in 1821 the Scot immediately realized the mistake he had made. Far from being a radical upstart like Hunt or Hazlitt, Haydon was clearly a man of his own stamp, that is, a pugnacious Tory. Thereafter the writer seems to have gone out of his way to help the painter, for as Haydon noted in his *Autobiography*, 'L[ockhart], when we became acquainted, felt so strongly how little I deserved what had been said of me, that his whole life has since been a struggle to undo the evil he was at the time party to.'[16] When Haydon was imprisoned in 1827 it was Lockhart who organized the public meeting (at the Crown and Anchor Tavern) to co-ordinate his release. And only a few months later he urged

Haydon to distance himself from the Cockney School once and for all by writing a vituperative review of Leigh Hunt's *Lord Byron and his Contemporaries* (1828).

Haydon did pen an attack on Hunt but then retracted it at the last moment, resolving to guard himself in future against what he called Lockhart's 'tricks':

March 2 1828. The more I reflect, the more I see the gulph I have escaped. I will venture to say it would have infallibly branded me for ever. Lockhart showed me a review by Lord Byron of Keats's work, in which Lord Byron called him a dirty little blackguard. I said 'This is shocking' & Lockhart took his pen and scratched it out. He said he had scratched out a good deal; Lord Byron called Keats 'The Masturbator of the human mind – the Onan of Literature' . . . The fact is, the cause of all the Cockney School of Poetry being so full of daisies and posies is because the Poets were brought up in brick walls and London fogs, and their minds fly to the very reverse for enjoyment.[17]

The concept of 'Cockneyism' was a subtle one in Lockhart's hands because although fuelled by political animus it wasn't *primarily* political. Nor was it a class term in any simple or straightforward sense. It referred instead to the dangerous metropolitan incongruities that he and his fellow Blackwoodsmen saw lurking in Hunt and Keats's poetry. The word 'Cockney', in Lockhart's formulation, was not targeted at the obviously or reassuringly low; its main aim was to gesture towards people or things that were indeterminate or ill-shapen in some way, amphibious, effeminate, neither popular nor polite. In social terms the word's natural habitat was not with the labouring class but among the new urban petite bourgeoisie: apprentices, seamstresses, clerks, and shopkeepers. In literary terms it homed in on the discomfiting discrepancies of style and social register in works such as Hazlitt's *Liber Amoris* and Hunt's *Story of Rimini*.

In his own mind at least Haydon was no Cockney radical: politically he had a profound respect for rank and title and aesthetically he was steadfastly devoted to that most classical and conservative of forms, large-scale history painting. This was the reason for his continued criticism of the Royal Academy: it was not that it was too conservative, as a body, but that it wasn't conservative enough. It refused to accept that proper public support was needed to preserve and support the art of history painting in England; it was too willing to acquiesce in the taste of the times.

But in spite of Haydon's ever-more apparent distance from his Cockney peers on matters of politics and aesthetics, the spring of 1828 found him strangely resistant to dishing them completely. When he penned his 2

March diary entry he had already had the idea for another metropolitan genre painting, *Punch, or May Day*, and shortly afterwards he started working on a sequel to *The Mock Election* entitled *Chairing the Member*. With this in mind, it is tempting to think that Haydon had his own recent prison experiences in view when he wrote so feelingly of 'brick walls and London fogs' and the desire to transcend them. Admittedly, Haydon's 'Cockney Moment' was a brief one, for when the king subsequently declined to purchase either *Punch* or *Chairing the Member* the painter flounced back to history painting feeling that he had prostituted his talents. But in spite of all this *The Mock Election* remains one of his most significant and characteristic performances: characteristic in its conscious assertions – which are Romantic and heroic; characteristic also in its underlying style, which is richly if reluctantly 'Cockney'. While at work on *The Mock Election* the painter himself had admitted: 'I should not wonder if this Picture has not awakened a faculty which has been dormant.'[18] No doubt the setting must take some of the credit for this, for as we shall see debtors' prison itself was, above all things, a superlatively 'Cockney' realm – in both Lockhart's and Hazlitt's sense of the word – a place of extraordinary paradox and incongruity, a veritable 'world within walls'.

   In the eighteenth and early nineteenth centuries, two kinds of imprisonment for debt were possible: pre-trial and post-trial, the first being called imprisonment on mesne process and the second imprisonment on final process, with the debtor detained on final process being, in normal circumstances, entirely dependent upon his creditor for his discharge. Because of this, as the historian Joanna Innes has pointed out, 'the process is less well described as a system of court-supervised arbitration than as a system of legalized bullying'.[19] But the law was not completely biased on the side of the creditor. There were certain loopholes that the debtor could exploit. Firstly, the bailiffs' power of arrest was fairly limited: they could not make arrests at night, or on Sundays; a fact that Thomas De Quincey made use of when slipping into Edinburgh to visit his family in the 1830s. Nor could they break into a house in order to make an arrest. Secondly, even when captured, the debtor was under no legal compulsion to surrender what he had, unless the creditor attempted the difficult course of proceeding against his property. So, given that imprisonment for debt actually offered the debtor legal protection for his assets, it was not unusual for people to arrange to have themselves detained by 'friendly actions'. Naturally enough, this only exacerbated creditors' frustrations, and led to frequent complaints during the eighteenth century that debtors' prisons were nothing but 'a haven for the spendthrift'.[20]

Nor was the life of an imprisoned debtor necessarily a miserable one. Officers would generally allow them out of the prison on day trips to help sort out their affairs. In the King's Bench debtors could actually live outside the prison: several square miles called 'The Rules' had been designated as an area in which prisoners and their families might settle, on payment of a weekly stipend. There were opportunities for debtors, especially tradesmen, to try and dig their way out of difficulty. Within the walls, debtors called meetings with their creditors and sought legal advice; and this advice helped create what Joanna Innes describes as 'a debtor ethos'. Debtors told themselves that the state of the law of debt was so weighted against them that their creditors had been able to make an arbitrary assault on their property and liberty, and that their own efforts to resist such tyranny were, by contrast, a vindication of the spirit of English law.[21] There was a lot of sympathy for this 'debtor ethos' in the eighteenth century especially; hence debtors were often on the receiving end of both public and private charity in this period, and were generally successful in presenting themselves to the world as not criminals, but victims.

By the late 1820s there was a growing consensus towards reform in the literature surrounding debtors' prisons, and increasing calls for the abolition of imprisonment for debt. It is this movement that Dickens gave added impetus to in the Fleet Prison section of his 1837 novel *Pickwick Papers*, and which prison veteran R. P. Gillies publicized further, first in a story for *Fraser's* entitled 'O'Hanlon and his Wife', and then in an article 'On the Law of Debtor and Creditor' for the *British and Foreign Review*.[22] In the short term, this campaign led to the dissolution of some of the smaller debtors' prisons (the Fleet and the Marshalsea were closed down in 1842). But it was not until the late 1860s, with the introduction of the new bankruptcy laws, that imprisonment for debt was seriously curtailed.

In this extract from an anonymous memoir, *Prison Reminiscences, or Whitecross Street and the Law of Imprisonment for Debt* (1859), the oft-repeated argument for abolition is put very powerfully and succinctly:

As the law of imprisonment for debt now stands, its operation saps the very foundations of honour and morality. It involves the honest and dishonest, the truthful and the habitually false, the accidentally unfortunate and the pre-determined cheat, in the meshes of the same net, returning them back upon society, in due time, all of the same colour . . . rogues all, in fact.[23]

There was, however, another current of feeling that ran alongside and even counter to this abolitionist position. It had been present in the eighteenth century, but seemed to gain in power during the Romantic period, perhaps because the world-view it expressed was so self-consciously archaic and sentimental. This current celebrated debtors' prisons as entertaining, instructive, strangely inviting places. Such sentiments were not necessarily in conflict with those of a reformist nature, but focused less on the prison as a breeding ground of vice and misery, and more on its status as a place of refuge, of freedom-in-imprisonment.[24]

In his autobiography of 1860 the hack journalist turned pub-owner and comedian Renton Nicholson had struck a delicate balance between the cautionary and the celebratory in his treatment of the King's Bench. Listing the extraordinary social mix of liars and cheats among the inmates he offered a facetious homage to the place as a 'little republic of ingenuity' and 'a commonwealth made up of errant and fugitive talent'. But he did also note how one could get addicted to the conviviality of the place, and that it had functioned for him personally as both a school and a shelter: 'The King's Bench, or Queen's Prison, is a great instructor. My knowledge of refined life has been mostly gleaned, and materially improved, by relations therein.'[25]

In the 'World Within Walls' chapter of John Bee's *Real Life in London* (1822) there was a similarly facetious mock-celebration of the King's Bench debtors as men of 'brilliant imagination', speculative over-reachers who had let their fantasy get the better of them:

It is generally speaking not your empty-headed fellows who can arrive at the honour of a residence here, it is rather those of brilliant imagination, of aspiring talent, who have been determined to have money for a time, without heeding the source from which it was derived – who have been up to snuff, till they have reduced themselves to the necessity of resting contented with the marrowbone stage instead of a phaeton or curricle, and twopenny in lieu of claret.[26]

Debtors' prison is here represented as a particular type of popular urban spectacle, a place where metropolitan ambition comes to ground, and is subject to innumerable ironies. But it is also viewed, with a certain paradoxical wit, as a haven for birth and talent, boasting a real community united by too-brilliant imagination.

There was a strong emphasis upon the prison as a friendly and much-needed resting-place in the various prospectuses that were sold to prisoners on their first arrival. 'The King's Bench,' insisted a guide from 1823, 'is for most debtors a happy and welcome asylum.'[27] The Marshalsea doctor who delivers Amy in Dickens's *Little Dorrit* (1855–7) couldn't agree more, for as he tells her bewildered father:

A little more elbow-room is all we want here. We are quiet here; we don't get badgered here; there's no knocker here, sir, to be hammered at by creditors and bring a man's heart into his mouth. Nobody comes here to ask if a man's at home, and to say he'll stand on the door mat till he is. Nobody writes threatening letters about money, to this place. It's freedom, sir, it's freedom![28]

Although Dickens himself was deeply unsympathetic to this position – if position it can be called – it was part of a long-standing tradition of celebrating debtors' prisons as little suburban utopias, bohemian backwaters miraculously freed from the commercial concerns of the outside world. This was such a strong current, particularly in the visual representations of the period, that one is tempted to think of debtors' prison imagery in the early 1800s in terms of a poetics of denial. Witness the golden glow in Pugin and Rowlandson's print of the King's Bench for Ackermann's *Microcosm of London* and the similarly Arcadian, and crepuscular, feel of their picture of the racket grounds of the Fleet. This latter image was of such attractiveness, it seems, that it was still being copied well over seventy years later, long after the Fleet itself had vanished, and debtors' prisons in general were on the way out.

The King's Bench was the largest and most socially respectable of the London debtors' prisons,[29] but as Ackermann's illustration and Haydon's painting clearly shows, its architecture and layout were still pretty basic. Debtors' prisons like the Fleet, the Marshalsea, Whitecross Street, and the King's Bench were all privately run. Each institution was headed by a marshal and administered by a series of officers, or turnkeys. Normally, the turnkeys were remarkably few in number, and had limited official duties that included escorting prisoners to trial and making sure that inmates did not leave without permission. The rest of their time was spent supplying the prisoners with goods and services, from which they generally drew an extremely healthy profit. Apart from that their role in the prisons was rather small, since much of the day-to-day running of these institutions was generally left to the prisoners themselves.[30]

Prisoners frequently resumed their trades in prison. 'Nearly all the lower or ground floor rooms were occupied by men who had turned them into places of business – into shops in fact,' the author of *Prison Reminiscences* tell us; 'here were cobblers – I beg their pardon, boot and shoe makers – tailors and barbers, who worked for inmates of the prison'.[31] Some prisoners even got chronically in arrears to their fellow prisoners, opening up

a new realm of debt within debt. Printers, journalists, and poets committed to the King's Bench (sometimes for seditious libel) often continued to work, sometimes selling pamphlets and newspapers from their
rooms.[32] There were hierarchical elements in prison society: different
classes had different living conditions, purchasing power, and living habits,
with the gentleman's world tending to revolve around the prison coffee
house, and that of the lower classes, the beer-house or tap. But if King's
Bench society was hierarchically structured, it was also knit together with
bonds of community and mutual aid. Renton Nicholson was not being
entirely facetious, therefore, when he referred to it as 'a commonwealth
made up of errant and fugitive talent'.[33]

The most important manifestations of the King's Benchers' sense of
community were the corporate bodies established among the prison
population, one for the 'masterside' of the main prison block, which
looked out on the main yard and contained the richer debtors, and the
other for the 'commonside', which faced the perimeter wall. The masterside corporation was called the King's Bench 'college', and each member
a 'collegian'. The college was a representative institution that facilitated
good order and harmony among the prison population by providing a
formal mechanism for making decisions and settling disputes. It met out
in the open, in the main yard of the prison. The officers of the college,
who were elected by the prisoners in general assembly, included the
president (also described as chairman, steward, and lord mayor), the clerk
or secretary, and the treasurer; there were also sheriffs, aldermen, and
constables. Hence, whether Haydon knew it or not, some of the titles
sported by the mock-electioneers in 1827 did correspond, in some sense,
to 'real' positions within the prison administration. Nor is it necessary to
assume that their prison-yard politicking was purely facetious. The King's
Bench college had actually petitioned parliament a number of times in
the previous century, one of its aims having been to encourage the government in its occasional habit of freeing large groups of honest debtors
in single *ad hoc* gestures of amnesty – the so-called 'Insolvency Acts'.

There were also more distant connections between the King's Bench
prison and outdoor political protest, which had to do with its rather
inadvertent role in both the Wilkesite and Gordon riots (of 1768 and 1780
respectively). In neither case had the disturbance in question been pre-
cipitated by the debtors, but in each the prison had been chosen as the
perfect place from which to assert the liberty and property rights of the
English subject. When the Bench was burnt down during the Gordon
disturbances the debtors themselves were in fact rather reluctant to leave,

and spent a good deal of their time securing their property before vacating the premises. It is incidents like this that have prompted historians to conclude that in spite of its democratic traditions the political ethos of the King's Bench prison was ultimately more like that of a medieval guild than a modern-day radical organization. 'Defensive conservatism' is the term Margot Finn uses to describe it, a phrase that perfectly sums up both its admirably stubborn yet also fundamentally static nature.[34]

Hence debtors' prisons were in many ways extraordinary places of paradox and even of inversion. The King's Bench in particular was an open prison, a prison that you could walk out of, a prison where you were, to some extent at least, looked after by your fellow prisoners, and could, if you chose, carry on your life very much as you would have done outside. It was a prison which was also a haven – and sometimes a hustings – and which was run, for the most part, by the prisoners themselves. As even the most reluctant inmate of little, down-at-heel Whitecross Street prison in the City of London was forced to admit, 'it appeared that the little community was a pure democracy, universal suffrage being the order of the day'.[35] Equally, the debtors' prison was a genuinely bohemian space, a place with its very own rhythm and humour, and, as such, offered a powerful, if implicit, resistance to the new time and work disciplines of the nineteenth century. Most intriguingly of all, the debtors' prison was a place in which losing might suddenly begin to look a little like winning – if you were capable of playing *misère*.

Haydon's *The Mock Election* registers this ambivalence strikingly well. Compositionally it presents the viewer with three groups placed on a dirty triangle of ground in the main prison yard. In the background, between the two apartment blocks, is a blustery blue patch of sky. The walls have not been insisted upon, and the prison's space is made to seem like a large one, as if it is the very idea of imprisonment that we are meant to focus upon, not its iron-and-brick reality. Regarding the prison itself, Haydon presents it as a space in which the distinction between public and private has all but ceased to exist. The masqueraders use the yard as a stage for their public meeting; Major Campbell treats it like a drawing-room. The respectable couple, however, could not look less at home: to them the prison is clearly a kind of purgatory, a realm of the unburied dead. By this means Haydon gives a powerful sense of imprisonment for debt as a kind of blank slate, like a theatre stage, an open space of the imagination, that could be inhabited – and furnished – in a variety of ways.

Regarding the actual burlesque upon which Haydon's painting was based, the initial media response was one of mild amusement. On 17 July

1827 *The Times* reported that 'for some days past a great deal of fun and merriment' had been going forward within the walls of the King's Bench prison 'in consequence of a mock election'.[36] But a couple of days later, as the unruliness of the festivities became evident, one of the paper's correspondents decided that enough was enough:

It is with great regret that we have observed the recent proceedings in the King's Bench Prison. Is it by mock elections, and the excesses attendant on such scenes, that the persons removed to that place of confinement mean to satisfy their honest creditors, and (in many cases we fear) make compensation to those they have wronged? What has the inside of a prison to do with elections?[37]

The writer then went on to praise William Jones, the marshal of the prison, for taking a firm hand with the carnival when it threatened to get out of hand, calling in the Grenadier Guards, and quick-marching all three candidates, the High Sheriff, and his poll-clerk to the King's Bench strong room. Not surprisingly, the prison collegians vehemently rejected this view of things; and indeed in the very same issue of *The Times* there was news of a prisoners' petition calling for Jones's resignation. The King's Bench college was outraged at his Peterloo-like introduction of the military and of his having treated their fellow debtors 'like criminals'.[38]

What *has* the inside of a prison to do with elections? Fundamentally facetious though it was, the King's Bench Mock Election of July 1827 was clearly drawing on a long-standing tradition of the debtors' prison as a site of political theatre and protest. What is interesting, however, is how very unsympathetic the commentators of the day were to this late flowering of the carnivalesque. Possible explanations are not hard to find. Firstly, the politics of political representation had become very heated by 1827: the campaign for Catholic Emancipation was reaching its height, with the political plight of poor Irish Catholics being very similar, in certain respects, to those of unjustly imprisoned debtors. The participation of several Irishmen in the King's Bench festivities may well have alerted people to this connection. More generally, the 'Mock Election' may also have served as an unwelcome reminder of the general riotousness and corruption surrounding the typical 'rotten borough' election, a state of affairs that was becoming ever more embarrassing to the establishment by the late 1820s. But at bottom the comparative lack of public sympathy for the King's Bench burlesque was probably due to the changed economic circumstances of the period. This was a time, after all, of burgeoning national debt. The king himself, George IV, was a notorious debtor, and there had been a great financial crash – the crash that ruined Sir Walter Scott – a couple of years before. There is a new puritanism in the attitude to insolvency during these years. Debtors were still viewed as unfortunate, but it was no longer so easy to celebrate them as martyrs to English liberty. The criminalization of debt that became so prevalent in the Victorian period was beginning to take hold.

Nor is this feeling absent from Haydon's painting: one has only to look at the soberly dressed middle-class family on the left-hand side of the canvas. As honest and industrious citizens who have been imprisoned under a corrupt legal system, they offer a powerful visual embodiment of the abolitionist argument. Secondly, in their evident disapproval of what is going on around them, Haydon's couple also represent respectable society's increasing distaste for the 'flash style' of the unreformed debtors' prison. It was this dual attitude that was to prevail in the later nineteenth century, for as the campaign to abolish debtors' prisons intensified, so too did the stigma of criminality surrounding debt. By the 1870s imprisonment for debt had ceased for everything except small debts, which meant that it was only the poor who were still subject to incarceration, and those convicted were no longer being sent to the King's Bench or the Fleet, but to grubby, cramped Whitecross Street, or, worse still, modern-style reformist penitentiaries like Holloway. This is one of the reasons cited by Margot Finn for the disappearance of debtors and debtors' prisons from English fiction after *Little Dorrit*: it was not that such places had ceased to exist, but that they no longer contained middle-class people.

On the left of the canvas Haydon shows a growing family rendered suddenly and dramatically abject by a mere accident of debt. And the fact that there are no names attached to these figures in the annotated catalogue only increases the suspicion that it is the painter's own family that has provided the model. While Haydon was working on *The Mock Election* his wife Mary gave birth to their sixth child, and despite being vehemently anti-Malthusian in theory, his burgeoning brood often left him anxious and depressed in practice. But if the group portrait on the left represents Haydon's intermittent acknowledgement of the brute facts of economic reality, the rest of the composition reflects his strenuous defiance of them.

In the central portion Haydon celebrates not only the debtors' burlesque spirit but also the vulgar self-advertisement that he himself always relied upon as a tool to get out of trouble. For the painter was not only the dejected father of a brood of children; he was also, like the Tory candidate in the picture, a vigorous petitioner and polemicist, with a gift for Cockney self-promotion. Only the year before *The Mock Election*

Haydon had begun a concerted campaign to mend his reputation with the Royal Academy, aggressively courting those members with whom he had argued in the past. He was also a regular petitioner of parliament, calling for English history painting to receive state support. Haydon always found public appeals and debates of this kind hugely energizing; and through them he indulged his idealism, his vanity, and his vulgarity. But to many of his artistic brethren they provided a grave distraction from his painting, and even in their own terms rarely had the desired effect. In both 1826 and 1827 Haydon had tried to cash in on his courtship of the Academy by putting himself up for election, but on neither occasion had he garnered a single vote.[39] While working on *The Mock Election* at the end of 1827 he joked in his diary that the Academicians might well see a satirical impulse in his current project, an attempt to bring elected authorities – all elected authorities – into contempt by painting mock Sheriffs and mock Mayors.[40] Nor, one might add, would they necessarily have been wrong to do so, for in the epigraph to the catalogue description Haydon had made a point of quoting *Measure for Measure* on 'man, proud man, dressed in little, brief, authority, most ignorant of what he's most assured'.

On the right-hand side of the painting, with the figure of the war hero Major Campbell, the painting moves beyond self-promotion to heroic defiance. In the catalogue Haydon links Campbell with Bonaparte, Byron, and Milton's Satan, all brilliant over-reachers, 'men of aspiring talent' who finished their careers in exile. One indication of Haydon's strong identification with this figure is the latter's striking profile, which closely resembles the painter's own; another is the following passage from the catalogue description, which whisks us abruptly away from the realm of Cockney satire and into the world of Byron's *Childe Harold*, Napoleon's *Memoirs* on St Helena, and general post-Waterloo disappointment:

We gaze after the eagle in his flight, and are bound by gravitation to the earth we tread on; we sail forth in pursuit of new worlds, and after a year or two return to the spot we started from, we weary our imaginations with hopes of something new, and find, after a long life, we can only embellish what we see: so that while our hopes are endless and our imagination unbounded, our faculties and being are limited; whether it be six thousand feet, or six thousand miles, a limit still marks the prison! (p. 4)

Major Campbell had spent nine years in prison by 1827, but Haydon himself had been in debt for even longer, and this passage is a painful, though oblique, acknowledgement of that fact. The eagle here, like the figure of Campbell in the painting, is a perfect image of the independent history painter, a man both heroic in himself and committed to heroic subjects, who has somehow found himself imprisoned in the world of genre painting. Genre, here, can be construed aesthetically, as that mode of low Dutch realism in which the artist is condemned to 'only embellish what he sees', and also economically, as the grubby world of everyday economic reality. Similarly, the Campbell figure registers Haydon's own contemptuous attitude to material difficulty, and his determination to go it alone, independently of parliaments or academies; he is in that sense an image of the painter's ideal self.

Pictorially, the Major is portrayed in a broader, brighter, less detailed style than everyone else. His physique is strongly reminiscent of the Illisus, one of the largest of the Elgin Marbles, and recalls Haydon's vehement championship of them in the previous decade. It was the Elgin Marbles, Haydon had argued, that were going to inspire a whole new generation of English artists, with the Illisus in particular representing a perfect synthesis of the natural and the ideal. The treatment of the respectable couple, by contrast, is much closer to that of contemporary genre painting, a point made by George IV himself when he pointed to the left-hand side of the canvas during his first perusal of the painting and said: 'This is our friend Wilkie out-and-out.'[41] The Royal Academician David Wilkie was one of Haydon's life-long friends, a brilliant genre painter who had first made his name in 1806 with a superbly conceived rustic scene called *Village Politicians* and then soared to even greater heights in 1822 with his history-cum-genre painting *Chelsea Pensioners reading the Waterloo Despatch*. Not long before his second incarceration Haydon had made an entry in his diary comparing himself to Wilkie, in which he employed a favourite analogy between artistic and military endeavour:

Wilkie's system was Wellington's: principle and prudence the groundwork of risk. Mine that of Napoleon: audacity, with defiance of principle, if principle was in the way. I got into prison. Napoleon died in St. Helena. Wellington is living and honoured, and Wilkie has had a public dinner given him in Rome, the seat of art and genius, and has secured a competence, while I am as poor and necessitous as ever.[42]

In his diary Haydon balanced a long-standing respect for Wilkie's gifts with an equally enduring contempt for the genre his friend specialized in. And its manifold popularity with the public only increased his anger. 'Nothing bold, or masculine, or grand, or powerful touches an English connoisseur,' he wrote in 1824. 'It must be small and highly wrought, and vulgar and humorous, and broad and palpable.'[43]

Haydon's *Mock Election* possesses many of the latter qualities, and owes a considerable amount to Wilkie's example, not only in the sober realism of the respectable family but also in the energy and naturalness of the central group, which is, in fact, something of a Cockney translation of *Village Politicians*, with the posturings of the impotent now transferred to the city. It is also, in its way, an ironic sequel to Wilkie's heart-warming image of veteran patriotism in the *Chelsea Pensioners*. Aesthetically, then, the painting is a deliberate confusion of genre painting, history painting, and Hogarthian graphic satire; something *The Times* reviewer may have been gesturing towards when he called it 'coarse and uneven'.[44] But narratively the painting is clear enough, with the visual composition describing what is in effect a left-to-right progress from abjection through protest to stoic defiance, a movement that is also, in its way, a progression from genre painting to history painting and from a purely economic understanding of things to one that is purely political.

In Haydon's hands history painting was a genre that specialized in extreme, even foolhardy, acts of will. In his first major painting, which was exhibited in 1809, he depicted Dentatus at the point of death still vigorously defending himself against his assassins, and in one of his last he showed Marcus Curtius leaping into the gulf to save the Roman republic. Haydon's favourite subjects are often creatures of suicidal heroism and self-sacrifice, and to that extent they appeal to the purest form of the political understanding. They appeal, that is, not to the party-political, but to politics as a pure discourse of the will. In *The Mock Election* Campbell's absolute refusal to negotiate with his creditors – even at the cost of remaining in the Bench for the rest of his life – is just such an act of pure voluntarism, and constitutes a heroic defiance of economics. And as in 'Marcus Curtius' so too in *The Mock Election* there is a politics of profile: by gazing directly offstage and refusing to meet anyone's eye the hero dramatizes the extent to which his thoughts are, quite literally, on a different plane from everyone else's. He alone, it seems, can see beyond the material confines of the canvas.

Such a defiant gesture was only possible, one could argue, because of the 'debtor ethos' that continued to surround early nineteenth-century debtors' prisons, for it rendered the King's Bench, ironically enough, the perfect place to insist upon the primacy of the political over the economic, the will over circumstance, personality over history. Three years after *The Mock Election* Benjamin Robert Haydon was imprisoned in the Bench once more, but by this time, as his biographer Eric George points out, he seems to have gotten used to the place, treating it almost as a second home.[45] Indeed something of the spirit of Ackermann's *Microcosm* engraving seems to have descended upon him during those July days of 1830. 'Waterloo Heroes absolutely abound here,' he wrote enthusiastically in his diary. 'On the racket ground at night [Major Bacon], I, and Colonel La Tour walk & talk. I excite them about Waterloo, and I never passed pleasanter evenings.'[46]

NOTES

1 Benjamin Robert Haydon, *The Autobiography and Memoirs of Benjamin Robert Haydon* (1853), ed. T. Taylor, 2 vols. (London: Peter Davies, 1926), vol. 1, p. 415.

2 Benjamin Robert Haydon, *The Diary of Benjamin Robert Haydon*, ed. W. Bissell Pope, 5 vols. (Cambridge, Mass.: Harvard University Press, 1963), vol. III, p. 215 (22 August 1827).

3 [Benjamin Robert Haydon], *Explanation of the Picture of the Mock Election which Took Place at the King's Bench Prison, July 1827* (London: James Bullock, 1828), p. 5. Price sixpence. Subsequent references are in parentheses in the text.

4 [Anon.], *Prison Reminiscences, or Whitecross Street and the Law of Imprisonment for Debt, with Facts showing its Cruelty and Impolicy* (London: A. W. Bennett, 1859), p. 148.

5 Haydon, *Diary*, vol. III, p. 216 (30 August 1827).

6 *Ibid.*, vol. III, pp. 215–16 (26 August 1827).

7 We know this because the British Library has Haydon's own copy of the 1828 *Explanation* of the picture, in which many of the names, and some biographical details, have been supplied. See also the article 'King's Bench Prison' in *The Times* (17 July 1827).

8 Haydon, *Diary*, vol. III, p. 218n.

9 *Ibid.*, p. 216n.

10 *Ibid.*, p. 215n.

11 Robert Cruikshank's 'Surrey Collegians giving a Lift to a Limb of the Law (Banco Regis, or King's Bench)' appeared in a *Life in London*-style metropolitan travelogue called *The English Spy* (London: Sherwood Jones and Co., 1825).

12 William Hazlitt, *Metropolitan Writings*, ed. Gregory Dart (Manchester: Carcanet, 2005), p. 84.

13 Pierce Egan, *Book of Sports and Mirror of Life*, 2nd edition (London: Tegg, Cheapside, 1836), p. 228.

14 Reckless with money in general, Haydon was especially extravagant in his outlay on props and models for his pictures. See William Bewick, *Life and Letters of William Bewick* (1871), ed. T. Landseer, 2 vols. (Wakefield: EP Publishing, 1978), vol. 1, pp. 268–9.

15 This is just one of the details inked into Haydon's own annotated copy of the *Explanation* (p. 3).
16 Haydon, *Autobiography and Memoirs*, p. 313.
17 Haydon, *Diary*, vol. III, pp. 257–8 (2 March 1828).
18 *Ibid.*, vol. III, p. 219 (12 September 1827).
19 Joanna Innes, 'The King's Bench in the Later Eighteenth Century: Law, Authority and Order in a London Debtors' Prison', in J. Brewer and J. Styles (eds.), *An Ungovernable People* (London: Hutchinson, 1980), p. 253.
20 The phrase is from Innes, 'The King's Bench', p. 255. Innes points out that on at least one occasion in the eighteenth century creditors got so frustrated about debtors using the prison as a refuge that they sought statutory powers to compel them to come out and make a settlement.
21 *Ibid.*, p. 257.
22 [R. Gillies], 'O'Hanlon and his Wife', *Fraser's Magazine* (August 1836), 184–202; 'On the Law of Debtor and Creditor', *British and Foreign Review* (July–October 1837). Gillies was also the author of the *Memoirs of a Literary Veteran*, 3 vols. (London, 1851), which gives an extensive account of his experiences in debtors' prison.
23 *Prison Reminiscences*, p. 4.
24 Margot Finn remarks that: 'Far from developing (with the criminal prison) from disorderly and archaic institutions of mere confinement into active, modern instruments of discipline and reform, fictional debtors' prisons continuously fluctuated between two extremes of representation, alternately figuring as venal sites of exploitation in which contractual oppression ran riot and as economic backwaters that served, worryingly, to protect their inmates from the demands of the modern market' (*The Character of Credit: Personal Debt in English Culture, 1740–1914* (Cambridge and New York: Cambridge University Press, 2003), p. 56).
25 Renton Nicholson, *Rogue's Progress: The Autobiography of Lord Chief Baron Nicholson* (1860), ed. J. Bradley (London: Longman, 1966), pp. 114–18.
26 John Bee, *Real Life in London* (London, 1822), p. 95.
27 *A Description of the King's Bench Prison, being a brief review of its Constitution, the Prison itself, the Day Rules &c.* (London: John McShee, 1823), p. 1.
28 Charles Dickens, *Little Dorrit*, ed. Helen Small and Stephen Wall (Harmondsworth: Penguin, 2003), pp. 78–9.
29 Hugh Barty-King, *The Worst Poverty* (London: Alan Sutton, 1991), p. 114.
30 Officers tended to think of their prisoners as customers, or clients, rather than reprobates, an ambience accurately captured in the relationship between Chivery the turnkey and Dorrit the long-term debtor in Charles Dickens's *Little Dorrit* (1855–7).
31 *Prison Reminiscences*, p. 133.
32 See Thackeray's portrait of Captain Shandon (William Maginn) in *Pendennis* (1848–50).
33 Nicholson, *Rogue's Progress*, p. 115.
34 Finn, *Character of Credit*, p. 145.

35 *Prison Reminiscences*, p. 28.
36 'King's Bench Prison', *The Times* No. 13333 (17 July 1827), 3.
37 *The Times* No. 13335 (19 July 1827), 2.
38 *The Times* No. 13387 (18 September 1827), 2.
39 See Clarke Olney, *Benjamin Robert Haydon, Historical Painter* (Atlanta: University of Georgia Press, 1952), p. 15.
40 Haydon, *Diary*, vol. III, p. 230 (14 November 1827).
41 Haydon, *Autobiography and Memoirs*, p. 438.
42 Haydon, *Diary*, vol. III, p. 182 (9 February 1827). See also Eric George, *The Life and Death of Benjamin Robert Haydon* (London: Geoffrey Cumberlege, Oxford University Press, 1948), p. 180.
43 Haydon, *Autobiography and Memoirs*, p. 386.
44 'Fine Arts', *The Times* No. 13483 (8 January 1828), 3.
45 George, *Life and Death*, p. 202.
46 Haydon, *Diary*, vol. III, p. 448 (3 June 1830).

PART V

Canon-formation and the common reader

Every-day poetry: William Hone, popular antiquarianism, and the literary anthology

Mina Gorji

In May 1825, Charles Lamb's 'Quatrains to the Editor of the Every-Day Book' appeared in *The London Magazine*. They describe and celebrate a neglected classic of Romantic popular culture:

> I like you, and your book, ingenious Hone!
> In whose capacious, all-embracing leaves
> The very marrow of tradition's shown;
> And all that history – much that fiction – weaves.
> By every sort of taste your work is graced.
> Vast stores of modern anecdote we find,
> With good old story quaintly interlaced –
> The theme as various as the reader's mind.
> . . .
> Rags, relics, witches, ghosts, fiends, crowd your page;
> Our fathers' mummeries we well-pleased behold;
> And, proudly conscious of a purer age,
> Forgive some fopperies in the times of old.[1]

William Hone's *Every-Day Book; or, Everlasting Calendar of Popular Amusements, Sports, Pastimes, Ceremonies, Manners, Customs and Events* was a truly 'capacious' work; part almanac, part encyclopaedia, part popular antiquarian miscellany, it was arranged according to the calendar year and listed the times of sunrise and sunset, the hours of full tide, feasts and fasts, and historical events, as well as miscellaneous facts, literary extracts, natural history, and accounts of 'the manners and customs of ancient and modern times, with descriptive accounts of the several seasons of popular pastime'.[2] *The Every-Day Book* was serially published from January 1825 to December 1826; each number was priced at three pence and made up of a sheet of thirty-two columns designed to be bound together into a book. These weekly numbers proved so successful that a collected two-volume edition was reissued throughout the nineteenth century. Although its admirers included 'individuals of high literary reputation', such as Scott, Dickens, and Christina Rossetti, Hone hoped that *The Every-Day Book* would appeal to 'every class of reader', to 'parents and children, teachers and pupils, master and servants'.[3]

Today, Hone is best remembered as an antiquarian and a radical publisher – champion of the free press, satirist, and anti-establishment pamphleteer tried for seditious blasphemy in 1817.[4] He was also an anthologist who, in the words of Robert Southey, had 'rendered good service in an important department of literature'.[5] Not only did 'this down-market publisher' give 'the urban crowd the concept of a popular cultural history', he also shaped a popular poetic canon.[6] *The Every-Day Book* was packed with extracts from Spenser, Shakespeare, Milton, Herrick, Browne, Wordsworth, Coleridge, Smith, Keats, and Clare. Printed on Hone's pages, poetry reached a large and socially diverse reading public, and was presented as part of a distinctively popular heritage. This chapter places *The Every-Day Book* in the print culture of its time and explores how it contributed to shaping and expanding a vernacular canon in the Romantic period. As we shall see, it was not only on the pages of literary anthologies and volumes of verse that the poetic canon found shape, but also in more miscellaneous works of popular culture and history: chapbooks, magazines, almanacs, literary digests, and antiquarian histories all included literary extracts.[7] Hone drew on and participated in this wider textual tradition, and reading *The Every-Day Book* in this context expands our understanding of the emerging canon and its relation to both popular culture and Romantic literary history.

The Every-Day Book was a *bricolage* of extracts from magazines and newspapers, volumes of verse (some within, some outside, copyright), rare antiquarian books and manuscripts, quotations from London barrow women's cries and chimney sweeps' songs, as well as hundreds of readers' letters.[8] Hone encouraged contributions, and his weekly publication was intended to facilitate 'the attainment of additional particulars during its progress'.[9] Correspondents' letters published in the December 1826 numbers, for example, detail Christmas observances in Ramsgate and Maidstone in Kent, Hornchurch in Essex, Avingham near Newcastle-on-Tyne, and Whitehaven in Yorkshire. John Clare wrote to Hone in April 1825 describing a ritual associated with St Mark's Eve in his own village, an account which was subsequently published on Hone's pages:

On St Mark's Eve, it is still the custom about us for young maids to make the *dumb cake*, a mystical ceremony which has lost its origin, and in some counties may have ceased altogether. The number of the party never exceeds three; they meet in silence to make the cake, and as soon as the clock strikes twelve, they each break a portion off to eat, and when done, they walk up to bed backwards without speaking a word, for if one speaks the spell shall be broken. Those that are to be married see the likeness of their sweethearts hurrying after them.[10]

The Every-Day Book was peppered with such first-hand accounts, sent in by common readers from all over the country; it thus presented a sociable, egalitarian model of collaborative authorship, and a truly popular cultural history.

Just as importantly, however, *The Every-Day Book* contributed to and extended a larger process of literary canon-formation in the Romantic period.[11] By the early decades of the nineteenth century, the nation's poetic tradition was available to a wider public than ever before. Cheaply produced multi-volume editions such as John Bell's *The Poets of Great Britain Complete from Chaucer to Churchill* (109 vols., 1776–82), John Anderson's *Complete Edition of the Poets of Great Britain* (1792–5; a fourteenth volume was added in 1807), Thomas Park's *The Works of the British Poets, Collated with the Best Editions* (1805–8), Chalmers's *The Works of the English Poets, From Chaucer to Cowper* (1790; reissued in 1801 and 1803), and Ellis's *Specimens of the Later British Poets* (1807) shaped a vernacular canon that stretched from Chaucer to Cowper and included Gay, Spenser, Smith, Shakespeare, and Milton.[12]

Anthologies of poetic extracts brought selections of verse to an even wider reading public. Ellis's *Specimens of the Early English Poets* (1811), Aiken's *Select Works of the British Poets* (1820), and Campbell's *Beauties of the British Poets* (1824) were just a few examples of a proliferating genre; of these, perhaps the most popular and influential was Vicesimus Knox's oft-reprinted *Elegant Extracts from the Most Eminent British Poets* (1784). Knox catered to existing tastes and reinforced current notions of literary popularity. In the preface to *Elegant Extracts*, he declared that he would include only 'famous and popular passages ... from Shakespeare, Milton, Pope, Gray'. It was his duty to present his young readers (the book was aimed primarily at school children) with a selection of the 'best pieces', from the 'most eminent' poets; those, he explained, were 'usually the most popular ... They are loudly recommended by the voice of Fame.' He went on to explain that:

the business of the Editor of a school-book like this, [is] not to insert scarce and curious works, such as please virtuoso readers, chiefly from their rarity, but to collect such as were publicly known and universally celebrated. The more known, the more celebrated, the better they were adapted to this Collection ... Private judgement, in a work like this, must often give way to public.[13]

The researches of private gentleman scholars, virtuoso readers, and antiquarians were certainly not part of the 'public' taste described by Knox. Other anthologists were more distrustful of the 'voice of Fame', and less certain of the correlation between commercial popularity and literary value. Alexander Chalmers, for example, in the introduction to his well-known collection *The Works of the English Poets, from Chaucer to Cowper; including the series edited with prefaces, biographical and critical, by Dr. Samuel Johnson* (21 vols., 1810), noted the slipperiness of the terms and their historical contingency:

There are perhaps two rules by which a collector of English poetry can be guided. He is either to give a series of the Best poets, or of the most Popular, but simple as these rules appear, they are not without difficulties, for whichever he choose to rely upon, the other will be found to interfere . . . the question 'who are the best poets' . . . will be . . . obstinately contested. On the other hand, he will not find more security in popularity, which is a criterion of uncertain duration, sometimes depending on circumstances very remote from taste or judgement, and, unless in some few happy instances, a mere fashion.[14]

Hone offered a more fundamental challenge to the distinction between commercial popularity and popular tradition. *The Every-Day Book was* a work of *popular* antiquarianism, aimed not at the 'virtuoso' reader but at a wide and socially diverse audience; as such, it is popular in two senses, concerned with the culture of 'the people', and possessing broad commercial appeal. In contrast to Knox, Hone set out to publish the 'scarce and curious' on his pages. *The Every-Day Book* 'introduced an entire generation to the literary inheritance that was previously locked up in costly and out-of-print volumes'.[15] In June 1825, Clare wrote to Hone once again, praising him for championing forgotten poetry: 'I perceive by the perusal of your Every day book that the neglected poetry of other days has found a friend in your taste.'[16]

Championing 'neglected poetry', Hone's collection expanded the canon, bringing poems that had remained in expensive antiquarian volumes to a wide and non-specialist audience. He popularized the researches of Percy and Scott, who had both published influential collections of ancient poetry. In Percy's *Reliques* (1765) and Scott's *English Minstrelsy: Being a Selection of Fugitive Poetry from the Best English Authors* (1810) an ancient common culture of ballad and song was framed for contemporary readers by footnotes, glosses, and scholarly apparatus. In *The Every-Day Book* Hone continued and extended this process of canonization by including not only popular songs and ballads, but also descriptions of popular customs and superstitions. And there was no sense of historical distance on Hone's pages: verses were not presented as 'reliques' of an ancient past, but as part of a living tradition. Hone was proud that the 'mothers of England' had enjoyed *The Every-Day Book* and 'had been pleased to entertain it as an every-day assistant in their families'.[17] If Addison's *Spectator* had brought philosophy into the coffee houses, Hone sought to bring antiquarian scholarship out of the libraries and into the more feminized domestic spaces of nineteenth-century England.

Not only did Hone expand the literary canon, he also presented poetry as part of popular culture. His literary extracts were neither 'popular' in Knox's sense of the word, nor were they 'elegant'. The poetry of *The Every-Day Book* was part of a collective national heritage, a cultural idea that was not shaped by notions of gentility or refinement, but shared by all ranks: milkmaids' and Mayers' songs shared space with Spenser and Milton, Dryden and Byron; the poems of Wordsworth and Cowper appeared in the same volume as self-taught poets Bloomfield, Kirke-White, and Clare. In distinct contrast to Hone's inclusive practice, Robert Southey's *Specimens of the Later English Poets* (London, 1807) and *Select Works of the British Poets from Chaucer to Jonson* (London, 1831) set those he described as 'uneducated poets', including Stephen Duck, Anne Yearsely, and John Jones, apart from the literary canon. Southey, who admired Hone's *Every-Day Book*, shaped his own literary anthologies according to very different principles, which find their clearest articulation in the preface to his *Lives and Works of the Uneducated Poets* (1831). Here Southey explained that after the Elizabethan age, 'the distinction between high and low life' became marked in British culture; henceforth, 'the mother tongue of the lower classes ceased to be the language of composition; that of the peasantry was antiquated, that of inferior citizens had become vulgar. It was not necessary that a poet should be learned in Greek and Latin, but it was vital that he should speak the language of polished society.'[18] No such 'distinction between high and low life' was apparent on Hone's pages; his anthology, in contrast, presented a common culture that extended to the present day and drew out continuities between the language used by poets from all ranks and periods, as well as antiquarians, journalists, milkmaids, mowers, and street vendors.

The entries for Maundy Thursday and Good Friday, for example, are typically wide-ranging and miscellaneous, including lines from Herrick,

Drayton, and Shakespeare alongside quotations from Dunton's *British Apollo*,[19] Archdeacon Nares's 'Glossary', an account of the custom of alms-giving, and common street cries.[20] On the following pages, London street cries appear in a description of Good Friday customs:

The dawn is awakened by a cry in the streets of 'Hot-cross-buns; one-a-penny buns, two-a-penny buns; one-a-penny, two-a-penny, hot-cross-buns!' This proceeds from some little 'peep-o'-day boy', willing to take the 'top of the morning' before the rest of his compeers. He carries his covered buns in a basket hanging on one arm, while his other hand is straightened like an open door, at the side of his mouth, to let forth his childish voice, and he 'pipes and trebles out the sound' to the extremity of his lungs. Scarcely has he departed before others come; 'another and another still succeeds', and at last the whole street is in one 'common cry of buns'.[21]

This juxtaposition of different accents and different kinds of writing calls into question distinctions between high and low cultural forms and registers. Textual voices mingle on Hone's pages into a 'common cry', so that Autolycus' song from *The Winter's Tale*:

> Lawn as white as driven snow;
> Cypress, black as e'er was crow;
> Gloves, as sweet as damask roses;
> Masks for faces, and for noses;
> Bugle bracelet, necklace-amber,
> Perfume for a lady's chamber;
> Golden quoits, and stomachers,
> For my lads to give their dears;
> Pins, and poking-sticks of steel,
> What maids lack from head to heel:
> Come, buy of me, come: come buy, come buy;
> Buy, lads, or else your lasses cry,
> Come, buy, &c[22]

finds an echo in the voice of a London barrow woman, recorded in the entry for 4 July 1826:

> Round and sound
> Two-pence a pound;
> Cherries! rare ripe cherries!
> . . .
> Cherries a ha'penny a strick!
> Come and pick! Come and pick
> Cherries! Big as plums!
> Who comes? Who comes?[23]

The barrow woman's voice, in turn, resounds in the following lines from Shenstone's 'The School Mistress', a pastoral portrait in Spenserian stanzas, which appeared on the facing page of *The Every-Day Book*:

> See! cherries here, ere cherries yet abound,
> With thread so white in tempting posies ty'd,
> Scatt'ring like blooming maid their glances round
> With pamper'd look draw little eyes aside,
> And must be bought.[24]

Shakespeare and a London barrow woman, Shenstone, Herrick, Drayton, and the hot-cross-bun seller are part of the same quotidian world. *The Every-Day Book* thus offered new ways of reading poetry that encouraged comparison and contrast, unsettled distinctions between high and low, polite and popular culture, and challenged notions of poetry as a genteel art. But Hone's book also suggests ways of expanding our understanding of the 'anthology' in this period, to include almanacs, antiquarian histories, newspapers, and magazines.

The Every-Day Book roots poetry in the everyday world, as a record of passing seasons, of daily life and the ritual calendar of work and festivals.[25] By presenting verse in this form, Hone was following the example of popular almanacs such as *Poor Robin's Almanac* (printed annually from the mid-1660s until the early nineteenth century), in drawing on poetic extracts to illustrate seasonal change.[26] Another example of the kind of almanac anthology that influenced Hone was *Time's Telescope, Or, a Complete Guide to the Almanack: Containing Explanations of Saint's Days and Holidays*. Its contents were more diverse, and include, for example, 'Illustration of British History and Antiquities' as well as 'Notices and Obsolete Rites and Customs', details of 'Astronomical Occurrences . . .' alongside select poetic extracts from a wide range of eighteenth- and early nineteenth-century poets. Thomson and Smith were among the most often cited in the 1818 number, and Akenside, Garth, Beattie, Charlotte Smith, Hurdis, Gray, Barbauld, Dyer, Cowper, and Bloomfield all appeared. In *Time's Telescope* poetry was called upon to illustrate seasonal changes, anniversaries, and notable dates, and also to describe natural history and geology.

While clearly indebted to the almanac tradition, Hone sought to publish a wider range of verse, including many lesser-known writers from the sixteenth and seventeenth centuries. An epigraph from Herrick appeared on the frontispiece of *The Every-Day Book*, setting out the plan of the entire work:

> I tell of festivals, and fairs, and plays,
> Of merriment, and mirth, and bonfire blaze;
> I tell of Christmas-mummings, new-year's day,
> Of twelfth-night king and queen, and children's play;
> I tell of Valentines, and true-love's-knots,
> Of omens, cunning men and drawing lots –
> I tell of brooks, of blossoms, birds and bowers,
> Of April, May, of June and July-flowers;
> I tell of May-poles, hock-carts, wassails, wakes,
> Of bridegrooms, brides, and of their bridal-cakes;
> I tell of groves, of twilights, and I sing
> The court of Mab, and of the fairy-king. – *Herrick*

Hone described Herrick as 'the poet of our festivals', and he is one of the most frequently quoted poets in *The Every-Day Book*. Extracts from his poems, and from the works of many of his contemporaries – Jonson, Spenser, Browne, and Drayton – were often used to illustrate traditional customs; poetry, Hone explained, was the 'history of ancient times', and poets were the 'annalists' of popular customs.[27]

In the early nineteenth century, there weren't such hard distinctions between literary anthologies and the kind of text we tend to characterize as antiquarian. 'Ancient' poetry appeared not just in Percy's *Reliques* and Scott's *English Minstrelsy*, but also in collections such as John Brand's *Observations on Popular Antiquities*. Hone, who was personally acquainted with Brand, was influenced by his antiquarian researches and by his practice of literary quotation.[28] In his *Observations*, Brand used poetic quotations to illustrate 'popular Notions and vulgar Ceremonies': Dryden, Browne, Shakespeare, Chaucer, Akenside, Dyer's *Fleece*, Thomson's *Seasons*, Ramsay's *Gentle Shepherd*, Skelton, and Gray all appeared, but by far the most frequently quoted poet in Brand's volume was John Gay, whose *Trivia* (1716) and *Shepherd's Week* (1714) provided examples of popular customs, song, and superstitions.[29]

There was some irony in using extracts from the *Shepherd's Week*, since the poem began as a burlesque. Yet it came to be seen as a genuine account of rural life by later readers, as Wordsworth explained in 1815:

though these Poems contain some detestable passages, the effect, as Dr. Johnson well observes, 'of reality and truth became conspicuous even when the intention was to show them grovelling and degraded'. The Pastorals, ludicrous to such as prided themselves upon their refinement, in spite of those disgusting passages, 'became popular, and were read with delight, as just representations of rural manners and occupations'.[30]

Brand's use of Gay to illustrate rural customs and superstitions offers a striking example of the changing cultural currency of his poem, and the ways in which different conceptions of popularity might apply to the same text as it circulated in different forms.

Brand's *Observations* was revised and augmented in 1813 by Henry Ellis, keeper of manuscripts of the British Museum. Ellis rearranged the contents of Brand's book into two main sections: a calendar of months with associated customs, and a separate collection of customs and ceremonies of common life, popular notions, sports, and errors. To this rearranged collection Ellis added many new literary quotations from writers of the sixteenth and seventeenth centuries (such as Herrick, Fletcher, Milton, and Browne) as well as extracts from popular songs and ballads, antiquarian volumes, manuscripts, magazines, and newspapers in his copious footnotes. Ellis's *Observations on Popular Antiquities* was an important example for Hone, and a source for many of the poetic extracts, historical facts, and anecdotes that appeared in *The Every-Day Book*, as he acknowledged in passing references. Hone thus popularized antiquarian researches, bringing material gathered from costly volumes to a wide, non-specialized audience and presenting it in a cheap and popular form.

And yet the canon of vernacular poetry that emerged on the pages of *The Every-Day Book* was more than a 'history of ancient times'. Hone was feeling his way past an illustrative (or more purely 'antiquarian') use of poetry, as an index of custom and tradition, towards a more presentist concern with the canon as a kind of *living* tradition, embodied and preserved in the minds of his readers. Whereas on Brand and Ellis's pages poetry is embedded within the past and presented to an educated scholarly audience, using footnotes, Latin quotations, and references to other learned volumes, Hone preferred to introduce quotations as part of the colloquial, lively texture of his prose, as part of a living tradition and a wider conversation taking place on his pages. For example, Herrick appears as an old friend in a description of Candlemas eve:

Hearken to the gay old man again, and participate in his joyous anticipations of pleasure from the natural products of the new year. His next little poem is a collyrium for the mind's eye:

> Ceremonies for Candlemasse Eve.
> Down with the Rosemary and Bayes,
> Down with the Misletoe;
> Instead of Holly, now up-raise
> The greener Box (for show).[31]

This extract, like so many others that appeared on Hone's pages, was culled from Ellis's edition of Brand's *Observations*. Reprinted in *The Every-Day Book*, it becomes part of a familiar and contemporary conversation, rather than a piece of historical evidence: Hone invites readers to 'hearken' to Herrick, and to 'participate in his joyous anticipations'. The archaic word 'hearken' calls on readers to hear Herrick's verses; this combination of immediacy, antique accent, and friendly tone is characteristic of the style and the spirit of Hone's volume.[32] His warm, colloquial manner of introducing quotations, and the convivial atmosphere of his pages, anticipated 'by a full generation the familial atmosphere' of Dickens's magazines *Master Humphrey's Clock* (1840–1), *Household Words* (1850–9), and *All the Year Round* in the 1860s.[33]

But although in this respect *The Every-Day Book* can be seen as proto-Dickensian, it was also shaped by the cultural politics of its own historical moment. Many of Hone's interests were shared by a circle of intimates that included Hazlitt, Lamb, and the Hunt brothers.[34] Leigh Hunt, whom Hone met during a brief spell editing the *Critical Review*, was a fellow champion of popular culture.[35] In a December 1817 edition of *The Examiner*, for example (a newspaper to which Hone himself had contributed), Hunt published an essay on 'Christmas and Other Old National Merry-Makings Considered, with Reference to the Nature of the Age, and to the Desireableness of their Revival'.[36] Here, Hunt celebrated 'The sports, the pastimes, the holidays, the Christmas greens, the archeries, May-mornings, the May-poles, the country-dances, the masks, the harvest homes' of merry England, and called for their revival.[37] In a later essay, 'New May-Day and Old May-Day' (1825), Hunt explained that the decline of folk festivals such as May-day was caused not only by 'trade' and 'fanaticism' (an old anti-puritan complaint), but also by the spread of 'politeness' imported from France. The 'pretended politeness and reasoning spirit of the French', he claimed, had rendered the nation 'unpoetical and effeminate' to the extent that '[w]e were to show our refinement by being superior to every rustic impulse'.[38]

That same year (1825), Hazlitt celebrated this 'rustic impulse' in 'Merry England', an essay which appeared in *The New Monthly Magazine*, and which was later reprinted in *The Every-Day Book* entry for 6 January 1827.[39] In that essay, Hazlitt described and celebrated a common culture of 'approved English games' such as 'Blindman's-buff, hunt-the-slipper, hot-cockles, and snap-dragon', traditional English fayre, 'roast-beef and plum-pudding, the spiced ale and roasted crab, thrown (hissing hot) into the foaming tankard', as well as the nation's literary past – Fielding, Walton, Shakespeare, and Robin Hood are all mentioned. Hone had published Hazlitt's *Political Essays* in 1819,[40] and the two men subsequently became firm friends and drinking companions, often spending afternoons together in the Southampton Arms on Chancery Lane.[41]

Of the London circle, Hone was perhaps closest to Lamb: 'My friend Charles Lamb,' he explained, 'is the only man who knows me intimately – all my intimacies have been with books.'[42] The two began corresponding in May 1823, but it was in 1825, shortly after Hone began to publish *The Every-Day Book*, that their friendship became established.[43] Lamb and Hone shared a fascination with the customs and literature of the past; they spent afternoons, together with Mary Lamb, exploring the villages around London, Highgate and Hampstead, Camden Town and Kentish Town, ever mindful that these districts were soon to be destroyed by property developers.[44] Several of Lamb's 'Elia' essays commemorate popular holidays such as 'New Year's Eve', 'All Fool's Day', and 'Valentine's Day', and extracts from some of these appeared in *The Every-Day Book*.

Hone dedicated the first volume of *The Every-Day Book* to Lamb (in 1826),[45] and he often quoted extracts from Lamb's essays and poems on its pages, as in the following description of New Year's Eve:[46]

Elia says, 'while that turncoat bell, that just now mournfully chanted the obsequies of the year departed, with changed notes lustily rings in a successor, let us attune to its peal the song made on a like occasion, by hearty, cheerful Mr. Cotton'. Turn gentle reader to the first page of the first sheet, which this hand presented to you, and you will find the first two and twenty lines of ELIA's 'song'. They tell us, that, of the two faces of Janus,

> – *that* which this way looks is clear,
> And smiles upon the New-born year.
> . . .

ELIA, having trolled this song to the sound of 'the merry, merry bells', breaks out: –

'How say you reader – do not these verses smack of the rough magnanimity of the old English vein? Do they not fortify like a cordial; enlarging the heart, and productive of sweet blood, and generous spirits in the concoction? – Another cup of the generous! and a merry New Year and many of them, to you all, my masters!'

The same to you, ELIA, – and 'to you *all* my masters!' – *Ladies*! think not yourselves neglected, who are chief among 'my masters' – you are the kindest, and therefore the most masterful, and most worshipful of 'my masters!'[47]

Here, Elia is included in a friendly conversation between living and dead authors, part of a convivial and demotic re-imagining of literary tradition conducted with 'the rough magnanimity of the old English vein'.[48]

Hazlitt shared this interest in reviving and popularizing the literature of the past: his *Lectures on the Literature of the Age of Elizabeth* (published in 1820) offers another example of this sociable figuring of literary tradition as part of a living conversation. The old authors, Hazlitt explains,

> sit with me at breakfast; they walk out with me before dinner. After a long walk through unfrequented tracks, after starting the hare from the fern, or hearing the wing of a raven rustling above my head, or being greeted by the woodman's 'stern goodnight', as he strikes into his narrow homeward path I can 'take mine ease at mine inn', beside the blazing hearth, and shake hands with Signor Orlando Friscobaldo, as the oldest acquaintance I have. Ben Jonson, learned Chapman, Master Webster, and Master Heywood, are there; and seated round, discourse the silent hours away. Shakespear is there himself, not in Cibber's manager's coat. Spenser is hardly yet returned from a ramble through the woods, or is concealed behind a group of nymphs, fawns, and satyrs.[49]

Readers would have recognized the phrase 'take mine ease at mine inn' from Henry IV Part I (3.iii). The words are Falstaff's, and they are addressed to Bardolph in a suitably convivial setting, the Boar's Head tavern. Calling up this icon of sociable, merry Englishness, Hazlitt builds into his lines through allusion the sense of literary community he describes.

In the writings of the Cockney circle, a canon of English poetry emerged, shaped and mediated through discussions of folk culture and popular customs. In Hunt's *The Months* (1821), for example, poetic extracts were embedded in descriptions of seasonal change and popular customs. It had originally been published as a series of essays 'Descriptive of the Successive Beauties of the Year' called 'The Calendar of Nature', which appeared in monthly instalments in the 1819 *Literary Pocket Book*. In each number, Hunt described the month's natural phenomena and farming activities and drew on poetic extracts, quotations from Keats, Jonson, Chaucer, Surrey, Shakespeare, Wordsworth, Herrick, Fletcher, and Drayton, to illustrate these observations. In the 'August' entry, for example, he describes the festival of harvest home and enlivens his description with a long passage from Herrick.[50] *The Months* provided Hone with a source and a model; he quoted lengthy extracts from it on the pages of *The Every-Day Book*.[51] He also followed Hunt's example and quoted stanzas from Spenser's Mutabilitie cantos to introduce entries for many of the months in *The Every-Day Book* (see Figure 11.1).

APRIL.

Next came fresh April, full of lustyhed,
And wanton as a kid whose horne new buds;
Upon a bull he rode, the same which led
Europa floating through th'Argolick fluds:
His hornes were gilden all with golden studs,
And garnished with garlands goodly dight
Of all the fairest flowers and freshest buds
Which th'earth brings forth; and wet he seem'd in sight
With waves, through which he waded for his love's delight.
    Spenser.

This is the fourth month of the year. Its Latin name is *Aprilis*, from *aperio*, to open or set forth. The Saxons called it, *Oster* or *Eastermonath*, in which month, the feast of the Saxon goddess, *Eostre*, *Eastre*, or *Eoster*, was by them celebrated. April, with us, is sometimes represented as a girl clothed in green, with a garland of myrtle and hawthorn buds; holding in one hand primroses and violets, and in the other the zodiacal sign, Taurus, or the bull, into which constellation the sun enters during this month. The Romans consecrated the first of April to Venus, the goddess of beauty, the mother of love, the queen of laughter, the mistress of the graces; and the Roman widows and virgins assembled in the temple of Virile Fortune, and dis-

closing their personal deformities, prayed the goddess to conceal them from their husbands.*

In this month the business of creation seems resumed. The vital spark rekindles in dormant existences; and all things "live, and move, and have their being." The earth puts on her livery to await the call of her lord; the air breathes gently on his cheek, and conducts to his ear the warblings of the birds, and the odours of new-born herbs and flowers; the great eye of the world "sees and shines" with bright and gladdening glances; the waters teem with life; man himself feels the reviving and all-pervading influence;
and his

  —— spirit holds communion sweet
  With the brighter spirits of the sky.
        * Lempriere.

    * Sayer's Disquisitions.

April 1.—All Fools' Day.

St. Hugh, Bp. a.d. 1132. St. Melito, Bp. a.d. 175. St. Gilbert, Bp. of Cathness, a.d. 1240.

On the first of April, 1712, Lord Bolingbroke stated, that in the wars, called the "glorious wars of queen Anne," the duke of Marlborough had not lost a single battle—and yet, that the French had carried their point, the succession to the Spanish monarchy, the pretended cause of these wars. Dean Swift called this statement "a due donation for 'All Fool' Day.'"

On the first of April, 1810, Napoleon married Maria Louisa, archduchess of Austria, on which occasion some of the waggish Parisians called him "*en prison d'Avril*," a term which answers to our *April fool*. On the occasion of his nuptials, Napoleon struck a medal, with Love bearing a thunderbolt for its device.

It is customary on this day for boys to practise jocular deceptions. When they succeed, they laugh at the person whom they think they have rendered ridiculous, and exclaim, "*Ah! you April fool!*"

Thirty years ago, when buckles were worn in shoes, a boy would meet a person in the street with—"Sir, if you please, your shoe's *unbuckled*," and the moment the accosted individual looked towards his feet, the informant would cry—"Ah! you April fool!" Twenty years ago, when buckles were wholly disused, the urchin-cry was—"Sir, your shoe's untied," and if the shoe-wearer lowered his eyes, he was hailed, as his buckled predecessor had been, with the said—"Ah! you April fool!" Now, when neither buckles nor strings are worn, because in the year 1825 no decent man "has a shoe to his foot," the waggery of the day is—"Sir, there's something *out of* your pocket," "Where?" "There!" "What?" "Your hand, sir—Ah! you April fool!"

No. 14.   AH! YOU APRIL FOOL!

Fig. 11.1 Pages from Hone's *Every-Day Book* (1826–7) showing a quotation from Spenser's *Faerie Queene* used to introduce the entry for April (pp. 407–10).

Hunt continued this practice of using Spenserian quotation to introduce and illustrate popular customs in essays. 'New May-Day and Old
May-Day', for example, published in the *Examiner* in 1825, was introduced with a quotation from *The Faerie Queene*:

> Then came faire May, the fayrest mayd on ground,
> Deckt all with dainties of her season's pryde,
> And throwing flowres out of her lap around.[52]

On Hunt's pages, Spenser both mediates and is mediated through a
discussion of popular culture.

Popular customs, folklore, and the old poets all shared space on the
pages of the *London Magazine*. Lines from Ben Jonson's 'Discoveries'
appeared as a motto on the title page, announcing a prevailing interest in
poetry of the past. An essay 'On May Day' appeared in the May 1820
number, and its anonymous author called on the same lines from Spenser
in its description of 'the ancient customs and pleasantries' associated with
that day:

The poets have ever been the great advocate and patrons of May. Spenser, and
Shakespeare, and Fletcher, and Milton, and all the greater spirits of England,
have stooped from their lofty places, without disdain, to do justice and honour to
this delicate month. Spenser, in his account of the months, thus introduces May:

> Then came faire May, the fairest Mayd on ground,
> Deck't all with dainties of her season's pryde,
> And throwing flow'rs out of her lap around.[53]

Spenser appears alongside Shakespeare, Marlow, and Milton as well as
contemporary writers such as Lamb. Folk heroes Robin Hood and
Marian also appear, since May-day, the anonymous author explained,
'had the additional recommendation of being called "Robin Hood's
day"', since on this festive occasion villagers would dress up as Robin
Hood and Maid Marian and preside over the May-day celebrations,
accompanied by villagers wearing Sherwood green, who would come to
celebrate and cheer the 'May-queen' who arrived garlanded in flowers.[54]
Hone's own entry for that day (1826), similarly, mingles extracts from
Spenser, Herrick, Browne, and Milton with extracts from Lamb and
traditional May songs about Robin Hood and Marian.[55]

For Hone and his London coterie, Spenser was one of a group of
Elizabethan poets that represented a sociable, convivial ideal of poetic and
political fellowship to Hunt and his London circle, an ideal that is vividly
described in Keats's 'Lines on the Mermaid Tavern' (1820). Elizabethan

poetry and folk culture come together in these lines, which describe a friendly meeting between Jonson and his coterie with the outlaw Robin Hood and his merry men:

> Souls of Poets dead and gone,
> What Elysium have ye known,
> Happy field or mossy cavern,
> Choicer than the Mermaid Tavern?
> Have ye tippled drink more fine
> Than mine host's Canary wine?
> Or are fruits of Paradise
> Sweeter than those dainty pies
> Of venison? Oh, generous food,
> Dressed as though bold Robin Hood
> Would, with his Maid Marian,
> Sup and bowse from horn and can.[56]

The poem was published beside 'Robin Hood' in *Lamia, Isabella, The Eve of St Agnes, and Other Poems* (1820), and registered a wider interest in the relationship between poetry and folk culture among Keats's circle. John Barnard has persuasively argued that Keats associated the 'great "old" Elizabethan poets with Robin Hood's England, the values of both of which were, in his view, denied by the modern world'.[57] Building on his work, Nicholas Roe has examined the radical significance of the Cockney taste for the Elizabethan poets and Robin Hood, which draws on Joseph Ritson's politicized reading of early modern song tradition.[58] English popular culture and poetry provide access to a vanished world of conviviality and fellow feeling, anticipating and influencing the later emergence of the notion of 'folklore' discussed in the introduction, yet also capable, in the hands of the Hunt circle, of a more radical political inflection.

The Every-Day Book both contributed to and extended this cultural agenda, printing accounts of festivals and customs, extracts from Robin Hood ballads, Spenser, Jonson, and Browne alongside lines from Lamb, Hazlitt, Hunt, and Keats. In the entry for 21 January 1825, Hone printed a long extract from Keats's 'Eve of St Agnes' in order to illustrate the popular customs and superstitions associated with that night:

Little is remembered of these homely methods for knowing 'all about sweet hearts', and the custom would scarcely have reached the greater number of readers, if one of the sweetest of our modern poets had not preserved its recollection in a delightful poem. Some stanzas are culled from it, with the hope that they may be read by a few to whom the poetry of Keates [*sic*] is unknown, and awaken a desire for further acquaintance with his beauties:-

The Eve of St. Agnes
St. Agnes Eve? Ah, bitter chill it was!
The owl, for all his feathers, was a-cold;
The hare limp'd trembling through the frozen grass,
And silent was the flock in woolly fold;[59]

Hone subtly alters the punctuation and orthography of the first line as it
was published in 1820, changing 'ST. Agnes' Eve – Ah, bitter chill it was!'
to 'St. Agnes Eve? Ah, bitter chill it was!' The shift from dash to question
mark introduces a spoken cadence to the phrase, so that the narrator
appears to be answering or responding to someone else, once again
introducing a sense of conversational immediacy. On Hone's pages Keats
takes his place in an English popular tradition, appearing both as a
preserver of popular culture, and as part of a poetic canon. He appears
'among the English poets'; lines from 'The Eve of St Agnes' were printed
beneath an extract from Ben Jonson's poetic account of St Agnes Eve:

And on sweet St. Agnes' night
Please you with the promis'd sight,
Some of husbands, some of lovers,
Which an empty dream discovers.[60]

Keats would have known these lines from his own reading of Ellis's
edition of Brand's *Observations*; it was from this antiquarian volume that
Keats himself learned of the 'popular superstition' associated with St
Agnes Eve.[61] On the same page, Hone printed another quotation gleaned
from Ellis, lines from John Aubrey's description of the customs associated
with St Agnes Eve. But whereas Ellis called on scholarly conventions to
introduce his source, both naming the work from which he quotes and
offering a page reference, Hone is more informal, introducing Aubrey in
a familiar manner:

Old Aubrey has a recipe, whereby a lad or lass was to attain a sight of the
fortunate lover. 'Upon St Agnes' night you take a row of pins, and pull out every
one, one after the other, saying Pater Noster, sticking a pin in your sleeve, and
you will dream of him or her you shall marry.'

Keats's poem appears underneath this extract, part of a lively intertextual
conversation about popular customs. Reading 'The Eve of St Agnes' in
The Every-Day Book thus places it in a context that acknowledges its
fruitful engagements with the popular antiquarian culture of its time.[62]
Not only does Keats adopt Spenser's stanza form in the poem, but by

doing so in a poem which describes a popular superstition he builds on a burgeoning association of Spenser with popular culture, an association which also found expression in Hone's pages.[63]

Keats was not yet widely known in the 1820s; it was not until several decades later that he began to achieve wider public recognition and lasting fame. By publishing a long extract from 'The Eve of St Agnes', Hone was playing a part in popularizing the poem and its author, establishing Keats's place in a popular literary tradition based on a shared common heritage. In doing so he was also responding to harsh critical accounts of Keats as a Cockney outsider, or what the *Blackwood's* critic John Gibson Lockhart had described as an 'uneducated and flimsy strapling'.[64] Such attacks were informed by class-based notions of poetry, according to which art was off-limits for the working and lower-middle classes.[65] On Hone's pages, by contrast, Keats is presented as part of a literary canon and a national culture, not as a vulgar intruder into the genteel realms of verse. If Keats lacked the cultural capital that would allow him admission into a polite literary pantheon, he shared a common heritage with poets such as Jonson, Herrick, and Spenser. In *The Every-Day Book* Keats's vulgarity is translated and redeemed: rather than a Cockney outcast, he is placed firmly within vernacular culture, participating in a popular and radical antiquarian revival. Hone contributed to the formation of a truly popular literary canon, one that both contributed to and drew on a shared common heritage in which poets from all ranks could participate. The success of *The Every-Day Book*, according to one later admirer, 'lay in [its] homely or vernacular character'.[66] Printed here, poetry was not part of a high and courtly sphere, nor was its enjoyment confined to gentlemen; it was one of the many forms and practices of everyday life.

NOTES

1 *The London Magazine* (1825 series) 2:5 (May 1825), 16. Hone reprinted this poem in *The Every-Day Book; or, Everlasting Calendar of Popular Amusements*, 2 vols. (London, 1826–7), vol. 1, pp. 927–30. Hone's reply, a poem in quatorzains, appeared just underneath Lamb's lines on the same page, in which he described his own humble origins ('No schools of science open'd to my youth; / No learned halls, no academic bowers; / No one had I to point my way to truth, / Instruct my ign'rance, or direct my powers' (vol. 1, p. 930)).

2 William Hone, 'Preface' to *The Every-Day Book*, vol. 1, p. vii.

3 *Ibid.*, 'Preface' (1826) and 'Explanatory Address to Readers of the Every-Day Book' (1824); both collated and reprinted in *The Every-Day Book* (1826).

4 Frederick Wm Hackwood, *William Hone: His Life and Times* (London, T. Fisher Unwin, 1912), pp. 194, 228. After his trial, he continued his radical pamphleteering; *The Political House that Jack Built* (1819), illustrated by George Cruikshank, sold a reputed 100,000 copies in 47 editions, an unprecedented circulation for this kind of popular publication. See also Ben Wilson, *The Laughter of Triumph: William Hone and the Fight for the Free Press* (London: Faber, 2005). D. R. Ewen and David A. Kent (eds.), *Regency Radical: Selected Writings of William Hone* (Detroit: Wayne State University Press, 2003), and Joss Marsh, *Word Crimes: Blasphemy, Culture, and Literature in Nineteenth-Century England* (Chicago: University of Chicago Press, 1998), discuss the trial in detail; see also Vic Gatrell, *City of Laughter: Sex and Satire in Eighteenth-Century London* (London: Atlantic, 2006), pp. 520–9. Although *The Every-Day Book* was in some respects a retreat from public controversy, it was continuous with Hone's radical antiquarian interests; during his trial, he had based his self-defence against the government prosecutors on that of the Leveller John Lilburn against Cromwell.

5 Robert Southey, *Life of Bunyan*, cited in Hackwood, *William Hone*, p. 298. In the same paragraph, Southey recommended *The Every-Day Book*, and its successor *The Table Book*, to 'those who are interested in the preservation of our national and local customs'. Despite an earlier quarrel between Southey and Hone after Hone's travesty of 'The Vision of Judgement', Southey admired Hone's *Every-Day Book* and, in 1830, he relented and wrote a 'good-natured letter' to Hone (Hackwood, *William Hone*, p. 277).

6 Marilyn Butler, 'Antiquarianism (Popular)', in Iain McCalman (ed.), *Oxford Companion to the Romantic Age: British Culture 1776–1832* (Oxford: Oxford University Press, 2001), p. 335.

7 For a discussion of popular antiquarianism in the period, see Butler, 'Antiquarianism (Popular)'. *The Mirror of Literature, Amusement, and Instruction*, for example, reprinted articles from journals like *Blackwoods*, the *Monthly*, *New Monthly*, *Edinburgh*, and *Quarterly*. It also published essays on diverse themes, including 'Customs and Whitsuntide' and 'The History of Manufacture of Writing Paper' (Jon Klancher, 'From "Crowd" to "Audience": The Making of an English Mass Readership in the Nineteenth Century', *ELH* 50:1 (Spring 1983), 155–73 (157)). It aimed at diffusion of useful knowledge and poetry to the poorest readers (it cost only 2d), and its pages were packed with facts and descriptions, as well as occasional verses; it helped popularize Byron and Scott. *The Every-Day Book* was distinct in that it was aimed not only at a 'mass' poor readership, but at 'all classes' of readers. For two different and authoritative discussions of reading audiences in the Romantic period see Klancher, *The Making of English Reading Audiences, 1790–1832* (Madison, Wisc.: University of Wisconsin Press, 1987), and William St Clair, *The Reading Nation in the Romantic Period* (Cambridge: Cambridge University Press, 2004).

8 Hone, *Every-Day Book*, vol. 1, pp. 570, 669, 1238.

9 Hone, 'Explanatory Address to the Reader of the Every-Day Book', *Every-Day Book*, vol. 1.

10 This was described as a 'communication respecting St Mark's day usages' in Northamptonshire by 'a correspondent near Peterborough', a 'Ben Barr of Helpstone' (Hone, *Every-Day Book*, vol. 1, pp. 523–5). Clare also described popular customs and superstitions in his long poem *The Shepherd's Calendar*, which he was composing during the mid 1820s. The poem was published in 1827, and numerous extracts from it were published in Hone's *The Year Book* (1832), a successful literary annual which followed the principles set out in *The Every-Day Book*.

11 For discussions of canon-making in the Romantic period, see Marilyn Butler, 'Revising the Canon', *Times Literary Supplement* (4 December 1987), 1349; Leah Price, *The Anthology and the Rise of the Novel* (Cambridge and New York: Cambridge University Press, 2000), pp. 67–77; St Clair, *Reading Nation*. For discussion of canon-formation in the eighteenth century, see Barbara Benedict, *Making the Modern Reader: Cultural Mediation in Early Anthologies* (Princeton, N. J.: Princeton University Press, 1996); Trevor Ross, 'Copyright and the Invention of Tradition', *Eighteenth Century Studies* 25 (1992), 1–27; Richard Terry, *Poetry and the Making of the English Literary Past, 1660–1781* (Oxford: Oxford University Press, 2001); Jonathan Brody Kramnick, *Making the English Literary Canon: Print-Capitalism and the Cultural Past, 1700–1770* (Cambridge: Cambridge University Press, 1998). See also John Guillory, *Cultural Capital: The Problem of Literary Canon Formation* (Chicago, Ill.: University of Chicago Press, 1993).

12 William St Clair describes this as the 'old Canon' (*Reading Nation*, pp. 128–9).

13 Vicesimus Knox, *Elegant Extracts from the Most Eminent British Poets* (London, 1784), 'Advertisement to the Eleventh Edition'.

14 Alexander Chalmers, *The Works of the English Poets, from Chaucer to Cowper; including the series edited with prefaces, biographical and critical, by Dr. Samuel Johnson*, 21 vols. (London: J. Johnson, 1810), vol. 1, 'Preface', pp. v–vi.

15 Marsh, *Word Crimes*, p. 51.

16 John Clare, *The Letters of John Clare*, ed. Mark Storey (Oxford: Clarendon Press, 1986), p. 335. Clare wrote this under a false name, James Gildroy, and in it he included a poem he said was by Marvell, found in an old book, which he himself had written; the poem appeared under Marvell's name in Hone, *The Every-Day Book*, vol. 1, p. 883, under the following heading: 'from "Miscellanies" published by Spalding Society for Antiquaries'. In another letter, written under the name of Frederic Roberts, of 2 August 1825, Clare offered an old poem he had written and fathered on Sir Henry Wooten (*Letters*, pp. 341–4).

17 Wilson, *Laughter of Triumph*, p. 354.

18 Robert Southey, *The Lives and Works of the Uneducated Poets* (1831), ed. J. S. Childers (London: H. Milford, 1925), p. 13.

19 Hone, *Every-Day Book*, vol. 1, pp. 400–2. *The British Apollo, or, Curious Amusements for the Ingenious, To Which are Added the Most Material Occurrences Foreign and Domestick; Perform'd by a Society of Gentlemen* was a witty eighteenth-century newspaper edited by Aaron Hill and Marshall Smith; it

included contributions from Gay. In some ways it anticipated *The Every-Day Book* in its variety; readers were invited to send in questions on any subject, and it devoted space to poetry, snippets of news, and announcements of new books. See David Nokes, *John Gay, A Profession of Friendship: A Critical Biography* (Oxford: Oxford University Press, 1995), p. 65.

20 These extracts were gleaned from a footnote by Henry Ellis in John Brand's *Observations on Popular Antiquities, Chiefly Illustrating the Origin of our Vulgar Customs, Ceremonies and Superstitions: Arranged and Revised, with Additions, by Sir Henry Ellis*, 2 vols. (London: F. C. and J. Rivington *et al.*, 1813), vol. 1, p. 125n.

21 Hone, *Every-Day Book*, vol. 1, pp. 402–3.

22 *Ibid.*, p. 8 (1 January 1826).

23 *Ibid.*, p. 905 (4 July 1826).

24 *Ibid.*, p. 903.

25 Hone engaged in the recuperation of the ritual calendar: see Bob Bushaway, *By Rite: Custom, Ceremony and Community, 1700–1880* (London: Junction, 1982); Ronald Hutton, *The Rise and Fall of Merry England: The Ritual Year, 1400–1700* (Oxford: Oxford University Press, 1994).

26 Hone quoted passages from that very almanac on his pages, as well as verses from the *Country Almanac* (1676) (Candlemas entry, *The Every-Day Book*, vol. 1, p. 207); *Time's Telescope* is cited in *The Every-Day Book*, vol. 1, pp. 53, 1472; and *Poor Robin* (1695 edition) is quoted in vol. 1, p. 1603.

27 Hone, *Every-Day Book*, vol. 1, pp. 53, 204. See Keith Stewart, 'Ancient Poetry as History in the Eighteenth Century', *Journal of the History of Ideas* 19:3 (1958), 335–47. Stewart has some useful material on this topic – especially on eighteenth-century discussions of the ballad in these terms by Addison *et al.*

28 Hone knew Brand, who died in 1806. He described him with affection as 'A tall, robust Johnsonian sort of man, without Johnsonian stoop. He loved his bottle of port and dessert, to loll over his wine with some noble friend, turn over his illustrated Pennant, and recall interesting anecdotes of the characters of past times.' Cited in Hackwood, *William Hone*, p. 258.

29 John Brand, 'Preface' to *Observations on Popular Antiquities* (Newcastle upon Tyne: T. Saint, 1777), p. iv. Careful to warn readers not to expect 'Elegance of Composition . . . in a work of this kind' (p. vii), Brand's use of the word 'vulgar' did not, however, convey the pejorative sense increasingly common in the late eighteenth century. See Janet Sorenson, 'Vulgar Tongues: Canting Dictionaries and the Language of the People in Eighteenth-Century Britain', *Eighteenth-Century Studies* 37:4 (2004), 435–54. Brand's book was a redaction of Henry Bourne's *Antiquitates Vulgares* of 1725, and his use of the word 'vulgar' calls on the word as it appeared in Bourne's title in its Latin sense, meaning popular.

30 William Wordsworth, 'Essay, Supplementary to the Preface' (1815), in *Prose Works of William Wordsworth*, 3 vols., ed. W. J. B. Owen and Jane Worthington Smyser (Oxford: Clarendon Press, 1974), vol. III, p. 72.

31 Hone, *Every-Day Book*, vol. 1, pp. 204–5 (2 February 1825).

32 *Ibid.*, p. 204.
33 Marsh, *Word Crimes*, p. 52. Like Hone before him, Dickens attempted a fusion of high and low audiences and subjects in his volumes.
34 Wilson, *Laughter of Triumph*, p. 6.
35 Gattrell, *City of Laughter*, pp. 521–2.
36 *The Examiner* (December 1817).
37 *Ibid.*
38 Leigh Hunt, 'New May-Day and Old May-Day', in *Leigh Hunt's Literary Criticism*, ed. Lawrence Huston Houtchens and Carolyn Washburn Houtchens (New York: Columbia University Press, 1956), pp. 215–29; this quote pp. 219–20.
39 Hone, *Every-Day Book*, vol. ii, pp. 36–7.
40 Hackwood, *William Hone*, p. 267.
41 Wilson, *Laughter of Triumph*, p. 7.
42 *Ibid.*, p. 357.
43 Hackwood, *William Hone*, pp. 266–8.
44 *The Every-Day Book* gave considerable space to chronicling this 'urban village culture' that was soon to be lost, as Wilson notes (*Laughter of Triumph*, p. 360).
45 Hackwood, *William Hone*, pp. 257–8.
46 Both Hone and Lamb wrote about the local culture of London villages such as Islington and Hampstead that was being lost (see Wilson, *Laughter of Triumph*, pp. 360–1). On the pages of *The Every-Day Book* some of these old customs were described and preserved, and Lamb recorded them in essays that were printed in the *London Magazine*. Lamb, Francis Place, and other friends ran a subscription to enable Hone to open The Grasshopper coffee house in Gracechurch Street. And although the venture had failed by 1833, its very name linked it with the Hunt circle and their culture of sociability.
47 Hone, *Every-Day Book*, vol. i, pp. 1654–5 (31 December 1825).
48 A sense of 'rough magnanimity' was also, as Hazlitt noted, a feature of Lamb's Elian style. In a *Table Talk* essay, 'On Familiar Style' (1821), Hazlitt explained: 'Mr Lamb is the only imitator of old English style I can read with pleasure; and he is so thoroughly imbued with the spirit of his authors, that the idea of imitation is almost done away. There is an inward unction, a marrowy vein both in the thought and in the feeling, an intuition, deep and lively, of his subject, that carries off any quaintness or awkwardness arising from an antiquated style and dress' (*Table Talk*, 2 vols. (London, 1821), vol. ii, pp. 191–2). Hone was later responsible for bringing Lamb's own antiquarian literary researches to a wide audience on the pages of his next anthologizing venture, *The Table Book*. To this monthly periodical, Lamb contributed extracts from the collections of rare plays which Garrick had bequeathed to the British Museum. Reproduced on Hone's pages, these extracts were part of popular culture, brought into lively conversation with living writers, ballads, and examples of dialect and street slang. These 'Garrick extracts' were later compiled and published together in 1835.

49 William Hazlitt, Lecture III, 'On Marston, Chapman, Deckar and Webster', *Lectures Chiefly on the Dramatic Literature of the Age of Elizabeth* (London, 1820), pp. 93–138; this quote pp. 136–7.

50 Leigh Hunt, *The Months: Descriptive of the Successive Beauties of the Year* (London, 1821), p. 92. Hone's pages were more copious and various than Hunt's, however, mingling poetic extracts with antiquarian sources and quotations from newspapers and magazines as well as readers' letters and illustrations. For a discussion of Hunt's *Months* and its wider cultural significance see Nicholas Roe, *Keats and the Culture of Dissent* (Oxford: Clarendon Press, 1997), pp. 258–67.

51 Hone, *Every-Day Book*, vol. 1, pp. 197, 738, for example.

52 Hunt, 'New May-Day and Old May-Day', p. 215.

53 'On May Day', *London Magazine* (1820 series) 1:5 (May 1820), 489–92 (491). See also 'A May Dream', *London Magazine* (1820 series) 3:17 (May 1821), 477–83; introduced with a quotation from Spenser, this 'dream' imagines a merry company made up of dead writers such as Walton, Webster, Drayton, and others all taking part in a lively conversation with the essay's (anonymous) author.

54 *London Magazine* (1820 series) 1:5 (May 1820), 490.

55 Hone, *Every-Day Book*, vol. 1, pp. 547–51.

56 John Keats, *The Poems of John Keats*, ed. Miriam Allott (London and New York: Longman, 1970), pp. 304–6, lines 1–12.

57 John Barnard, 'Keats's "Robin Hood", John Hamilton Reynolds, and the "Old Poets"', *Proceedings of the British Academy* 75 (1989), 181–200.

58 See Roe, *Culture of Dissent*.

59 Hone, *Every-Day Book*, vol. 1, p. 136. The word 'homely' carried a class inflection; it was distinct from 'genteel'; in 1780, Adam Smith had observed, 'It is the duty of a poet to write like a gentleman. I dislike that homely style which some think fit to call the language of nature and simplicity and so forth' (John Roe, *Life of Adam Smith* (New York: Kelly, 1965), p. 369). See the discussion of this passage in the introduction to this volume. As this quotation suggests, homeliness had a social inflection, associated with common speech and set against the elegance and refinement associated with genteel speech. Hone's use of the word here might be read as a subtle intertextual response to class-based critical attacks on Keats's poetry.

60 Hone, *Every-Day Book*, vol. 1, p. 136.

61 Keats used this phrase to describe the poem in a letter, noting the poem's popular roots (*The Letters of John Keats 1814–1821*, ed. Hyder Edward Rollins, 2 vols. (Cambridge: Cambridge University Press, 1958), vol. 11, p. 139). See Keats, *Poems*, ed. Allott, p. 450n.

62 Roe has shown that placing Keats's writing in the print culture of its time restores lost meanings; reading Keats's 'Autumn' ode as it was published in Hunt's *Months* drew out the poem's engagements with contemporary historical events (see Roe, *Culture of Dissent*). My argument draws on and extends his observation in a new context.

63 For a more detailed account of this neglected aspect of Spenser's popular reception in the Romantic period see Mina Gorji, *John Clare and the Place of Poetry* (Liverpool: Liverpool University Press, 2008), Chapter 4.

64 John Wilson Croker, Review of *Endymion* in the *Quarterly Review* (April 1818); John Gibson Lockhart, Review of *Endymion* in *Blackwood's Edinburgh Magazine* (August 1818); both cited in G. M. Matthews (ed.), *John Keats: The Critical Heritage* (London: Routledge and Kegan Paul, 1971), pp. 111, 101. See also Lynda Mugglestone, 'The Fallacy of the Cockney Rhyme: From Keats and Earlier to Auden', *Review of English Studies* 42 (1991), 57–66 (59).

65 Hone alluded to this critical attack in his entry for 23 February 1827, the anniversary of Keats's death in 1820. Hone describes how the 'Virulent and unmerited attack upon his literary ability, by an unprincipled and malignant reviewer, injured his rising reputation, overwhelmed his spirit, and he sank into consumption'. He goes on to quote 'Ode to a Nightingale' (*Every-Day Book*, vol. 11, pp. 250–4). For a recent critical discussion of the attacks see Jeffrey N. Cox, *Poetry and Politics in the Cockney School: Keats, Shelley, Hunt and their Circle* (Cambridge: Cambridge University Press, 1998), p. 28. For a discussion of Keats's 'Eve of St Mark' and its sources in popular antiquarian culture see David Pirie's essay 'Old Saints and Young Lovers: Keats's Eve of St Mark and Popular Culture', in Michael O'Neill (ed.), *Keats: Bicentenary Readings* (Edinburgh: Edinburgh University Press, 1997), pp. 48–70. Pirie proposes that Keats's source was John Brand's *Popular Antiquities*, and that Bertha, the poem's heroine, may in fact have cheated herself by ignoring far jollier traditions related to St Mark's Eve that 'celebrate youth as the time to find and enjoy a lover' (p. 60) and focusing only on the morbid superstition that on that day the ghosts of those destined to die would appear.

66 John Timbs, *Leisure Hour* (29 July 1871), 470; cited in Marsh, *Word Crimes*, p. 51.

CHAPTER 12

How to popularize Wordsworth

Philip Connell

Looking back in 1879, Matthew Arnold remarked, with some regret, on the vagaries of Wordsworth's nineteenth-century reputation. 'The poetry-reading public was very slow to recognize him,' noted Arnold, 'and was very easily drawn away from him'; first by Scott and Byron, and latterly by Tennyson with the 'decisive appearance' of the 1842 *Poems*.[1] Wordsworth's 'diminution of popularity' since the 1830s had been both 'visible' and prolonged. Yet the tone of Arnold's remarks is predominantly polemical, rather than elegiac. It is the injustice of the poet's contemporary standing which is at issue; and that injustice prompts a vigorous defence of his place within the nation's literary canon: 'I firmly believe that the poetical performance of Wordsworth is, after that of Shakespeare and Milton . . . undoubtedly the most considerable in our language from the Elizabethan age to the present time.'[2] The boldness of Arnold's claims is partly a matter of temperament, but his confidence also reflects the fact that a revival of critical interest in Wordsworth's verse was already under way – a revival to which Arnold's essay made a significant contribution, particularly when reprinted as the Preface to his selected *Poems of Wordsworth* shortly afterwards. Throughout the 1870s and 1880s, a steady stream of appreciations and revaluations of the poet flowed from the Victorian 'higher' periodicals.[3] Critics and cultural commentators of this period struggled to define the precise nature – and limits – of Wordsworth's genius. But beyond the question of his intrinsic literary merits, the broader social and cultural function of Wordsworth's verse was also very much at issue. More specifically, the Wordsworth revival raised the question of Wordsworth's 'popularity' (or lack of it), his status as a national poet, and the role of his 'followers' and 'disciples' in sustaining his reputation. Arnold, for one, was clear that Wordsworth needed to be rescued from the 'Wordsworthians', even as he included himself in their number. The bard of Rydal Mount, he urged, 'is something more than the pure and sage master of a small band of devoted followers'.[4]

Arnold's essay was answered by Richard Holt Hutton, one of the poet's most acute nineteenth-century critics (and a 'Wordsworthian' by any definition), in a piece for the *Spectator* called 'How to Popularize Wordsworth'. The irony of the title quickly becomes apparent, but it is in the service of a rather more subtle semantic distinction. 'Wordsworth is not, and probably never will be, a popular poet,' insisted Hutton. 'And here we use the word "popular" not in the sense of appealing to the homeliest hearts, as Burns appeals, but in the sense of having the power to haunt the cultivated fancy, as Byron's "Isles of Greece" and Shelley's "Ode to a Skylark" haunt the fancy of the literary multitude.' Hutton's passing reference here to two of the most widely read Romantic lyrics carries a hint of fastidious superiority, as well as approval; the phrases 'cultivated fancy' and the 'literary multitude' imply a curious combination of the refined and the lowbrow, the elitist and the inclusive. The source of these equivocations can be traced back to Hutton's self-consciousness about the very idea of the 'popular', and his sense that, to be truly worthy of this epithet, Wordsworth should appeal not merely to the 'homeliest hearts' but to the quotidian sensibilities of 'the average cultivated man'.[5]

To some extent, Hutton's awkwardness on this point merely signals the perennial tendency of 'the popular' to evoke a whole range of highly evaluative, and potentially divisive, connotations. Yet his comments also suggest a more specific awareness, shared by many late-Victorian critics, that the category of popular taste now extended well beyond its traditional associations with the 'homeliest hearts' – the plebeian instincts in which the polite culture of the eighteenth century had discovered the contradictory extremes of coarse vulgarity and primitivist authenticity. To 'popularize' Wordsworth now required an additional appeal to the recreational predilections of the 'average cultivated man' and a growing lower middle class whose powers of literary discrimination were often far from assured, but whose aspirational tastes could not always be straightforwardly dissociated from those of a more securely genteel sensibility.

Such sentiments might be considered quite typical of a certain kind of progressive Victorian intellectual. There is something in Hutton's remarks reminiscent of the assertion by his friend and fellow liberal, Walter Bagehot, that 'public opinion', the guardian of English liberties, is also necessarily 'the opinion of the bald-headed man at the back of the omnibus'.[6] But Hutton's differences with Arnold are also indicative of the increasingly precarious cultural authority of the higher journalistic critic in the final decades of the nineteenth century, poised between an emergent mass market and the institutionalized critical judgements of the university. Hereafter, the incipient professionalization of literary studies would make the writer's popularity – however defined – increasingly marginal to the business of academic criticism and scholarship, displacing such concerns into the rather different (but closely related) sphere of 'cultural' commentary. Nonetheless, the relationship between canonicity and popular taste continued to inform the practice of criticism throughout the nineteenth century. In the case of Wordsworth, that relationship played a particularly significant, and revealing, role in determining critical responses to the poet and his work. This was, in large part, a result of the changing audience for his verse. But it was also conditioned by Wordsworth's own public declarations on his poetic debt to the amorphous field of discourse and practice that we now might term 'popular culture'.

This aspect of his work had been apparent to many readers almost from the start of Wordsworth's public career. The *Lyrical Ballads*, above all, linked his poetic inspiration with a class of verse that was increasingly familiar to audiences of the late eighteenth century: literary imitations of old popular song, or what one guide to the genre called the 'rude original pastoral poetry of our country ... the popular pieces called ballads'.[7] Contemporary reviews of the volume, whether hostile or appreciative, were largely united in assuming that it contained '*imitations* of antique versification', inspired by the popular ballad and the ancient minstrelsy.[8] And while such a conclusion was not explicitly confirmed by the Advertisement and Preface to the collection, it was by no means ruled out. Wordsworth's famous claims to have employed the language of 'Low and rustic life'; his repeated references to our 'elder writers'; his identification with the 'earliest poets of all nations'; and his professed admiration for the metrical forms of 'the old ballads' – all seemed to justify a reading which located his contributions to the *Lyrical Ballads* firmly within the milieu of eighteenth-century aesthetic primitivism and the popular ballad revival.[9]

This impression was reinforced in 1815, when Wordsworth published the first collected edition of his poems, including both a new Preface to his works, and an 'Essay, Supplementary to the Preface'. In the latter document, Wordsworth declared himself 'proud to acknowledge his obligations' to Thomas Percy's influential *Reliques of Ancient English Poetry*, the key text of the English ballad revival. It was the authenticity of Percy's work, he suggested, that had allowed the *Reliques*, unlike Ossian, to 'amalgamate with the literature of the Island' (despite the *Reliques'* distinctly tenuous relation to oral tradition), and on this basis Wordsworth implicitly claimed for himself a comparable place in the national canon, while carefully distinguishing the artificial literary taste of 'the PUBLIC' from the unfeigned poetic instincts of 'the PEOPLE'.[10] There was an element of conscious artifice in all this, of course. Some of Wordsworth's experiments with 'common' diction and balladic metre were extreme, by the standards of contemporary poetic taste. But they were, nevertheless, intended for a 'polite', respectable reading public – just like Percy's *Reliques*. The resulting contradictions impelled Wordsworth to identify his ideal reader with neither public nor people, but rather to submit his work to the future judgement of an idealized audience, 'that Vox Populi which the Deity inspires ... the People, philosophically characterised'.[11]

Wordsworth's 'Essay' offers a fascinating demonstration of the way in which discourse on literary popularity in this period could shift, almost imperceptibly, between the quantitative enumeration of appreciative readers, and a more complex, normative assessment of those qualities in a given work which might mark it out as an authentic manifestation of 'the people'. Throughout the nineteenth century, this conceptual instability would lend a distinct ideological significance to the changing nature, and extent, of Wordsworth's audience – particularly after some examples of his poetry did begin to attract a numerous, and socially diffuse, readership during the 1810s and 1820s. The remarkable, and continuing, success of so-called 'simple' poems such as 'We are Seven', 'Susan Gray', and 'The Pet Lamb' would go on to present a significant challenge to the conventions of contemporary critical discourse on 'the popular'. Moreover, by raising some awkward questions about the relationship between popular taste and aesthetic value, such poems also played a crucial, and often contentious, role in the critical debates surrounding his literary canonization.

'We are Seven' is perhaps the best example – a reported conversation in verse, between an obtuse narrator and a bereaved 'cottage girl' who, apparently refusing to acknowledge the mortality of her two dead siblings, counters her interlocutor's 'ye are only five' with the insistent refrain of the title.

> "Two of us in the church-yard lie,
> "My sister and my brother,
> "And in the church-yard cottage, I
> "Dwell near them with my mother."

"You say that two at Conway dwell,
"And two are gone to sea,
"Yet you are seven; I pray you tell
"Sweet Maid, how this may be?"

Then did the little Maid reply,
"Seven boys and girls are we;
"Two of us in the church-yard lie,
"Beneath the church-yard tree."[12]

The poem's apparent artlessness immediately divided readers when it appeared in the first edition of *Lyrical Ballads*. It is among 'the simplest stories in the book', judged the *British Critic* in 1799, 'yet he must be a very fastidious reader who will deny that it has great beauty and feeling'. According to the *Monthly Review*, on the other hand, 'We are Seven' was simply 'innocent and pretty infantine prattle'.[13] For those modern readers inclined to agree with this latter comment, the poem's subsequent success might do no more than confirm certain prejudices about Victorian sentimental excess and the idealization of childhood. In its identification of infantile beauty and innocence with an ambiguous boundary between life and death, the poem certainly foreshadowed some of the central symbolic functions of childhood in Victorian culture.[14] It was frequently reprinted in selections of Wordsworth's verse, including Palgrave's, and although excluded from the *Golden Treasury* (presumably on the grounds that its overly 'dramatic' qualities ran counter to Palgrave's primary interest in the lyric), 'We are Seven' repeatedly appears in other nineteenth-century poetry anthologies, for both children and adult readers.[15]

But the poem's appeal crossed boundaries of class, as well as age. John Clare, who counted 'We are Seven' among his favourite Wordsworth verse, recalled coming across the poem in the form of a penny ballad, hawked around Northamptonshire villages by itinerant sellers. Reproduction in this form, he suggested, had brought the poem a truly 'common fame', a claim that can be graphically substantiated by a comparison of Birket Foster's elaborate illustration of 'We are Seven' for the Routledge *Poetical Works* of 1858 with the crude blockprints that embellished its (illicit) chapbook publication around 1820 (Figures 12.1 and 12.2).[16] If any poem could vindicate Wordsworth's claims to speak the universal language of the human heart, it seemed it was this one. As early as 1812, Wordsworth himself pointed to the success of 'We are Seven' in response to his detractors, and nearly eighty years later, William Knight, his editor and biographer, could still refer to it as amongst the 'most popular' of his poems.[17]

The widespread audience for Wordsworth's 'simple' verse went some way towards justifying his claim to be regarded as a poet of common life; but it also lent credence to a powerful strain of critical discourse which saw in both the poet's work, and its reception, a symbolic transcendence of social difference. Wordsworth himself had expressed the hope that his poetry might have an edifying effect upon plebeian readers, and by the latter half of the century this ambition appeared to have been at least partly fulfilled.[18] Wordsworth's 'universality', declared Charles Knight in 1865, 'has sent his poetry into the homes of the poor and lowly, and that vital quality will keep him fresh and green for the few, and possibly for the many, of coming ages'.[19] The poet's continued appeal to both refined and plebeian taste apparently depended on a 'vitality' that was conferred and sustained by the 'universal' quality of his poetry. But this commonality of poetic taste could also figure a much broader sense of class harmony, as John Ruskin suggested during a typically homiletic address to the lower orders in his *Fors Clavigera*. After recommending the life of the 'true worker', and the 'fellowship' between classes promised by a shared commitment to labour, Ruskin illustrated his argument with the aspirational description of a respectable, hard-working family amongst whom a social superior could find both courteous hospitality and

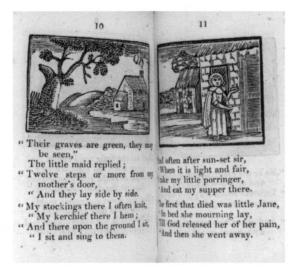

Figs. 12.1 and 12.2 *The Little Maid and the Gentleman; or, We are Seven* (York, n.d. [*c.* 1820]). Copyright British Library Board. (*Overleaf*) Birket Foster's illustration for 'We are Seven' in Wordsworth's *Poetical Works* (London, 1858).

WE ARE SEVEN.

" And often after sunset, Sir,
When it is light and fair,
I take my little porringer,
And eat my supper there."

Figs. 12.1 and 12.2 *(cont.)*

a charming daughter who 'was conversant with her poets, quoted Wordsworth and Burns'.[20] For many Victorian readers, Wordsworth amounted to a kind of honorary peasant poet; a status suggesting, conversely, that within each plebeian breast lurked the hidden potential to attain his nobility of soul. 'Give a homely English peasant that brooding and meditative spirit,' claimed Hutton, 'that deep musing joy in watching his own life and the life of nature around, and you might almost have another Wordsworth.' If for Hutton the peculiarly 'meditative' quality of Wordsworth's mind put him largely beyond the reach of 'plain men', he nevertheless retained the quality of 'common universality', a symbolic 'community of mind with every-day man'.[21]

Yet despite such rhetoric, and the undoubted appeal of many of his poems to lower-class audiences, Wordsworth's Victorian canonization as a 'poet of the people' was always rather precarious. For one thing, it was difficult to maintain a faith in the intrinsic nobility of a working-class taste for Wordsworth's verse – and thus, by implication, of 'the real language of men' – when so many of his most popular poems were also commonly reprinted as children's verse. The apparent 'babyism' of poems such as 'We are Seven' and 'The Pet Lamb' may have been rather less objectionable to Victorian audiences than to their original readers.[22] But the complaint that Wordsworth's subjects were drawn from 'vulgar ballads and plebeian nurseries' (as Francis Jeffrey had put it in 1807) continued to inform a certain unease among the poet's more self-consciously serious admirers, tainting Wordsworth's experiments in conversational and 'low' diction with the suggestion of asinine infantilism.[23] As late as 1896, George Saintsbury was still prepared to exploit this demeaning conflation of the juvenile and the demotic, in a pained reference to Wordsworth's 'namby-pamby dialect'.[24]

Nor was it particularly easy to defend the idiosyncrasies of Wordsworth's simple style by continued reference to the primitive authenticity of the 'old ballad'. Collectors and editors (most notably F. J. Child) continued to lay claim to a vanishing tradition of popular song.[25] But the cultural significance of the ballad in Victorian Britain was considerably more diverse than this. With a few notable exceptions, the literary ballad of the later nineteenth century tended towards an ever-greater degree of artistic licence in relation to its ostensible sources and was, moreover, increasingly associated with the 'fleshly' aestheticism of Swinburne and Rossetti. Meanwhile, the Victorian 'drawing-room ballad' successfully domesticated the form, reducing it to a branch of light musical composition with scant investment in the primitivist ideology which had governed the eighteenth-century ballad revival. 'We are Seven' was itself set to music more than once in the 1860s, joining the Savoy operatics of Gilbert and Sullivan in the repertoire of the Victorian amateur musician.[26] The less genteel form of the 'popular ballad' was now more likely to be associated with either the vulgar temptations of the Music Hall, or the garrulous entrepreneurship of the street balladeer – a plebeian version of the Grub Street hack whose apparent decline was now cause for the same romanticizing nostalgia that had once been reserved for the ancient minstrelsy.[27]

It is hardly surprising that, in such circumstances, the earnest simplicity of Wordsworth's 'balladic' verse should have fallen victim to parody. And just as it was one of the most popular, so 'We are Seven' was also one of the most parodied of all Wordsworth's poems. Walter Scott was the first to burlesque the poem in print, in 1826, but the true apogee of Words-worthian parody coincided with what has sometimes been described, with a rather different object in view, as the 'Wordsworth renaissance' of the 1870s.[28] The poem was sent up in *Punch*, and ridiculed by university wits in the *Cambridge Fortnightly* and *Oxford Magazine*.[29] But many Wordsworthian parodies also appeared in mass-circulation illustrated comic magazines with titles such as *Figaro* and *Funny Folks*, published weekly and selling for only a penny. These were typically burlesque versions of the comic ballad – a genre that positively encouraged the knowing exploitation of balladic 'vulgarity' to humorous effect. *Fun* magazine, for example, not only published a number of parodies of Wordsworth's balladic verse (including 'We are Seven'), but also pro-duced a series of 'Plebeian Ballads Adapted (For the First Time) to Aristocratic Circles'.[30] Here the aesthetic and social conventions of the upper and lower classes were simulated, stereotyped, and combined, in much the same way as the Music Hall 'Champagne Charlie' aspired to a carnivalesque blend of 'cockney' and 'aristocratic' social codes.[31] Within this context, the popular parodies of Wordsworth's balladic verse suggest an implicit inversion of his poetics, for if the latter could be said to have ennobled the language of common life, so the parodies in turn vulgarized Wordsworth's pretensions to poetic canonicity, exploding the spurious literary seriousness of critics such as Arnold and Hutton with the jovial irreverence of plebeian and lower-middle-class humour.[32]

Weakened by parody, and increasingly unsupported by the cultural authority of the ballad revival, the 'universality' of Wordsworth's simple verse was clearly in danger of being achieved at the expense of his pro-fundity. His democratization of poetic diction, consecration of humble life, and association with 'old ballads' all seemed to ground the poet's claims to canonicity in a determinedly 'popular' aesthetic. Yet the inclusion of his simple balladic poems within that canon was increasingly problematic, not despite, but rather precisely *because* of, their 'popularity', a term that could now tend to connote, in Hutton's terms, the tenuous aesthetic enfranchisement of the 'average cultivated man', in addition to the unformed but noble tastes of the 'homeliest hearts'. The contradictions in Wordsworth's poetics first suggested by the 1815 'Essay' were thus made both urgent and embarrassingly obvious. Their rationalization prompted a systematic devaluation of Wordsworth's experiments with 'simple' diction, and the widespread critical consensus that the poet's work was grotesquely – almost incredibly – uneven.

The fitfulness of Wordsworth's genius had been subject for comment at least since Coleridge's exposition of his 'characteristic defects' in the *Biographia Literaria*.[33] But its pronouncement became a virtual imperative for his late-Victorian critics. Throughout the seven volumes of Wordsworth's collected poems, Arnold noted, 'the pieces of high merit are mingled with a mass of pieces very inferior to them; so inferior to them that it seems wonderful how the same poet should have produced both'.[34] Walter Pater, whose response to Wordsworth differed fundamentally from Arnold's in other respects, concurred that, despite his excellencies, 'nowhere is there so perplexed a mixture as in Wordsworth's own poetry, of work touched with intense and individual power, with work of almost no character at all'. For Pater, as for Arnold, this was not simply a result of the didacticism of much of Wordsworth's poetry, but also derived from his 'conventional sentiment' and 'insincere poetic diction'.[35] Hutton, meanwhile, identified the 'affectation of simplicity' as Wordsworth's 'special weakness' and set out to rescue the poet's genius from a wayward tendency to 'puerility and dullness'.[36] By 1897 it was possible for George Milner to make the quite remarkable claim that the 'work of Wordsworth has in it an educational value, a certain power of testing the capacity of the reader, with reference to the determination of what is, and what is not, true poetry, which is over and above its importance as an addition to the bulk of our poetical literature'. For this critic, then, the intrinsic merits of Wordsworth's best poetry were actually of less importance than the 'astounding inequality' of his output, since it was by virtue of the latter quality that Wordsworth's work was so peculiarly well adapted to testing the cultural competence of an aspirant to true 'poetic taste'.[37]

Such arguments raised problems of their own. For Wordsworth himself had effectively prohibited any measure of selectivity in the assessment of his work, by stating quite categorically in 1815 that all his 'small pieces' should 'be regarded under a two-fold view; as composing an entire work within themselves; and as adjuncts to the philosophical Poem, "The Recluse"'.[38] Clearly Wordsworth would never have countenanced the idea that his slighter, simpler verses might be peripheral to his lasting poetic reputation, and nor had he wished to maintain any fundamental distinction between the 'popular' and 'philosophical' aspects of his work. Moreover, it was hard to see how Wordsworth's canonical status could be credibly preserved from the assaults of parodists and philistines if a small but significant portion of his output was acknowledged, even by his staunchest defenders, to have sunk to such a complete poetic nadir.

Arnold's response to these difficulties, in his selected edition of Wordsworth's *Poems*, was to retain a form of presentation that superficially recalled the poet's own comprehensive categorization of his works into distinct classes ('Poems of the Imagination', 'Poems Founded on the Affections', and so on), but to recast those categories into a generic hierarchy. Arnold's Oxford lectures on Homer had already made clear that 'the supreme form of epic poetry' could not credibly be reduced to a mere collection of ballads and lays, as Homer's most recent translators had claimed. The 'ballad-style' purchased 'vigour and spirit' only 'by resigning all pretensions to the highest, to the grand manner', a claim that Arnold attempted to substantiate later in the lectures by reference to Wordsworth's 'Lucy Gray'.[39] It is unsurprising, then, that 'Poems of Ballad Form' constitute the first, and lowest, of Arnold's generic categories in his edition of Wordsworth's verse. Yet several poems that seem, in certain respects, distinctly 'balladic' – 'Simon Lee' and 'Hart-Leap Well', for example – are reserved for the more dignified category of 'Narrative Poems'. Indeed, Arnold seems to have identified the 'ballad form' almost exclusively with the short, 'simple' verse, of largely juvenile subject matter, that had proved so appealing to Wordsworth's parodists: poems such as 'Lucy Gray', 'Anecdote for Fathers', 'Alice Fell', and, of course, 'We are Seven'. In this respect, Arnold's editorial practice represents a particularly striking example of the apparent ease with which the formal requirements of generic classification could be subordinated to broader questions of taste, as Wordsworth's smaller and simpler poems became damagingly associated with the juvenile, the vulgar, and the ridiculous. Yet although, as Arnold explained in his Preface, the 'ballad kind' of poetry 'is a lower kind', he was prepared to concede some merits to the simple verse. It could never be of 'equal value' to more noble poetic forms. But Wordsworth's best examples demanded inclusion by virtue of the poet's distinctive 'power and importance'.[40] The 'ballad kind' thereby assumed a peculiarly liminal relation to the Wordsworth canon, as an intrinsically minor class of poetry, but one which was nevertheless imbued with its author's characteristic 'power'.

Arnold thus anticipated an increasingly influential reading of Wordsworth's poetic development, wherein he attained the high form of meditative blank verse without diluting his lived connection to popular, but inevitably lesser, literary genres. A few powerful detractors such as Arthur Quiller-Couch continued to deny that Wordsworth's simple verse possessed any merit whatsoever.[41] It was A. C. Bradley, however, who most clearly anticipated the subsequent, much more positive, response of academic critics to such pieces as 'We are Seven'. It 'has long been one of the most popular of the ballad poems, and I do not think I have ever heard it ridiculed', Bradley declared, perhaps a little disingenuously, in a note on the poem in his Oxford lectures, before going on to reveal the intellectual kinship of 'We are Seven' with 'the consciousness or forefeeling of immortality' to be found in such texts as the 'Essays on Epitaphs' and the 'Intimations of Immortality' ode.[42] For Bradley, there was clearly a redemptive continuity of purpose between the 'simple' and 'serious' poetry, justifying Wordsworth's own claims for the aesthetic unity of his shorter pieces, considered as 'adjuncts' to the great (and unfinished) philosophical poem *The Recluse*.

A similar pattern emerged within schoolroom literary histories, which likewise began to insist upon the wisdom and seriousness of Wordsworth's simplest verse.[43] Students were increasingly enjoined to progress beyond the naive reading they might have given such verse in the nursery, and to discover instead its spiritual and philosophical depths. Indeed, while journalistic and academic critics could still remark on the startling unevenness of Wordsworth's work, in pedagogic contexts this disparity was gradually transferred to the individual responses which the ballad poetry was capable of eliciting from the reader, responses which could now demonstrate analogous extremes of childish superficiality and mature intellectual penetration. 'We are Seven' thus became a staging post in the cultural education of the Victorian child, a particularly ironic development given its infant protagonist's stubborn resistance to the poem's catechizing adult narrator.[44] Indeed, the poem's problematic representation of the encounter between adult and child, the polite and the plebeian, not only contradicts the more anodyne readings of contemporary school-books; it also suggests some of the broader contradictions of Wordsworth's nineteenth-century reception.

This, at least, seems to have been the opinion of Max Beerbohm, who ended the nineteenth-century tradition of Wordsworthian parody with a devastating visual satire on 'We are Seven', entitled 'William Wordsworth in the Lake District, at Cross-Purposes' (Figure 12.3). For Beerbohm, the frustrated interrogatory moment of 'We are Seven' stands as the parodic primal scene of the Wordsworthian imagination itself. From behind heavy spectacles, the poet peers through the Lakeland rain, his pinched, decrepit expression sagging into a mixture of stern condescension and baffled yearning before the gawping face of the girl. A dull burst of sublimity from behind the mountains completes the picture, rising at the same angle as the girl's occluded gaze, and reinforcing our sense of the encounter as comically emblematic of Wordsworth's broader poetics of nature. The child-like, the natural, and the plebeian are all bound together in the object of the poet's attention – just as they are in 'We are Seven'. But rather than the young author of the *Lyrical Ballads*, Wordsworth is represented here as a septuagenarian laureate, the dod-dering literary patriarch of Victorian culture. This inspired substitution reinforces our sense of incongruity between the *éminence grise* of nine-teenth-century poetry and the simple, 'natural' sensibilities to which his early poems claimed to give voice, while succinctly delineating, in the two opposed figures, the two faults most commonly identified by Wordsworth's detractors: humourless didacticism and juvenile inanity. Although Beerbohm's image is still well known today, its original satiric context is not always fully appreciated. By taking 'We are Seven' as the inspiration for his caricature, Beerbohm demonstrated an acute awareness of the extent to which this particular poem had provided a focus for Victorian anxieties about the relationship between poetic canonicity and popular taste. The poem's ambivalent representation of childhood – undefiled, spiritually receptive, yet simultaneously naive, untutored, and potentially disruptive of adult categories of judgement – also suggests some of the enduring ambiguities of Wordsworth's appeal to 'the people'. Like the old man and the Lakeland child, Wordsworth's popular verse was caught at cross-purposes for much of the nineteenth century, between the values and expectations of the respectable literary world, and a recalcitrant, protean cultural demotic.

Defenders of Wordsworth are usually quick to point out that Beer-bohm misreads 'We are Seven', by mistaking the voice of the Words-worthian narrator for that of the poet himself. Indeed, critics and teachers now tend to identify the literary merits of Wordsworth's simple, balladic poems precisely with the way in which they foreground, and

Fig. 12.3 Max Beerbohm, 'William Wordsworth in the Lake District, at Cross-Purposes',
The Poet's Corner (London: William Heinemann, 1904).

problematize, the relationship between narrator, subject, and reader. The enduring interest and value of such verse can thus be established by reference to the often ambiguous narrative voice with which Wordsworth frames such tales, dramatizing not just the encounter between a more or less 'respectable' narrator and his plebeian subjects, but also the act of narration itself. In 'We are Seven', for example, the poem's speaker not only undertakes the condescending correction of the cottage child's naive spirituality, but also seeks to make a pretty tale of this 'simple girl' and her artless charm. The narration of Wordsworth's poem thereby takes on a troubling social inflection, jarring against a readerly *habitus* conditioned to complacent acquiescence in the aesthetic appeal of common life. To appreciate the poem as many of its Victorian readers appear to have done, as an affecting tale of childish beauty and innocence, is to overlook the way in which 'We are Seven' implicitly challenges the subordination of 'low and rustic life' to the ends of cultivated literary pleasure. The real subject of Wordsworth's balladic experiments, we might conclude, is as much the teller, and his audience, as the tale.

But it also seems possible that this latter approach to the poem reflects a continued, vestigial anxiety about the place of the 'simple' verse within the canon of Wordsworth's work – an anxiety that has, once again, effectively been resolved by its displacement onto the relationship between narrator and reader, thereby identifying the reader's hermeneutic unease as the self-reflexive subject of the poetry. Faced by the troubling simplicity of Wordsworth's popular verse, the critic is always tempted to make the vexed act of interpretation itself the subject of his reading. Such a strategy does not, however, escape the force of Beerbohm's parody. For 'Wordsworth in the Lake District' implicitly satirizes every attempt to discover some kind of deep truth in the little maid – and by extension 'We are Seven' itself – as a form of potentially absurd condescension on the part of the self-consciously literary reader. For this poem, as perhaps for the rest of Wordsworth's simple verse, every act of critical interpretation courts exposure as an act of spurious *over*-interpretation.[45]

In the case of 'We are Seven', this kind of critical *impasse* can be further illuminated (if not overcome) by considering, in conclusion, a further visual analogue for the poem. 'We are Seven' shares its title, and refrain, with a type of pictorial riddle that was commonly reproduced as a cheap print from the sixteenth to the nineteenth centuries. An enduring favourite of printsellers throughout Europe, it is variously titled 'Nous Sommes Sept' in France; in Italy, 'Noi siamo sette'; and in England, 'We are Seven' (Figure 12.4).[46] The riddle could be represented in a number of

WE ARE SEVEN.

Sold in Bow-Church-Yard.

Welcome my frind thus long wee haue bin even | A perfect number foe men doe it call
Now thou art come thou makest our number feven | As perfect are wee in our follies all

Fig. 12.4 *We are Seven* [n.d.], British Museum Department of Prints and Drawings. Copyright Trustees of the British Museum.

different ways, but it is, in essence, disarmingly simple: the viewer scans the figures in the print, counting (in this case) the three fools on three asses, then looking, again, for the elusive seventh, apparently hidden somewhere in the image. Craning forward, perhaps prompted by the picture's caption, he sooner or later realizes that the seventh figure,

joining these fools and asses, is – himself. This moment of comic anag-
norisis is characterized by an embarrassed consciousness of one's own
perspective. Unaware of his own ridiculousness, the viewer discovers that
he has been looking for (and at) himself all along. An unselfconscious,
incorporeal gaze suddenly collapses into grotesque embodiment. But this
effect is itself a function of the most basic mechanism of the joke: that
is, *metalepsis*, or a slippage between 'diegetic levels', in the language of
narratology, between the 'world in which one tells, [and] the world of
which one tells'.[47]

Cheap popular prints such as these enjoyed a tremendous social
penetration in early modern England: pasted to the walls of taverns and
homes, hawked in the streets, and displayed in shop windows, they
formed part of the visual fabric of everyday life for both plebeian and
genteel society. Nevertheless, the cheap pictorial print failed to attract
middle-class collectors of popular cultural products, whose attentions
were directed instead at those printed artefacts, such as the broadside
ballad, which could be considered the tangible repositories of an older,
and more authentic, oral tradition.[48] As a result, relatively few examples
have survived, our knowledge of this area of early modern visual culture is
still imperfect, and the direct allusiveness of Wordsworth's poem in this
respect must therefore remain suggestively indeterminate. Certainly the
light-hearted atmosphere that apparently surrounded the poem's original
composition seems far closer to the mood of the 'We are Seven' print
than more ponderous readings of the poem might allow.[49] Most interestingly, however, the 'We are Seven' print also seems to provide a very
suggestive gloss, not just on Wordsworth's poem, but also on the terms of
its critical reception.

On the one hand, the mechanism of the joke seems, rather like
Beerbohm's print, to provide a teasing, proleptic metaphor for the
manner in which Wordsworth's later critics would strive to discover
profound metaphysical truths in the short, 'ballad' poems, only to be
confounded by their recalcitrant, mocking simplicity. If Beerbohm seems
specifically preoccupied by the patronizing 'literary' gaze of Wordsworth
and his critics when faced with the demotic subject, the 'We are Seven'
print derides all acts of interpretation, however sophisticated and self-
reflexive, as ineluctably foolish. But the way in which the print ridicules
the viewer, by foregrounding and subverting the assumed autonomy of
the gaze, also corresponds very closely to the impression of many modern
readers that Wordsworth's ballad experiments seem intent, in Mary
Jacobus's words, on 'questioning the very basis of narrative convention,

and finally subverting it altogether'.[50] The exhortation, in the middle of a volume of poems, to 'quit your books'; the frustration of balladic narrative with the sly confession that 'It is no tale; but should you think, / Perhaps a tale you'll make it': such moments have a disruptive effect – comically so, at times – drawing attention both to the fact of narration, and the uneasy complicity of the polite reader in sustaining the sentimental conventions of the literary ballad.[51] These devices effect much the same kind of metaleptic jolt, within the context of poetic narrative, that the 'We are Seven' print accomplishes through a combination of visual and verbal prompts. Thus Wordsworth's 'We are Seven' implicitly extends the patronizing presumption of the poem's narrator to the polite reader, just as the print draws the unwitting viewer into its company of fools. The indeterminate ontological distinction between the living and the dead, upon which the cottage girl insists, mirrors the similarly absolute, but never unquestionable, division between fictive narrator and empirical reader.

Such a conclusion offers a clear alternative to our common tendency to differentiate between naive, popular form (whether 'authentic' or 'imitative' ballad) and the sophisticated literary techniques with which Wordsworth purportedly defamiliarizes such forms. For here at least, in a poem in which Wordsworth sets out to challenge the polite reader's expectations of the literary ballad, he appears to do so by allusion to a popular cultural product which plays on a similarly subversive, disconcerting relation to its audience. The changing Victorian reputation of 'We are Seven' might provide a particularly striking perspective on the place of popular or simple verse within the emergent Wordsworthian canon; but the poem itself seems to have both anticipated, and challenged, the unstable fault-line dividing 'popular' and 'polite' culture in nineteenth-century society.

NOTES

1 Matthew Arnold, 'Wordsworth', *Macmillan's Magazine* 40 (1879), 193.
2 *Ibid.*, 194–6, 204.
3 Stephen Gill, *Wordsworth and the Victorians* (Oxford: Clarendon Press, 1998), pp. 211–21.
4 Arnold, 'Wordsworth', 204.
5 [Richard Holt Hutton], 'How to Popularize Wordsworth', *Spectator* (12 July 1879), 879–80.
6 Walter Bagehot, *The English Constitution* (London, 1867), p. 50.
7 [John Aikin], *Essays on Song-Writing* (London, n.d. [1772]), p. 22.

8 [Charles Burney], 'Lyrical Ballads', *Monthly Review*, 2nd ser. 29 (1799), 203; see also *Analytical Review* 28 (1798), 583; *Monthly Magazine* 6 (1799), 514; *New London Review* 1 (1799), 34.

9 William Wordsworth, 'Preface' and 'Advertisement' to *Lyrical Ballads*, in *Prose Works*, ed. W. J. B. Owen and Jane Worthington Smyser, 3 vols. (Oxford: Clarendon Press, 1974), vol. I, pp. 124, 116, 128, 160, 147. On the relationship between Wordsworth's *Lyrical Ballads* and the traditions of popular and broadside balladry, see, *inter alia*, Paul G. Brewster, 'The Influence of the Popular Ballad on Wordsworth's Poetry', *Studies in Philology* 35 (1938), 588–612; Albert B. Friedman, *The Ballad Revival: Studies in the Influence of Popular on Sophisticated Poetry* (Chicago: University of Chicago Press, 1961), pp. 270–84; Mary Jacobus, *Tradition and Experiment in Wordsworth's 'Lyrical Ballads' (1798)* (Oxford: Clarendon Press, 1976), pp. 209–61; Linda Venis, 'The Problem of Broadside Balladry's Influence on the *Lyrical Ballads*', *Studies in English Literature 1500–1900* 24 (1984), 617–32.

10 Wordsworth, *Prose Works*, vol. III, pp. 78, 84. On the question of Percy's editorial integrity, see Nick Groom, *The Making of Percy's 'Reliques'* (Oxford: Clarendon Press, 1999).

11 Wordsworth, *Prose Works*, vol. III, p. 84.

12 William Wordsworth, *Lyrical Ballads and Other Poems, 1797–1800*, ed. James Butler and Karen Green (Ithaca, N.Y.: Cornell University Press, 1992), pp. 73–5, lines 21–32.

13 'Lyrical Ballads', *British Critic* 14 (1799), 367; [Burney], 'Lyrical Ballads', 207.

14 U. C. Knoepflmacher, 'Mutations of the Wordsworthian Child of Nature', in U. C. Knoepflmacher and G. B. Tennyson (eds.), *Nature and the Victorian Imagination* (Berkeley: University of California Press, 1977), pp. 391–425; Carl Woodring, 'Wordsworth and the Victorians', in Kenneth R. Johnston and Gene W. Ruoff (eds.), *The Age of William Wordsworth: Critical Essays in the Romantic Tradition* (New Brunswick: Rutgers University Press, 1987), p. 261.

15 *A Selection from the Works of William Wordsworth*, ed. Francis Turner Palgrave (London, 1865); *Selections from Wordsworth*, ed. J. S. Fletcher (London, 1883); *The Lyric Poems of William Wordsworth*, ed. Ernest Rhys (London, n.d. [1896]); *Wordsworth*, ed. Andrew Lang, Selections from the Poets (London, 1897); *Selections from the Poems of William Wordsworth, Esq. Chiefly for the Use of Schools and Young Persons* (London, 1831); *Poetical Selections for the Use of Young People*, 2nd edition (London, 1836); *Beauties of Poetry and Art* (London, n.d. [1866]); N. Stephen Bauer, 'Wordsworth and the Early Anthologies', *The Library*, 5th ser. 27 (1972), 37–45.

16 John Clare, *Prose*, ed. J. W. and Anne Tibble (London: Routledge, 1951), pp. 118, 208; Helen Sard Hughes, 'Two Wordsworthian Chapbooks', *Modern Philology* 25 (1927), 207–10. On Wordsworth's Chartist and working-class readers, see Richard D. Altick, *The English Common Reader: A Social History of the Mass Reading Public 1800–1900* (Chicago: University of Chicago Press, 1957), p. 207; Gary Harrison, *Wordsworth's Vagrant Muse: Poetry, Poverty and Power* (Detroit: Wayne State University Press, 1994), pp. 190–3.

17 Henry Crabb Robinson, *Books and Their Writers*, ed. Edith J. Morley, 3 vols. (London: J. M. Dent, 1938), vol. I, pp. 93–4; William Knight, 'Life of William Wordsworth', in Wordsworth, *Poetical Works*, ed. William Knight, 11 vols. (Edinburgh, 1882–9), vol. X, p. 198.

18 Dorothy Wordsworth and William Wordsworth, *Letters*, ed. Ernest de Selincourt, 2nd edn, rev. and ed. Chester L. Shaver *et al.*, 8 vols. (Oxford: Clarendon Press, 1967–88), vol. II, p. 248 (5 June 1808).

19 Charles Knight, *Passages of a Working Life during Half a Century*, 3 vols. (London, 1864–5), vol. III, p. 27.

20 John Ruskin, *Fors Clavigera: Letters to the Workmen and Labourers of Great Britain*, 9 vols. (Orpington, Kent, 1871–87), vol. VIII, p. 226.

21 [Richard Holt Hutton], 'William Wordsworth', *National Review* 4 (1857), 3. Cf. Harrison, *Wordsworth's Vagrant Muse*, p. 188.

22 Nicola Trott, 'Wordsworth and the Parodic School of Criticism', in Steven E. Jones (ed.), *The Satiric Eye: Forms of Satire in the Romantic Period* (Basingstoke: Palgrave, 2003), pp. 71–97; Barbara Garlitz, 'The Baby's Debut: The Contemporary Reaction to Wordsworth's Poetry of Childhood', *Boston University Studies in English* 4 (1960), 85–94.

23 [Francis Jeffrey], 'Poems by W. Wordsworth', *Edinburgh Review* 11 (1807), 218.

24 George Saintsbury, *A History of Nineteenth Century Literature (1780–1895)* (London, 1896), p. 53.

25 Francis James Child (ed.), *English and Scottish Ballads*, 8 vols. (Boston, 1857–9).

26 *We are Seven*, music by 'Emilia' (Reading, n.d. [1861]); *We are Seven*, music by Eliza Davis (London, n.d. [1867]).

27 [Thomas Hughes], 'Street Ballads', *National Review* 13 (1861), 397–419; John Ashton, *Modern Street Ballads* (London, 1888), pp. v, ix; Leslie Shepard, *The History of Street Literature* (Newton Abbot, Devon: David and Charles, 1973), pp. 103–4. For a typically misty-eyed identification of Music Hall song as 'the genuine successor of the ancient national lay', see C. D. Stuart and A. J. Park, *The Variety Stage* (London, n.d. [1895]), p. 168; quoted in Laurence Senlick, 'Politics as Entertainment: Victorian Music-Hall Songs', *Victorian Studies* 19 (1975), 151.

28 'Malachi Malagrowther' [Walter Scott], *A Second Letter to the Editor of the Edinburgh Weekly Journal* (Edinburgh, 1826), p. 10. For early parodies of Wordsworth's verse, see Trott, 'Wordsworth and the Parodic School'; and Graeme Stones and John Strachan (eds.), *Parodies of the Romantic Age*, 5 vols. (London: Pickering and Chatto, 1999).

29 Walter Hamilton (ed.), *Parodies of the Works of English and American Authors*, 6 vols. (London, 1884–9), vol. V, pp. 88–106.

30 'Plebeian Ballads', *Fun* 1 (21 September 1861–14 December 1861), 4, 20, 31, 51, 62, 69, 79, 91, 95, 119, 129; J. S. Bratton, *The Victorian Popular Ballad* (London: Macmillan, 1975), pp. 208–9.

31 Peter Bailey, *Popular Culture and Performance in the Victorian City* (Cambridge: Cambridge University Press, 1998), pp. 101–27.

32 Cf. Mark Jones, 'Parody and its Containments: The Case of Wordsworth', *Representations* 54 (1996), 57–79.

33 Samuel Taylor Coleridge, *Biographia Literaria* (1817), ed. James Engell and W. Jackson Bate, 2 vols. (Princeton, N. J.: Princeton University Press, and London: Routledge and Kegan Paul, 1983), vol. II, Chapter 22.

34 Arnold, 'Wordsworth', 197.

35 Walter Pater, 'Wordsworth' (1874), in *Appreciations: With an Essay on Style* (London, 1889), p. 38.

36 [Richard Holt Hutton], 'The Weak Side of Wordsworth', *Spectator* (27 May 1882), 687–8. See also George Saintsbury, *A Short History of English Literature* (London, 1898), p. 658.

37 George Milner, 'The Criticism of Wordsworth and Some Recent Additions to Wordsworth Literature', *Manchester Quarterly* 16 (1897), 195–6.

38 Wordsworth, 'Preface' to *Poems* (1815); reprinted in *Prose Works*, vol. III, p. 28.

39 Matthew Arnold, 'On Translating Homer' (1861), in *Complete Prose Works*, ed. R. H. Super, 11 vols. (Ann Arbor: University of Michigan Press, 1960–77), vol. I, pp. 126, 129, 208.

40 Matthew Arnold, 'Preface' to *Poems of Wordsworth*, ed. Matthew Arnold (London, 1879), pp. xiii–xiv.

41 [Arthur Quiller-Couch], 'A Literary Causerie', *The Speaker* (13 March 1897), 300; and 'Anecdote for Fathers', *Oxford Magazine* 4 (1886), 406–7.

42 A. C. Bradley, *Oxford Lectures on Poetry* (London: Macmillan, 1909), pp. 146–8.

43 See, for example, Anna Buckland, *The Story of English Literature* (London, 1882), pp. 490–2; J. Marshall Mather, *Popular Studies of Nineteenth Century Poets* (London, 1892), pp. 14–16.

44 Cf. Alan Richardson, 'The Politics of Childhood: Wordsworth, Blake, and Catechistic Method', *English Literary History* 56 (1989), 853–68.

45 For a series of related reflections, see Umberto Eco *et al.*, *Interpretation and Overinterpretation* (Cambridge: Cambridge University Press, 1992); on the poem's challenge to readerly proprieties, see also Peter de Bolla, *Art Matters* (Cambridge, Mass.: Harvard University Press, 2001), pp. 95–128.

46 Sheila O'Connell, *The Popular Print in England 1550–1850* (London: British Museum, 1999), p. 122; Malcolm Jones, 'The English Print, c. 1550–c. 1650', in Michael Hattaway (ed.), *A Companion to English Renaissance Literature and Culture* (Oxford: Blackwell, 2000), pp. 356–7. I am grateful to both these authors for their advice.

47 Gérard Genette, *Narrative Discourse*, trans. Jane E. Lewin (Oxford: Blackwell, 1980), p. 236.

48 O'Connell, *The Popular Print*, pp. 9–15.

49 See the account offered in William Wordsworth, *The Fenwick Notes*, ed. Jared Curtis (London: Bristol Classical Press, 1993), pp. 3–4.

50 Jacobus, *Tradition and Experiment*, p. 234.

51 Wordsworth, 'The Tables Turned', line 3, and 'Simon Lee, The Old Huntsman', lines 79–80; in *Lyrical Ballads*, pp. 109, 67.

Bibliography

PRIMARY SOURCES

[Aikin, John.] *Essays on Song-Writing*. London, n.d. [1772].

Akenside, Mark. *The Pleasures of the Imagination*. London, 1744.

[Anon.] *Prison Reminiscences, or Whitecross Street and the Law of Imprisonment for Debt, with Facts showing its Cruelty and Impolicy*. London, 1859.

[Anon.] *The Dens of London Exposed*. London, 1835.

Antient Scotish Poems, Never Before in Print. But now published from the MS Collection of Sir Richard Maitland, 2 vols. London, 1786.

Arnold, Matthew. *Complete Prose Works*, ed. R. H. Super, 11 vols. Ann Arbor, Mich.: University of Michigan Press, 1960–77.

'Wordsworth', *Macmillan's Magazine* 40 (1879), 193–204.

Ashton, John. *Modern Street Ballads*. London, 1888.

Association for Preserving Liberty and Property against Republicans and Levellers. *Association Papers*. London, 1793.

Bagehot, Walter. *The English Constitution*. London, 1867.

Beattie, James. *Original Poems and Translations*. London, 1760.

Beauties of Poetry and Art. London, n.d. [1866].

Bee, John. *Real Life in London*. London, 1822.

Beerbohm, Max. *The Poet's Corner*. London: William Heinemann, 1904.

Bewick, William. *Life and Letters of William Bewick* (1871), ed. T. Landseer, 2 vols. Wakefield: E.P. Publishing, 1978.

Blackner, John. *The History of Nottingham, Embracing its Antiquities, Trade, and Manufactures, from the Earliest Authentic Records, to the Present Period*. Nottingham, 1815.

Boaden, James. *Memoirs of Mrs. Siddons* (1827). London, 1893.

Bolg an tSolair: A Reprint of the Gaelic Magazine of the United Irishmen, ed. Brendan Clifford and Pat Muldowney. Belfast: Athol Books, 1999.

Brand, John. *Observations on Popular Antiquities: Including the Whole of Mr Bourne's 'Antiquitates Vulgares'*. Newcastle upon Tyne, 1777. Rev. edn published as *Observations on Popular Antiquities, Chiefly Illustrating the Origin of Our Vulgar Customs, Ceremonies and Superstitions: Arranged and Revised, with Additions, by Sir Henry Ellis*, ed. Henry Ellis, 2 vols. London: F. C. and J. Rivington, 1813.

Brooke, Charlotte. *Reliques of Irish Poetry Consisting of Heroic Poems, Odes, Elegies, and Songs Translated into English Verse with Notes Explanatory and Historical; and the Originals in the Irish Character. To Which is Subjoined An Irish Tale by Miss Brooke.* Dublin, 1789.

    Reliques of Irish Poetry ... To Which is Prefixed A Memoir of Her Life and Writings by Aaron Crossley Seymour. Dublin, 1816.

Buckland, Anna. *The Story of English Literature.* London, 1882.

Burke, Edmund. *The Writings and Speeches of Edmund Burke*, ed. Paul Langford et al., 9 vols. Oxford: Clarendon Press, 1981–.

[Burney, Charles.] 'Lyrical Ballads', *Monthly Review*, 2nd ser. 29 (1799), 202–10.

Burns, Robert. *Commonplace Book 1783–5*, ed. with intro. by Raymond Lamont Brown. Wakefield: S. R. Publishers Ltd, 1969.

    Letters, ed. J. Lancey Ferguson and G. Ross Roy, 2 vols. Oxford: Clarendon Press, 1985.

    Poems and Songs of Robert Burns, ed. James Kinsley, 3 vols. Oxford: Clarendon Press, 1968.

    Robert Burns's Commonplace Book 1783–1785, ed. David Daiches. Sussex: Centaur Press, 1965.

    The Scots Musical Museum, ed. D. A. Low, 2 vols. Aldershot: Scolar Press, 1991.

Busby, T. L. *Costume of the Lower Orders of London.* London, n.d. [1820].

Byng, John. *The Torrington Diaries: A Selection from the Tours of the Hon. John Byng*, ed. C. Bruyn Andrews and Fanny Andrews. London: Eyre and Spottiswoode, 1954.

Chambers, Robert. *Biographical Dictionary of Eminent Scotsmen*, rev. by Thomas Thomson, 3 vols. London, 1875.

    Man of Letters: The Early Life and Love Letters of Robert Chambers, ed. C. H. Layman. Edinburgh: Edinburgh University Press, 1990.

    Reekiana: Minor Antiquities of Edinburgh. Edinburgh, 1833.

    Select Writings of Robert Chambers, 7 vols. Edinburgh, 1847.

    Traditions of Edinburgh, 2 vols. Edinburgh, 1825; new edn, Edinburgh, 1868.

'Chambers' Traditions of Edinburgh', *The Edinburgh Magazine* n.s. 17 (1825), 130.

Child, Francis James, ed. *English and Scottish Ballads*, 8 vols. Boston, 1857–9.

    The English and Scottish Popular Ballads, 5 vols. New York: Dover Publications, 1965.

Clare, John. *Prose*, ed. J. W. and Anne Tibble. London: Routledge, 1951.

    The Letters of John Clare, ed. Mark Storey. Oxford: Clarendon Press, 1986.

Cockburn, Henry. *Memorials of His Time.* Edinburgh, 1856.

Coleridge, Samuel Taylor. *Biographia Literaria*, ed. James Engell and W. Jackson Bate, 2 vols. London: Routledge and Kegan Paul, and Princeton, N. J.: Princeton University Press, 1983.

    Biographia Literaria, ed. Nigel Leask. London: Everyman, 1997.

    Collected Letters, ed. Earl Leslie Griggs, 6 vols. Oxford: Clarendon Press, 1956–71.

    Essays on His Times, ed. David V. Erdman, 3 vols. London: Routledge and Kegan Paul, and Princeton, N. J.: Princeton University Press, 1978.

Lay Sermons, ed. R. J. White. London: Routledge and Kegan Paul, and Princeton, N.J.: Princeton University Press, 1972.

On the Constitution of Church and State, ed. John Colmer. London: Routledge and Kegan Paul, and Princeton, N.J.: Princeton University Press, 1976.

Table Talk, ed. Carl Woodring, 2 vols. London: Routledge and Kegan Paul, and Princeton, N.J.: Princeton University Press, 1990.

The Friend, ed. Barbara E. Rooke, 2 vols. London: Routledge and Kegan Paul, and Princeton, N.J.: Princeton University Press, 1969.

Crabbe, George. *The Complete Poetical Works*, ed. Norman Dalrymple-Champneys and Arthur Pollard, 3 vols. Oxford: Clarendon Press, 1988.

Cromek, R. H. *Remains of Nithsdale and Galloway Song: with Historical and Traditional Notices relative to the Manners and Customs of the Peasantry.* London, 1810.

A Description of the King's Bench Prison, being a brief review of its Constitution, the Prison itself, the Day Rules &c. London, 1823.

Dibdin, Charles. *Observations on a Tour through the Whole of England*, 2 vols. London, 1802.

Dibdin, Charles, Moorehead, John, and Attwood, Thomas. *The Songs, Chorusses, Duets, &c. in 'The Waterman.' Or, the First of August. And in the Interlude of Plutus and Wit.* N.p., n.d. [London?, 1774?].

Dickens, Charles. *Little Dorrit*, ed. Helen Small and Stephen Wall. Harmondsworth: Penguin, 2003.

Douglas, Robert. *General View of the Agriculture in the Counties of Roxburgh and Selkirk*. Edinburgh, 1798.

Egan, Pierce. *Book of Sports and Mirror of Life*, 2nd edn. London, 1836.

Life in London. London, 1821.

The English Spy. London, 1825.

Gillies, Robert Pearse. *Memoirs of a Literary Veteran*, 3 vols. London, 1851.

'O'Hanlon and his Wife', *Fraser's Magazine* 2 (1836), 184–202.

'On the Law of Debtor and Creditor', *British and Foreign Review* 5 (1837), 64–89.

'Great Fire of Edinburgh', *Blackwood's Magazine* 16 (1824), 707.

Griffith, Amyas. *Miscellaneous Tracts*. Dublin, 1788.

Hadden, James Cuthbert. *George Thomson, the Friend of Burns: His Life and Correspondence*. London, 1898.

Hamilton, Walter, ed. *Parodies of the Works of English and American Authors*, 6 vols. London, 1884–9.

Harrall, Thomas. *Scenes of Life*, 3 vols. London, 1805.

Haydon, Benjamin Robert. *Explanation of the Picture of the Mock Election which Took Place at the King's Bench Prison, July 1827*. London, 1828.

The Autobiography and Memoirs of Benjamin Robert Haydon (1853), ed. T. Taylor, 2 vols. London: Peter Davies, 1926.

The Diary of Benjamin Robert Haydon, ed. W. Bissell Pope, 5 vols. Cambridge, Mass.: Harvard University Press, 1963.

Hazlitt, William. *Complete Works*, ed. P. P. Howe, 21 vols. London: Dent, 1930–4.

Lectures Chiefly on the Dramatic Literature of the Age of Elizabeth. London, 1820.

Metropolitan Writings, ed. Gregory Dart. Manchester: Carcanet, 2005.

Herd, David. *Ancient and Modern Scottish Songs, Heroic Ballads, etc., collected by David Herd*, 2 vols. 1776; rpt Edinburgh and London: Scottish Academic Press, 1973.

Hogg, James, *Altrive Tales, Featuring a 'Memoir of the Author's Life'*, ed. Gillian Hughes. Edinburgh: Edinburgh University Press, 2005.

The Private Memoirs and Confessions of a Justified Sinner, ed. P. D. Garside. Edinburgh: Edinburgh University Press, 2002.

Hone, William. *'Don John', or Don Juan Unmasked*, 2nd edn. London, 1819.

The Every-Day Book; or, Everlasting Calendar of Popular Amusements, 2 vols. London, 1826–7.

The Table Book. London, 1827.

[Hughes, Thomas.] 'Street Ballads', *National Review* 13 (1861), 397–419.

Hunt, Leigh. 'Christmas and Other Old National Merry-Makings Considered, with Reference to the Nature of the Age, and to the Desireableness of their Revival', *Examiner* (Dec. 1817), 801–3, 817–19.

Leigh Hunt's Literary Criticism, ed. Lawrence Huston Houtchens and Carolyn Washburn Houtchens. New York: Columbia University Press, 1956.

Table-Talk. London, 1882.

The Months: Descriptive of the Successive Beauties of the Year. London, 1821.

The Poetical Works of Leigh Hunt, 3 vols. London, 1819.

Hush the Mouse Off of the Hob. Dublin, 1788.

[Hutton, Richard Holt.] 'How to Popularize Wordsworth', *Spectator* (12 July 1879), 879–80.

'The Weak Side of Wordsworth', *Spectator* (27 May 1882), 687–8.

'William Wordsworth', *National Review* 4 (1857), 1–30.

Iliff, Edward. *A Summary of the Duties of Citizenship! Written expressly for the Members of the London Corresponding Society*. London, 1795.

Jamieson, Robert. *Popular Ballads and Songs*. Edinburgh, 1806.

[Jeffrey, Francis.] 'Poems by W. Wordsworth', *Edinburgh Review* 11 (1807), 214–31.

[Jones, William.] *John Bull in Answer to His Brother Thomas*. London, n.d. [1792?].

One Penny-worth More, or, A Second Letter from Thomas Bull to his Brother John. London, 1792.

Kay, John. *Kay's Edinburgh Portraits, Being Original Engravings of About Four Hundred Various Personages, by John Kay, Caricaturist, Engraver, and Miniature Painter*. Edinburgh, 1836.

Keating, Geoffrey. *The General History of Ireland*, trans. Dermod O'Connor. London, 1723.

Keats, John. *Poems*, ed. Miriam Allott. London: Longman, 1970.

Poems, ed. Jack Stillinger. London: Heinemann, 1978.

The Letters of John Keats 1814–1821, ed. Hyder Edward Rollins, 2 vols. Cambridge: Cambridge University Press, 1958.

Knight, Charles. *Passages of a Working Life during Half a Century*, 3 vols. London, 1864–5.

Lamb, Charles. *Elia: and, the Last Essays of Elia*, ed. Jonathan Bate. Oxford: Oxford University Press, 1987.

Lamb, Charles and Mary. *Works*, ed. E. V. Lucas, 7 vols. London: Methuen, 1903–5.

Lee, Richard. *On the Death of Mrs. Hardy, Wife of Mr. Thomas Hardy, of Piccadilly; Imprisoned in the Tower for High Treason*. London, 1794.

London Corresponding Society. *The Moral and Political Magazine of the London Corresponding Society*, 2 vols. London, 1796–7.

   The Report of the Committee of Constitution, of the London Corresponding Society. [London, 1794].

'Lyrical Ballads', *British Critic* 14 (1799), 364–9.

Macpherson, James. *The Poems of Ossian, and Related Works*, ed. Howard Gaskill, intro. by Fiona Stafford. Edinburgh: Edinburgh University Press, 1996.

Mather, J. Marshall. *Popular Studies of Nineteenth Century Poets*. London, 1892.

Matthews, G. M., ed. *John Keats: The Critical Heritage*. London: Routledge and Kegan Paul, 1971.

Mill, John Stuart. *Collected Works*, ed. J. M. Robson *et al.*, 33 vols. Toronto: University of Toronto Press, 1981–91.

Milner, George. 'The Criticism of Wordsworth and Some Recent Additions to Wordsworth Literature', *Manchester Quarterly* 16 (1897), 195–216.

'Miss Brooke', *Dublin Penny Journal* (1 September 1832), 74–5.

[More, Hannah.] *Village Politics. Addressed to all the Mechanics, Journeymen, and Day Labourers, in Great Britain. By Will Chip, a Country Carpenter*, 2nd edn. London, 1792.

Moss, Thomas. *Poems on Several Occasions*. Wolverhampton and London, 1769.

Motherwell, William. *Minstrelsy: Ancient and Modern, with an Historical Introduction and Notes*. Glasgow, 1827.

Neale, John and William. *A Colection [sic] of the most Celebrated Irish Tunes*. Dublin, 1724.

Nicholson, Renton. *Rogue's Progress: The Autobiography of Lord Chief Baron Nicholson* (1860), ed. J. Bradley. London: Longman, 1966.

O'Conor, Charles. *Dissertations on the History of Ireland*. Dublin, 1753.

O'Halloran, Sylvester. *A General History of Ireland*, 2 vols. London, 1778.

'On May Day', *London Magazine* 1 (1820), 489–92.

One Pennyworth of Pig's Meat; or, Lessons for the Swinish Multitude, 3 vols. London, 1793–5.

Pater, Walter. *Appreciations: With an Essay on Style*. London, 1889.

Percy, Thomas. *Reliques of Ancient English Poetry: Consisting of Old Heroic Ballads, Songs, and Other Pieces of Our Earlier Poets*, 3 vols. London, 1765.

   Reliques of Ancient English Poetry, 3 vols. Dublin, 1766.

   Reliques of Ancient English Poetry, 4th edn, 3 vols. London, 1794.

   The Percy Letters: The Correspondence of Thomas Percy and John Pinkerton, ed. Harriet Harvey Wood. New Haven, Conn.: Yale University Press, 1985.

The Philanthropist; or, Philosophical Essays on Politics, Government, Morals and Manners. London, 1795–6.

Pinkerton, John. *A Dissertation on the Origin and Progress of the Scythians or Goths*. London, 1787.

    Scottish Tragic Ballads. London, 1781.

    Select Scotish Ballads. London, 1783.

'Plebeian Ballads Adapted (For the First Time) to Aristocratic Circles', *Fun* 1 (21 September 1861–14 December 1861), 4, 20, 31, 51, 62, 69, 79, 91, 95, 119, 129.

Poetical Selections for the Use of Young People, 2nd edn. London, 1836.

Politics for the People: or, A Salmagundy for Swine, 2 vols. London, 1794–5.

The Poor Man's Prayer. Addressed to the Earl of Chatham. An Elegy. By Simon Hodge, a Kentish Labourer. London, 1766.

'Proceedings of the People', *Black Dwarf* 3 (24 February 1819), 114.

Pye, Henry. *Poems on Various Subjects*, 2 vols. London, 1787.

[Quiller-Couch, Arthur.] 'A Literary Causerie', *Speaker* (13 March 1897), 300.

    'Anecdote for Fathers', *Oxford Magazine* 4 (1886), 406–7.

Ramsay, Allan. *The Ever Green: Being a Collection of Scots Poems Wrote by the Ingenious before 1600*. Edinburgh, 1724.

    The Tea-Table Miscellany. Edinburgh, 1724.

The Register of the Times, 8 vols. London, 1794–5.

Ritson, Joseph. *A Select Collection of English Songs* (1783), 2nd edn with notes by Thomas Parks, 3 vols. London, 1813.

    Observations on the Three First Volumes of the History of English Poetry. London, 1782.

    Scotish Song, 2 vols. London, 1794.

Roberts, William. *Memoirs of the Life and Correspondence of Mrs Hannah More*, 4 vols. London, 1834.

    Poems by Dr. Roberts of Eton College. London, 1774.

Robinson, Henry Crabb. *Books and Their Writers*, ed. Edith J. Morley, 3 vols. London: J. M. Dent, 1938.

Rousseau, Jean-Jacques. *Lettre à d'Alembert sur les Spectacles* (1758), ed. Michel Launay. Paris: Garnier-Flammarion, 1967.

Ruskin, John. *Fors Clavigera: Letters to the Workmen and Labourers of Great Britain*, 9 vols. Orpington, Kent, 1871–87.

Saintsbury, George. *A History of Nineteenth Century Literature (1780–1895)*. London, 1896.

    A Short History of English Literature. London, 1898.

'Saunders, Henry Martin'. *The Crimps, or the Death of Poor Howe: A Tragedy in One Act*. London, 1794.

Scott, Walter. *Minstrelsy of the Scottish Border, consisting of Historical and Romantic Ballads*, ed. J. G. Lockhart (1833), vols. I–IV of *The Poetical Works of Sir Walter Scott*, 12 vols. Edinburgh, 1861.

    Poetical Works of Sir Walter Scott, ed. J. Logie Robertson. London, 1913.

Provincial Antiquities and Picturesque Scenery of Scotland, with Descriptive Illustrations, 2 vols. London and Edinburgh, 1826.

The Heart of Midlothian, ed. Claire Lamont. Oxford: Oxford University Press, 1982.

The Letters of Sir Walter Scott and Charles Kirkpatrick Sharpe to Robert Chambers 1821–45, ed. C. E. S. Chambers. London: W. & R. Chambers, 1904.

Scott, Walter [as 'Malachi Malagrowther']. *A Second Letter to the Editor of the Edinburgh Weekly Journal*. Edinburgh, 1826.

Scrivener, Michael, ed. *Poetry and Reform: Periodical Verse from the English Democratic Press 1792–1824*. Detroit, Mich.: Wayne State University Press, 1992.

Shelley, Percy Bysshe. *Poetry and Prose*, 2nd edn, ed. Neil Fraistat and Donald H. Reiman. New York: W. W. Norton, 2002.

The Complete Poetical Works of Percy Bysshe Shelley, ed. Thomas Hutchinson. London: Oxford University Press, 1934.

The Letters of Percy Bysshe Shelley, ed. Frederick L. Jones, 2 vols. Oxford: Clarendon Press, 1964.

The Poetical Works of Percy Bysshe Shelley, Edited by Mrs Shelley, 4 vols. London, 1839.

The Prose Works of Percy Bysshe Shelley, vol. 1, ed. E. B. Murray. Oxford: Clarendon Press, 1993.

Smith, John Thomas. *Vagabondiana; or, Anecdotes of Mendicant Wanderers through the Streets of London*. London, 1817.

Smollett, Tobias. *The Expedition of Humphrey Clinker*, 3 vols. London, 1771.

Southey, Robert. *Essays, Moral and Political*, 2 vols. London, 1832.

Letters of Robert Southey, ed. Maurice H. Fitzgerald. London: Henry Frowde, 1912.

The Lives and Works of the Uneducated Poets (1831), ed. J. S. Childers. London: H. Milford, 1925.

Wat Tyler; A Dramatic Poem. A New Edition. With a Preface, suitable to Recent Circumstances. London, 1817.

Stark, John. *Picture of Edinburgh: Containing a History and Description of the City, With a Particular Account of Every Remarkable Object in, or Establishment Connected with, the Scottish Metropolis*. Edinburgh, 1806.

Stones, Graeme and Strachan, John, eds. *Parodies of the Romantic Age*, 5 vols. London: Pickering and Chatto, 1999.

Stuart, C. D. and Park, A. J. *The Variety Stage*. London, n.d. [1895].

Suffolk to Wit. Notice to the Inn-Holders and Ale-House-Keepers in the Hundred of Mutford and Lothingland in the said County of Suffolk. N.p., n.d. [Suffolk, 1792].

Swift, Jonathan. *Miscellanies, in Prose and Verse. Volume the fifth*. London, 1735.

Thale, Mary, ed. *Selections from the Papers of the London Corresponding Society*. Cambridge: Cambridge University Press, 1983.

Thelwall, John. *Poems written in Close Confinement in the Tower and Newgate, under a Charge of High Treason*. London, 1795.

Political Lectures. Volume the first, part the first: Containing the Lecture on Spies and Informers. London, 1795.

The Peripatetic, ed. Judith Thompson. Detroit, Mich.: Wayne State University Press, 2001.

The Tribune, 3 vols. London, 1795.

Thomson, George. *A Select Collection of Original Scotish Airs*, first set. London, 1793.

A Select Collection of Original Scottish Airs for the Voice. With Introductory & Concluding Symphonies & Accompaniments for the Piano Forte, Violin & Violoncello By Pleyel, Kozeluch & Haydn. With Select & Characteristic Verses both Scottish and English adapted to the Airs, including upwards of One Hundred New Songs by Burns, 2 vols. London, 1817.

A Select Collection of Original Welsh Airs. London and Edinburgh, 1811.

Thomson's Collection of the Songs of Burns, Sir Walter Scott Bart. and other eminent Lyric Poets Ancient and Modern united to The Select Melodies of Scotland and of Ireland and Wales with Symphonies and Accompaniments for the Piano Forte by Pleyel, Haydn, Beethoven &c, 6 vols. London, 1825.

Thornton, Henry. 'Cheap Repository for Moral & Religious Publications', in *Cheap Repository Tracts, Published during the Year 1795.* London, n.d. [1797].

Trant, Dominick. *Considerations on the Present Disturbances in the Province of Munster, Their Causes, Extent, Probable Consequences and Remedies.* Dublin, 1787.

Tytler, William. 'Dissertation on the Scottish Music', in *Transactions of the Society of Antiquaries of Scotland.* Edinburgh and London, 1792, pp. 468–98.

Vallancey, Charles. *A Vindication of the Ancient History of Ireland.* Dublin, 1786.

Walker, Joseph Cooper. *Historical Memoirs of the Irish Bards.* London, 1786.

Wardlaw, Elizabeth. *Hardyknute: A Fragment of an old Heroick Ballad.* Edinburgh, 1719.

Watson, James. *A Choice Collection of Comic and Serious Scots Poems*, 3 vols. Edinburgh, 1706–11.

Wilson, C. H. *Brookiana*, 2 vols. London, 1804.

Wilson, Daniel. *Memorials of Edinburgh in the Olden Time*, 2 vols. Edinburgh, 1848.

Wilson, J. *The Land of Burns: A Series of Landscapes and Portraits illustrative of the Life and Writings of the Scottish Poet.* Edinburgh, 1840.

[Winston, James.] *The Theatric Tourist.* London, 1805.

Wordsworth, Dorothy and William. *Letters*, ed. Ernest de Selincourt, 2nd edn, rev. and ed. Chester L. Shaver *et al.*, 8 vols. Oxford: Clarendon Press, 1967–88.

Wordsworth, William. *A Selection from the Works of William Wordsworth*, ed. Francis Turner Palgrave. London, 1865.

Lyrical Ballads and Other Poems, 1797–1800, ed. James Butler and Karen Green. Ithaca, N.Y.: Cornell University Press, 1992.

Poems of Wordsworth, ed. Matthew Arnold. London, 1879.

Poetical Works. London, 1858.

Poetical Works, ed. William Knight, 11 vols. Edinburgh, 1882–9.

Prose Works, ed. W. J. B. Owen and Jane Worthington Smyser, 3 vols. Oxford: Clarendon Press, 1974.

Selections from the Poems of William Wordsworth, Esq. Chiefly for the Use of Schools and Young Persons. London, 1831.

Selections from Wordsworth, ed. J. S. Fletcher. London, 1883.

The Fenwick Notes, ed. Jared Curtis. London: Bristol Classical Press, 1993.

The Little Maid and the Gentleman; or, We are Seven. York, n.d. [*c.* 1820].

The Lyric Poems of William Wordsworth, ed. Ernest Rhys. London, n.d. [1896].

The Prelude: 1799, 1805, 1850, ed. Jonathan Wordsworth *et al.* New York: Norton, 1979.

The Salisbury Plain Poems, ed. Stephen Gill. Ithaca, N.Y.: Cornell University Press, 1975.

Wordsworth, ed. Andrew Lang. Selections from the Poets. London, 1897.

Wordsworth, William and Coleridge, Samuel Taylor. *The Lyrical Ballads*, ed. R. L. Brett and A. R. Jones, 2nd edn. London and New York: Routledge, 1991.

SECONDARY SOURCES

Adorno, Theodor and Horkheimer, Max. *Dialectic of Enlightenment* (1944), trans. John Cumming. London: Verso, 1979.

Altick, Richard D. *The English Common Reader: A Social History of the Mass Reading Public, 1800–1900*. Chicago, Ill.: University of Chicago Press, 1957.

The Shows of London. Cambridge, Mass.: Harvard University Press, 1978.

Andersen, Flemming G., Holzapfel, O. and Pettit, T., eds. *The Ballad as Narrative*. Odense: Odense University Press, 1982.

Anderson, Patricia. *The Printed Image and the Transformation of Popular Culture, 1790–1860*. Oxford: Clarendon Press, 1991.

Bailey, Peter. *Popular Culture and Performance in the Victorian City*. Cambridge: Cambridge University Press, 1998.

Baker, Jean N. 'Theatre, Law and Society in the Provinces: The Case of Sarah Baker', *Cultural and Social History* 1 (2004), 159–78.

Bakhtin, Mikhail. *Rabelais and his World*, trans. Helene Iswolsky. Bloomington, Ind.: Indiana University Press, 1984.

Baldick, Chris. *The Social Mission of English Criticism, 1848–1932*. Oxford: Clarendon Press, 1983.

Barnard, John. 'Keats's "Robin Hood", John Hamilton Reynolds, and the "Old Poets"', *Proceedings of the British Academy* 75 (1989), 181–200.

Barrell, John. *Imagining the King's Death: Figurative Treason, Fantasies of Regicide, 1793–1796*. Oxford: Oxford University Press, 2000.

'London and the London Corresponding Society', in James Chandler and Kevin Gilmartin, eds., *Romantic Metropolis: The Urban Scene of British Culture, 1780–1840*. Cambridge: Cambridge University Press, 2005, pp. 85–112.

The Dark Side of the Landscape: The Rural Poor in English Painting, 1730–1840. Cambridge: Cambridge University Press, 1980.

The Spirit of Despotism: Invasions of Privacy in the 1790s. Oxford: Oxford University Press, 2006.

Barry, Jonathan. 'Literacy and Literature in Popular Culture: Reading and Writing in Historical Perspective', in Tim Harris, ed., *Popular Culture in England, c.1500–1850*. Basingstoke: Macmillan, 1995, pp. 69–94.

Barty-King, Hugh. *The Worst Poverty*. London: Alan Sutton, 1991.

Bate, Jonathan. *John Clare: A Biography*. London: Picador, 2003.

Shakespearean Constitutions: Politics, Theatre, Criticism 1730–1830. Oxford: Clarendon Press, 1989.

Bauer, N. Stephen. 'Wordsworth and the Early Anthologies', *The Library*, 5th ser. 27 (1972), 37–45.

Beaudry, Harry R. *The English Theatre and John Keats*. Salzburg: Universität Salzburg, 1973.

Behrendt, Stephen. *Royal Mourning and Regency Culture: Elegies and Memorials of Princess Charlotte*. Basingstoke: Macmillan, 1997.

Shelley and His Audiences. Lincoln, Nebr.: University of Nebraska Press, 1989.

Benedict, Barbara. *Making the Modern Reader: Cultural Mediation in Early Anthologies*. Princeton, N. J.: Princeton University Press, 1996.

Bindman, David. 'Prints', in Iain McCalman, ed., *An Oxford Companion to the Romantic Age*. Oxford: Oxford University Press, 1999, pp. 207–13.

'The English Apocalypse', in Frances Carey, ed., *The Apocalypse and the Shape of Things to Come*. London: British Museum, 1999, pp. 208–69.

The Shadow of the Guillotine: Britain and the French Revolution. London: British Museum, 1989.

Bold, Valentina. ' "Nouther right spelled nor right setten down": Scott, Child and the Hogg Family Ballads', in Edward J. Cowan, ed., *The Ballad in Scottish History*. East Lothian: Tuckwell Press, 2000, pp. 116–41.

Bolla, Peter de. *Art Matters*. Cambridge, Mass.: Harvard University Press, 2001.

Borsay, Peter. 'All the Town's a Stage: Urban Ritual and Ceremony, 1600–1800', in Peter Clark, ed., *The Transformation of English Provincial Towns, 1600–1800*. London: Hutchinson, 1984, pp. 228–56.

The English Urban Renaissance: Culture and Society in the Provincial Town 1660–1770. Oxford: Clarendon Press, 1989.

Borsay, Peter, ed. *The Eighteenth-Century Town: A Reader in English Urban History 1688–1820*. London: Longman, 1990.

Boulton, James T. *The Language of Politics in the Age of Wilkes and Burke*. London: Routledge and Kegan Paul, 1963.

Bourdieu, Pierre. *Distinction: A Social Critique of the Judgement of Taste*, trans. Richard Nice. London: Routledge, 1994.

The Field of Cultural Production, trans. Richard Nice, ed. with intro. by Randal Johnson. Cambridge: Polity, 1993.

Bradley, A. C. *Oxford Lectures on Poetry*. London: Macmillan, 1909.

Bratton, J. S. *New Readings in Theatre History*. Cambridge: Cambridge University Press, 2003.

The Victorian Popular Ballad. London: Macmillan, 1975.

Brewer, John. 'Commercialization and Politics', in John Brewer, J. H. Plumb, and Neil McKendrick, *The Birth of a Consumer Society: The Commercialization of Eighteenth-Century England*. London: Hutchinson, 1983, pp. 197–262.

'Sensibility and the Urban Panorama', *Huntington Library Quarterly* 70 (2007), 229–49.

'Theatre and Counter-Theatre in Georgian Politics: The Mock Elections at Garrat', *Radical History Review* 22 (1979–80), 7–40.

The Common People and Politics 1750–1790s. Cambridge: Chadwyck-Healey, 1986.

Brewster, Paul. 'The Influence of the Popular Ballad on Wordsworth's Poetry', *Studies in Philology* 35 (1938), 588–612.

Bric, Maurice. 'Priests, Parsons and Politics: The Rightboy Protest in County Cork 1785–1788', *Past and Present* 100 (1983), 100–23.

Briggs, Asa. 'The Language of "Mass" and "Masses" in Nineteenth-Century England', in D. E. Martin and D. Rubinstein, eds., *Ideology and the Labour Movement*. London: Croom Helm, 1979, pp. 62–83.

Brown, Mary Ellen. *William Motherwell's Cultural Politics*. Lexington, Ky.: University Press of Kentucky, 2001.

Bruster, Douglas and Weimann, Robert. *Prologues to Shakespeare's Theatre: Performance and Liminality in Early Modern Drama*. London: Routledge, 2004.

Buchan, Norman. *The Ballad and the Folk*. East Lothian: Tuckwell Press, 1997.

Burchell, Jenny. *Polite or Commercial Concerts? Concert Management and Orchestral Repertoire in Edinburgh, Bath, Oxford, Manchester, and Newcastle, 1730–1799*. New York: Garland, 1996.

Burke, Peter. *Popular Culture in Early Modern Europe* (1978), rev. reprint, Aldershot: Scolar Press, 1994.

'The Discovery of Popular Culture', in Raphael Samuel, ed., *People's History and Socialist Thought*. London: Routledge and Kegan Paul, 1981, pp. 216–26.

Bushaway, Bob. *By Rite: Custom, Ceremony and Community, 1700–1880*. London: Junction, 1982.

Butler, Marilyn. 'Antiquarianism (Popular)', in McCalman, ed., *An Oxford Companion to the Romantic Age*, pp. 328–38.

'Revising the Canon', *Times Literary Supplement* (4 Dec. 1987), 1349, 1359–60.

Butler, Marilyn, ed. *Burke, Paine, Godwin, and the Revolution Controversy*. Cambridge: Cambridge University Press, 1984.

Cairns, David and Richards, Shaun. *Writing Ireland: Colonialism, Nationalism, and Culture*. Manchester: Manchester University Press, 1988.

Carlson, Julie. *In the Theatre of Romanticism: Coleridge, Nationalism, Women*. Cambridge: Cambridge University Press, 1994.

Castle, Terry. 'Phantasmagoria: Spectral Technology and the Metaphorics of Modern Reverie', *Critical Inquiry* 15 (1988), 26–60.

Certeau, Michel de. *The Practice of Everyday Life*, trans. Steven Rendall. Berkeley, Calif.: University of California Press, 1984.

Chandler, James. 'A Discipline in Shifting Perspective: Why We Need Irish Studies', *Field Day Review* 2 (2006), 19–39.

England in 1819: The Politics of Literary Culture and the Case of Romantic Historicism. Chicago, Ill.: University of Chicago Press, 1998.

Chandler, James and Gilmartin, Kevin, eds. *Romantic Metropolis: The Urban Scene of British Culture, 1780–1840.* Cambridge: Cambridge University Press, 2005.

Chartier, Roger. 'Culture as Appropriation: Popular Cultural Uses in Early Modern France', in Steven L. Kaplan, ed., *Understanding Popular Culture.* New York: Mouton, 1984, pp. 229–54.

Clark, Anna. 'Queen Caroline and the Sexual Politics of Popular Culture in London', *Representations* 31 (1990), 47–68.

Clark, Peter. *British Clubs and Societies, 1580–1800: The Origins of an Associational World.* Oxford: Clarendon Press, 2000.

'Migrants in the City: The Process of Social Adaptation in English Towns 1500–1800', in Peter Clark and David Souden, eds., *Migration and Society in Early Modern England.* London: Hutchinson, 1987, pp. 267–91.

The English Alehouse: A Social History, 1200–1830. New York: Longman, 1983.

'The Alehouse and Alternative Society', in Donald Pennington and Keith Thomas, eds., *Puritans and Revolutionaries.* Oxford: Clarendon Press, 1978, pp. 47–72.

'Visions of the Urban Community: Antiquarians and the English City before 1800', in Derek Fraser and Anthony Sutcliffe, eds., *The Pursuit of Urban History.* London: Edward Arnold, 1983, pp. 105–24.

Colby, Elbridge. 'A Supplement on Strollers', *Publications of the Modern Language Association of America* 39 (1924), 642–54.

'Strolling Players in the Eighteenth Century', *Notes and Queries* 11th ser., 12 (1915), 454–7.

'Strolling Players of the Eighteenth Century', *Notes and Queries* 12th ser., 9 (1921), 168.

Conlin, Jonathan. 'Vauxhall Revisited: The Afterlife of a London Pleasure Garden, 1770–1859', *Journal of British Studies* 45 (2006), 718–43.

Connell, Philip. 'British Identities and the Politics of Ancient Poetry in Later Eighteenth-Century England', *Historical Journal* 49 (2006), 161–92.

Romanticism, Economics and the Question of 'Culture'. Oxford: Oxford University Press, 2001.

Connolly, Sean. ' "Ag Déanamh *Commanding*": Elite Responses to Popular Culture, 1660–1850', in Donnelly and Miller, eds., *Irish Popular Culture*, pp. 1–29.

Constantine, Mary-Ann. *The Truth against the World: Iolo Morganwg and Romantic Forgery.* Cardiff: University of Wales Press, 2007.

Corfield, P. J. *The Impact of English Towns.* Oxford: Oxford University Press, 1982.

Cowan, Edward J., ed. *The Ballad in Scottish History.* East Lothian: Tuckwell Press, 2000.

Cowan, Edward J. and Paterson, Mike, eds. *Folk in Print: Scotland's Chapbook Heritage, 1750–1850.* Edinburgh: John Donald, 2007.

Cox, Jeffrey N. *Poetry and Politics in the Cockney School: Keats, Shelley, Hunt and their Circle.* Cambridge: Cambridge University Press, 1998.

Crawford, Thomas. *Society and the Lyric: A Study of the Song Culture of Eighteenth-Century Scotland.* Edinburgh: Scottish Academic Press, 1979.

Cross, Ashley J. '"What a World We Make the Oppressor and the Oppressed": George Cruikshank, Percy Shelley, and the Gendering of Revolution in 1819', *English Literary History* 71 (2004), 167–207.

Cullen, Michael J. *The Statistical Movement in Early Victorian Britain: The Foundations of Empirical Social Research.* Hassocks: Harvester, 1975.

Cunningham, Hugh. *Leisure in the Industrial Revolution, c. 1780–c. 1880.* London: Croom Helm, 1980.

Dahlhaus, Carl. *Ninteenth-Century Music*, trans. J. Bradford Robinson. Berkeley, Calif.: University of California Press, 1989.

Daiches, David. *Robert Burns.* Edinburgh: Spurbooks, 1981.

Dalton, R. and Hamer, S. H. *The Provincial Token-Coinage of the Eighteenth Century.* London: B. A. Seaby, 1967.

Dart, Gregory. '"Flash Style": Pierce Egan and Literary London 1820–28', *History Workshop Journal* 51 (2001), 180–205.

Rousseau, Robespierre and English Romanticism. Cambridge: Cambridge University Press, 1999.

Daunton, Martin. *Progress and Poverty: An Economic and Social History of Britain 1700–1850.* Oxford: Oxford University Press, 1995.

Davis, Leith. *Acts of Union: Scotland and the Literary Negotiation of the British Nation, 1707–1830.* Stanford, Calif.: Stanford University Press, 1998.

Music, Postcolonialism and Gender: The Construction of Irish National Identity, 1724–1874. Notre Dame, Ind.: University of Notre Dame Press, 2005.

Davis, Michael. 'The Mob Club? The London Corresponding Society and the Politics of Civility in the 1790s', in Michael Davis and Paul Pickering, eds., *Unrespectable Radicals? Popular Politics in the Age of Reform.* Aldershot: Ashgate, 2008, pp. 21–40.

Davis, Tracy C. '"Reading Shakespeare by Flashes of Lightning": Challenging the Foundations of Romantic Acting Theory', *English Literary History* 62 (1995), 933–54.

The Economics of the British Stage 1800–1914. Cambridge: Cambridge University Press, 2000.

Day, James and Huray, Peter le, eds. *Music and Aesthetics in the Eighteenth and Early-Nineteenth Centuries.* Cambridge: Cambridge University Press, 1987.

Deacon, George. *John Clare and the Folk Tradition.* London: Francis Boutle, 2002.

Deane, Seamus. *Strange Country: Modernity and Nationhood in Irish Writing since 1790.* Oxford: Clarendon Press, 1997.

Devine, T. M. *The Scottish Nation 1700–2000.* London: Allen Lane, 1999.

Dickinson, H. T. *The Politics of the People in Eighteenth-Century Britain.* Basingstoke: Macmillan, 1994.

Donald, Diana. *The Age of Caricature: Satirical Prints in the Age of George III.* New Haven, Conn.: Yale University Press, 1996.

Donaldson, William. *The Jacobite Song: Political Myth and National Identity*. Aberdeen: Aberdeen University Press, 1988.

Donnelly, James and Miller, Kerby, eds. *Irish Popular Culture*. Dublin: Irish Academic Press, 1998.

Dresser, Madge. 'Britannia', in Raphael Samuel, ed., *Patriotism: The Making and Unmaking of British National Identity*, vol. III *National Fictions*. London: Routledge, 1989, pp. 26–49.

Dugaw, Dianne. 'Anglo-American Folksong Reconsidered: The Interface of Oral and Written Forms', *Western Folklore* 43 (1984), 83–103.

'On the "Darling Songs" of Poets, Scholars and Singers: An Introduction', *Eighteenth Century: Theory and Interpretation* 47 (2006), 97–113.

'The Popular Marketing of "Old Ballads": The Ballad Revival and Eighteenth-Century Antiquarianism Reconsidered', *Eighteenth-Century Studies* 21 (1987), 71–90.

Warrior Women and Popular Balladry, 1650–1850. Cambridge: Cambridge University Press, 1989.

'Women and Popular Culture: Gender, Cultural Dynamics, and Popular Prints', in Vivien Jones, ed., *Women and Literature in Britain 1700–1800*. Cambridge: Cambridge University Press, 2000, pp. 263–84.

Duncan, Ian. 'Edinburgh, Capital of the Nineteenth Century', in Chandler and Gilmartin, eds., *Romantic Metropolis*, pp. 45–64.

Scott's Shadow: The Novel in Romantic Edinburgh. Princeton, N.J. and Oxford: Princeton University Press, 2007.

Dyck, Ian. *William Cobbett and Rural Popular Culture*. Cambridge: Cambridge University Press, 1992.

Dyck, Ian and Hawkins, Alun. ' "The Time's Alteration": Popular Ballads, Rural Radicalism and William Cobbett', *History Workshop Journal* 23 (1987), 20–38.

Eagleton, Terry. *The Function of Criticism: From the Spectator to Post-Structuralism*. London: Verso, 1984.

Eagleton, Terry, Jameson, Frederic and Said, Edward, eds. *Nationalism, Colonialism, and Literature*. Minneapolis: University of Minnesota Press, 1990.

Eastwood, David. 'Patriotism and the English State in the 1790s', in Mark Philp, ed., *The French Revolution and British Popular Politics*. Cambridge: Cambridge University Press, 1991, pp. 146–68.

'Robert Southey and the Intellectual Origins of Romantic Conservatism', *English Historical Review* 104 (1989), 308–31.

Eco, Umberto *et al*. *Interpretation and Overinterpretation*. Cambridge: Cambridge University Press, 1992.

Epstein, James A. ' "Equality and No King": Sociability and Sedition: The Case of John Frost', in Gillian Russell and Clara Tuite, eds., *Romantic Sociability: Social Networks and Literary Culture in Britain, 1770–1840*. Cambridge: Cambridge University Press, 2002, pp. 43–61.

Radical Expression: Political Language, Ritual, and Symbol in England, 1790–1850. Oxford: Oxford University Press, 1994.

Evans, Hilary and Evans, Mary. *John Kay of Edinburgh: Barber, Miniaturist, and Social Commentator, 1742–1826.* Aberdeen: Impulse Publications, 1973.

Ewen, D. R. and Kent, David A., eds. *Regency Radical: Selected Writings of William Hone.* Detroit, Mich.: Wayne State University Press, 2003.

Fahrner, Robert. *The Theatre Career of Charles Dibdin the Elder (1745–1814).* New York: Lang, 1989.

Fielding, Penny. *Writing and Orality: Nationality, Culture, and Nineteenth-Century Scottish Fiction.* Oxford: Clarendon Press, 1996.

Finn, Margot. *The Character of Credit: Personal Debt in English Culture, 1740–1914.* Cambridge: Cambridge University Press, 2003.

Finnegan, Ruth. *Oral Poetry: Its Nature, Significance, and Social Context.* Cambridge: Cambridge University Press, 1977.

Fiske, Roger. *Scotland in Music: A European Enthusiasm.* Cambridge: Cambridge University Press, 1982.

Fox, Adam. *Oral and Literate Culture in England 1500–1700.* Oxford: Clarendon Press, 2000.

Fraistat, Neil. 'Illegitimate Shelley: Radical Piracy and the Textual Edition as Cultural Performance', *Publications of the Modern Language Association of America* 109 (1994), 409–23.

Friedman, Albert B. *The Ballad Revival: Studies in the Influence of Popular on Sophisticated Poetry.* Chicago, Ill.: Chicago University Press, 1961.

Frith, Simon. 'The Good, the Bad, and the Indifferent: Defending Popular Culture from Populists', *Diacritics* 21 (Winter 1991), 101–15.

Gamer, Michael and Mandell, Laura, eds. 'On Romanticism, the Canon, and the Web', *Romanticism on the Net* 10 (1998), http://www.erudit.org/revue/ron/1998/v/n10/index.html

Garlitz, Barbara. 'The Baby's Debut: The Contemporary Reaction to Wordsworth's Poetry of Childhood', *Boston University Studies in English* 4 (1960), 85–94.

Gatrell, V. A. C. *City of Laughter: Sex and Satire in Eighteenth-Century London.* London: Atlantic, 2006.

Gelder, Ken. *Subcultures: Cultural Histories and Social Practice.* London: Routledge, 2007.

Genette, Gérard. *Narrative Discourse,* trans. Jane E. Lewin. Oxford: Blackwell, 1980.

George, Eric. *The Life and Death of Benjamin Robert Haydon.* London: Oxford University Press, 1948.

George, M. Dorothy. *English Political Caricature 1798–1832: A Study of Opinion and Propaganda.* Oxford: Clarendon Press, 1959.

Gibbons, Luke. *Transformations in Irish Culture.* Notre Dame, Ind.: University of Notre Dame Press, 1996.

Gill, Stephen. *Wordsworth and the Victorians.* Oxford: Clarendon Press, 1998.

Gillespie, Stuart and Rhodes, Neil, eds. *Shakespeare and Elizabethan Popular Culture.* London: Arden Shakespeare, 2006.

Gilmartin, Kevin. *Print Politics: The Press and Radical Opposition in Early Nine-teenth-Century England.* Cambridge: Cambridge University Press, 1996.
　　Writing against Revolution: Literary Conservatism in Britain, 1790–1832. Cambridge: Cambridge University Press, 2007.
Gladden, Samuel. 'Shelley's Agenda Writ Large: Reconsidering *Oedipus Tyrannus; or, Swellfoot the Tyrant*', in Michael Scrivener, ed., *Reading Shelley's Interventionist Poetry, 1819–20.* Romantic Circles Praxis Series (May 2001), www.rc.umd.edu/praxis/interventionist/
Goddard, Kathleen S. 'A Case of Injustice? The Trial of John Bellingham', *American Journal of Legal History* 46 (2004), 1–25.
Goldby, J. M. and Purdue, A. W. *The Civilisation of the Crowd: Popular Culture in England 1750–1900.* London: Batsford, 1984.
Gorji, Mina. *John Clare and the Place of Poetry.* Liverpool: Liverpool University Press, 2008.
Graves, Thornton S. 'Strolling Players in the Eighteenth Century', *Notes and Queries* 13th ser., 1 (1923), 6–7.
Gray, Denis. *Spencer Perceval: The Evangelical Prime Minister, 1762–1812.* Manchester: Manchester University Press, 1963.
Griffin, Emma. 'Popular Culture in Industrializing England', *Historical Journal* 45 (2002), 619–35.
Groom, Nick. *The Making of Percy's 'Reliques'.* Oxford: Clarendon Press, 1999.
　　' "The Purest English": Ballads and the English Literary Dialect', *Eighteenth Century: Theory and Interpretation* 47 (2006), 179–202.
Guillory, John. *Cultural Capital: The Problem of Literary Canon Formation.* Chicago, Ill.: Chicago University Press, 1993.
Habermas, Jürgen. *The Structural Transformation of the Public Sphere: An Inquiry into a Category of Bourgeois Society*, trans. Thomas Burger. Cambridge: Polity, 1989.
Hackwood, Frederick Wm. *William Hone: His Life and Times.* London: T. Fisher Unwin, 1912.
Hall, Stuart. 'Notes on Deconstructing the Popular', in Raphael Samuel, ed., *People's History and Socialist Theory.* London: Routledge, 1981, pp. 227–40.
Harker, Dave. *Fakesong: The Manufacture of British 'Folksong' from 1700 to the Present Day.* Milton Keynes: Open University Press, 1985.
Harmer, James L. 'Jane Shore in Literature: A Checklist', *Notes and Queries* n.s. 28 (1981), 496–507.
Harris, Tim, ed. *Popular Culture in England, c.1500–1850.* Basingstoke: Macmillan, 1995.
Harrison, Gary. *Wordsworth's Vagrant Muse: Poetry, Poverty and Power.* Detroit: Wayne State University Press, 1994.
Harrison, Mark. *Crowds and History: Mass Phenomena in English Towns, 1790–1835.* Cambridge: Cambridge University Press, 1988.
Haywood, Ian. *Bloody Romanticism: Spectacular Violence and the Politics of Representation 1776–1832.* Basingstoke: Palgrave, 2006.

The Revolution in Popular Literature: Politics, Print, and the People, 1790–1860. Cambridge: Cambridge University Press, 2004.

Herzog, Don. *Poisoning the Minds of the Lower Orders.* Princeton, N.J.: Princeton University Press, 1998.

Hillebrand, H. N. *Edmund Kean.* New York: AMS Press, 1966.

Hitchcock, Tim. 'Begging on the Streets of Eighteenth-Century London', *Journal of British Studies* 44 (2005), 478–98.

Holmes, Richard. *Coleridge: Darker Reflections, 1804–1834.* New York: Pantheon, 1998.

Hopkinson, Cecil and Oldman, C. B. 'Thomson's Collections of National Song', *Transactions of the Edinburgh Bibliographical Society* 2 (1940), 3–64 and 3 (1954), 123–4.

Houston, R. A. *Scottish Literacy and Scottish Identity: Illiteracy and Society in Scotland and Northern England, 1600–1800.* Cambridge: Cambridge University Press, 1985.

Social Change in the Age of Enlightenment: Edinburgh 1660–1760. Oxford: Clarendon Press, 1994.

Hughes, Helen Sard. 'Two Wordsworthian Chapbooks', *Modern Philology* 25 (1927), 207–10.

Hunt, Tamara L. *Defining John Bull: Political Caricature and National Identity in Georgian England.* Aldershot: Ashgate, 2003.

Hustvedt, S. B. *Ballad Books and Ballad Men.* Cambridge, Mass.: Harvard University Press, 1930.

Ballad Criticism in Scandinavia and Great Britain during the Eighteenth Century. New York: Oxford University Press, 1916.

Hutton, Ronald. *The Rise and Fall of Merry England: The Ritual Year, 1400–1700.* Oxford: Oxford University Press, 1994.

Innes, Joanna. 'Politics and Morals: The Reformation of Manners Movement in Later Eighteenth-Century England', in Eckhart Hellmuth, ed., *The Transformation of Political Culture: England and Germany in the Late Eighteenth Century.* Oxford: Oxford University Press, 1990, pp. 57–118.

'The King's Bench in the Later Eighteenth Century: Law, Authority and Order in a London Debtors' Prison', in J. Brewer and J. Styles, eds., *An Ungovernable People.* London: Hutchinson, 1980, pp. 250–98.

Jacobus, Mary. *Tradition and Experiment in Wordsworth's 'Lyrical Ballads' (1798).* Oxford: Clarendon Press, 1976.

Janowitz, Anne. *Lyric and Labour in the Romantic Tradition.* Cambridge: Cambridge University Press, 1998.

Jennings, Paul. *The Public House in Bradford, 1770–1970.* Keele: Keele University Press, 1995.

Jones, Gareth Stedman. *Languages of Class: Studies in English Working Class History, 1832–1982.* Cambridge: Cambridge University Press, 1983.

Jones, Malcolm. 'The English Print, c. 1550–c. 1650', in Michael Hattaway, ed., *A Companion to English Renaissance Literature and Culture.* Oxford: Blackwell, 2000, pp. 352–66.

Jones, Mark. 'Parody and its Containments: The Case of Wordsworth', *Representations* 54 (1996), 57–79.

Jones, Steven E. *Shelley's Satire: Violence: Exhortation, and Authority*. Dekalb, Ill.: Northern Illinois University Press, 1994.

Kandl, John. 'Plebeian Gusto, Negative Capability, and the Low Company of "Mr. Kean": Keats' Dramatic Review for *The Champion* (21 December 1817)', *Nineteenth-Century Prose* 28 (2001), 130–41.

Kearney, Richard. *Postnationalist Ireland: Literature, Culture, Philosophy*. London: Routledge, 1997.

Keen, Paul. *The Crisis of Literature in the 1790s: Print Culture and the Public Sphere*. Cambridge: Cambridge University Press, 1999.

Kelley, Theresa M. *Reinventing Allegory*. Cambridge: Cambridge University Press, 1997.

Kerrigan, John. *Archipelagic English: Literature, History, and Politics, 1603–1707*. Oxford: Oxford University Press, 2008.

Kiberd, Declan. *Inventing Ireland: The Literature of the Modern Nation*. Cambridge, Mass.: Harvard University Press, 1995.

Kidd, Colin. 'Race, Theology and Revival: Scots Philology and its Contexts in the Age of Pinkerton and Jamieson', *Scottish Studies Review* 3 (2002), 20–33.

Klancher, Jon. 'From "Crowd" to "Audience": The Making of an English Mass Readership in the Nineteenth Century', *English Literary History* 50 (1983), 155–73.

The Making of English Reading Audiences, 1790–1832. Madison, Wisc.: University of Wisconsin Press, 1987.

Knoepflmacher, U. C. 'Mutations of the Wordsworthian Child of Nature', in U. C. Knoepflmacher and G. B. Tennyson, eds., *Nature and the Victorian Imagination*. Berkeley: University of California Press, 1977, pp. 391–425.

Kramnick, Jonathan Brody. *Making the English Literary Canon: Print-Capitalism and the Cultural Past, 1700–1770*. Cambridge: Cambridge University Press, 1998.

Langan, Celeste. *Romantic Vagrancy: Wordsworth and the Simulation of Freedom*. Cambridge: Cambridge University Press, 1995.

'Scotch Drink & Irish Harps: Mediations of the National Air', in Phyllis Weliver, ed., *The Figure of Music in Nineteenth-Century British Poetry*. Aldershot: Ashgate, 2005, pp. 25–49.

'Understanding Media in 1805: Audiovisual Hallucination in *The Lay of the Last Minstrel*', *Studies in Romanticism* 40 (2001), 49–70.

Leask, Nigel. 'Burns, Wordsworth and the Politics of Vernacular Poetry', in Peter de Bolla, Nigel Leask, and David Simpson, eds., *Land, Nation and Culture, 1740–1840: Thinking the Republic of Taste*. Basingstoke: Palgrave Macmillan, 2005, pp. 202–22.

Curiosity and the Aesthetics of Travel Writing 1770–1840. Oxford: Oxford University Press, 2002.

Ledger, Sally. *Dickens and the Popular Radical Tradition*. Cambridge: Cambridge University Press, 2007.

Leerssen, Joep. *Mere Irish and Fíor-Ghael: Studies in the Idea of Irish Nationality, Its Development and Literary Expression Prior to the Nineteenth Century.* Notre Dame, Ind.: Notre Dame University Press, 1986.

Lefebvre, Henri. *Writings on Cities*, trans. and ed. Eleonore Kofman and Elizabeth Lebas. Oxford: Blackwell, 1996.

Lloyd, David. *Anomalous States: Irish Writing and the Post-Colonial Moment.* Durham, N.C.: Duke University Press, 1993.

    Ireland after History. Notre Dame, Ind.: University of Notre Dame Press, 1999.

Lowenthal, Leo. *Literature and Mass Culture.* New Brunswick: Transaction, 1984.

Lyle, Emily. ' "Thus began with me Love and Poesy": Burns's First Song and "I am a man unmarried" ', in Kenneth Simpson, ed., *Love & Liberty. Robert Burns: A Bicentenary Celebration.* East Lothian: Tuckwell Press, 1997, pp. 334–40.

McCalman, Iain. *Radical Underworld: Prophets, Revolutionaries, and Pornographers in London, 1795–1840.* Oxford: Clarendon Press, 1993.

McCalman, Iain, ed. *An Oxford Companion to the Romantic Age: British Culture 1776–1832.* Oxford: Oxford University Press, 1999.

McCarthy, William Bernard. *The Ballad Matrix: Personality, Milieu, and the Oral Tradition.* Bloomington and Indianapolis: Indiana University Press, 1990.

MacCraith, Mícheál. 'Charlotte Brooke and James MacPherson', *Litteraria Pragensia: Studies in Literature and Culture* 10 (2000), 5–17.

McCue, K. C. 'George Thomson (1757–1851): His Collections of National Airs in their Scottish Cultural Context', unpublished PhD thesis, University of Oxford (1993).

    ' "The most intricate bibliographical enigma": Understanding George Thomson (1757–1851) and his Collections of National Airs', in Richard Turbet, ed., *Music Librarianship in the United Kingdom.* Aldershot: Ashgate, 2003, pp. 99–120.

McDowell, Paula. 'The Manufacture and Lingua-Facture of Ballad Making', *Eighteenth Century: Theory and Interpretation* 47 (2006), 151–78.

McEathron, Scott. 'Wordsworth, *Lyrical Ballads* and the Problem of Peasant Poetry', *Nineteenth-Century Literature* 54 (1999), 1–26.

Mackay, James. *Burns: A Biography of Robert Burns.* Edinburgh: Mainstream, 1992.

MacLaine, Allan H., ed. *The Christis Kirk Tradition: Scots Poems of Folk Festivity.* Glasgow: ASLS, 1996.

McLane, Maureen. 'Dating Orality, Thinking Balladry: Of Milkmaids and Minstrels in 1771', *Eighteenth Century: Theory and Interpretation* 47 (2006), 131–49.

McVeigh, Simon. *Concert Life in London from Mozart to Haydn.* Cambridge: Cambridge University Press, 1993.

Magnusson, Paul. *Reading Public Romanticism.* Princeton, N.J.: Princeton University Press, 1998.

Malcolmson, Robert W. *Popular Recreations in English Society 1700–1850*. Cambridge: Cambridge University Press, 1973.

Marsh, Joss. *Word Crimes: Blasphemy, Culture, and Literature in Nineteenth-Century England*. Chicago, Ill.: University of Chicago Press, 1998.

Matheson, C. Suzanne. 'Viewing', in McCalman, ed., *An Oxford Companion to the Romantic Age*, pp. 187–96.

Mekie, Margeorie. *The Heart of Old Edinburgh*. Catrine, Ayrshire: Stenlake, 2004.

Money, John. 'Taverns, Coffee Houses and Clubs: Local Politics and Popular Articulacy in the Birmingham Area, in the Age of the American Revolution', *Historical Journal* 14 (1971), 15–47.

Moody, Jane. *Illegitimate Theatre in London, 1770–1840*. Cambridge: Cambridge University Press, 2000.

Morgan, Prys. 'The Hunt for the Welsh Past in the Romantic Period', in Eric Hobsbawm and Terence Ranger, eds., *The Invention of Tradition*. Cambridge: Cambridge University Press, 1983, pp. 43–100.

Mugglestone, Lynda. 'The Fallacy of the Cockney Rhyme: From Keats and Earlier to Auden', *Review of English Studies* 42 (1991), 57–66.

Mullan, John and Reid, Christopher, eds. *Eighteenth-Century Popular Culture: A Selection*. Oxford: Oxford University Press, 2000.

Mulrooney, Jonathan. 'Keats in the Company of Kean', *Studies in Romanticism* 42 (2003), 227–50.

Nelson, Alfred Lewis. 'James Winston's *Theatric Tourist*, A Critical Edition with a Biography and Census of Winston Material', unpublished PhD thesis, George Washington University (1968).

Newman, Steve. *Ballad Collecting, Lyric and the Canon: The Call of the Popular from the Restoration to the New Criticism*. Philadelphia, Penn.: University of Pennsylvania Press, 2007.

   'The Scots Songs of Allan Ramsay: "Lyrick" Transformation, Popular Culture, and the Boundaries of the Scottish Enlightenment', *Modern Language Quarterly* 63 (2002), 277–314.

Nicoll, Allardyce. *A History of Early Nineteenth Century Drama 1800–1850*, 2 vols. Cambridge: Cambridge University Press, 1930.

Nokes, David. *John Gay: A Profession of Friendship. A Critical Biography*. Oxford: Oxford University Press, 1995.

Ó Ciosáin, Niall. *Print and Popular Culture in Ireland, 1750–1850*. Basingstoke: Macmillan, 1997.

O'Connell, Sheila. *The Popular Print in England 1550–1850*. London: British Museum, 1999.

Oliver, Susan. *Scott, Byron and the Poetics of Cultural Encounter*. Basingstoke: Palgrave Macmillan, 2005.

Olney, Clarke. *Benjamin Robert Haydon, Historical Painter*. Atlanta, Ga.: University of Georgia Press, 1952.

Paley, Morton D. *Apocalypse and Millenium in English Romantic Poetry*. Oxford: Clarendon Press, 1999.

Parsons, Coleman O. 'Serial Publication of *Traditions of Edinburgh*', *Transactions of the Bibliographical Society* 14 (1933), 207–11.

Pedersen, Susan. 'Hannah More Meets Simple Simon: Tracts, Chapbooks and Popular Culture in Late Eighteenth-Century England', *Journal of British Studies* 25 (1986), 84–113.

Peltz, Lucy. 'Aestheticizing the Ancestral City: Antiquarianism, Topography and the Representation of London in the Long Eighteenth Century', in Dana Arnold, ed., *The Metropolis and its Image: Constructing Identities for London, c. 1750–1950*. Oxford: Blackwell, 1999, pp. 6–28.

Phillips, Mark Salber. 'Relocating Inwardness: Historical Distance and the Transition from Enlightenment to Romantic Historiography', *Publications of the Modern Language Association of America* 118 (2003), 436–49.

Society and Sentiment: Genres of Historical Writing in Britain, 1740–1820. Princeton, N.J.: Princeton University Press, 2000.

Philp, Mark. 'Revolution', in McCalman, ed., *An Oxford Companion to the Romantic Age*, pp. 17–25.

'Vulgar Conservatism, 1792–3', *English Historical Review* 110 (1995), 42–59.

Philpin, C. H. E., ed. *Nationalism and Popular Protest in Ireland*. Cambridge: Cambridge University Press, 1987.

Pirie, David. 'Old Saints and Young Lovers: Keats's Eve of St Mark and Popular Culture', in Michael O'Neill, ed., *Keats: Bicentenary Readings*. Edinburgh: Edinburgh University Press, 1997, pp. 48–70.

Pittock, Murray. *Poetry and Jacobite Politics in Eighteenth-Century Britain and Ireland*. Cambridge: Cambridge University Press, 1994.

Pocock, J. G. A. *The Discovery of Islands: Essays in British History*. Cambridge: Cambridge University Press, 2005.

Poovey, Mary. *Making a Social Body: British Cultural Formation 1830–1864*. Chicago, Ill.: University of Chicago Press, 1995.

Porter, Roy. *London: A Social History*. London: Penguin, 1996.

Price, Leah. *The Anthology and the Rise of the Novel*. Cambridge: Cambridge University Press, 2000.

Pugliatti, Paola. *Beggary and Theatre in Early Modern England*. Aldershot: Ashgate, 2003.

Rauser, Amelia. 'The Butcher-Kissing Duchess of Devonshire: Between Caricature and Allegory in 1784', *Eighteenth-Century Studies* 36 (2002), 23–46.

Richardson, Alan. 'The Politics of Childhood: Wordsworth, Blake, and Catechistic Method', *English Literary History* 56 (1989), 853–68.

Rigney, Ann. 'Portable Monuments: Literature, Cultural Memory, and the Case of Jeanie Deans', *Poetics Today* 25 (2004), 361–96.

Roe, John. *Life of Adam Smith*. New York: Kelly, 1965.

Roe, Nicholas. *John Keats and the Culture of Dissent*. Oxford: Clarendon Press, 1997.

Rogers, Helen. *Women and the People: Authority, Authorship, and the Radical Tradition in Nineteenth-Century England*. Aldershot: Ashgate, 2000.

Rogers, Nicholas. *Crowds, Culture, and Politics in Georgian Britain*. Oxford: Clarendon Press, 1998.

Rose, Jonathan. *The Intellectual Life of the British Working Classes*. New Haven, Conn.: Yale University Press, 2001.

Rosen, Charles. *The Classical Style*. London: Faber and Faber, 1984.

Rosenfeld, Sybil. *Strolling Players and Drama in the Provinces, 1660–1765*. Cambridge: Cambridge University Press, 1939.

Ross, Trevor. 'Copyright and the Invention of Tradition', *Eighteenth-Century Studies* 25 (1992), 1–27.

Rowland, Ann Wierda. ' "The false nourice sang": Childhood, Child Murder, and the Formalism of the Scottish Ballad Revival', in Leith Davis, Ian Duncan, and Janet Sorensen, eds., *Scotland and the Borders of Romanticism*. Cambridge: Cambridge University Press, 2004, pp. 225–44.

Russell, Gillian. *The Theatres of War: Performance, Politics, and Society, 1793–1815*. Oxford: Clarendon Press, 1995.

   Women, Sociability and Theatre in Georgian London. Cambridge: Cambridge University Press, 2007.

Rycroft, Marjorie E. 'Haydn's Welsh Songs: George Thomson's Musical and Literary Sources', in S. Harper and W. Thomas, eds., *Bearers of Song*, Welsh Music Studies 7. Cardiff: University of Wales Press, 2007, pp. 92–160.

Said, Edward. *Orientalism*. London: Routledge and Kegan Paul, 1978.

St Clair, William. *The Reading Nation in the Romantic Period*. Cambridge: Cambridge University Press, 2004.

Samuel, Raphael. *Theatres of Memory, Vol. 1: Past and Present in Contemporary Culture*. London: Verso, 1994.

Scholnick, Robert J. ' "The Fiery Cross of Knowledge": *Chambers's Edinburgh Journal*, 1832–1844', *Victorian Periodical Review* 32 (1999), 324–58.

Scrivener, Michael. *Radical Shelley: The Philosophical Anarchism and Utopian Thought of Percy Bysshe Shelley*. Princeton, N.J.: Princeton University Press, 1982.

Secord, James A. *Victorian Sensation: The Extraordinary Publication, Reception, and Secret Authorship of the Vestiges of the Natural History of Creation*. Chicago, Ill.: University of Chicago Press, 2000.

Senlick, Laurence. 'Politics as Entertainment: Victorian Music-Hall Songs', *Victorian Studies* 19 (1975), 149–80.

Sennett, Richard. *Flesh and Stone: The Body and the City in Western Civilization*. New York and London: W. W. Norton, 1994.

Shepard, Leslie. *The History of Street Literature*. Newton Abbot: David and Charles, 1973.

Shiach, Morag. *Discourse on Popular Culture: Class, Gender, and History in Cultural Analysis, 1730 to the Present*. Cambridge: Polity Press, 1989.

Slote, Bernice. *Keats and the Dramatic Principle*. Lincoln, Nebr.: University of Nebraska Press, 1958.

Smiles, Sam. *Eye Witness: Artists and Visual Documentation in Britain 1770–1830*. Aldershot: Ashgate, 2000.

Smyth, Jim. *The Men of No Property: Irish Radicals and Popular Politics in the Late Eighteenth Century*. Basingstoke: Macmillan, 1992.

Sorenson, Janet. 'Vulgar Tongues: Canting Dictionaries and the Language of the People in Eighteenth-Century Britain', *Eighteenth-Century Studies* 37 (2004), 435–54.

Stallybrass, Peter and White, Allon. *The Politics and Poetics of Transgression*. London: Methuen, 1986.

Stephens, W. B. 'Literacy in England, Scotland and Wales, 1500–1900', *History of Education Quarterly* 30 (1990), 545–71.

Stevenson, John. *Popular Disturbances in England 1700–1780*. London: Longman, 1979.

  'The London "Crimp" Riots of 1794', *International Review of Social History* 16 (1971), 40–58.

Stewart, Keith. 'Ancient Poetry as History in the Eighteenth Century', *Journal of the History of Ideas* 19 (1958), 335–47.

Stewart, Susan. *Crimes of Writing: Problems in the Containment of Representation*. New York: Oxford University Press, 1991.

Storey, Mark. *Robert Southey: A Life*. Oxford: Oxford University Press, 1997.

Strong, L. A. G. *The Minstrel Boy: A Portrait of Tom Moore*. London: Hodder and Stoughton, 1937.

Sweet, Rosemary. *Antiquaries: The Discovery of the Past in Eighteenth-Century Britain*. London and New York: Hambledon, 2004.

  The Writing of Urban Histories in Eighteenth-Century England. Oxford: Clarendon Press, 1997.

Symonds, Deborah. *Weep Not for Me: Women, Ballads, and Infanticide in Early Modern Scotland*. University Park, Penn.: Pennsylvania State University Press, 1997.

Taylor, Miles. 'John Bull and the Iconography of Public Opinion in England, c. 1712–1929', *Past and Present* 134 (1992), 93–128.

Temperley, Nicholas. 'Ballroom and Drawing-Room Music', in Nicholas Temperley, ed., *The Romantic Age 1800–1914*. London: Athlone Press, 1981, pp. 109–34.

Terry, Richard. *Poetry and the Making of the English Literary Past, 1660–1781*, Oxford: Oxford University Press, 2001.

Thompson, E. P. *Customs in Common*. London: Merlin Press, 1991.

  The Making of the English Working Class. New York: Vintage Books, 1966.

Thomson, Robert S. 'The Development of the Broadside Ballad and Its Influence upon the Transmission of English Folksongs', unpublished PhD thesis, University of Cambridge, 1974.

Trott, Nicola. 'Wordsworth and the Parodic School of Criticism', in Steven E. Jones, ed., *The Satiric Eye: Forms of Satire in the Romantic Period*. Basingstoke: Palgrave, 2003, pp. 71–97.

Trumpener, Katie. *Bardic Nationalism: The Romantic Novel and the British Empire*. Princeton, N.J.: Princeton University Press, 1997.

Vaughan Williams, Ralph. *National Music and Other Essays*. Oxford: Oxford University Press, 1963.

Venis, Linda. 'The Problem of Broadside Balladry's Influence on the *Lyrical Ballads*', *Studies in English Literature 1500–1900* 24 (1984), 617–32.

Vincent, David. *Literacy and Popular Culture: England, 1750–1914*. Cambridge: Cambridge University Press, 1989.

Wahrman, Dror. *Imagining the Middle Class: The Political Representation of Class in Britain, c. 1780–1840*. Cambridge: Cambridge University Press, 1995.

'Public Opinion, Violence and the Limits of Constitutional Politics', in James Vernon, ed., *Re-reading the Constitution: New Narratives in the Political History of England's Long Nineteenth Century*. Cambridge: Cambridge University Press, 1996, pp. 83–122.

Walker, Carol Kyros. *Walking North with Keats*. New Haven, Conn.: Yale University Press, 1992.

Whelan, Kevin. *The Tree of Liberty: Radicalism, Catholicism and the Construction of Irish Identity 1760–1830*. Cork: Cork University Press, 1996.

Williams, Raymond. *Culture and Society 1780–1950*. London: Chatto and Windus, 1958.

Keywords. London: Fontana, 1988.

The Country and the City. London: Hogarth Press, 1993.

Wilson, Ben. *The Laughter of Triumph: William Hone and the Fight for the Free Press*. London: Faber and Faber, 2005.

Wilson, Kathleen. *The Sense of the People: Politics, Culture and Imperialism in England, 1715–1785*. Cambridge: Cambridge University Press, 1995.

This Island Race: Englishness, Empire and Gender in the Eighteenth Century. London and New York: Routledge, 2003.

Wolfson, Susan. 'Poetical Form and Political Reform: *The Mask of Anarchy* and "England in 1819"', in Percy Shelley, *Poetry and Prose*, ed. Fraistat and Reiman, pp. 722–35.

Wood, Marcus. *Radical Satire and Print Culture 1790–1822*. Oxford: Clarendon Press, 2004.

Woodring, Carl. 'Wordsworth and the Victorians', in Kenneth R. Johnston and Gene W. Ruoff, eds., *The Age of William Wordsworth: Critical Essays in the Romantic Tradition*. New Brunswick: Rutgers University Press, 1987, pp. 261–75.

Worrall, David. *Theatric Revolution: Drama, Censorship, and Romantic Period Subcultures 1773–1832*. Oxford: Oxford University Press, 2006.

Yeo, Eileen and Yeo, Stephen, eds. *Popular Culture and Class Conflict 1590–1914: Explorations in the History of Labour and Leisure*. Sussex: Harvester, 1981.

Index